eat

Time Stranger Kyoko

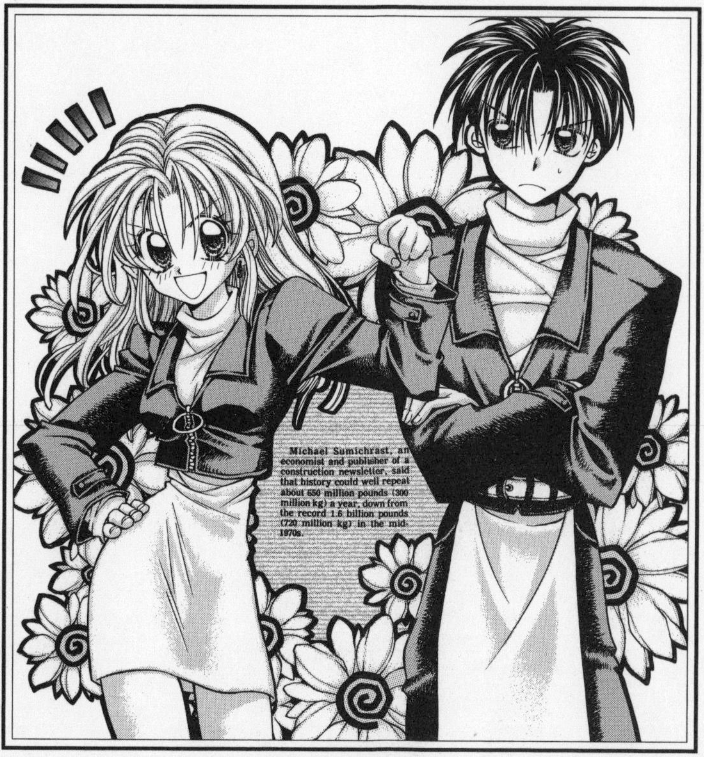
Michael Sumichrast, an economist and publisher of a construction newsletter, said that history could well repeat about 650 million pounds (300 million kg) a year, down from the record 1.6 billion pounds (720 million kg) in the mid-1970s.

Vol. 1

Story & Art by

Arina Tanemura

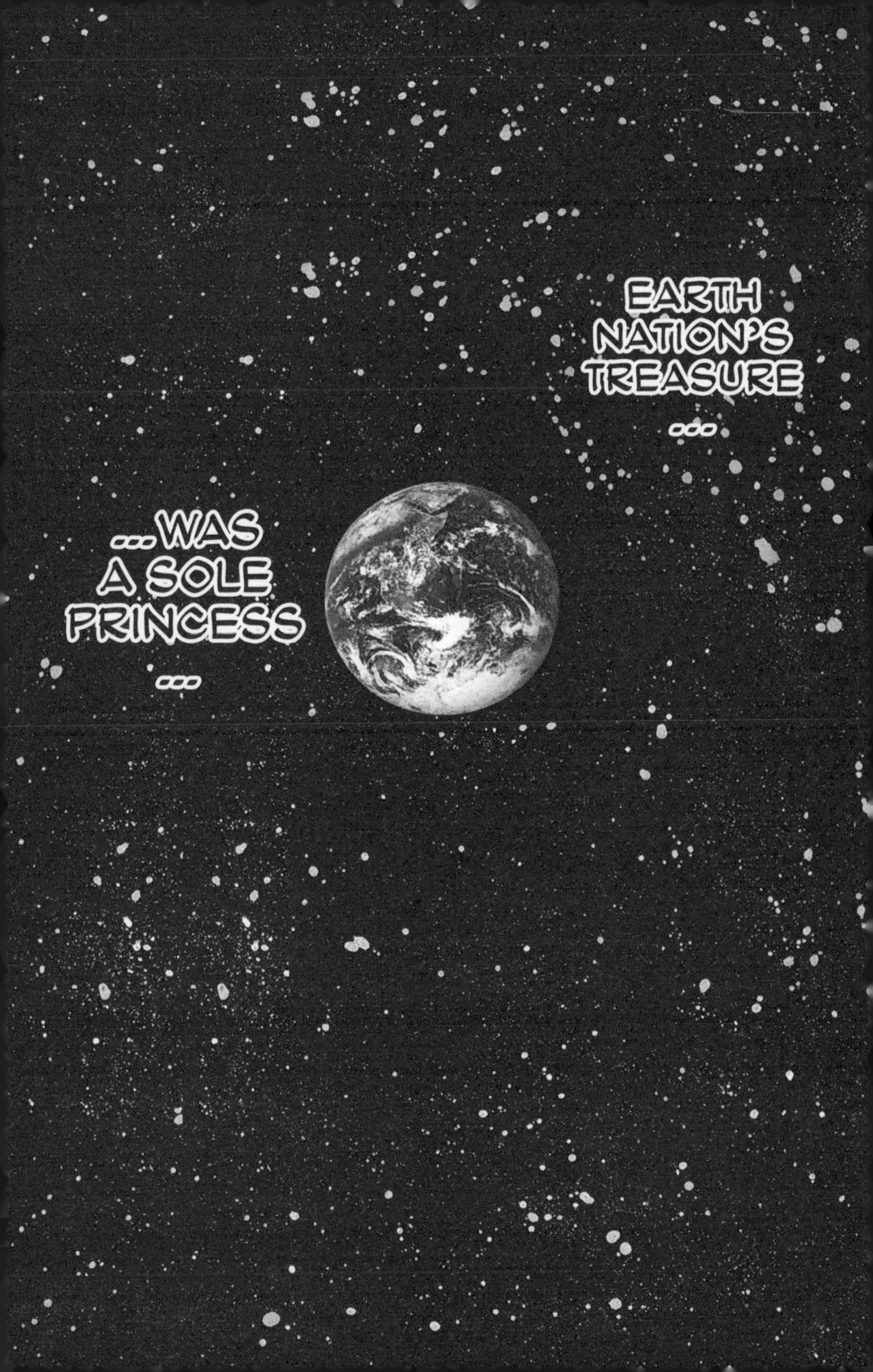
EARTH NATION'S TREASURE ...
...WAS A SOLE PRINCESS ...

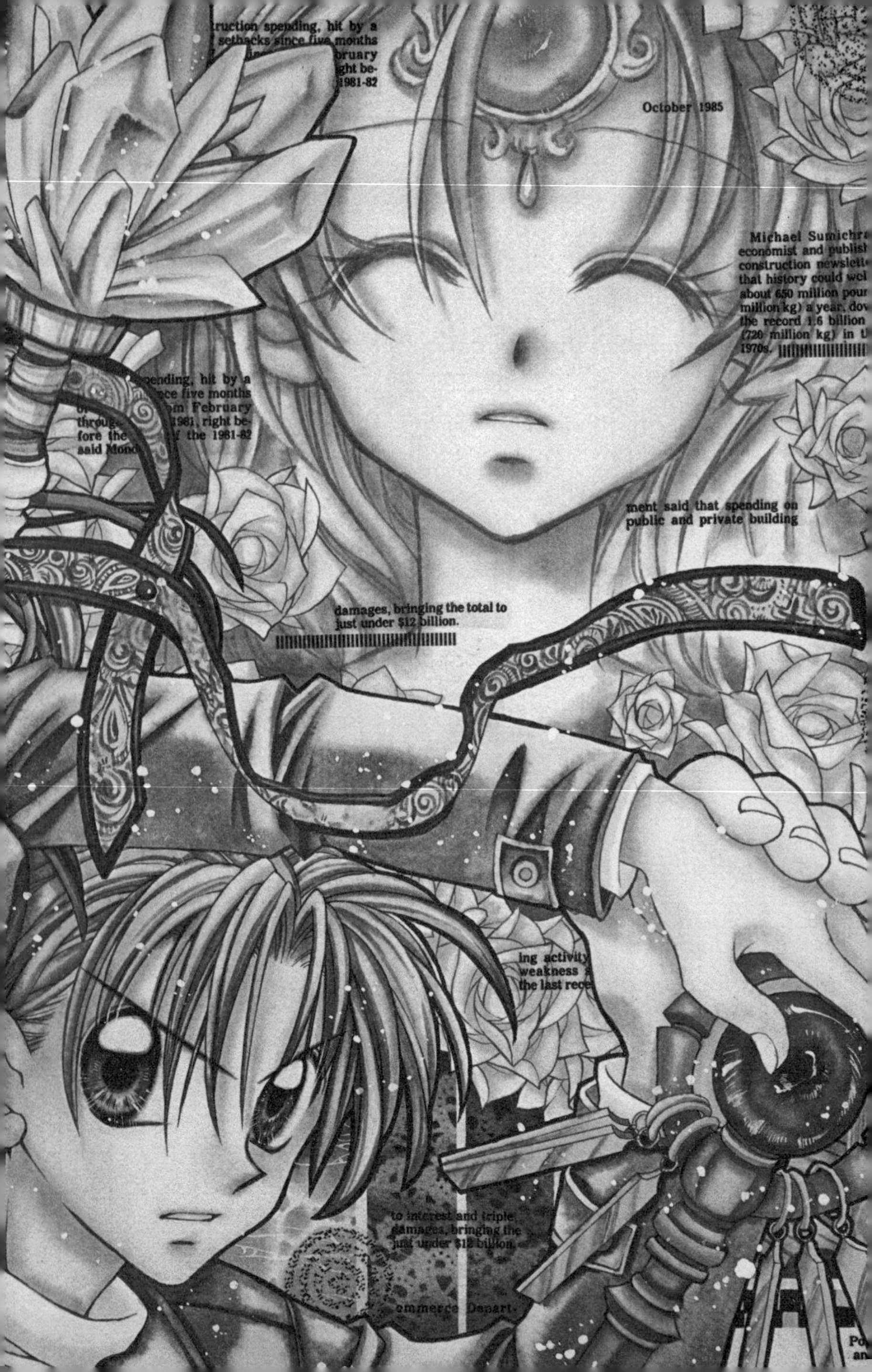
ruction spending, hit by a
setbacks since five months
1981-82
October 1985
Michael Sumichra
economist and publish
construction newslette
that history could wel
about 650 million pour
million kg) a year, dov
the record 1.6 billion
(720 million kg) in t
1970s.
pending, hit by a
nce five months
om February
1981, right be-
fore the
f the 1981-82
said Mond
ment said that spending on
public and private building
damages, bringing the total to
just under $12 billion.
ing activity
weakness
the last rece
to interest and triple
damages, bringing the
just under $12 billion.
ommerce Depart-

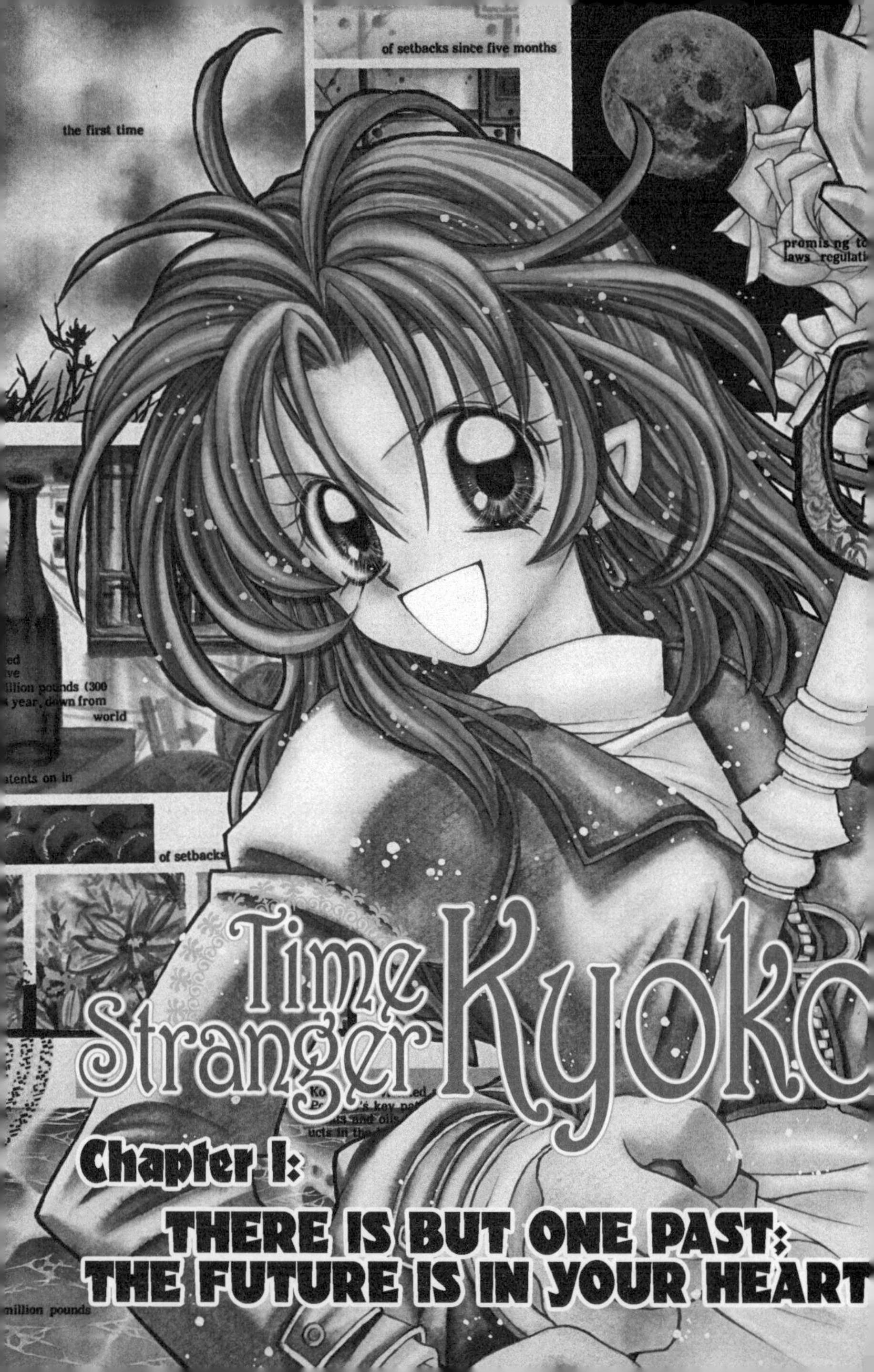
of setbacks since five months
the first time
promising to
laws regulati
million pounds (300
year, down from
world
atents on in
of setbacks
Time Stranger Kyoko
Chapter 1:
THERE IS BUT ONE PAST;
THE FUTURE IS IN YOUR HEART
million pounds

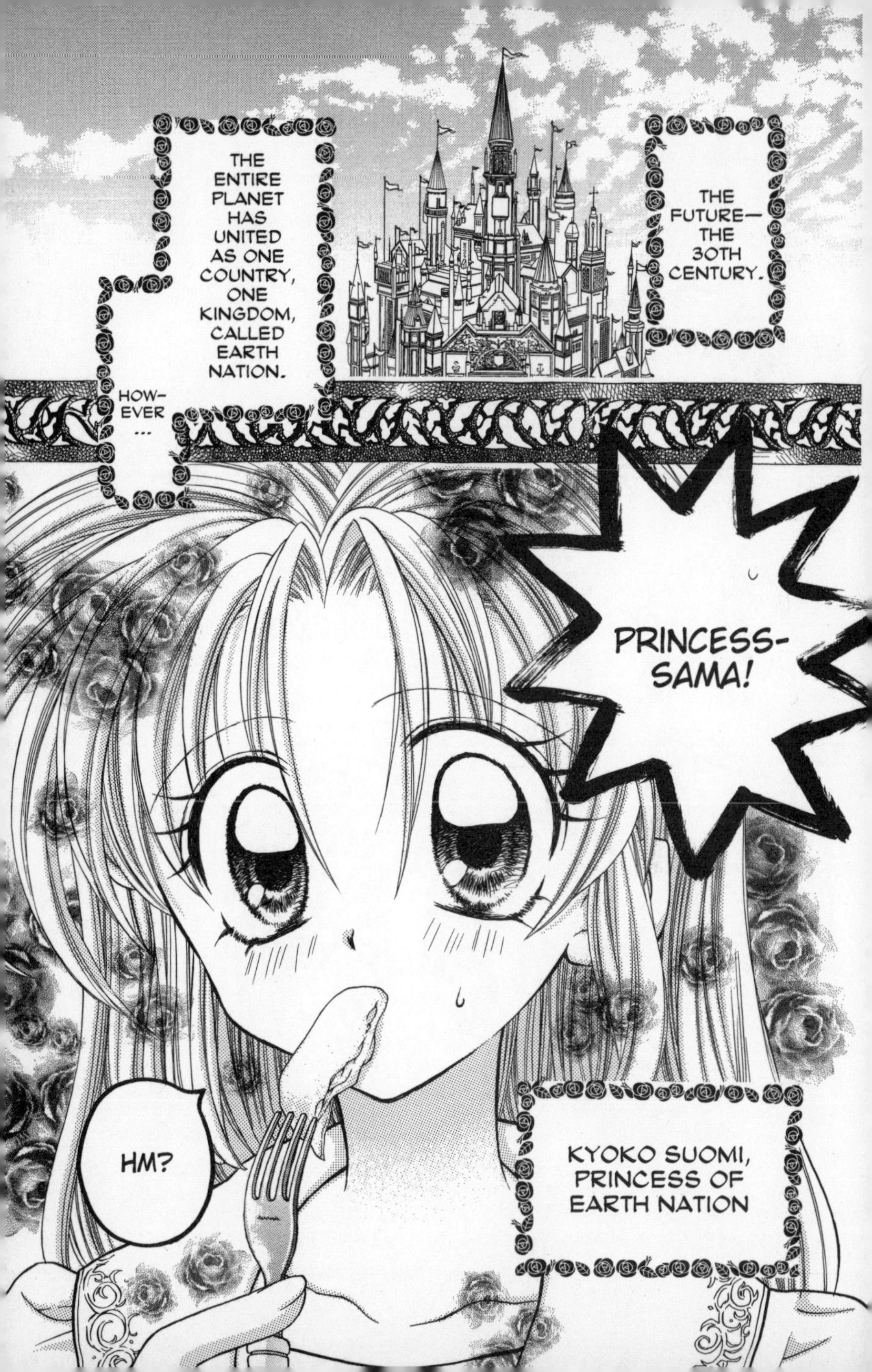
THE FUTURE— THE 30TH CENTURY.
THE ENTIRE PLANET HAS UNITED AS ONE COUNTRY, ONE KINGDOM, CALLED EARTH NATION.
HOW-EVER ...
PRINCESS-SAMA!
KYOKO SUOMI, PRINCESS OF EARTH NATION
HM?

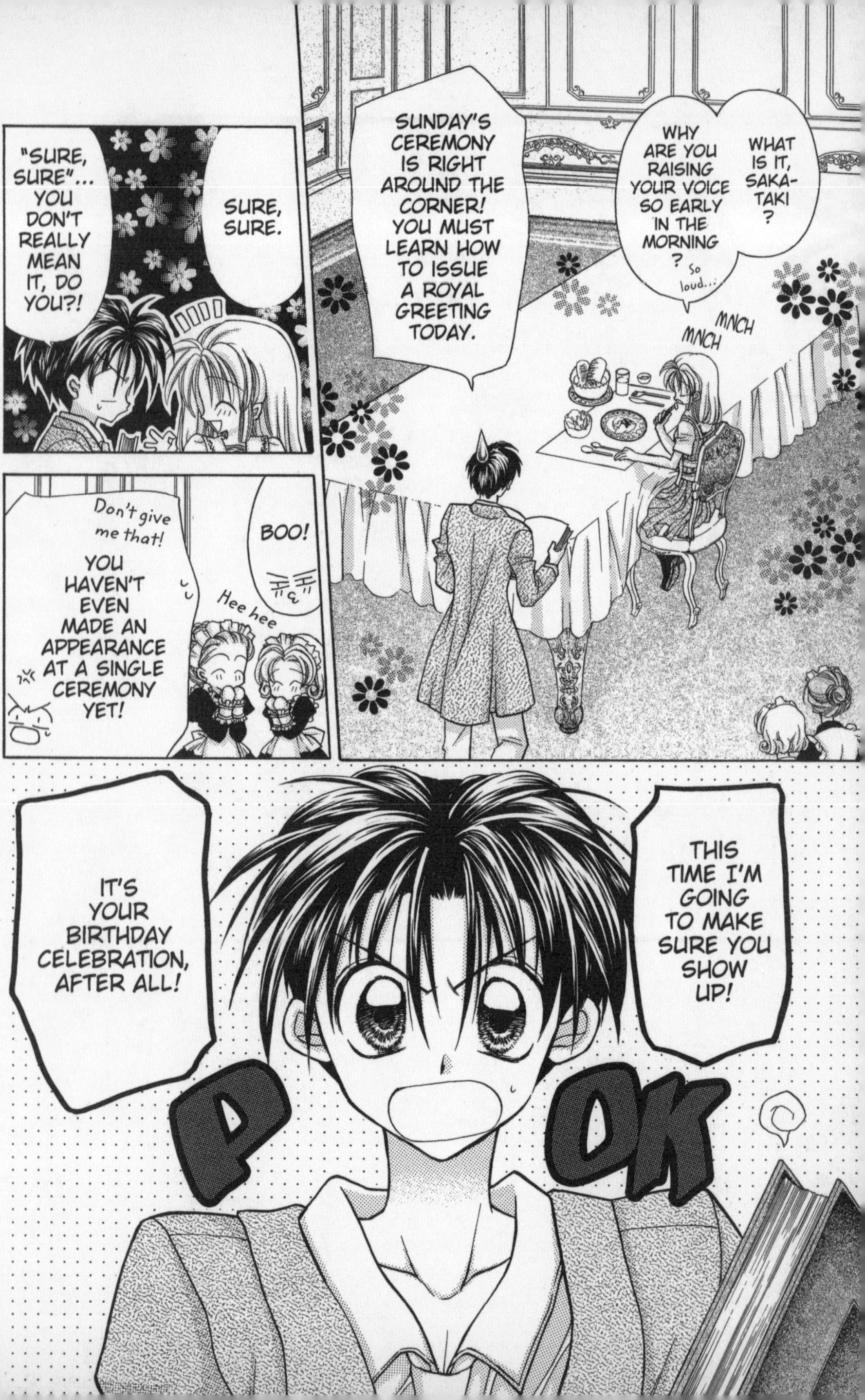
WHAT IS IT, SAKATAKI?
WHY ARE YOU RAISING YOUR VOICE SO EARLY IN THE MORNING?
So loud...
MNCH MNCH
SUNDAY'S CEREMONY IS RIGHT AROUND THE CORNER! YOU MUST LEARN HOW TO ISSUE A ROYAL GREETING TODAY.
SURE, SURE.
"SURE, SURE"... YOU DON'T REALLY MEAN IT, DO YOU?!
BOO!
Hee hee
Don't give me that!
YOU HAVEN'T EVEN MADE AN APPEARANCE AT A SINGLE CEREMONY YET!
THIS TIME I'M GOING TO MAKE SURE YOU SHOW UP!
IT'S YOUR BIRTHDAY CELEBRATION, AFTER ALL!
POK

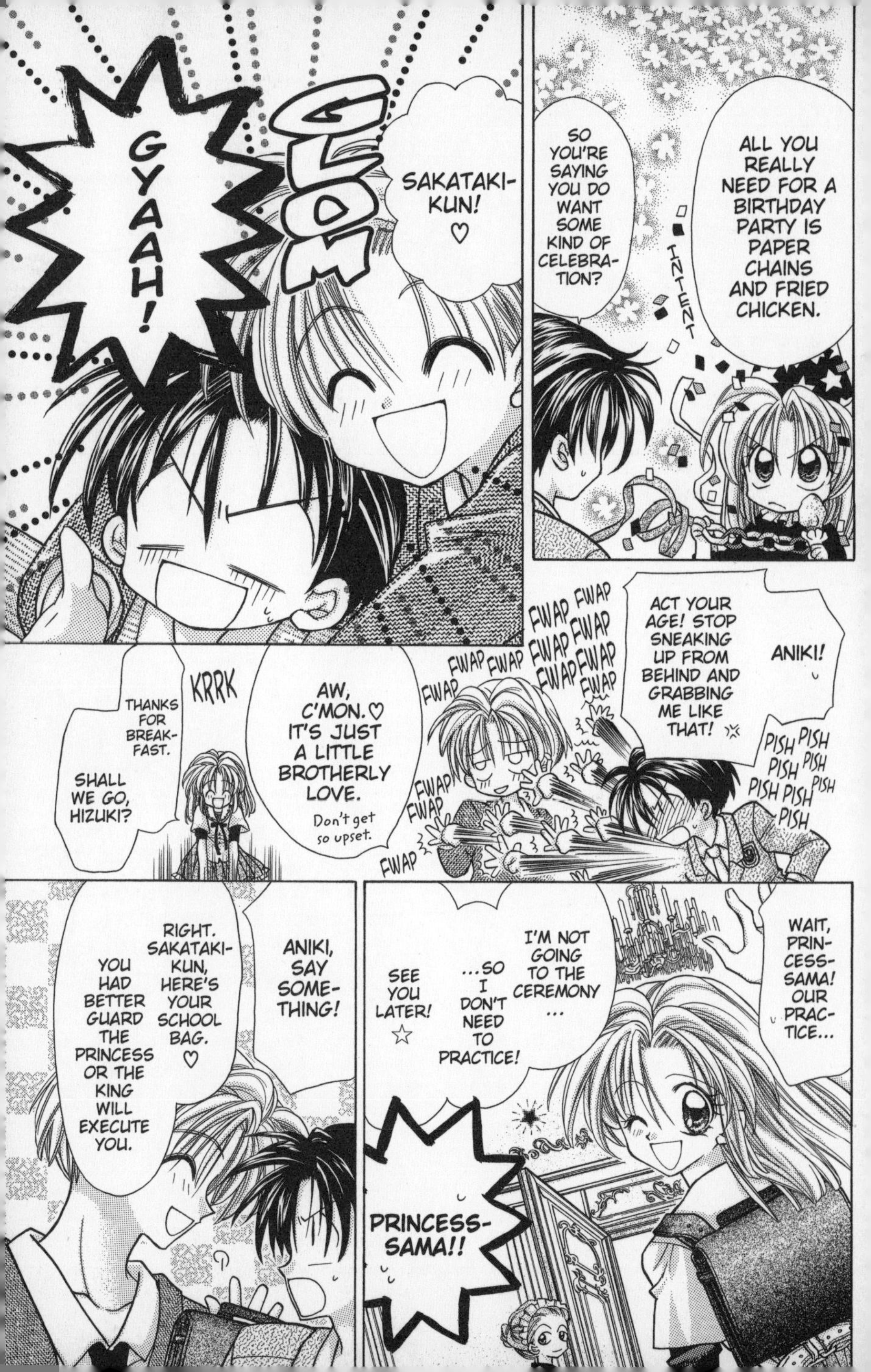
ALL YOU REALLY NEED FOR A BIRTHDAY PARTY IS PAPER CHAINS AND FRIED CHICKEN.
INTENT
SO YOU'RE SAYING YOU DO WANT SOME KIND OF CELEBRATION?
SAKATAKI-KUN! ♡
GLOM
GYAAH!
ANIKI!
ACT YOUR AGE! STOP SNEAKING UP FROM BEHIND AND GRABBING ME LIKE THAT!
PISH PISH PISH PISH PISH PISH PISH PISH PISH
FWAP FWAP FWAP FWAP FWAP FWAP FWAP FWAP FWAP FWAP FWAP FWAP FWAP
AW, C'MON. ♡ IT'S JUST A LITTLE BROTHERLY LOVE.
Don't get so upset.
KRRK
THANKS FOR BREAKFAST.
SHALL WE GO, HIZUKI?
WAIT, PRINCESS-SAMA! OUR PRACTICE...
I'M NOT GOING TO THE CEREMONY...
...SO I DON'T NEED TO PRACTICE!
SEE YOU LATER! ☆
PRINCESS-SAMA!!
ANIKI, SAY SOMETHING!
RIGHT. SAKATAKI-KUN, HERE'S YOUR SCHOOL BAG. ♡
YOU HAD BETTER GUARD THE PRINCESS OR THE KING WILL EXECUTE YOU.

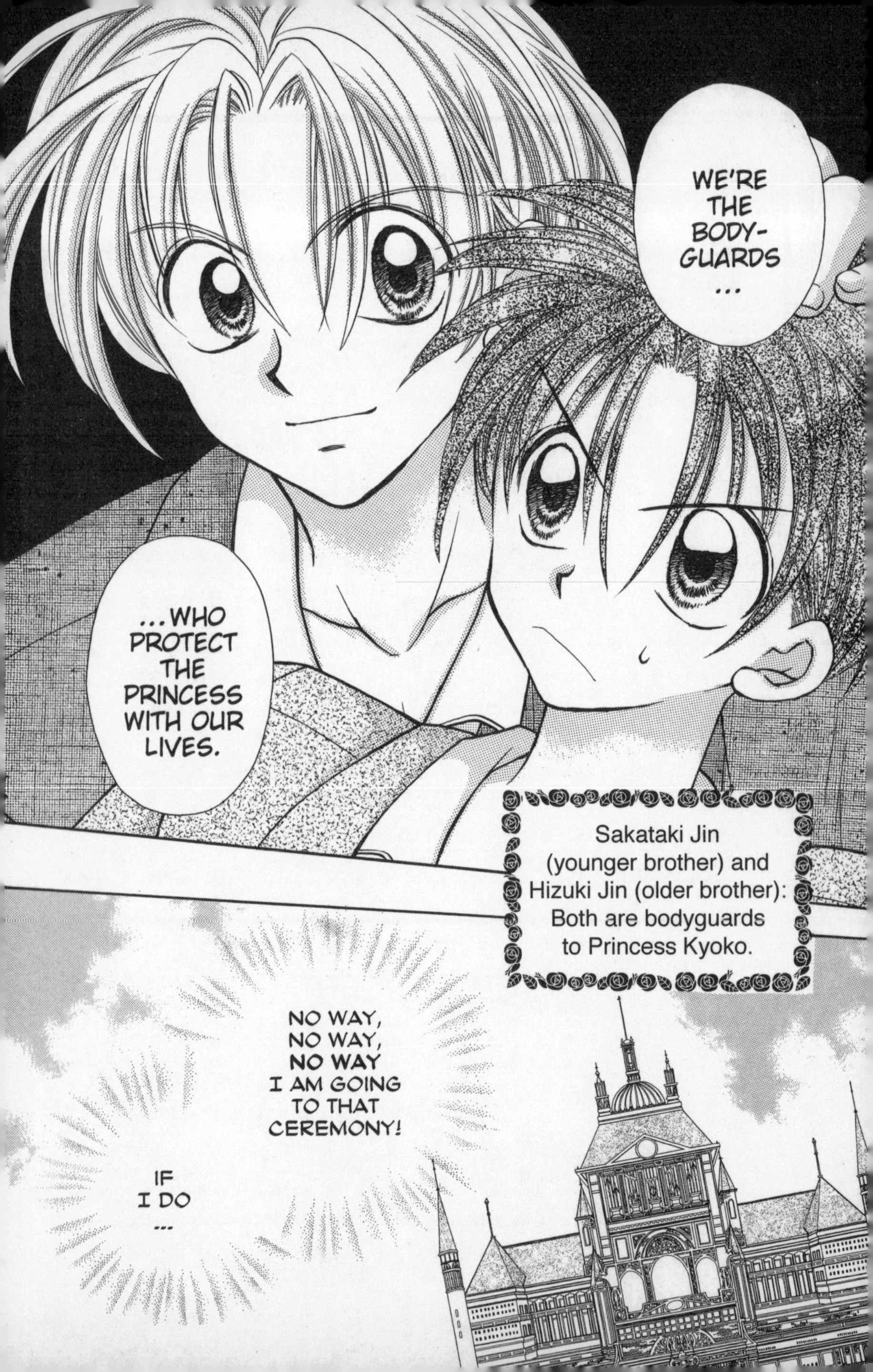
WE'RE THE BODY-GUARDS ...
...WHO PROTECT THE PRINCESS WITH OUR LIVES.
Sakataki Jin (younger brother) and Hizuki Jin (older brother): Both are bodyguards to Princess Kyoko.
NO WAY, NO WAY, NO WAY I AM GOING TO THAT CEREMONY!
IF I DO ...

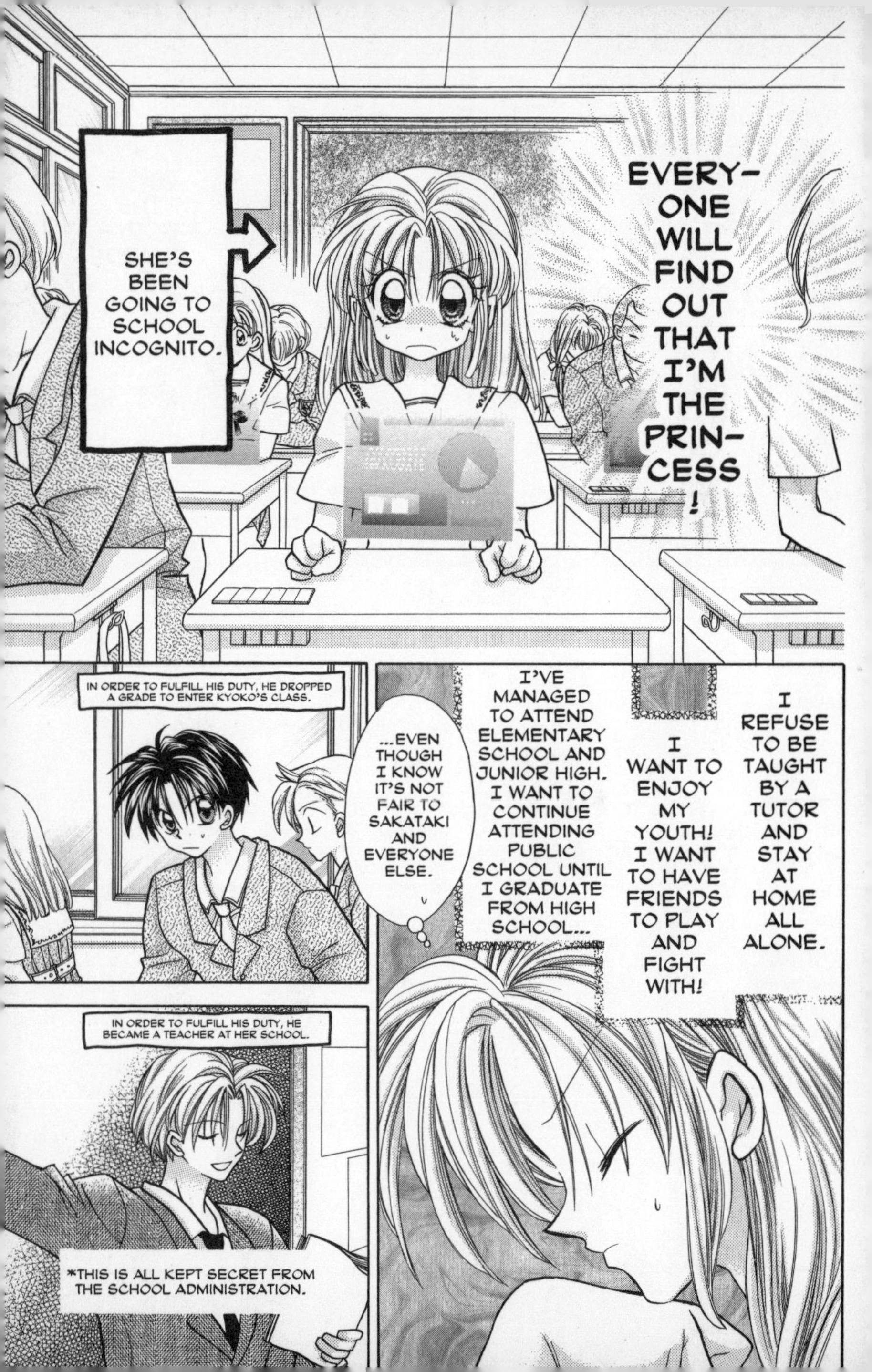
EVERY-ONE WILL FIND OUT THAT I'M THE PRIN-CESS!
SHE'S BEEN GOING TO SCHOOL INCOGNITO.
I REFUSE TO BE TAUGHT BY A TUTOR AND STAY AT HOME ALL ALONE.
I WANT TO ENJOY MY YOUTH! I WANT TO HAVE FRIENDS TO PLAY AND FIGHT WITH!
I'VE MANAGED TO ATTEND ELEMENTARY SCHOOL AND JUNIOR HIGH. I WANT TO CONTINUE ATTENDING PUBLIC SCHOOL UNTIL I GRADUATE FROM HIGH SCHOOL...
...EVEN THOUGH I KNOW IT'S NOT FAIR TO SAKATAKI AND EVERYONE ELSE.
IN ORDER TO FULFILL HIS DUTY, HE DROPPED A GRADE TO ENTER KYOKO'S CLASS.
IN ORDER TO FULFILL HIS DUTY, HE BECAME A TEACHER AT HER SCHOOL.
*THIS IS ALL KEPT SECRET FROM THE SCHOOL ADMINISTRATION.

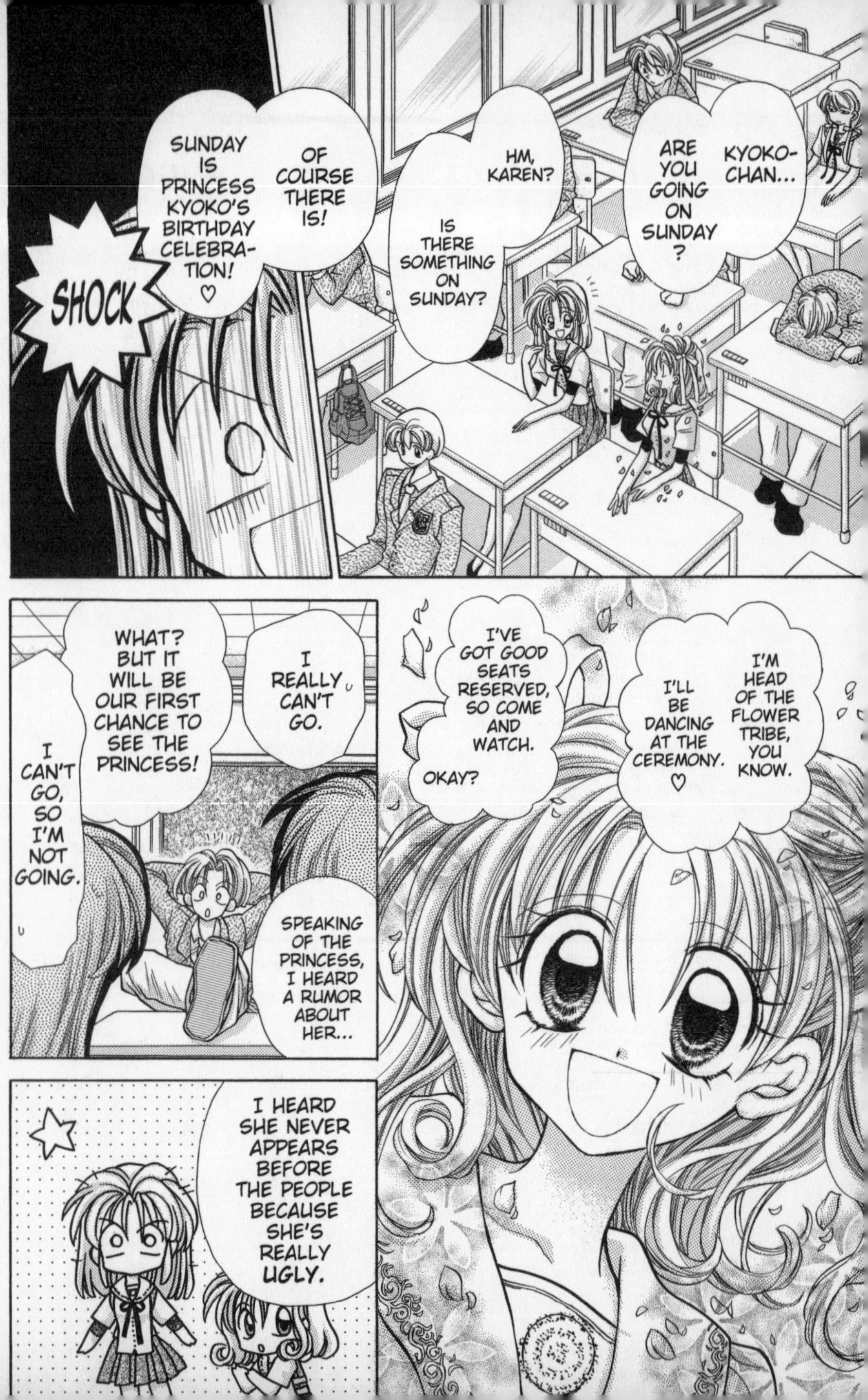
KYOKO-CHAN...
ARE YOU GOING ON SUNDAY?
HM, KAREN?
IS THERE SOMETHING ON SUNDAY?
OF COURSE THERE IS!
SUNDAY IS PRINCESS KYOKO'S BIRTHDAY CELEBRATION! ♡
SHOCK
I'M HEAD OF THE FLOWER TRIBE, YOU KNOW.
I'LL BE DANCING AT THE CEREMONY. ♡
I'VE GOT GOOD SEATS RESERVED, SO COME AND WATCH.
OKAY?
I REALLY CAN'T GO.
WHAT? BUT IT WILL BE OUR FIRST CHANCE TO SEE THE PRINCESS!
I CAN'T GO, SO I'M NOT GOING.
SPEAKING OF THE PRINCESS, I HEARD A RUMOR ABOUT HER...
I HEARD SHE NEVER APPEARS BEFORE THE PEOPLE BECAUSE SHE'S REALLY UGLY.

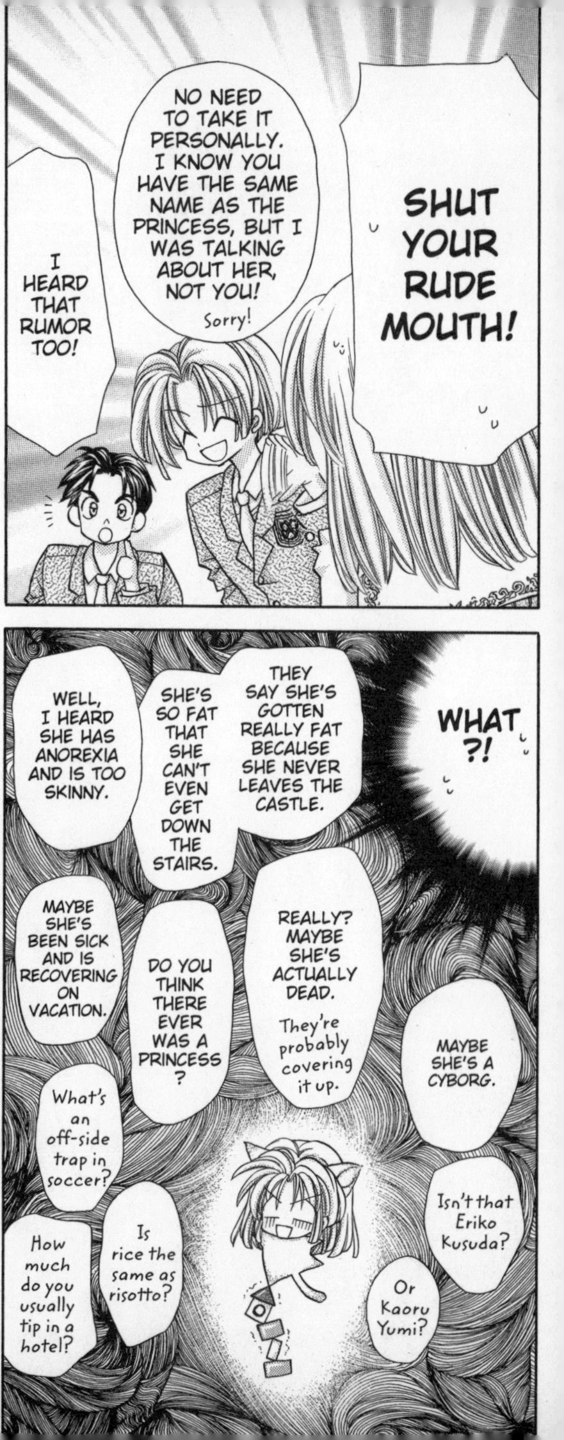
SHUT YOUR RUDE MOUTH!
NO NEED TO TAKE IT PERSONALLY. I KNOW YOU HAVE THE SAME NAME AS THE PRINCESS, BUT I WAS TALKING ABOUT HER, NOT YOU!
Sorry!
I HEARD THAT RUMOR TOO!
WHAT?!
THEY SAY SHE'S GOTTEN REALLY FAT BECAUSE SHE NEVER LEAVES THE CASTLE.
SHE'S SO FAT THAT SHE CAN'T EVEN GET DOWN THE STAIRS.
WELL, I HEARD SHE HAS ANOREXIA AND IS TOO SKINNY.
MAYBE SHE'S A CYBORG.
REALLY? MAYBE SHE'S ACTUALLY DEAD.
They're probably covering it up.
DO YOU THINK THERE EVER WAS A PRINCESS?
MAYBE SHE'S BEEN SICK AND IS RECOVERING ON VACATION.
Isn't that Eriko Kusuda?
Or Kaoru Yumi?
Is rice the same as risotto?
What's an off-side trap in soccer?
How much do you usually tip in a hotel?

HELLO.

HELLO TO ALL MY READERS, BOTH NEW AND OLD! MY NAME IS ARINA TANEMURA, AND I'M WRITING THIS MANGA FOR SHUEISHA'S *RIBON* MAGAZINE. HOW ARE YOU ALL?! TO TELL YOU THE TRUTH, IT'S ALREADY BEEN FIVE YEARS SINCE I BECAME A MANGA ARTIST...WOW! *TIME STRANGER KYOKO* VOL. 1 IS MY TENTH MANGA!! Yay! klap klap

SO, ANYWAY, HERE'S THE FIRST *KYOKO* VOLUME. I'M VERY HAPPY!

DRAWING KYOKO-CHAN IS LIKE A DREAM COME TRUE FOR ME, AND ALTHOUGH I'M NOT SURE I'LL BE ABLE TO SEE IT THROUGH TO THE END, I'LL GIVE IT MY ALL.

Send fan letters here → Arina Tanemura
C/O VIZ Media
P.O. Box 77010
San Francisco, CA 94107

THERE ARE QUITE A LOT OF CHARACTERS IN *KYOKO*. (IT'S ACTUALLY VERY GOOD OF YOU ALL TO STILL BE WITH ME.) IT'S HARD TO REMEMBER THEM ALL, SO I PLAN TO DO PROPER CHARACTER INTRODUCTIONS IN THIS VOLUME. However, I haven't written any recently...

ALSO, PLEASE BE SURE TO READ "LITTLE PRINCESS," THE BONUS STORY AT THE END. LITTLE KYOKO IS MY FAVORITE CHARACTER, AND THERE ARE SOME IMPORTANT PLOT POINTS IN IT.

I love drawing young characters!

NOW, ON TO THE MAIN EVENT. →

START THE MAGIC THAT ALLOWS US TO SEE TOMORROW: TIME TRAVEL!!

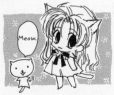

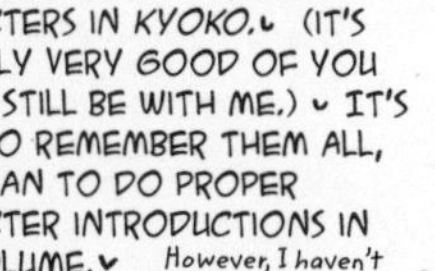
Meow.

↑ This is a picture of me and my cat. We will be explaining things in the story.

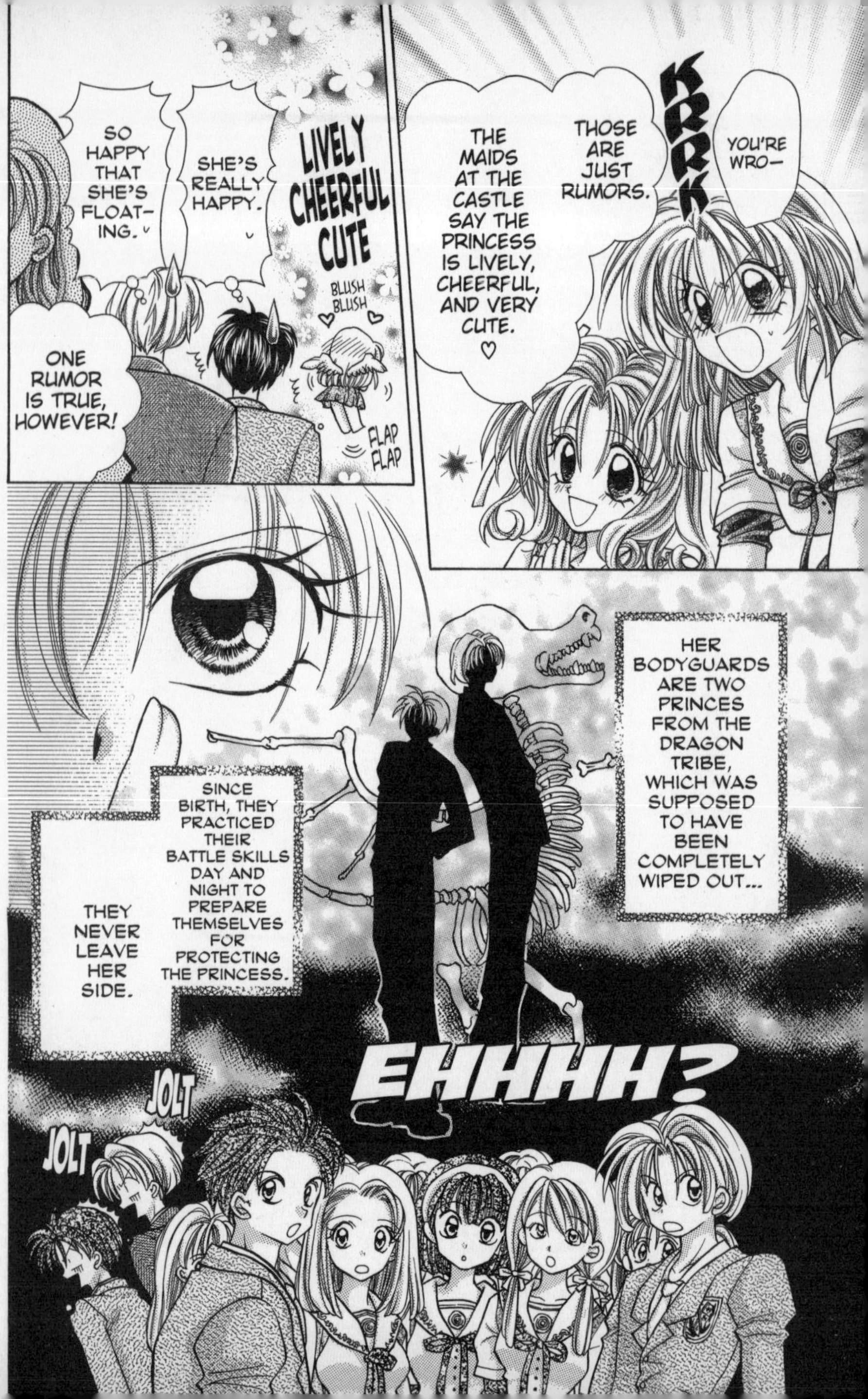
YOU'RE WRO—
KRRK
THOSE ARE JUST RUMORS.
THE MAIDS AT THE CASTLE SAY THE PRINCESS IS LIVELY, CHEERFUL, AND VERY CUTE. ♡
LIVELY CHEERFUL CUTE
BLUSH BLUSH
SHE'S REALLY HAPPY.
SO HAPPY THAT SHE'S FLOAT-ING.
ONE RUMOR IS TRUE, HOWEVER!
FLAP FLAP
HER BODYGUARDS ARE TWO PRINCES FROM THE DRAGON TRIBE, WHICH WAS SUPPOSED TO HAVE BEEN COMPLETELY WIPED OUT...
SINCE BIRTH, THEY PRACTICED THEIR BATTLE SKILLS DAY AND NIGHT TO PREPARE THEMSELVES FOR PROTECTING THE PRINCESS.
THEY NEVER LEAVE HER SIDE.
EHHHH?
JOLT
JOLT

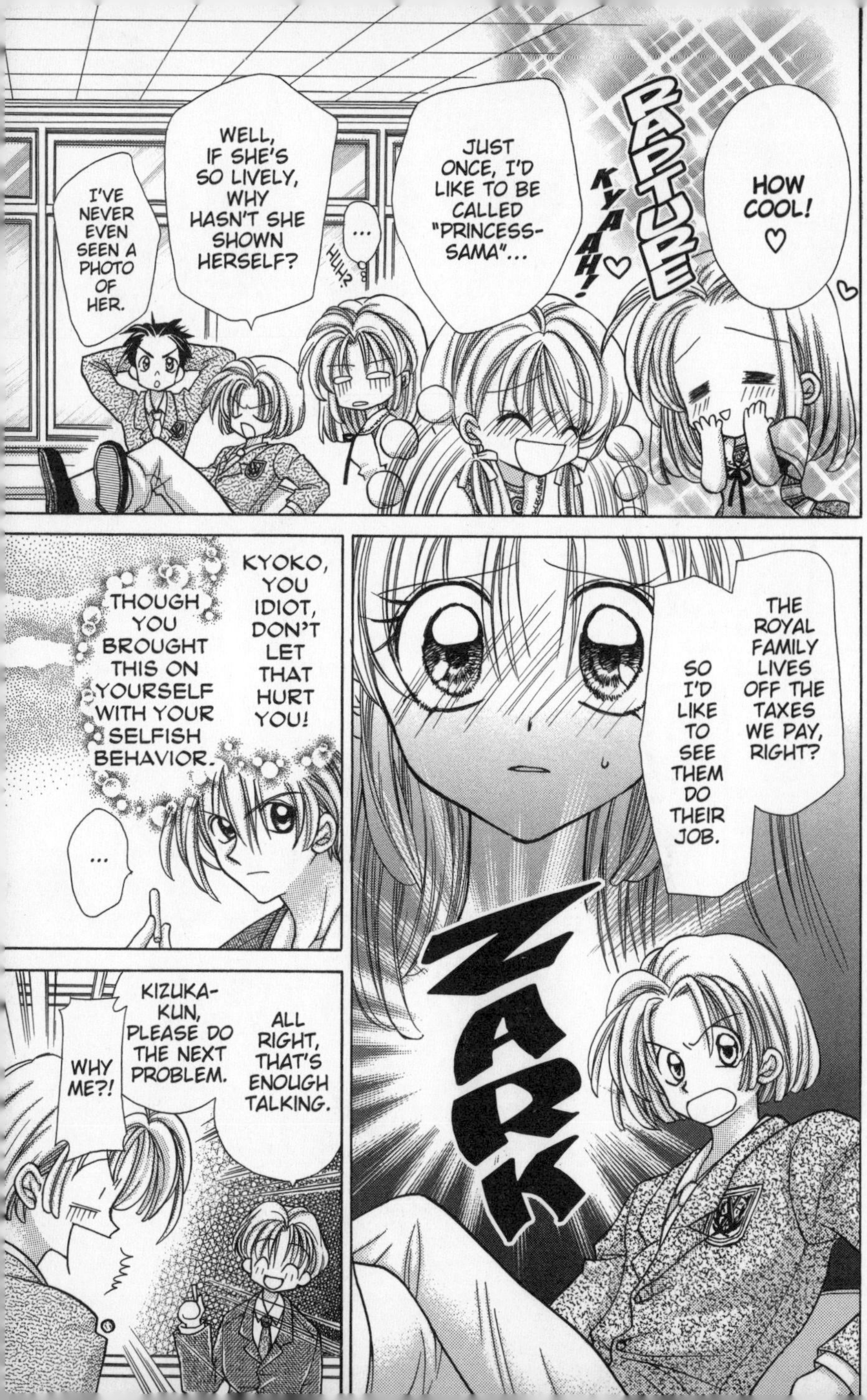

HOW COOL! ♡
RAPTURE
KYAAH! ♡
JUST ONCE, I'D LIKE TO BE CALLED "PRINCESS-SAMA"...
...
HUH?
WELL, IF SHE'S SO LIVELY, WHY HASN'T SHE SHOWN HERSELF?
I'VE NEVER EVEN SEEN A PHOTO OF HER.
THE ROYAL FAMILY LIVES OFF THE TAXES WE PAY, RIGHT?
SO I'D LIKE TO SEE THEM DO THEIR JOB.
ZARK
KYOKO, YOU IDIOT, DON'T LET THAT HURT YOU!
THOUGH YOU BROUGHT THIS ON YOURSELF WITH YOUR SELFISH BEHAVIOR.
...
ALL RIGHT, THAT'S ENOUGH TALKING.
KIZUKA-KUN, PLEASE DO THE NEXT PROBLEM.
WHY ME?!

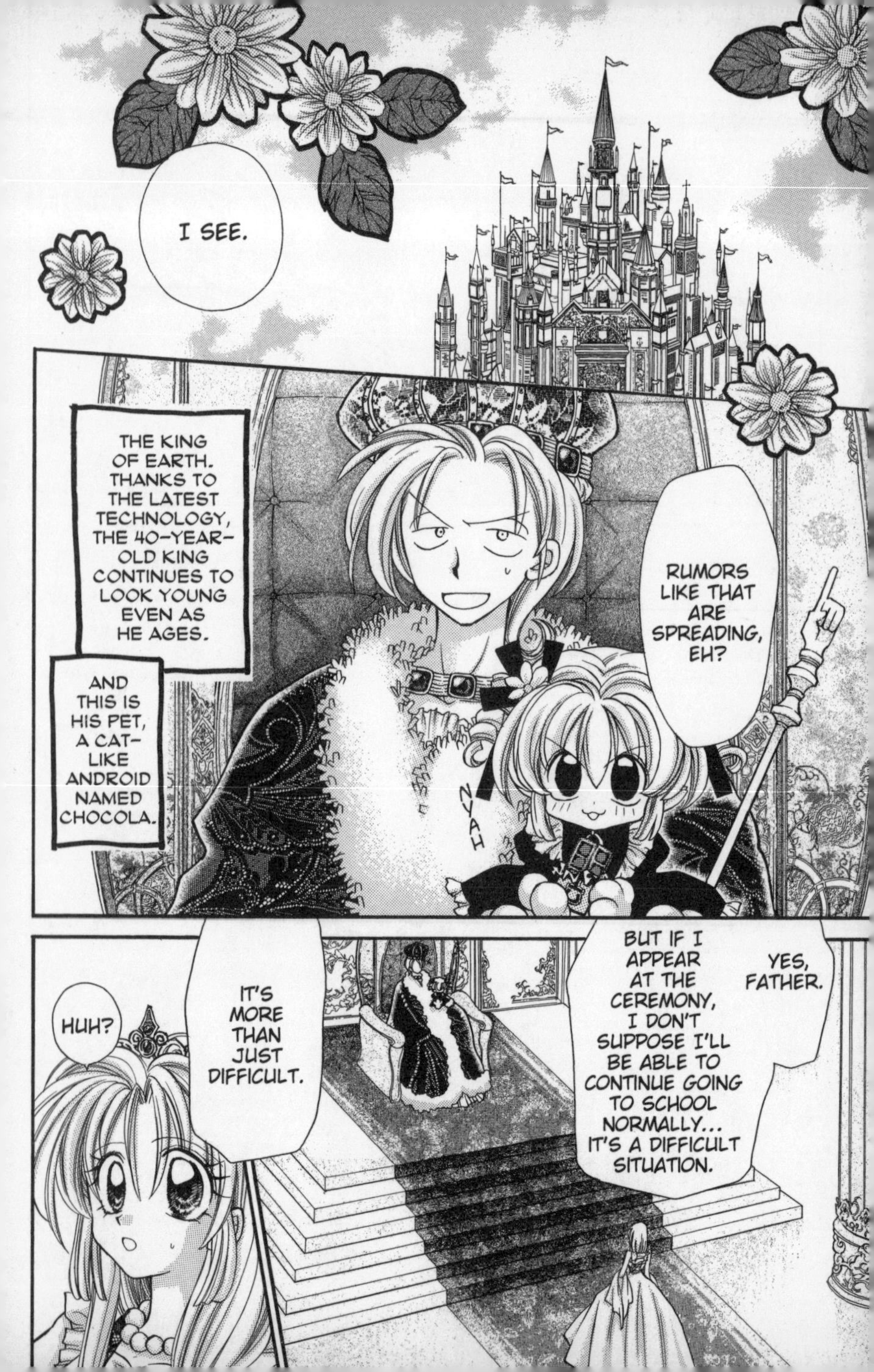
I SEE.
RUMORS LIKE THAT ARE SPREADING, EH?
THE KING OF EARTH. THANKS TO THE LATEST TECHNOLOGY, THE 40-YEAR-OLD KING CONTINUES TO LOOK YOUNG EVEN AS HE AGES.
AND THIS IS HIS PET, A CAT-LIKE ANDROID NAMED CHOCOLA.
NYAH
YES, FATHER.
BUT IF I APPEAR AT THE CEREMONY, I DON'T SUPPOSE I'LL BE ABLE TO CONTINUE GOING TO SCHOOL NORMALLY... IT'S A DIFFICULT SITUATION.
IT'S MORE THAN JUST DIFFICULT.
HUH?

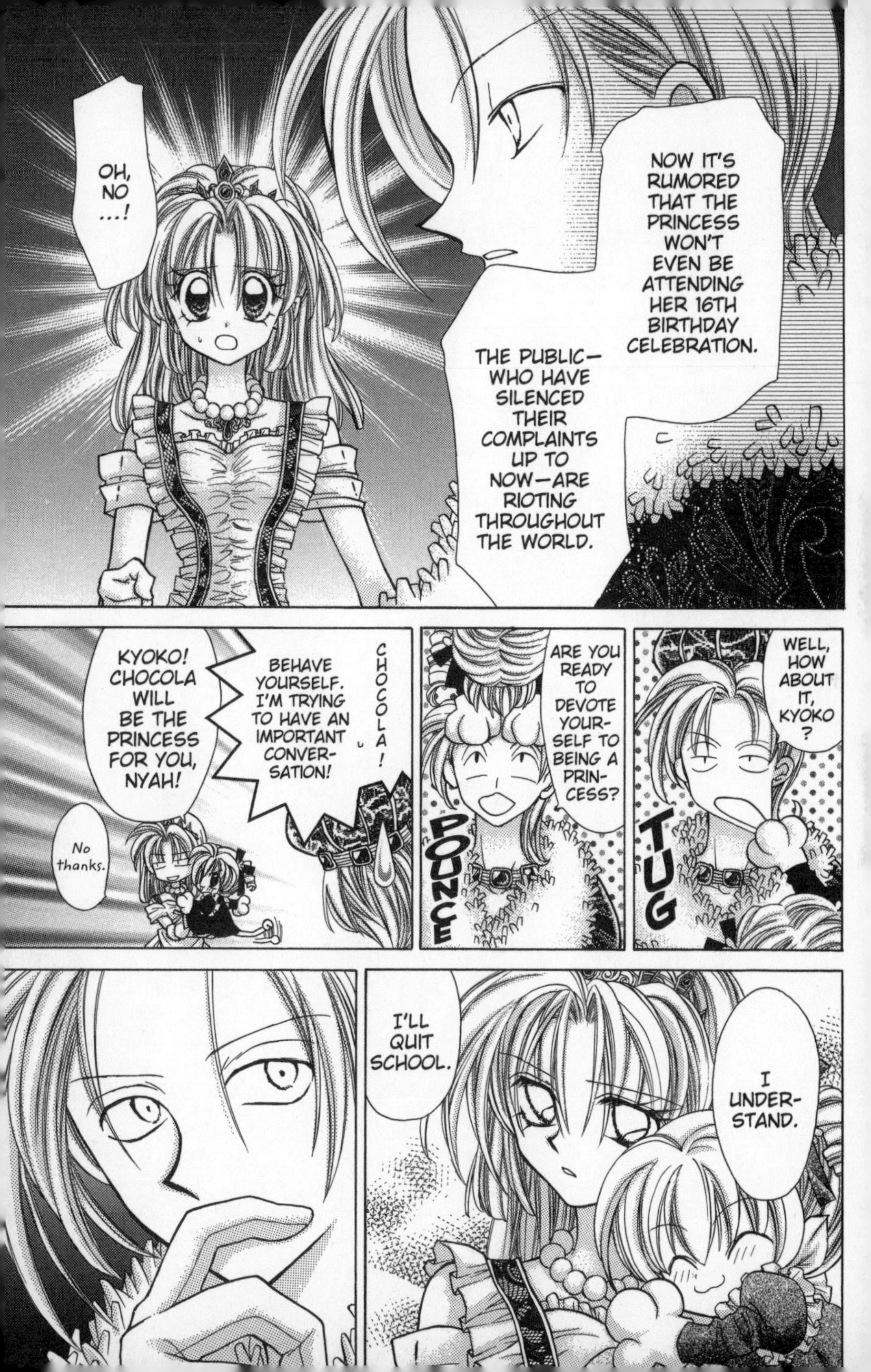
NOW IT'S RUMORED THAT THE PRINCESS WON'T EVEN BE ATTENDING HER 16TH BIRTHDAY CELEBRATION.
THE PUBLIC—WHO HAVE SILENCED THEIR COMPLAINTS UP TO NOW—ARE RIOTING THROUGHOUT THE WORLD.
OH, NO ...!
WELL, HOW ABOUT IT, KYOKO?
TUG
ARE YOU READY TO DEVOTE YOURSELF TO BEING A PRINCESS?
POUNCE
CHOCOLA!
BEHAVE YOURSELF. I'M TRYING TO HAVE AN IMPORTANT CONVERSATION!
KYOKO! CHOCOLA WILL BE THE PRINCESS FOR YOU, NYAH!
No thanks.
I UNDERSTAND.
I'LL QUIT SCHOOL.

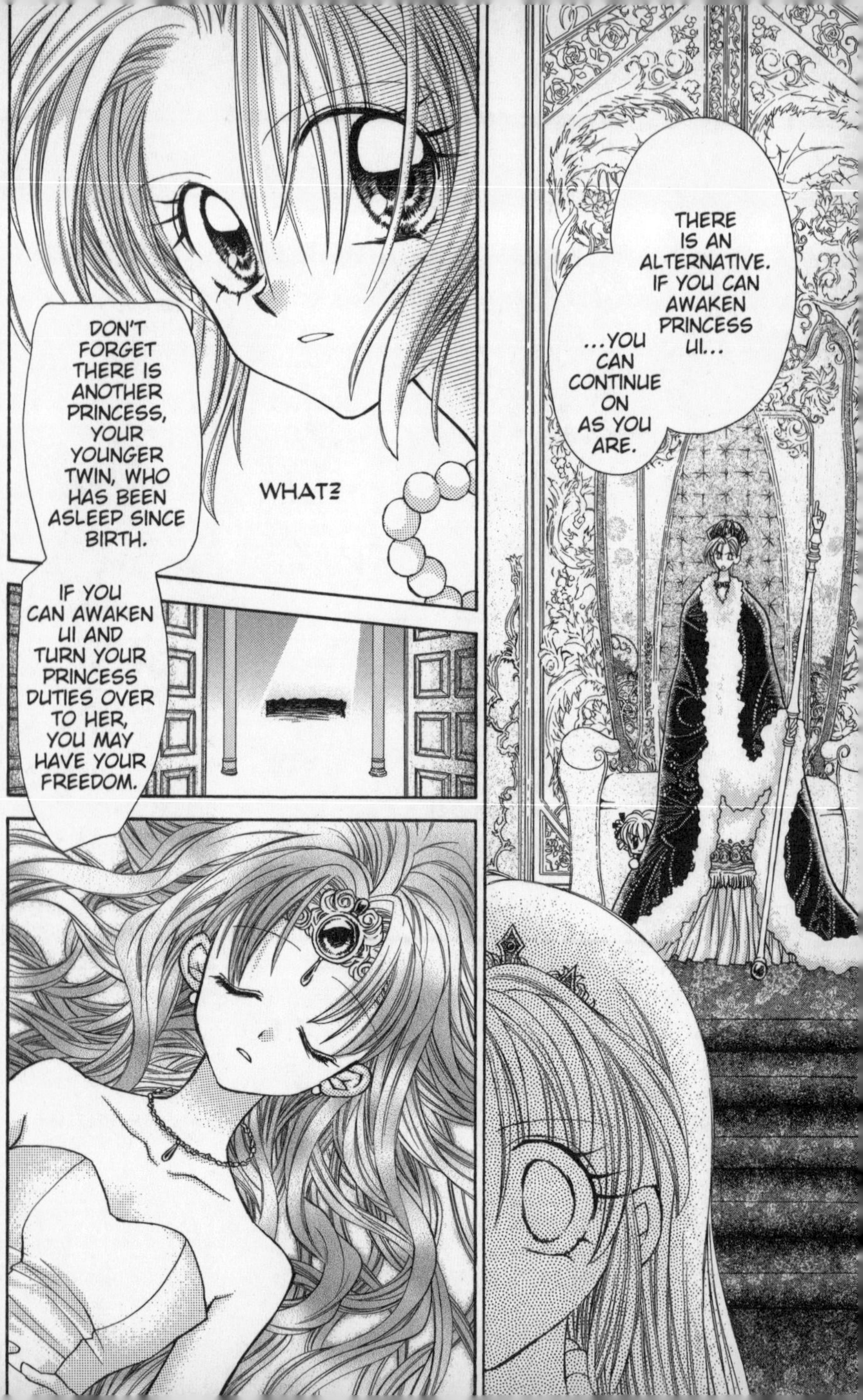
THERE IS AN ALTERNATIVE. IF YOU CAN AWAKEN PRINCESS UI...
...YOU CAN CONTINUE ON AS YOU ARE.
WHAT?
DON'T FORGET THERE IS ANOTHER PRINCESS, YOUR YOUNGER TWIN, WHO HAS BEEN ASLEEP SINCE BIRTH.
IF YOU CAN AWAKEN UI AND TURN YOUR PRINCESS DUTIES OVER TO HER, YOU MAY HAVE YOUR FREEDOM.

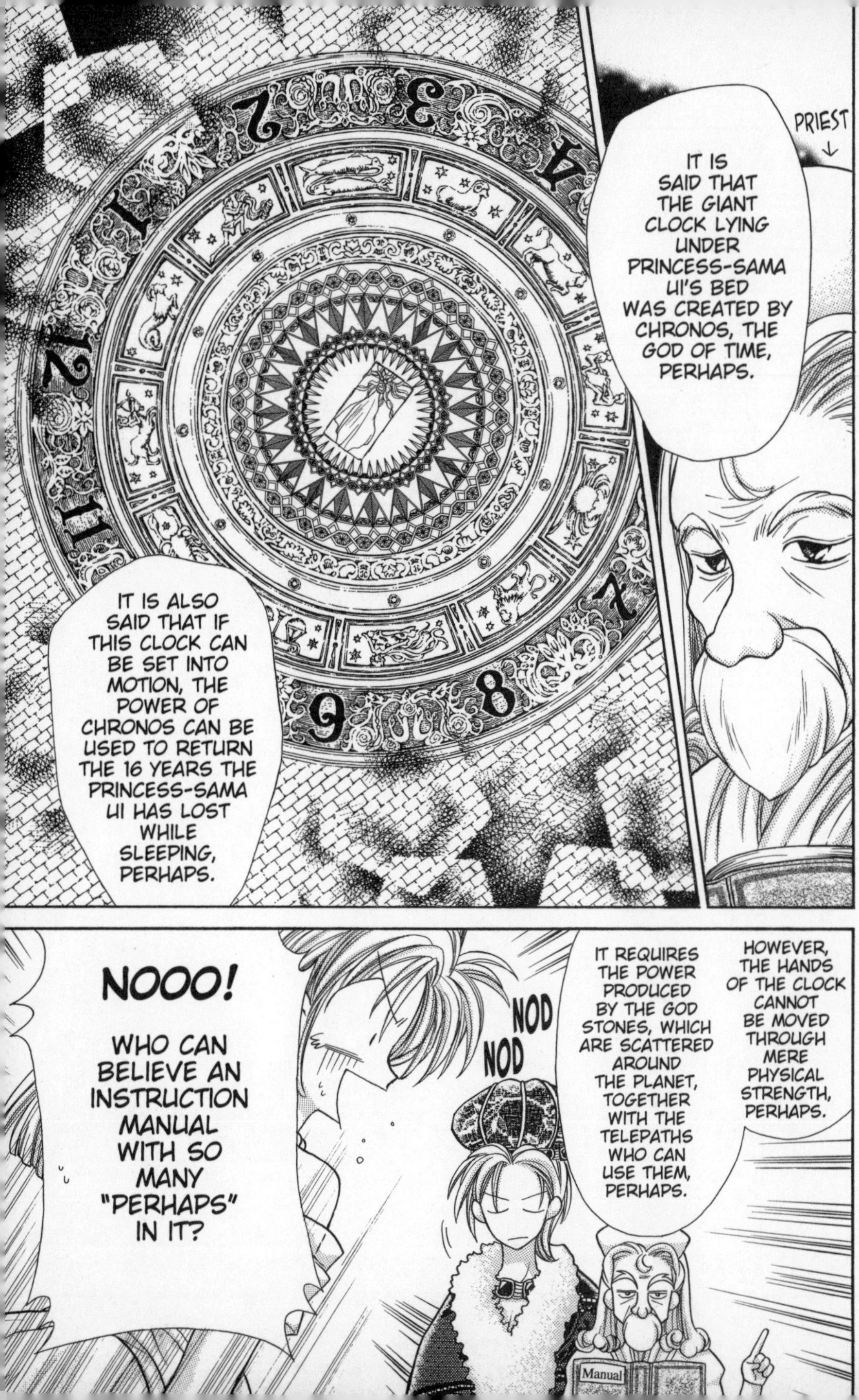
PRIEST
IT IS SAID THAT THE GIANT CLOCK LYING UNDER PRINCESS-SAMA UI'S BED WAS CREATED BY CHRONOS, THE GOD OF TIME, PERHAPS.
IT IS ALSO SAID THAT IF THIS CLOCK CAN BE SET INTO MOTION, THE POWER OF CHRONOS CAN BE USED TO RETURN THE 16 YEARS THE PRINCESS-SAMA UI HAS LOST WHILE SLEEPING, PERHAPS.
HOWEVER, THE HANDS OF THE CLOCK CANNOT BE MOVED THROUGH MERE PHYSICAL STRENGTH, PERHAPS.
IT REQUIRES THE POWER PRODUCED BY THE GOD STONES, WHICH ARE SCATTERED AROUND THE PLANET, TOGETHER WITH THE TELEPATHS WHO CAN USE THEM, PERHAPS.
NOD
NOD
NOOO!
WHO CAN BELIEVE AN INSTRUCTION MANUAL WITH SO MANY "PERHAPS" IN IT?
Manual

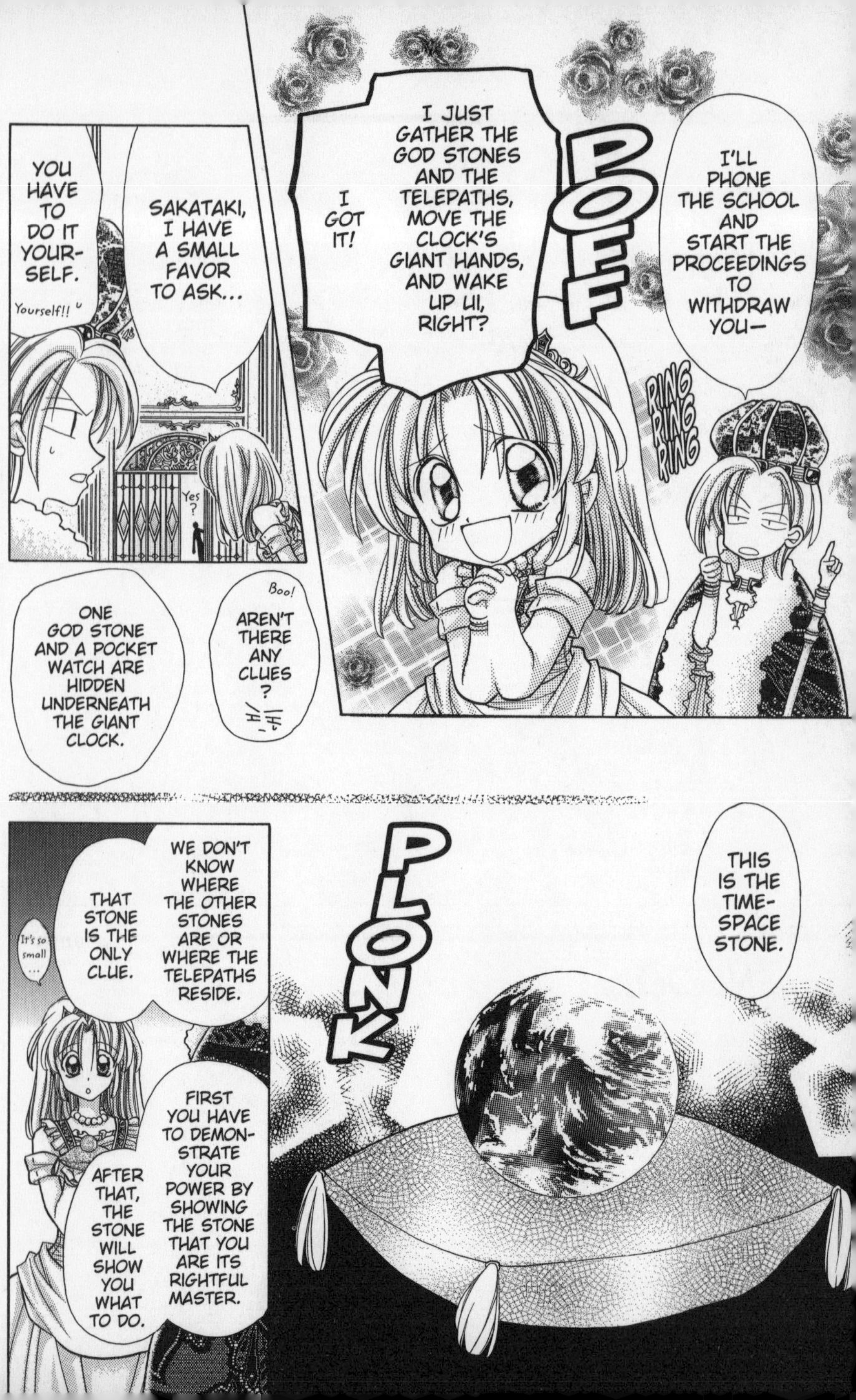
I'LL PHONE THE SCHOOL AND START THE PROCEEDINGS TO WITHDRAW YOU—
POFF
RING RING RING
I JUST GATHER THE GOD STONES AND THE TELEPATHS, MOVE THE CLOCK'S GIANT HANDS, AND WAKE UP UI, RIGHT?
I GOT IT!
SAKATAKI, I HAVE A SMALL FAVOR TO ASK...
YOU HAVE TO DO IT YOURSELF.
Yourself!!
Yes?
Boo!
AREN'T THERE ANY CLUES?
ONE GOD STONE AND A POCKET WATCH ARE HIDDEN UNDERNEATH THE GIANT CLOCK.
THIS IS THE TIME-SPACE STONE.
PLONK
WE DON'T KNOW WHERE THE OTHER STONES ARE OR WHERE THE TELEPATHS RESIDE.
THAT STONE IS THE ONLY CLUE.
It's so small...
FIRST YOU HAVE TO DEMONSTRATE YOUR POWER BY SHOWING THE STONE THAT YOU ARE ITS RIGHTFUL MASTER.
AFTER THAT, THE STONE WILL SHOW YOU WHAT TO DO.

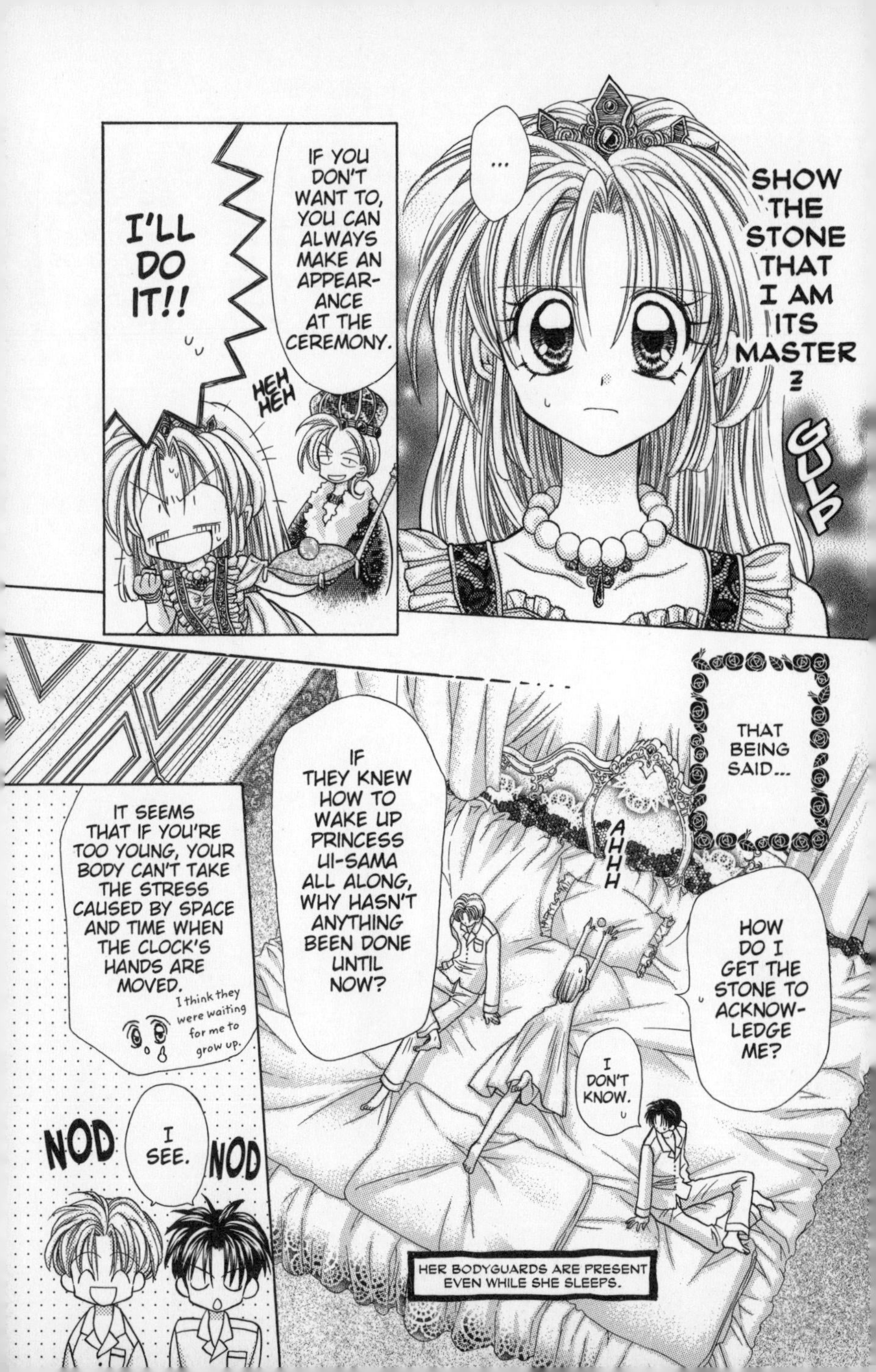
...
SHOW THE STONE THAT I AM ITS MASTER?
GULP
IF YOU DON'T WANT TO, YOU CAN ALWAYS MAKE AN APPEARANCE AT THE CEREMONY.
I'LL DO IT!!
HEH HEH
THAT BEING SAID...
AHHH
HOW DO I GET THE STONE TO ACKNOWLEDGE ME?
I DON'T KNOW.
IF THEY KNEW HOW TO WAKE UP PRINCESS UI-SAMA ALL ALONG, WHY HASN'T ANYTHING BEEN DONE UNTIL NOW?
HER BODYGUARDS ARE PRESENT EVEN WHILE SHE SLEEPS.
IT SEEMS THAT IF YOU'RE TOO YOUNG, YOUR BODY CAN'T TAKE THE STRESS CAUSED BY SPACE AND TIME WHEN THE CLOCK'S HANDS ARE MOVED.
I think they were waiting for me to grow up.
NOD
I SEE.
NOD

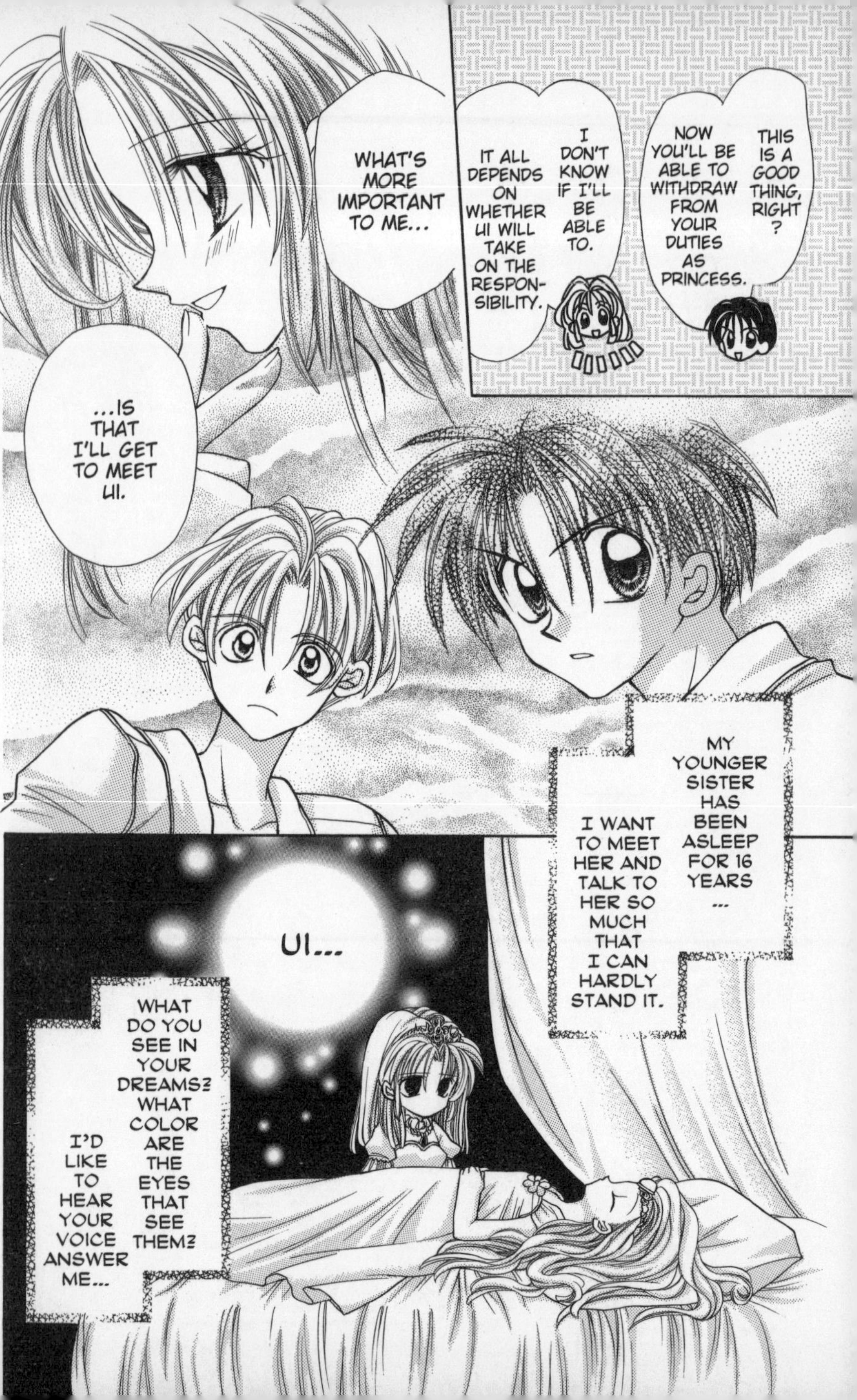
THIS IS A GOOD THING, RIGHT?
NOW YOU'LL BE ABLE TO WITHDRAW FROM YOUR DUTIES AS PRINCESS.
I DON'T KNOW IF I'LL BE ABLE TO.
IT ALL DEPENDS ON WHETHER UI WILL TAKE ON THE RESPONSIBILITY.
WHAT'S MORE IMPORTANT TO ME...
...IS THAT I'LL GET TO MEET UI.
MY YOUNGER SISTER HAS BEEN ASLEEP FOR 16 YEARS...
I WANT TO MEET HER AND TALK TO HER SO MUCH THAT I CAN HARDLY STAND IT.
UI...
WHAT DO YOU SEE IN YOUR DREAMS? WHAT COLOR ARE THE EYES THAT SEE THEM?
I'D LIKE TO HEAR YOUR VOICE ANSWER ME...

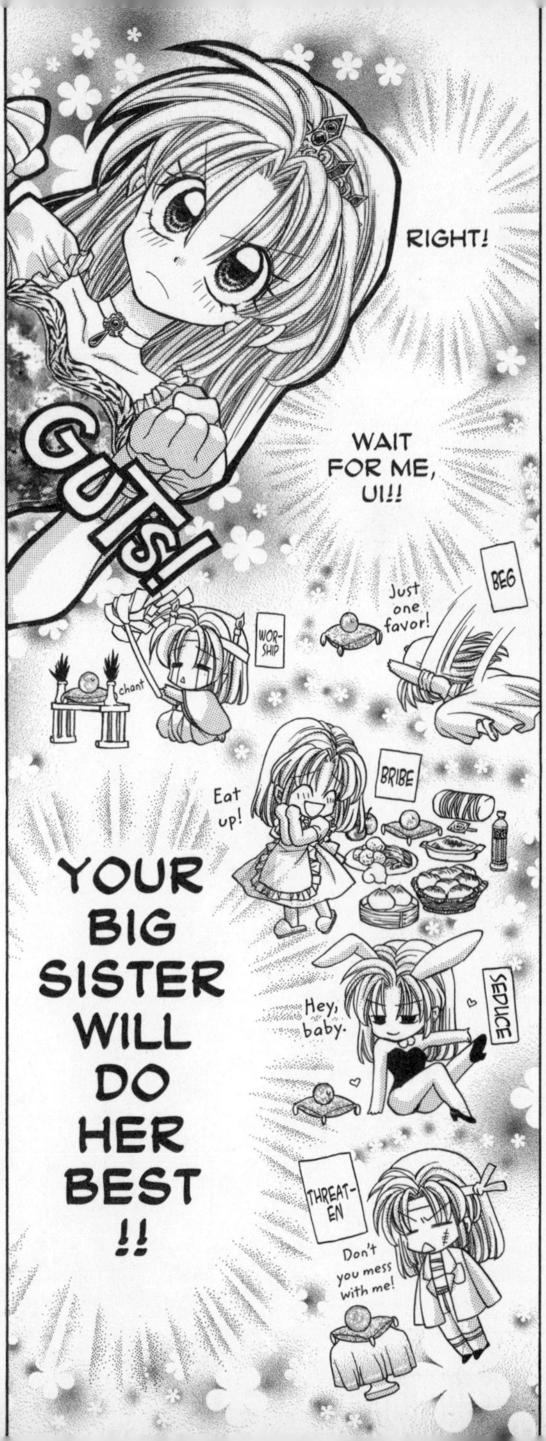
RIGHT!
GUTS!
WAIT FOR ME, UI!!
BEG
Just one favor!
WOR-SHIP
chant
BRIBE
Eat up!
YOUR BIG SISTER WILL DO HER BEST!!
SEDUCE
Hey, baby.
THREAT-EN
Don't you mess with me!

SHE'S INNOCENT BUT BRAVE!
WAY TO GO, PRINCESS-SAMA!

KYOKO SUOMI

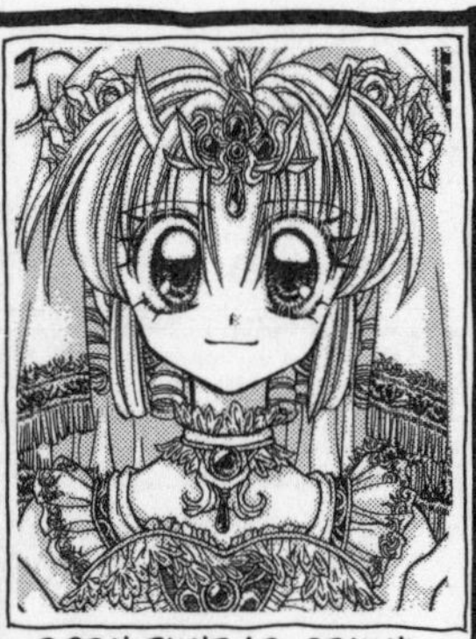

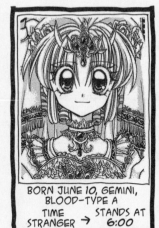

BORN JUNE 10, GEMINI, BLOOD-TYPE A

TIME STRANGER → STANDS AT 6:00

I LIKE HER FOOLISH SIDE. I THINK SHE LIKES TO TEASE. HER FEMININE SIDE IS SHOWN BY HER LOVE OF THE LACE-THEMED WESTERN CLOTHING BRAND AI·SHI. (SOME OF YOU MAY ALREADY KNOW THIS, BUT THE BRAND IS A PLAY ON THE NAME OF THE SCREENTONE MAKER, AISHI.)

I also used the AI·SHI lace motif ♥ in a furoku letter set...

KYOKO WANTS TO AWAKEN UI SO THAT SHE CAN HAND OVER HER DUTIES TO UI AND STOP BEING A PRINCESS. (IF THAT'S ALL YOU KNOW, YOU NO DOUBT THINK SHE IS SUPREMELY SELFISH. HOWEVER, SHE JUST MAY HAVE SOME SORT OF PLAN, SO PLEASE STICK WITH US UNTIL THE NEXT VOLUME.)

long-term plan

OF THE TWO BROTHERS, HIZUKI IS THE ONE WHO IS IN ON HER JOKES. SAKATAKI, ON THE OTHER HAND, COMES ACROSS AS A BOSSY PAIN IN THE NECK.

KYOKO IS THE MAIN CHARACTER. SHE TURNS 16 IN CHAPTER 1. PLEASE ENJOY!

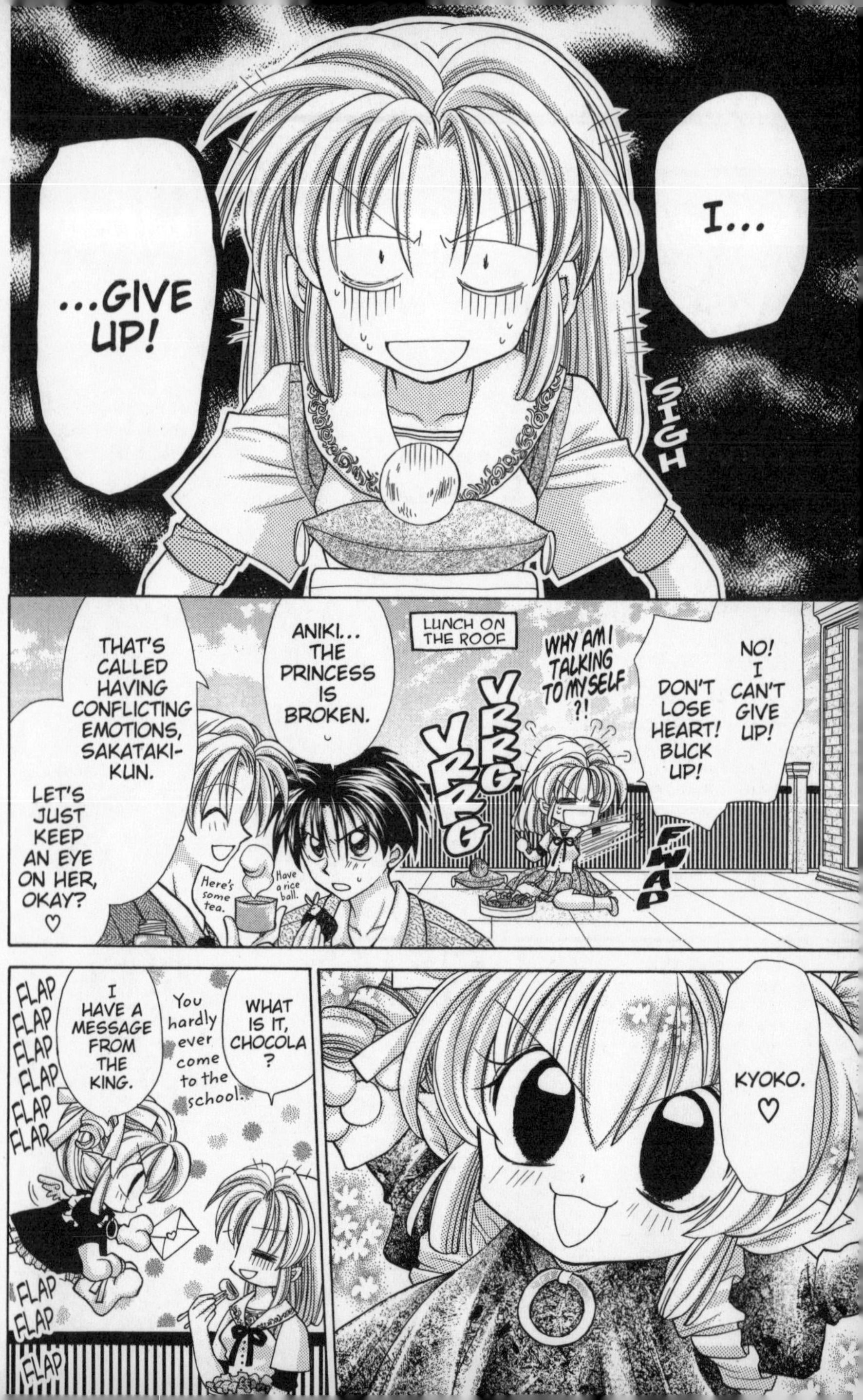
I...
...GIVE UP!
SIGH
LUNCH ON THE ROOF
NO! I CAN'T GIVE UP!
DON'T LOSE HEART! BUCK UP!
FWAP
WHY AM I TALKING TO MYSELF ?!
VRRG VRRG
ANIKI... THE PRINCESS IS BROKEN.
Have a rice ball.
THAT'S CALLED HAVING CONFLICTING EMOTIONS, SAKATAKI-KUN.
Here's some tea.
LET'S JUST KEEP AN EYE ON HER, OKAY? ♡
KYOKO. ♡
WHAT IS IT, CHOCOLA?
You hardly ever come to the school.
I HAVE A MESSAGE FROM THE KING.
FLAP FLAP FLAP FLAP FLAP FLAP
FLAP FLAP
FLAP

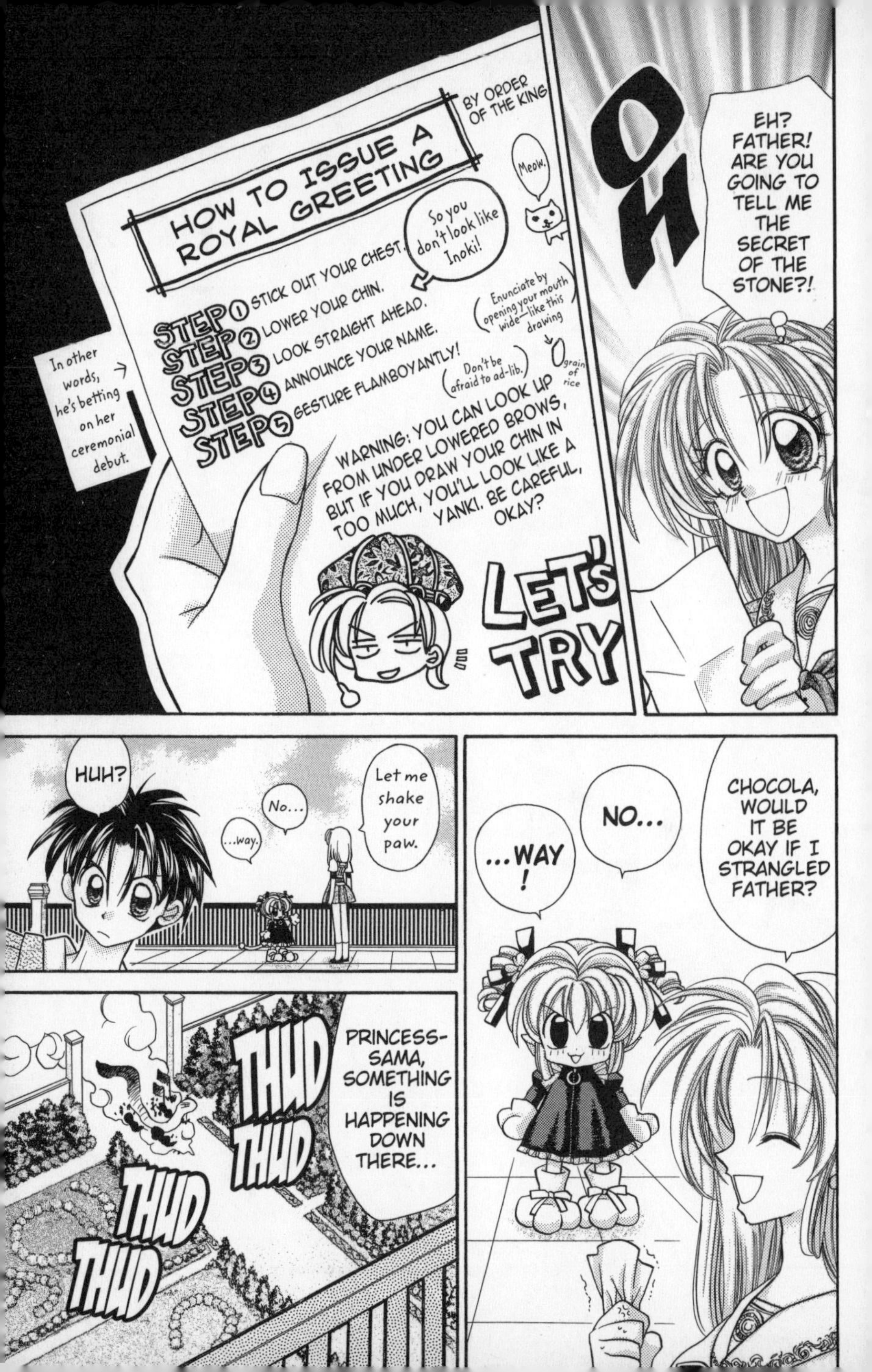
OH
EH? FATHER! ARE YOU GOING TO TELL ME THE SECRET OF THE STONE?!
BY ORDER OF THE KING
HOW TO ISSUE A ROYAL GREETING
Meow.
So you don't look like Inoki!
STEP ① STICK OUT YOUR CHEST.
STEP ② LOWER YOUR CHIN.
STEP ③ LOOK STRAIGHT AHEAD.
STEP ④ ANNOUNCE YOUR NAME.
STEP ⑤ GESTURE FLAMBOYANTLY!
Enunciate by opening your mouth wide—like this drawing
grain of rice
Don't be afraid to ad-lib.
WARNING: YOU CAN LOOK UP FROM UNDER LOWERED BROWS, BUT IF YOU DRAW YOUR CHIN IN TOO MUCH, YOU'LL LOOK LIKE A YANKI. BE CAREFUL, OKAY?
LET'S TRY
In other words, he's betting on her ceremonial debut.
CHOCOLA, WOULD IT BE OKAY IF I STRANGLED FATHER?
NO...
...WAY!
Let me shake your paw.
No...
...way.
HUH?
PRINCESS-SAMA, SOMETHING IS HAPPENING DOWN THERE...
THUD THUD
THUD THUD

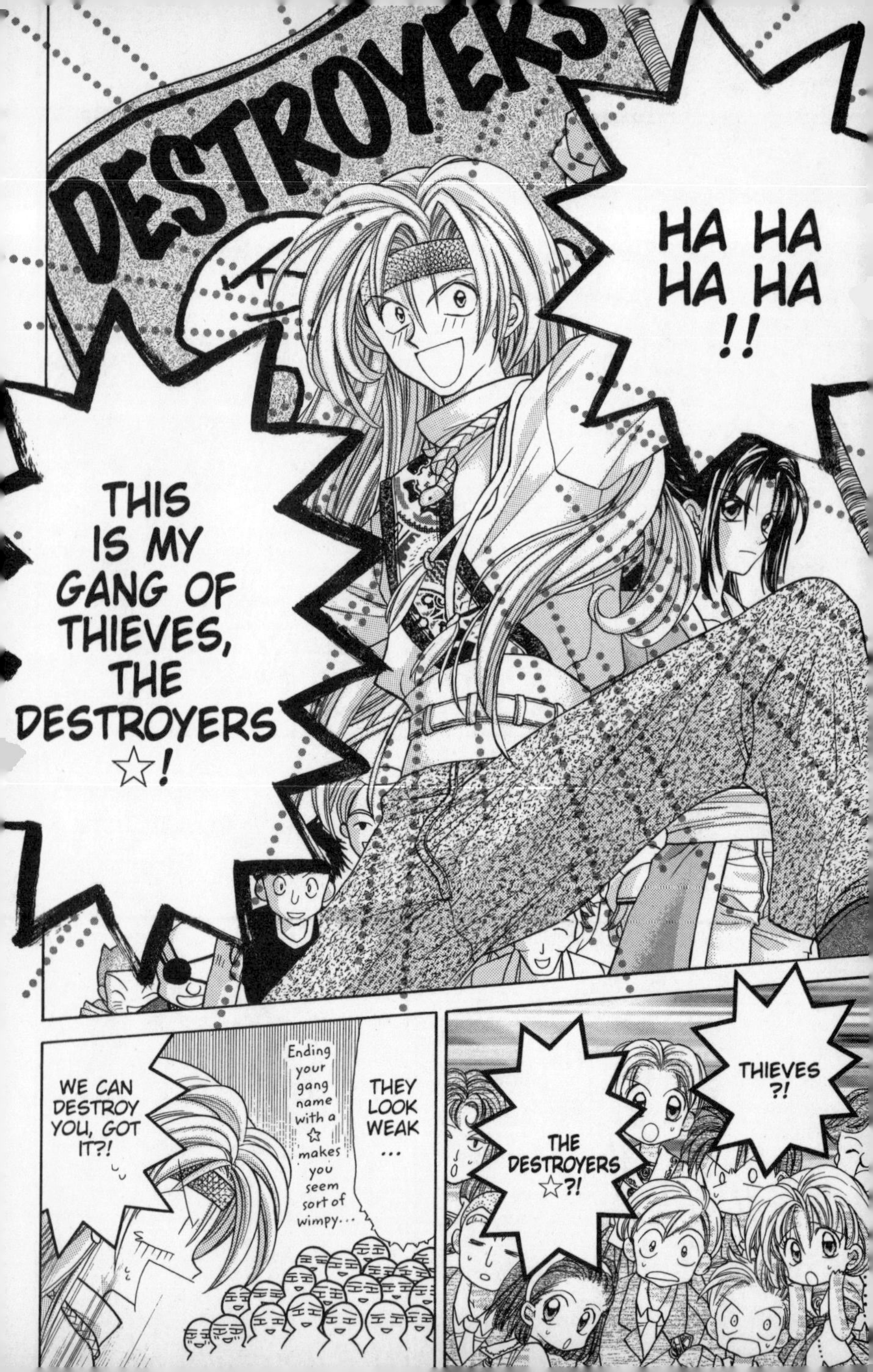
DESTROYERS
HA HA HA HA!!
THIS IS MY GANG OF THIEVES, THE DESTROYERS☆!
THIEVES?!
THE DESTROYERS☆?!
THEY LOOK WEAK...
Ending your gang name with a ☆ makes you seem sort of wimpy...
WE CAN DESTROY YOU, GOT IT?!

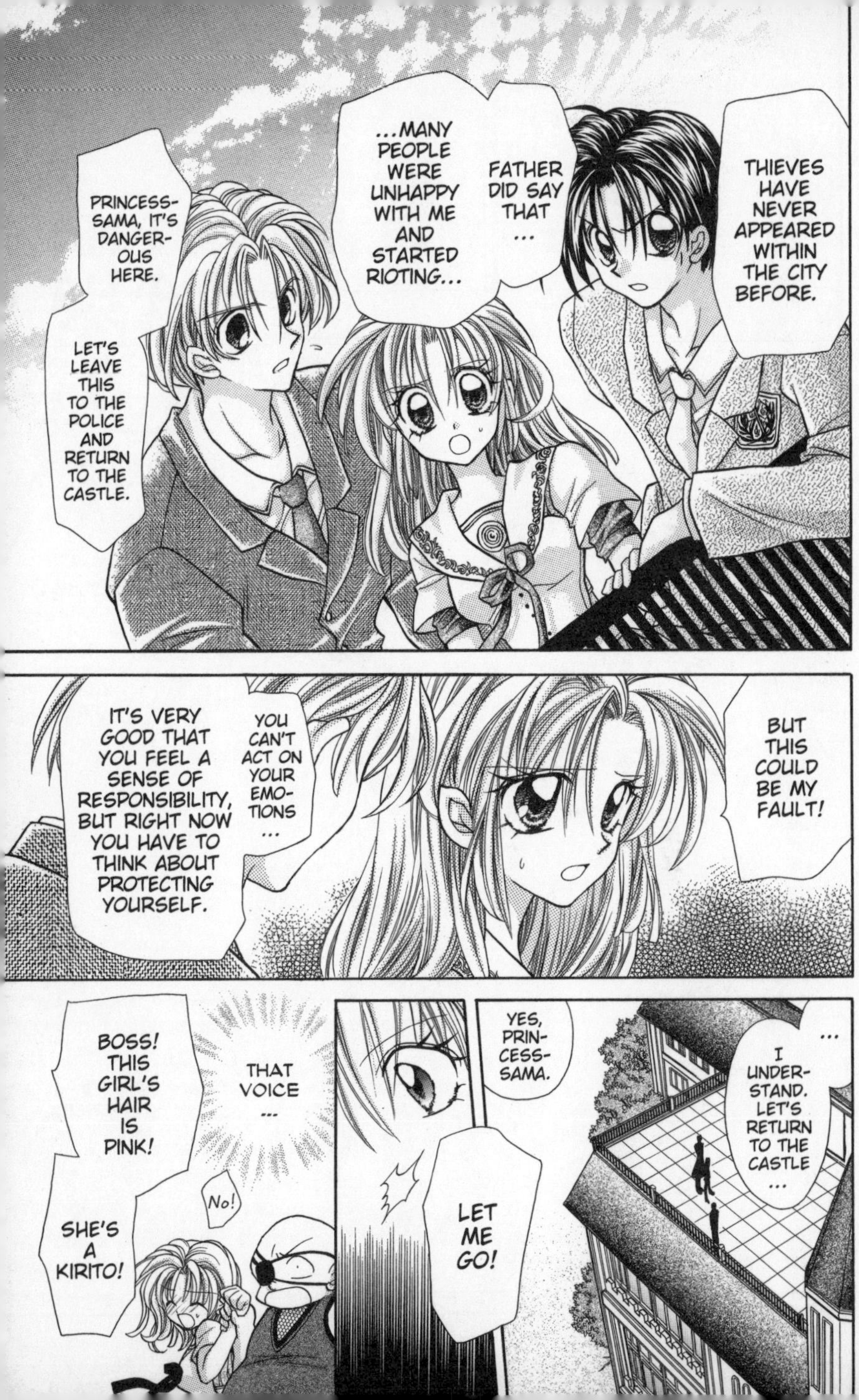
THIEVES HAVE NEVER APPEARED WITHIN THE CITY BEFORE.
FATHER DID SAY THAT ...
...MANY PEOPLE WERE UNHAPPY WITH ME AND STARTED RIOTING...
PRINCESS-SAMA, IT'S DANGEROUS HERE.
LET'S LEAVE THIS TO THE POLICE AND RETURN TO THE CASTLE.
BUT THIS COULD BE MY FAULT!
YOU CAN'T ACT ON YOUR EMOTIONS ...
IT'S VERY GOOD THAT YOU FEEL A SENSE OF RESPONSIBILITY, BUT RIGHT NOW YOU HAVE TO THINK ABOUT PROTECTING YOURSELF.
... I UNDERSTAND. LET'S RETURN TO THE CASTLE ...
YES, PRINCESS-SAMA.
LET ME GO!
THAT VOICE ...
BOSS! THIS GIRL'S HAIR IS PINK!
No!
SHE'S A KIRITO!

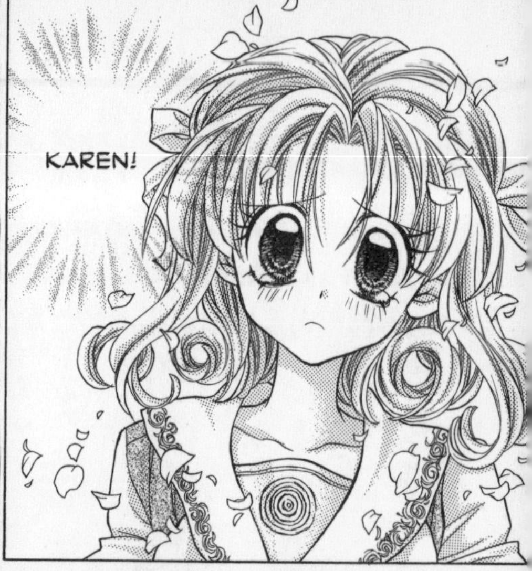
KAREN!

Kyoko's Glossary ①

●KIRITO●

The designation for new types of humans resulting from the combination of human DNA with that of Earth's animals and plants.

Human + Fish = Merpeople (Fish Tribe)
Human + Flower = Flowerpeople (Flower Tribe)
There are many such types.

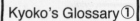

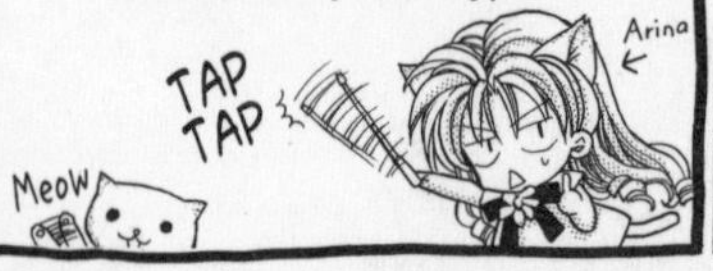
Arina
TAP TAP
Meow

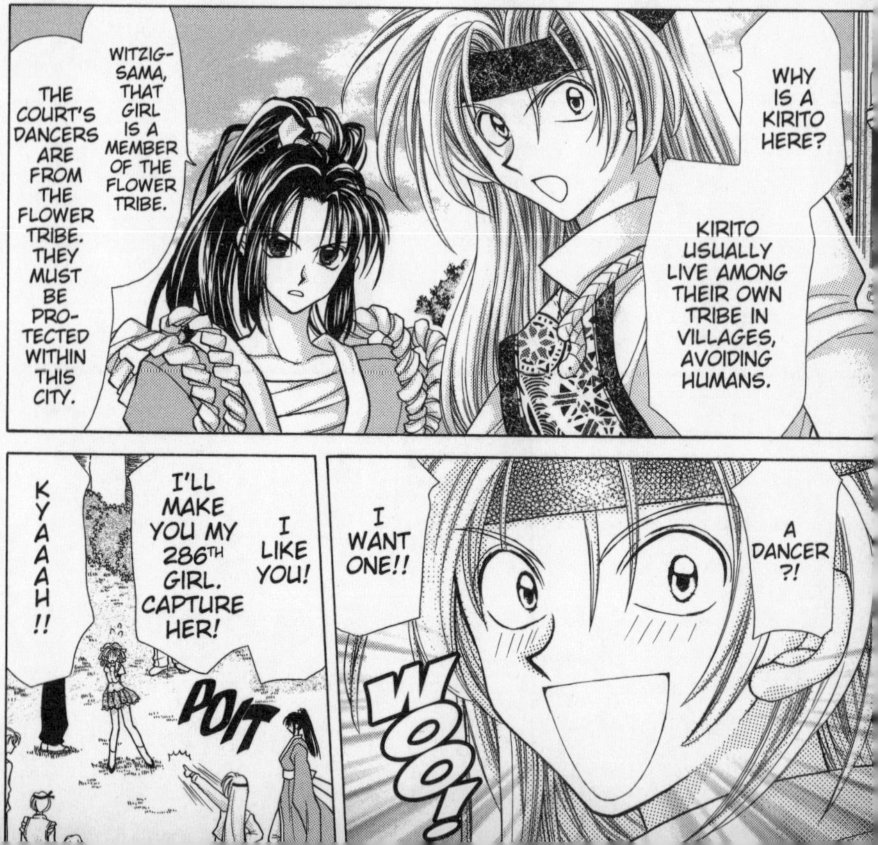
WHY IS A KIRITO HERE?
KIRITO USUALLY LIVE AMONG THEIR OWN TRIBE IN VILLAGES, AVOIDING HUMANS.
WITZIG-SAMA, THAT GIRL IS A MEMBER OF THE FLOWER TRIBE.
THE COURT'S DANCERS ARE FROM THE FLOWER TRIBE. THEY MUST BE PRO-TECTED WITHIN THIS CITY.
A DANCER?!
I WANT ONE!!
WOO!
I LIKE YOU!
I'LL MAKE YOU MY 286TH GIRL. CAPTURE HER!
KYAAAAH!!
POIT

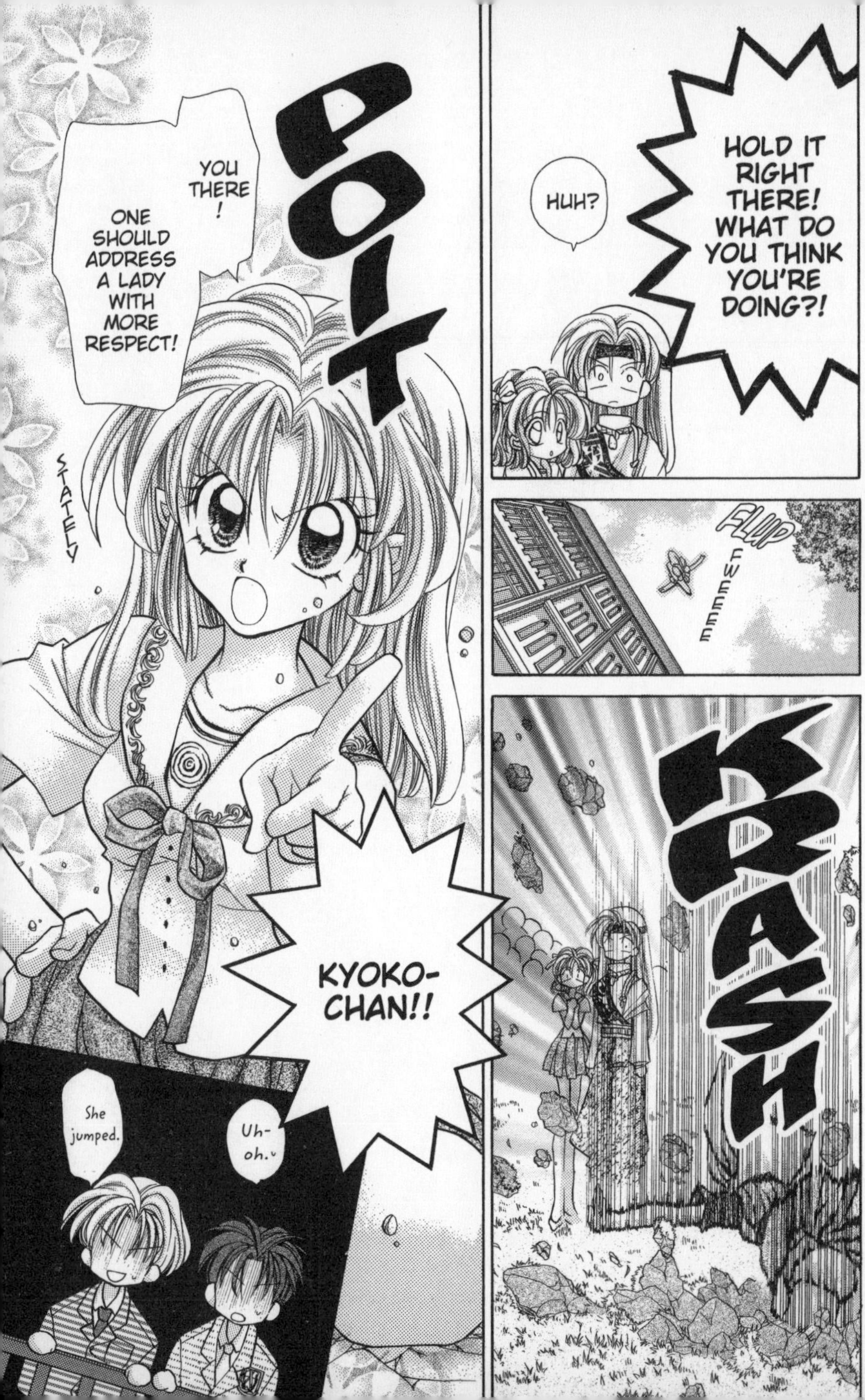
HOLD IT RIGHT THERE! WHAT DO YOU THINK YOU'RE DOING?!
HUH?
FLIP
FWEEEE
KRASH
POIT
YOU THERE!
ONE SHOULD ADDRESS A LADY WITH MORE RESPECT!
STATELY
KYOKO-CHAN!!
Uh-oh.
She jumped.

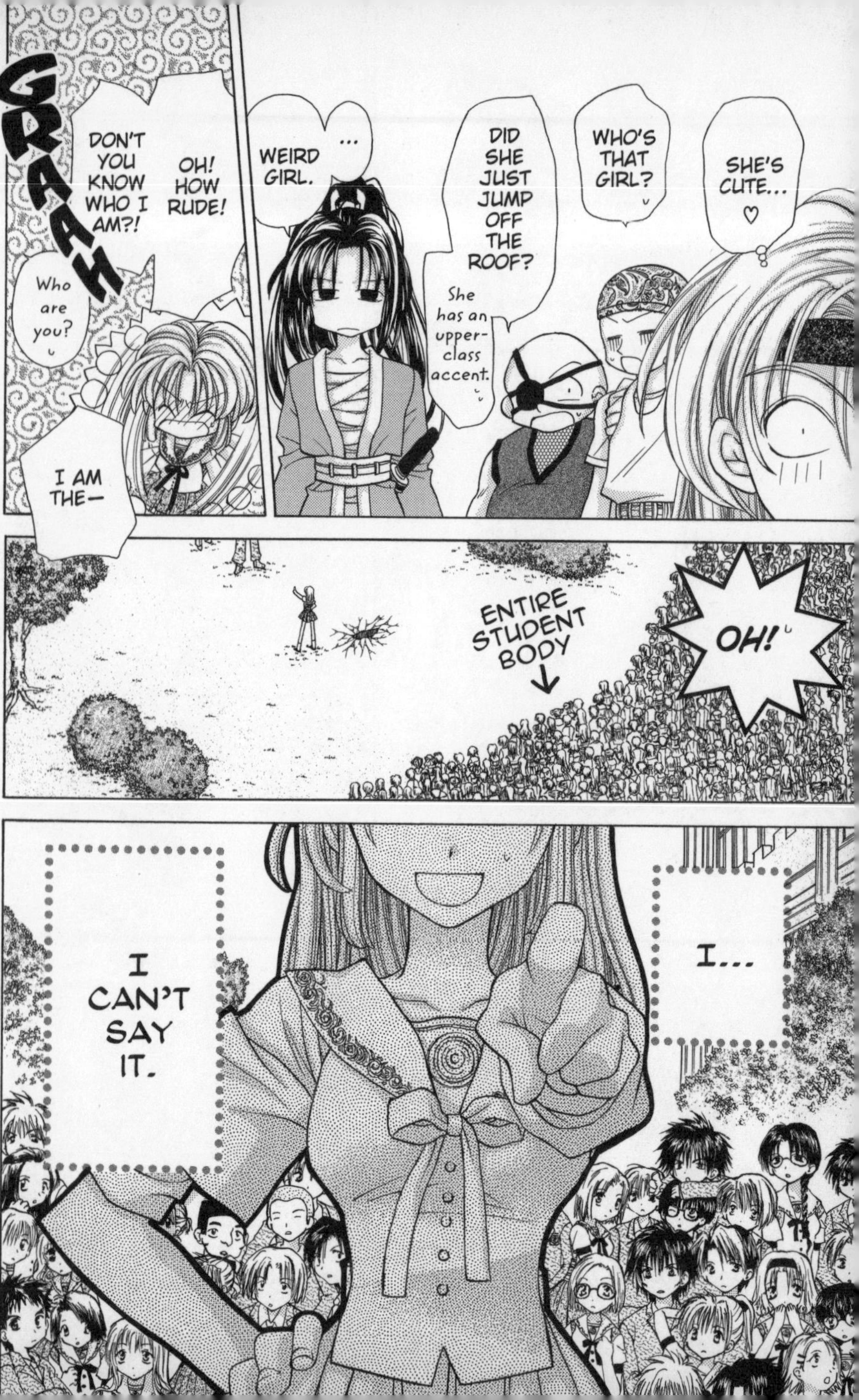
SHE'S CUTE... ♡
WHO'S THAT GIRL?
DID SHE JUST JUMP OFF THE ROOF?
She has an upper-class accent.
...
WEIRD GIRL.
OH! HOW RUDE!
DON'T YOU KNOW WHO I AM?!
GRAAAH
Who are you?
I AM THE—
OH!
ENTIRE STUDENT BODY
I...
I CAN'T SAY IT.

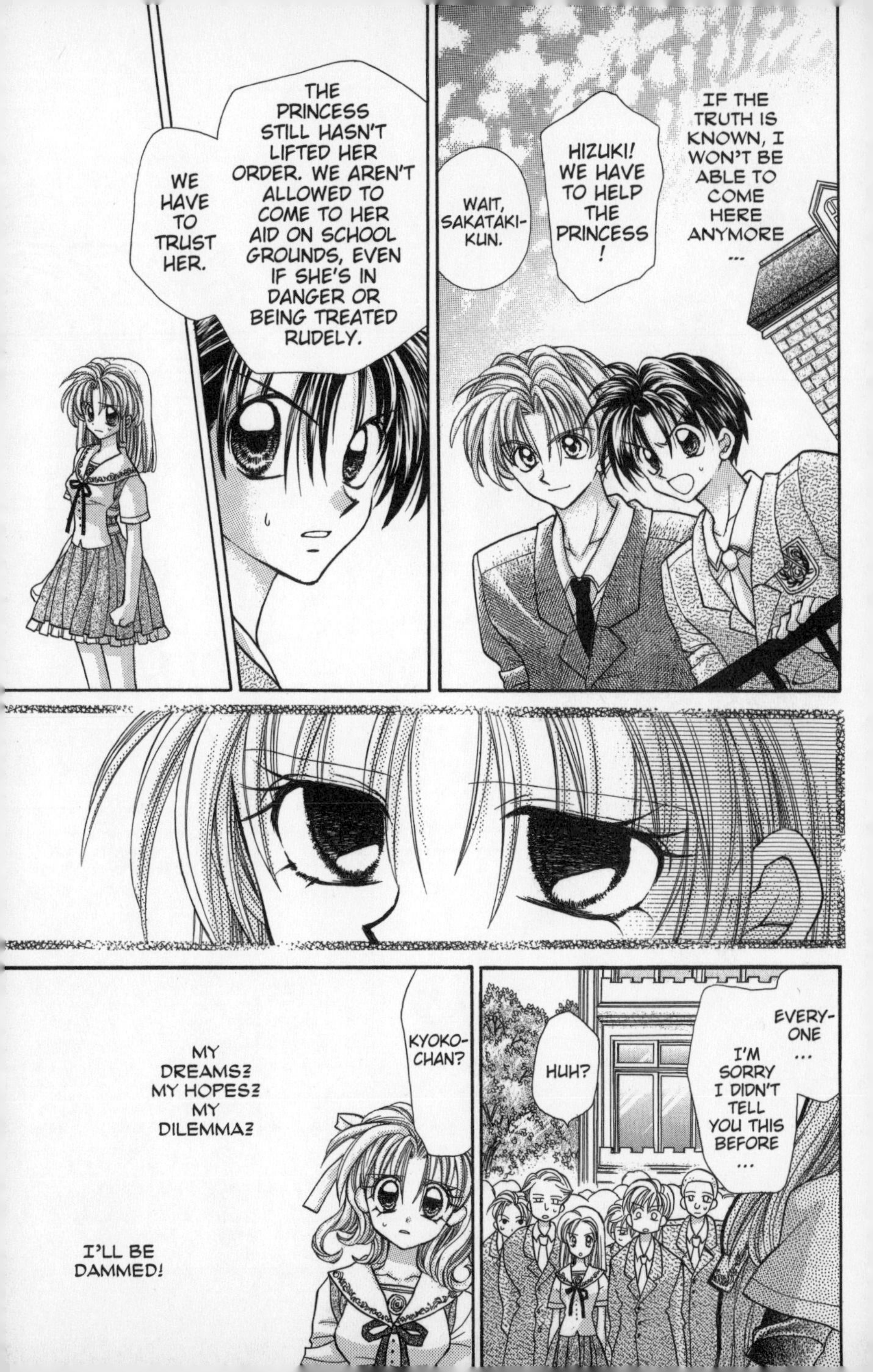
IF THE TRUTH IS KNOWN, I WON'T BE ABLE TO COME HERE ANYMORE...
HIZUKI! WE HAVE TO HELP THE PRINCESS!
WAIT, SAKATAKI-KUN.
THE PRINCESS STILL HASN'T LIFTED HER ORDER. WE AREN'T ALLOWED TO COME TO HER AID ON SCHOOL GROUNDS, EVEN IF SHE'S IN DANGER OR BEING TREATED RUDELY.
WE HAVE TO TRUST HER.
EVERY-ONE...
I'M SORRY I DIDN'T TELL YOU THIS BEFORE...
HUH?
KYOKO-CHAN?
MY DREAMS? MY HOPES? MY DILEMMA?
I'LL BE DAMMED!

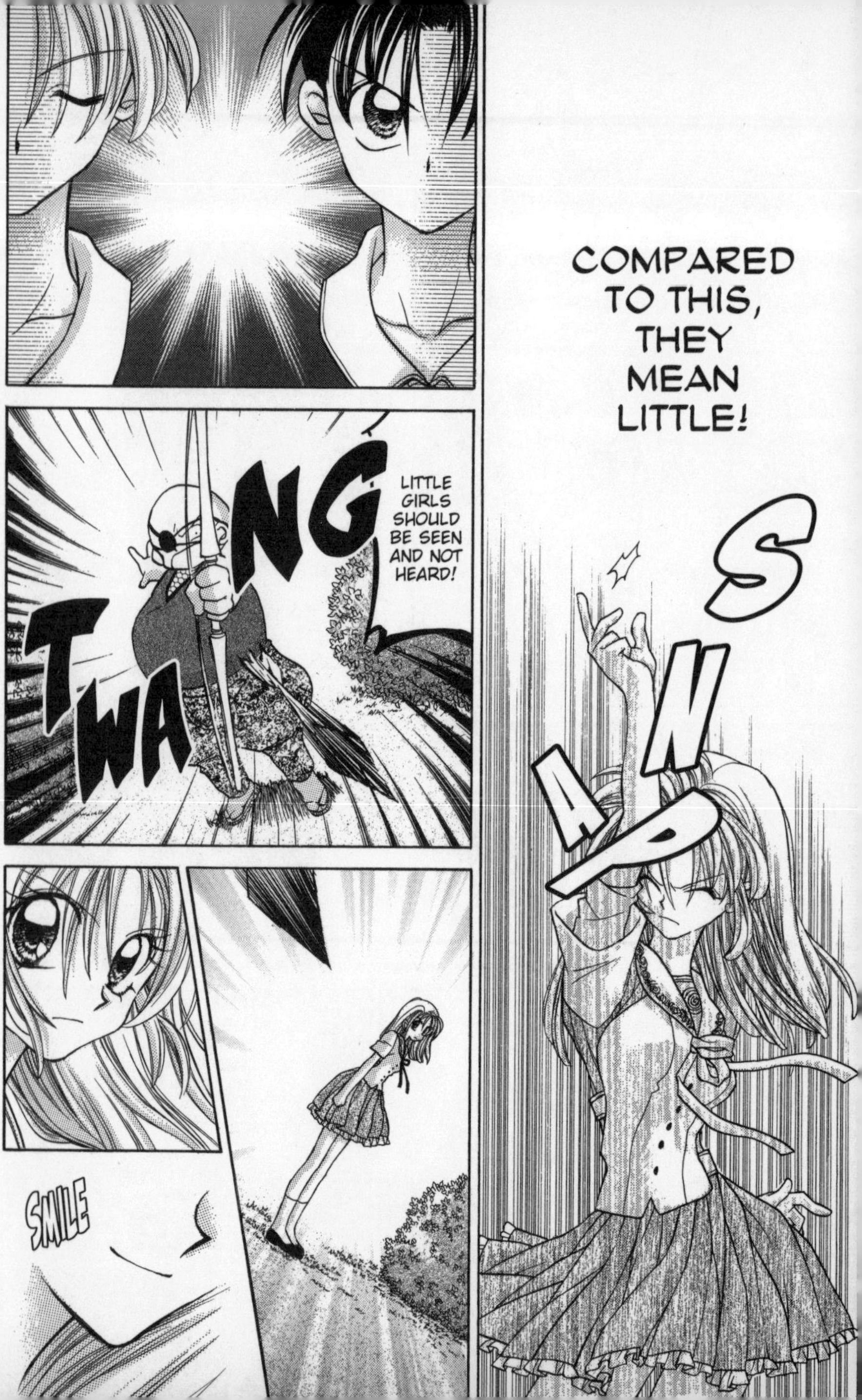
COMPARED TO THIS, THEY MEAN LITTLE!
SNAP
TWANG
LITTLE GIRLS SHOULD BE SEEN AND NOT HEARD!
SMILE

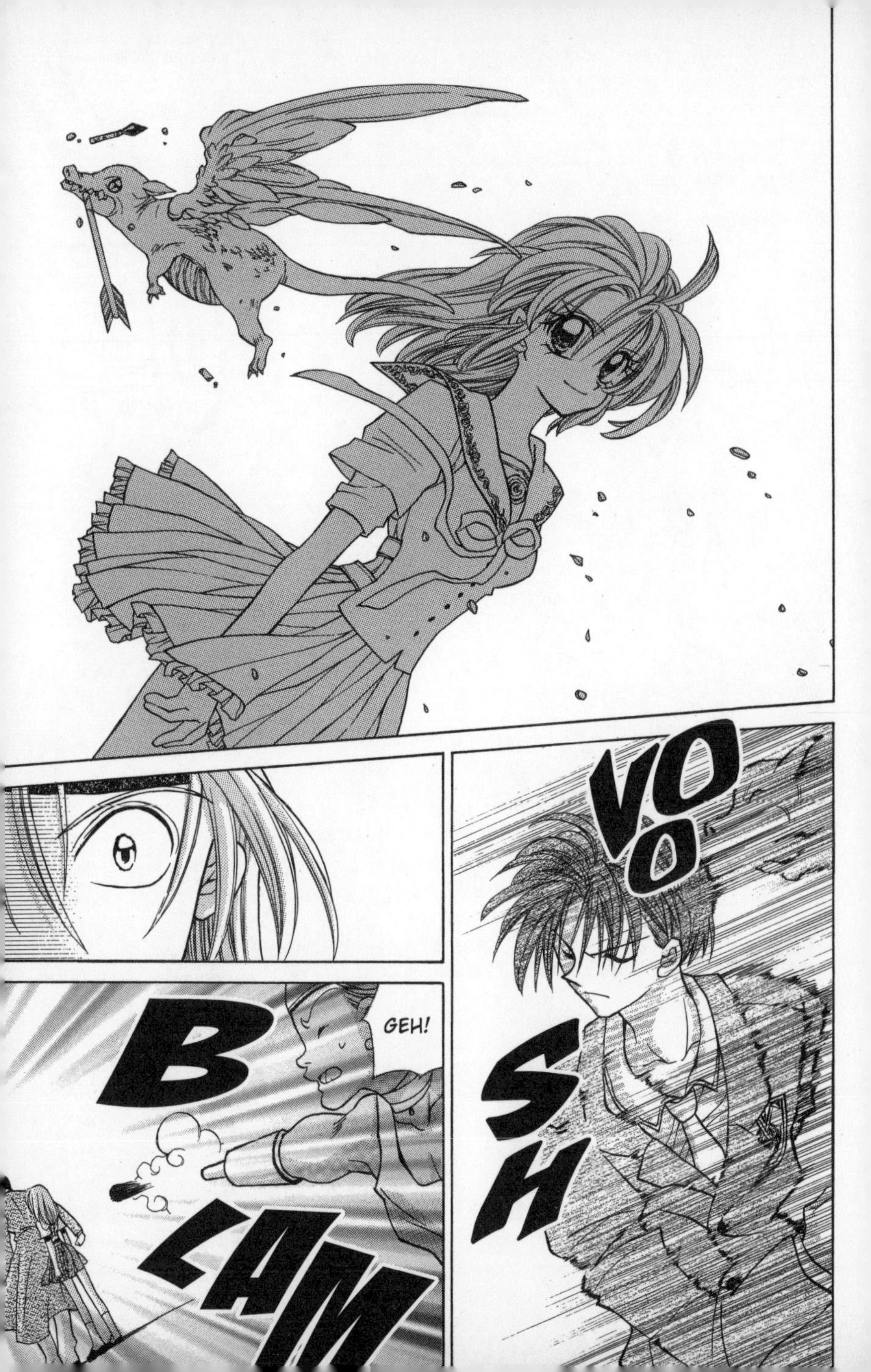
VOOSH
GEH!
BLAM

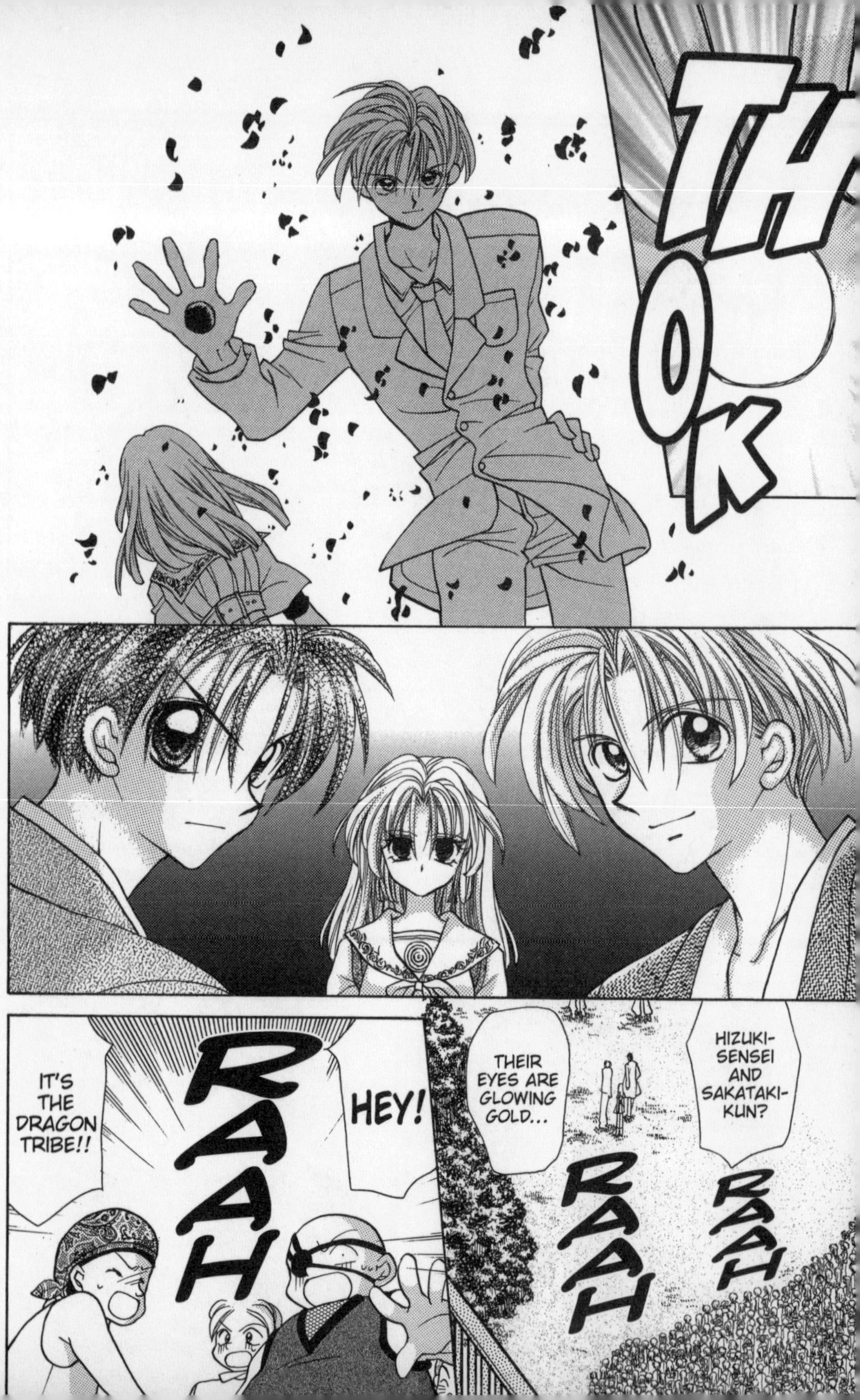
THOOK
HIZUKI-SENSEI AND SAKATAKI-KUN?
RAAH
THEIR EYES ARE GLOWING GOLD...
RAAH
HEY!
RAAH
IT'S THE DRAGON TRIBE!!

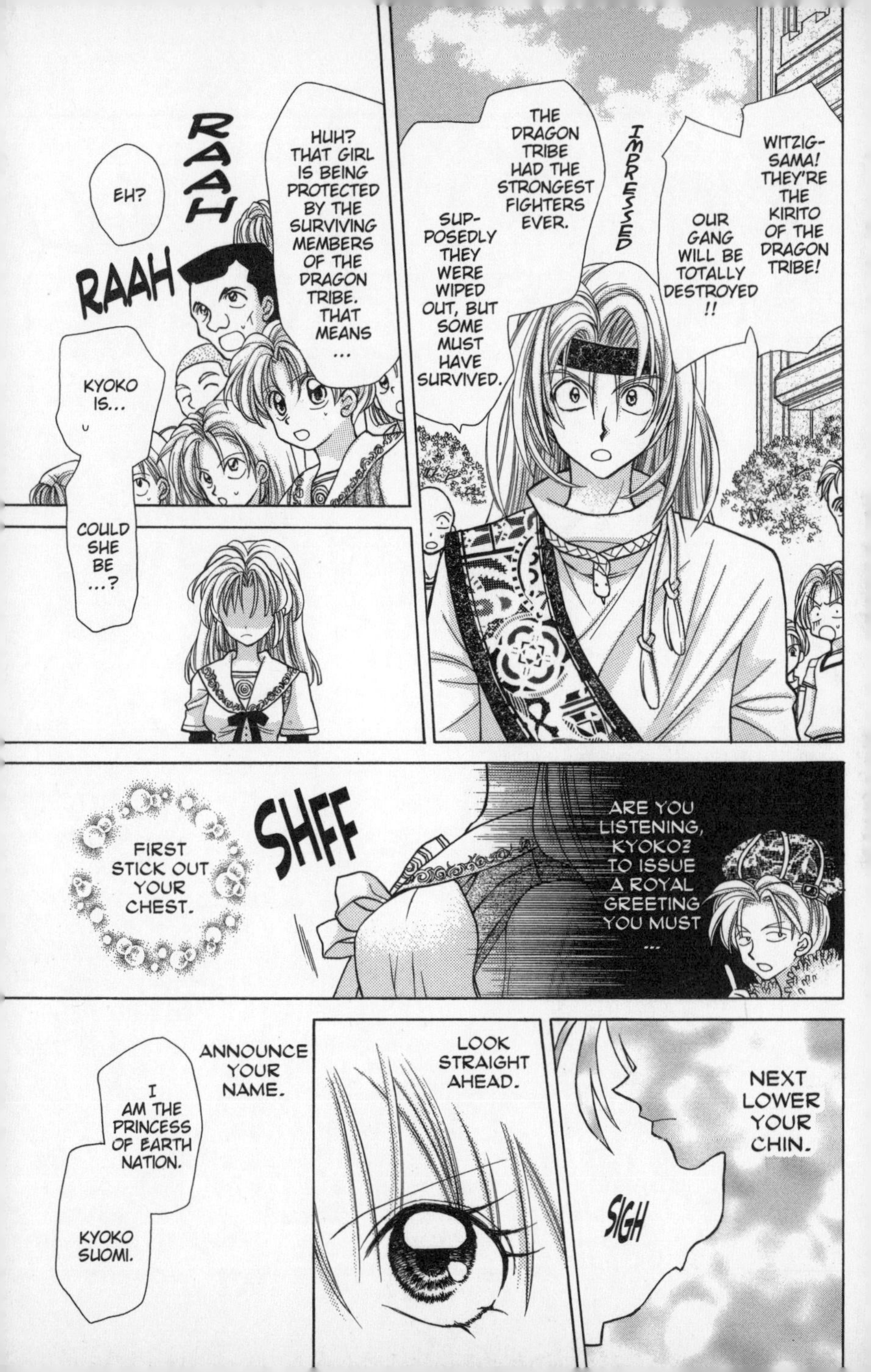
WITZIG-SAMA! THEY'RE THE KIRITO OF THE DRAGON TRIBE!
OUR GANG WILL BE TOTALLY DESTROYED!!
IMPRESSED
THE DRAGON TRIBE HAD THE STRONGEST FIGHTERS EVER.
SUP-POSEDLY THEY WERE WIPED OUT, BUT SOME MUST HAVE SURVIVED.
HUH? THAT GIRL IS BEING PROTECTED BY THE SURVIVING MEMBERS OF THE DRAGON TRIBE. THAT MEANS ...
RAAH
RAAH
EH?
KYOKO IS...
COULD SHE BE ...?
ARE YOU LISTENING, KYOKO? TO ISSUE A ROYAL GREETING YOU MUST ...
SHFF
FIRST STICK OUT YOUR CHEST.
NEXT LOWER YOUR CHIN.
SIGH
LOOK STRAIGHT AHEAD.
ANNOUNCE YOUR NAME.
I AM THE PRINCESS OF EARTH NATION.
KYOKO SUOMI.

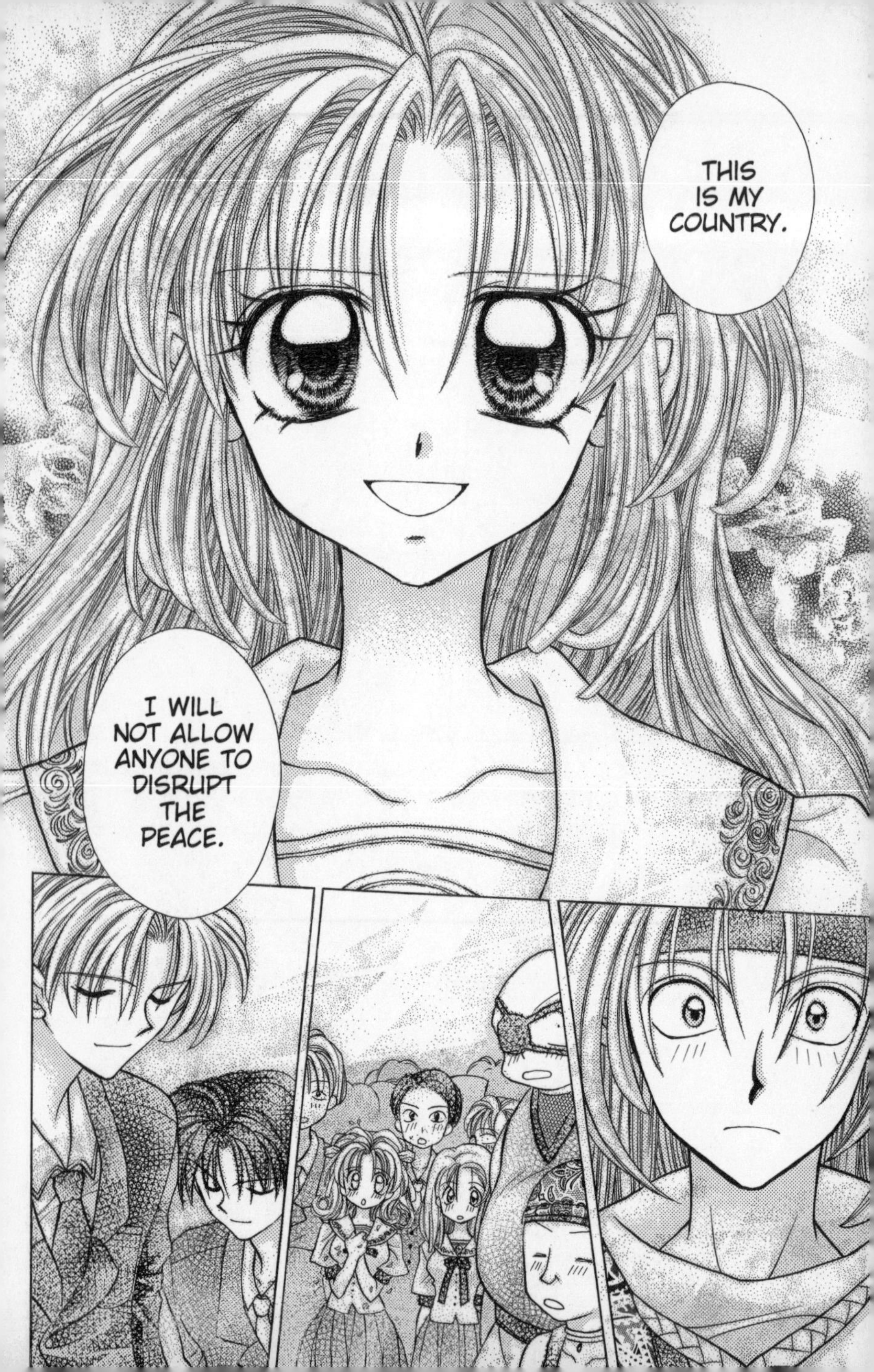
THIS IS MY COUNTRY.
I WILL NOT ALLOW ANYONE TO DISRUPT THE PEACE.

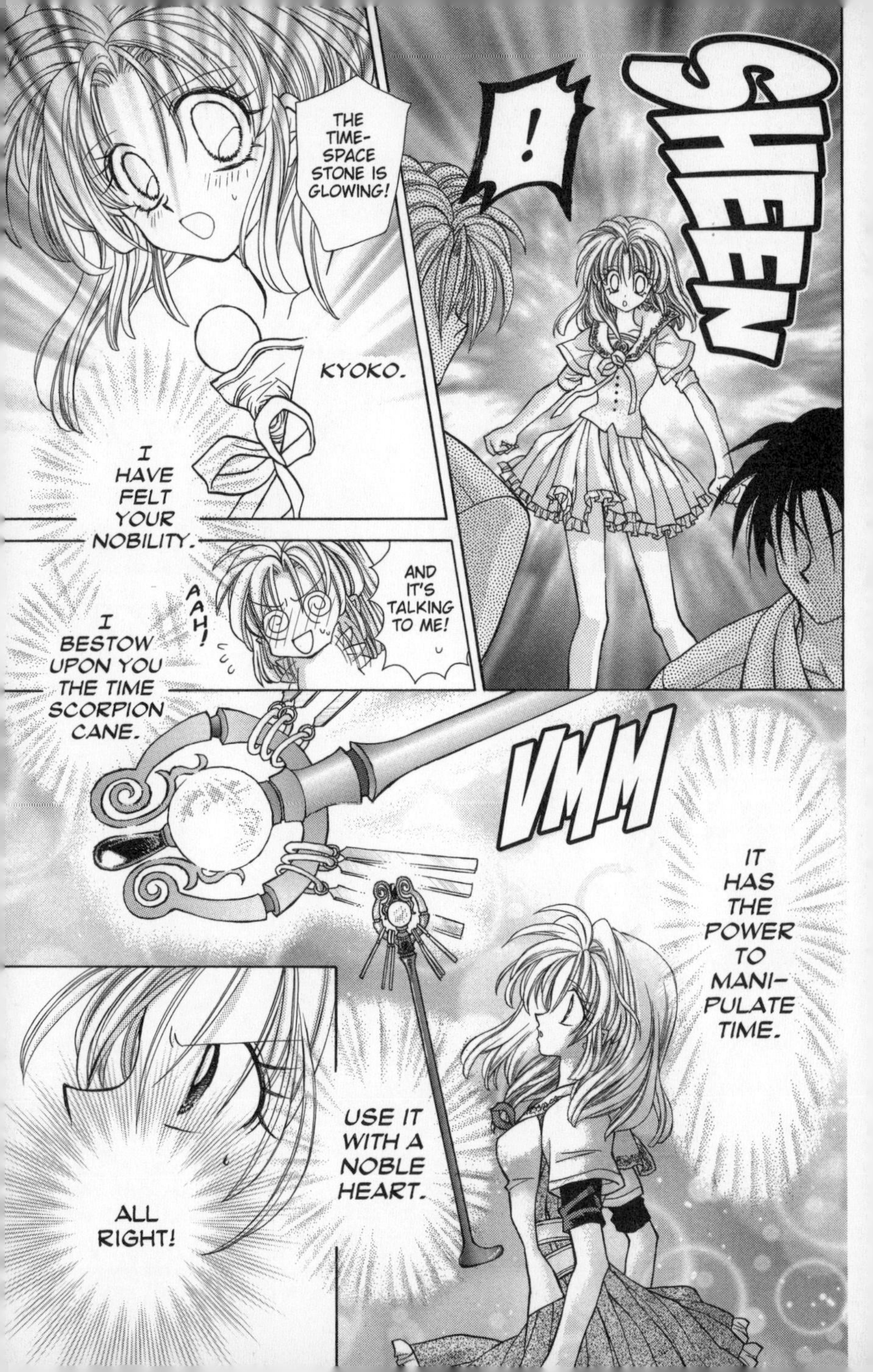
SHEEN
!
THE TIME-SPACE STONE IS GLOWING!
KYOKO.
I HAVE FELT YOUR NOBILITY.
AND IT'S TALKING TO ME!
AAH!
I BESTOW UPON YOU THE TIME SCORPION CANE.
VMM
IT HAS THE POWER TO MANI-PULATE TIME.
USE IT WITH A NOBLE HEART.
ALL RIGHT!

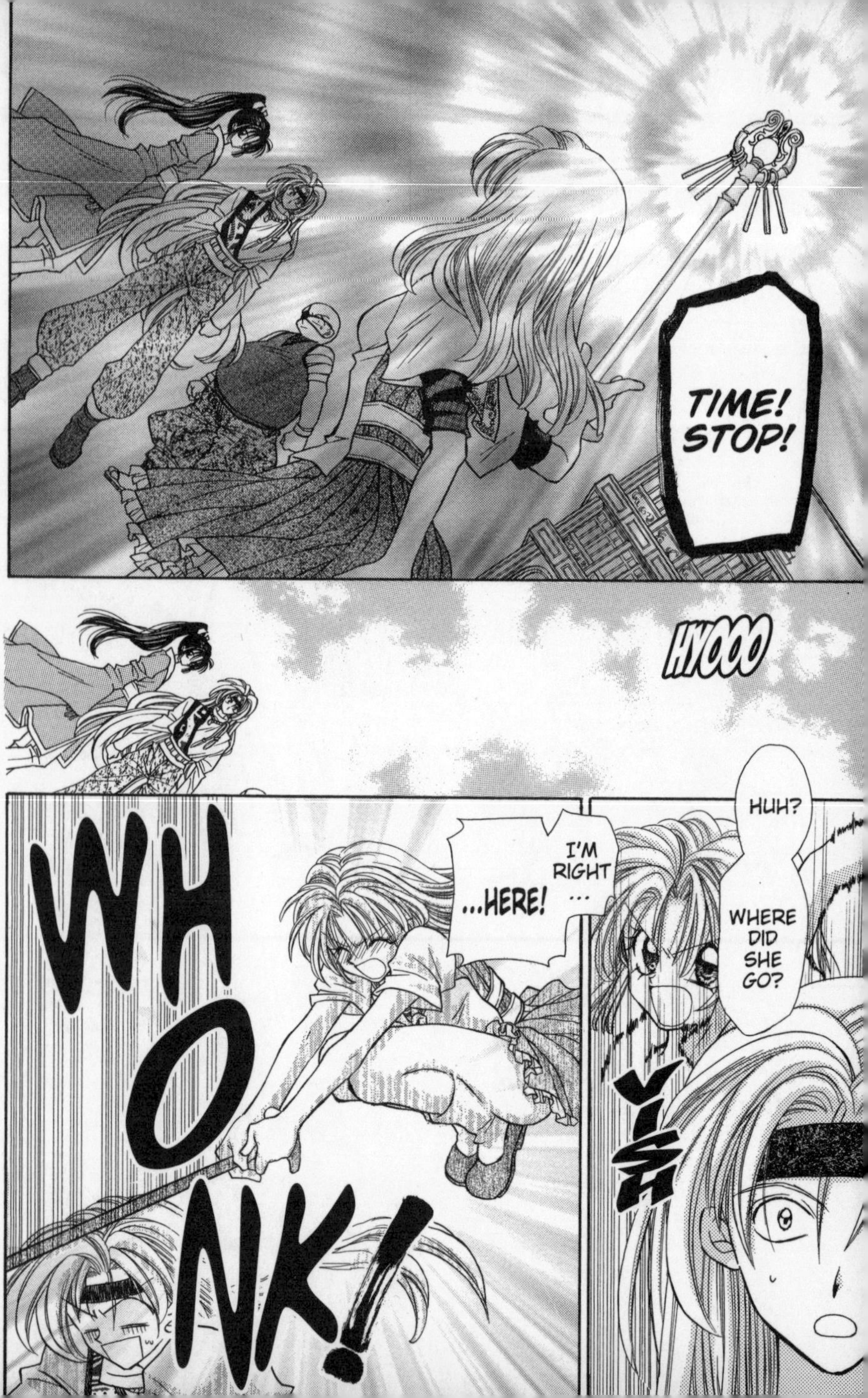
TIME! STOP!
HYOOO
HUH?
WHERE DID SHE GO?
YISH
I'M RIGHT ...
...HERE!
WHONK!

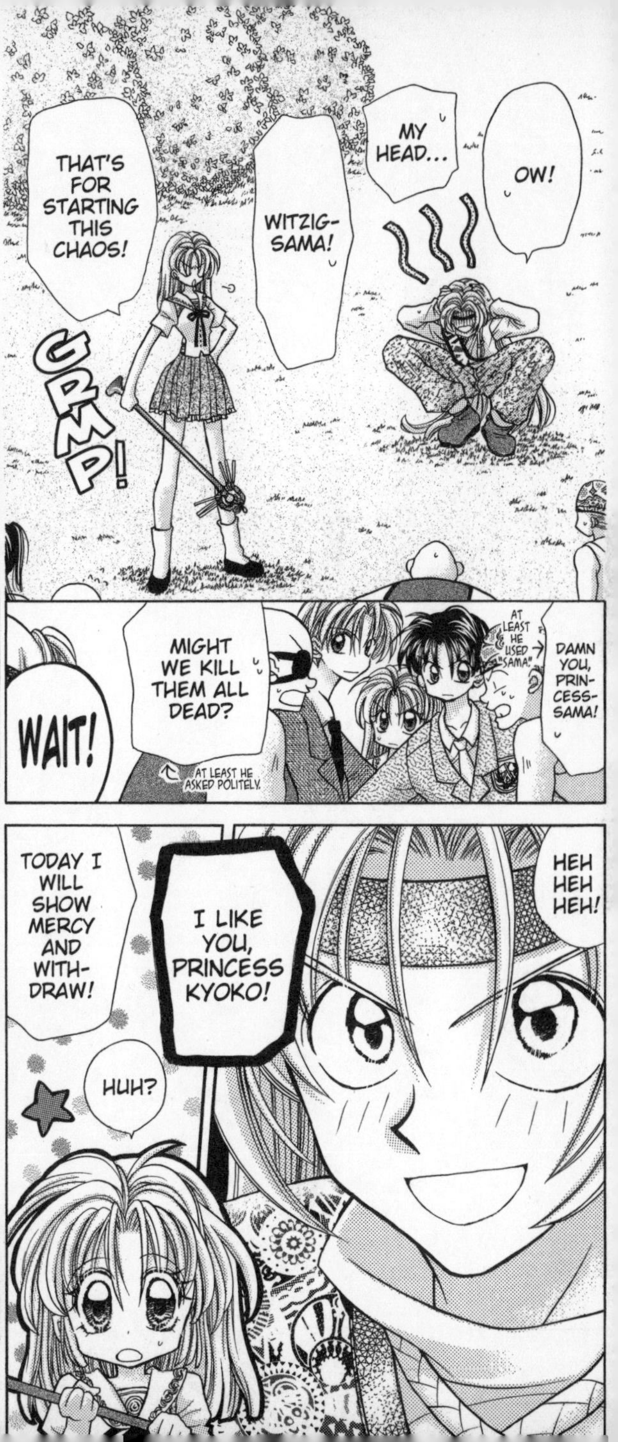
OW!
MY HEAD...
WITZIG-SAMA!
THAT'S FOR STARTING THIS CHAOS!
GRMP!
DAMN YOU, PRINCESS-SAMA!
AT LEAST HE USED "SAMA!"
MIGHT WE KILL THEM ALL DEAD?
AT LEAST HE ASKED POLITELY.
WAIT!
HEH HEH HEH!
I LIKE YOU, PRINCESS KYOKO!
TODAY I WILL SHOW MERCY AND WITHDRAW!
HUH?

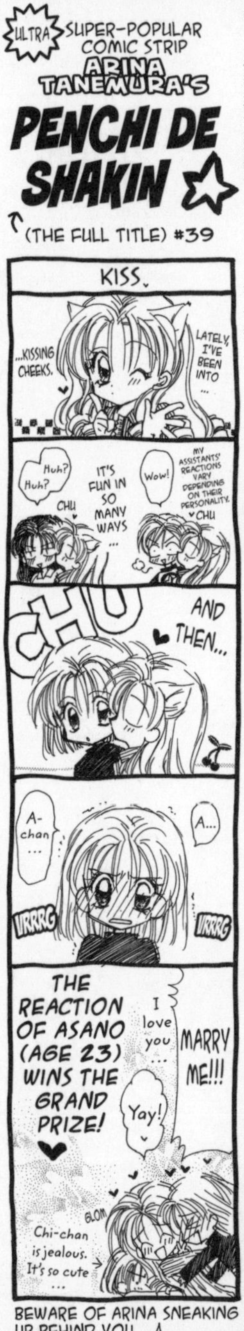
ULTRA SUPER-POPULAR COMIC STRIP
ARINA TANEMURA'S
PENCHI DE SHAKIN
(THE FULL TITLE) #39
KISS
LATELY, I'VE BEEN INTO ...
...KISSING CHEEKS.
MY ASSISTANTS' REACTIONS VARY DEPENDING ON THEIR PERSONALITY.
CHU
Wow!
IT'S FUN IN SO MANY WAYS ...
Huh? Huh?
CHU
AND THEN...
CHU
A...
A-chan ...
VRRRG
VRRRG
MARRY ME!!!
I love you ...
Yay!
THE REACTION OF ASANO (AGE 23) WINS THE GRAND PRIZE!
GLOM
Chi-chan is jealous. It's so cute ...
BEWARE OF ARINA SNEAKING UP BEHIND YOU...
(especially you, fans)

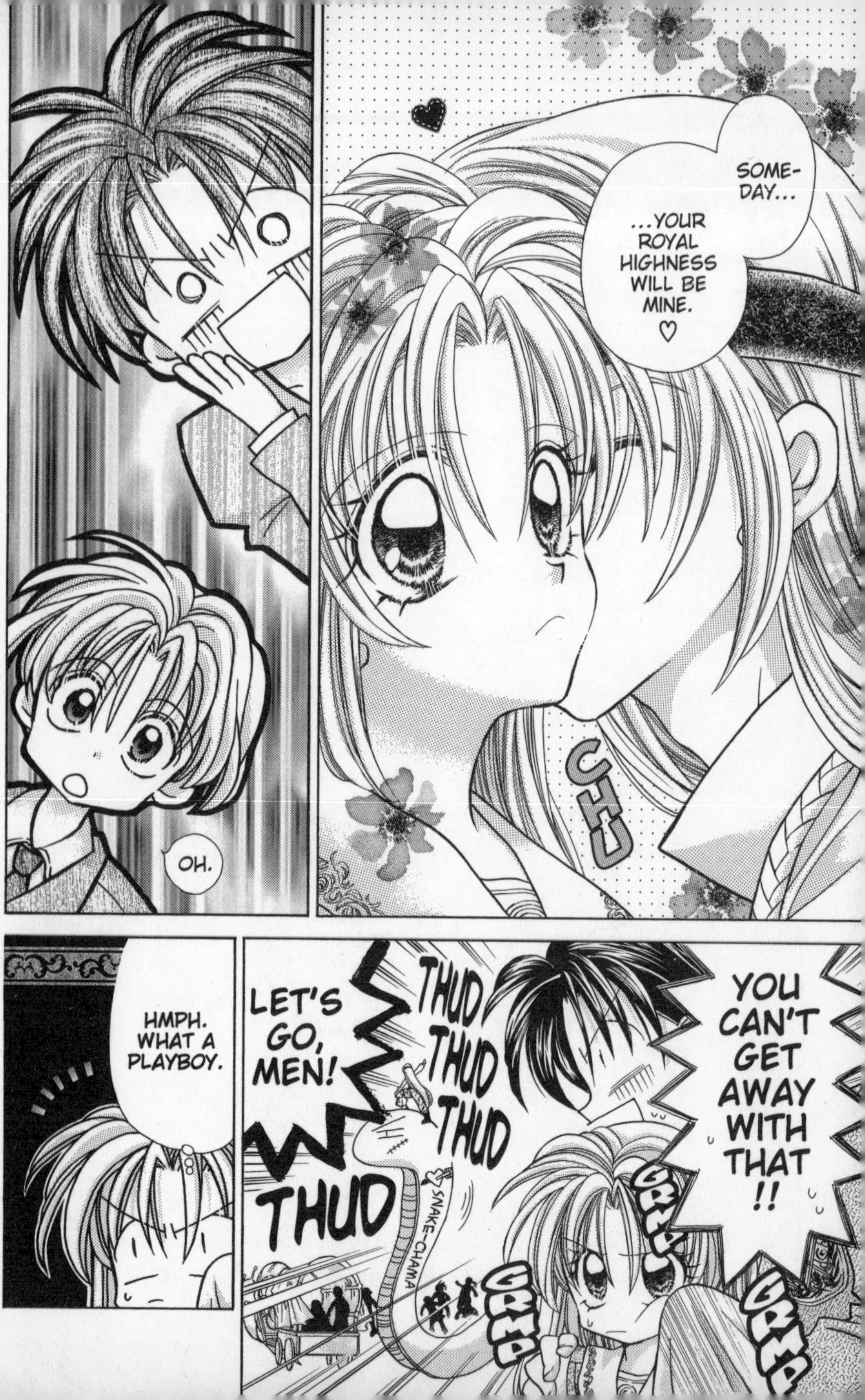
SOME-DAY...
...YOUR ROYAL HIGHNESS WILL BE MINE. ♡
CHU
OH.
YOU CAN'T GET AWAY WITH THAT!!
THUD THUD THUD
THUD
LET'S GO, MEN!
THUD
SNAKE-CHAMA
HMPH. WHAT A PLAYBOY.

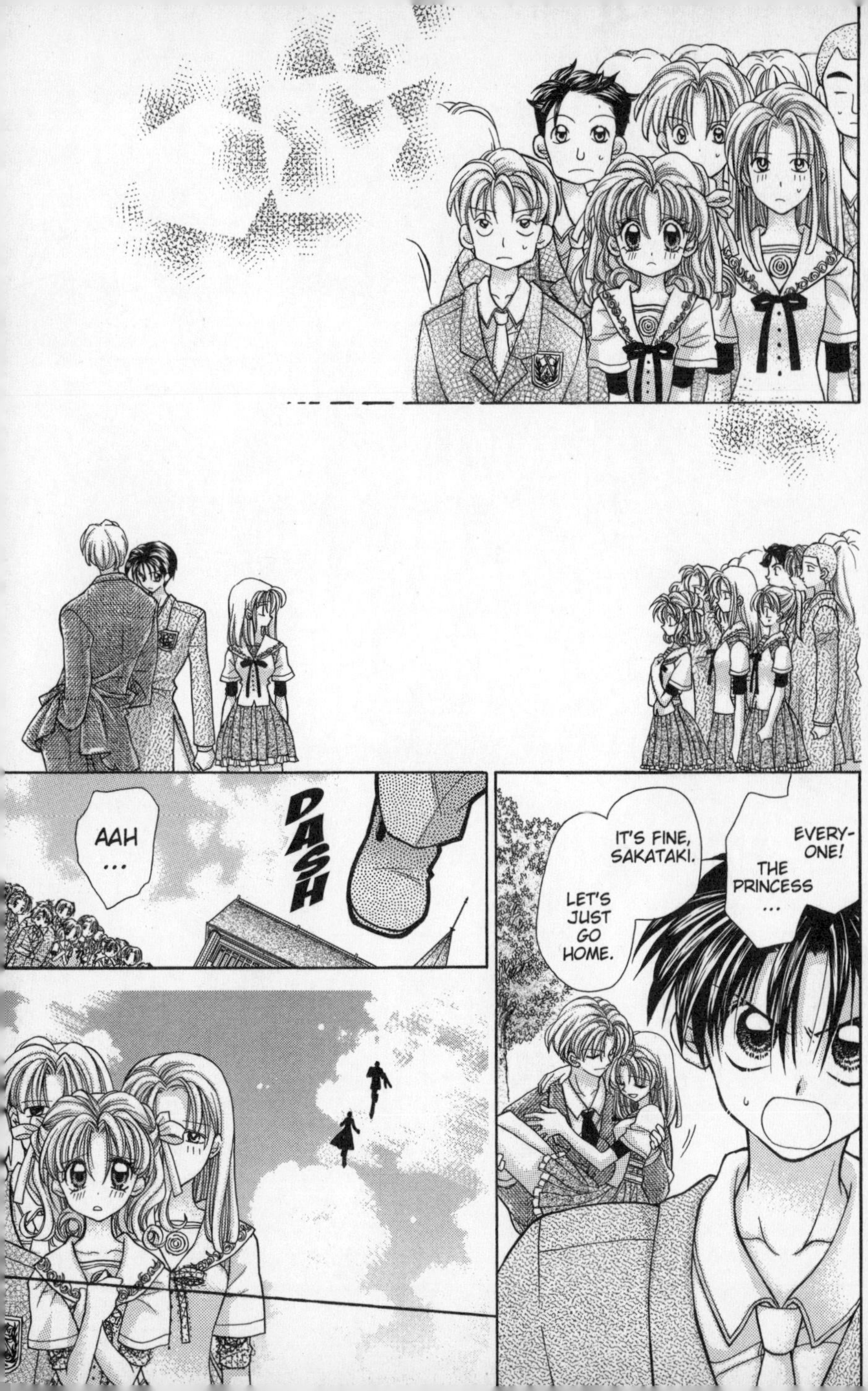
EVERY-ONE! THE PRINCESS ...
IT'S FINE, SAKATAKI.
LET'S JUST GO HOME.
DASH
AAH ...

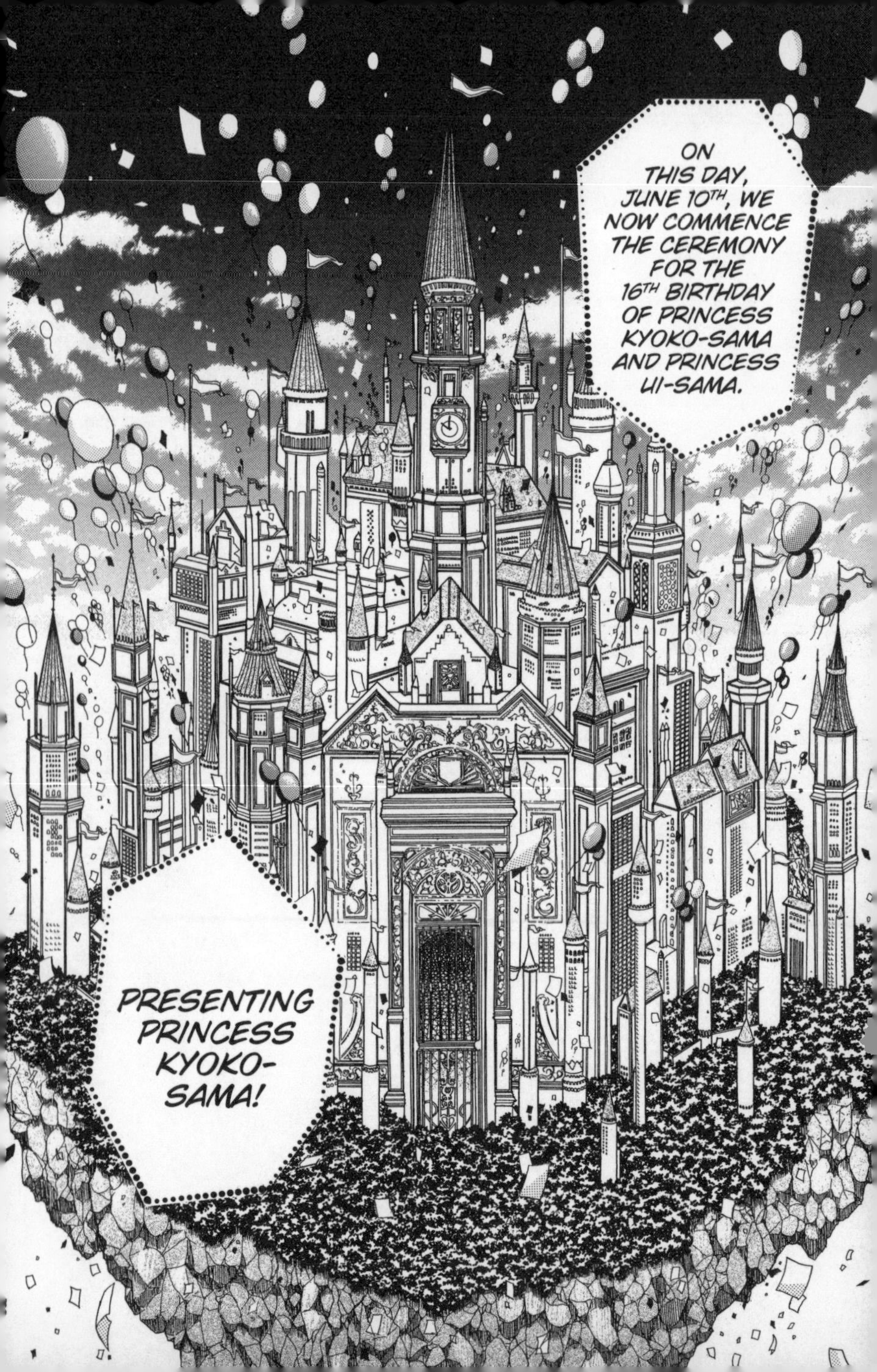
ON THIS DAY, JUNE 10TH, WE NOW COMMENCE THE CEREMONY FOR THE 16TH BIRTHDAY OF PRINCESS KYOKO-SAMA AND PRINCESS UI-SAMA.
PRESENTING PRINCESS KYOKO-SAMA!

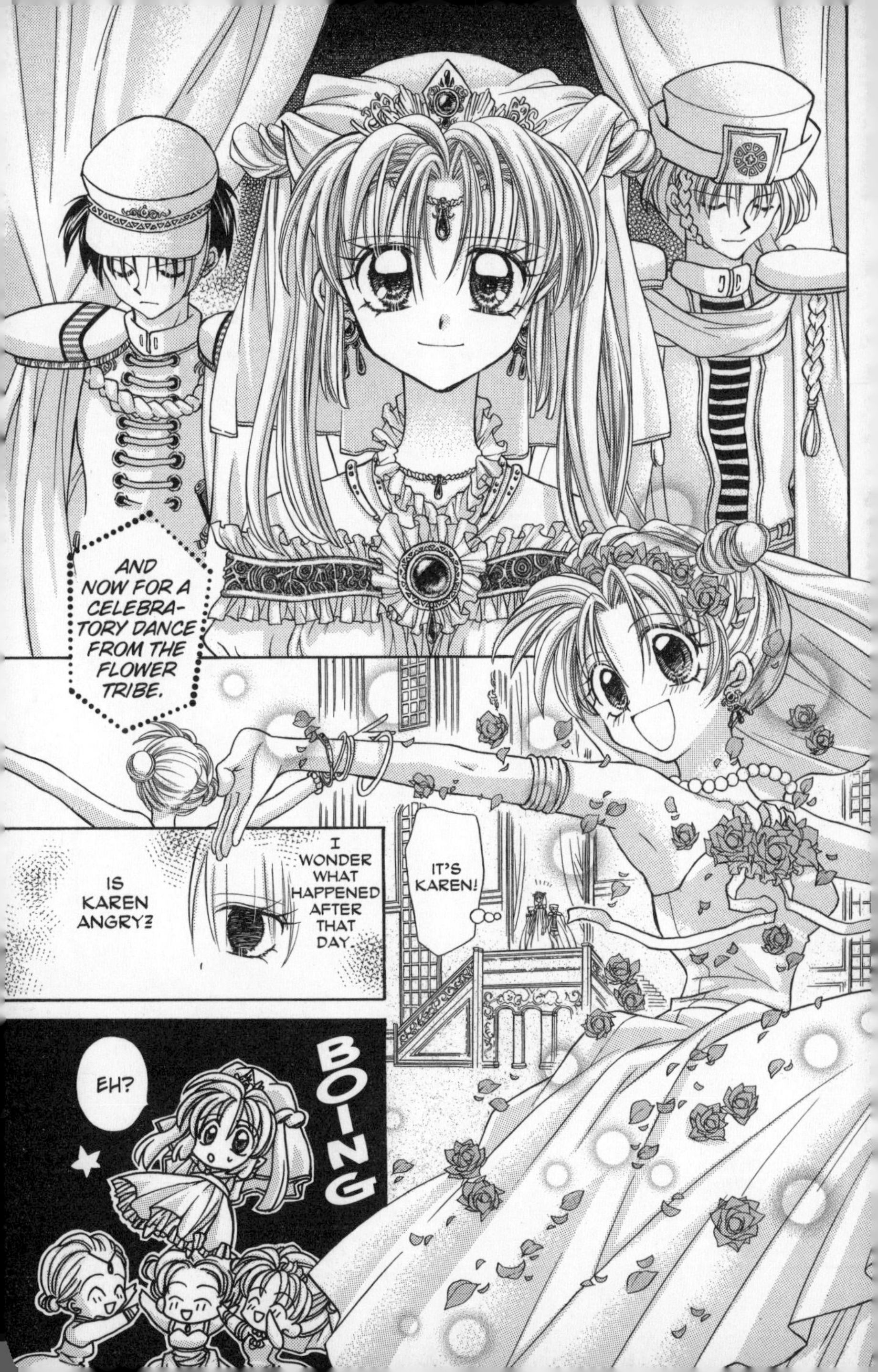
AND NOW FOR A CELEBRATORY DANCE FROM THE FLOWER TRIBE.
IT'S KAREN!
I WONDER WHAT HAPPENED AFTER THAT DAY.
IS KAREN ANGRY?
BOING
EH?

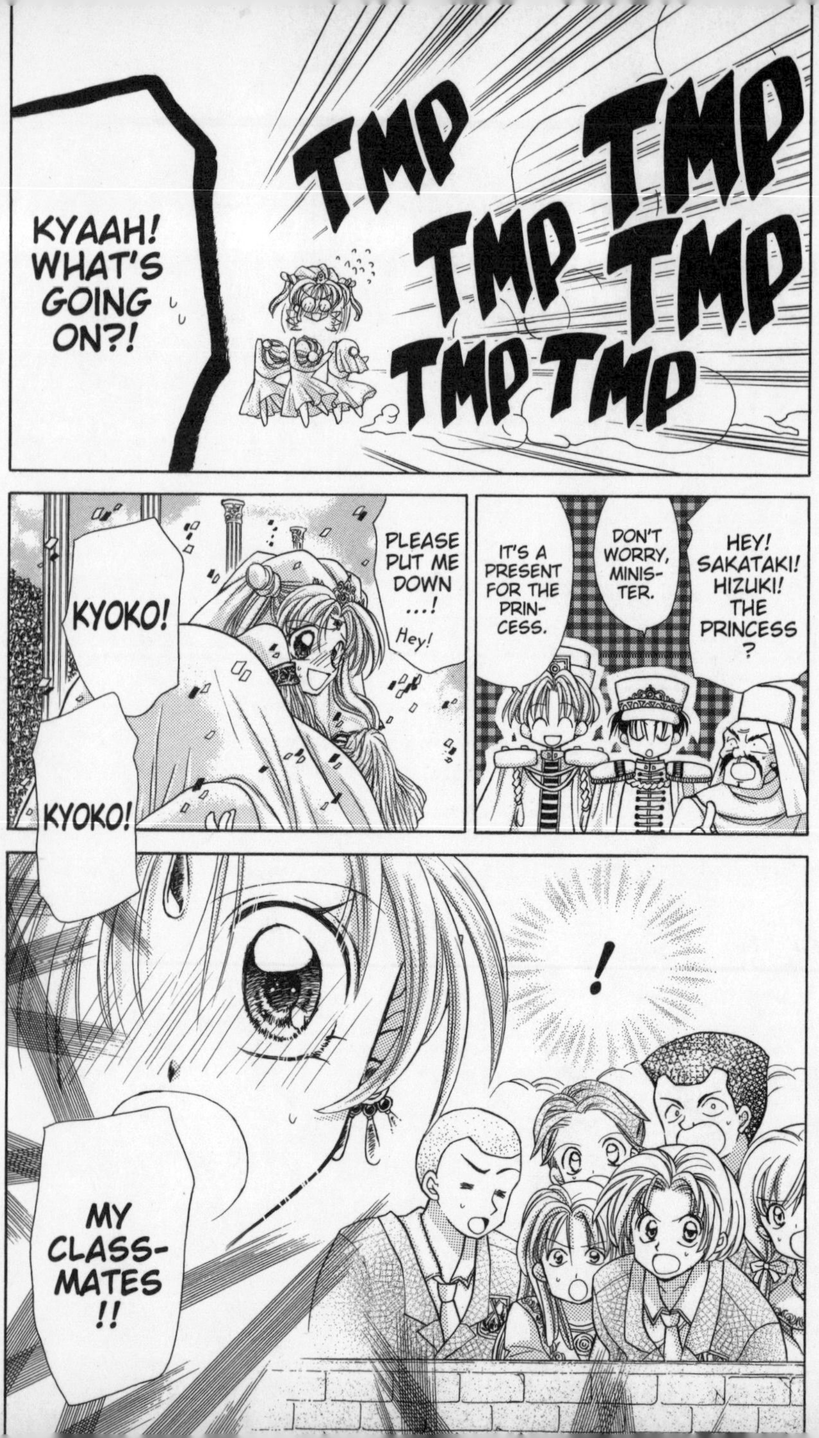
TMP TMP TMP TMP TMP TMP TMP
KYAAH! WHAT'S GOING ON?!
HEY! SAKATAKI! HIZUKI! THE PRINCESS?
DON'T WORRY, MINISTER.
IT'S A PRESENT FOR THE PRINCESS.
PLEASE PUT ME DOWN ...!
Hey!
KYOKO!
KYOKO!
!
MY CLASSMATES!!

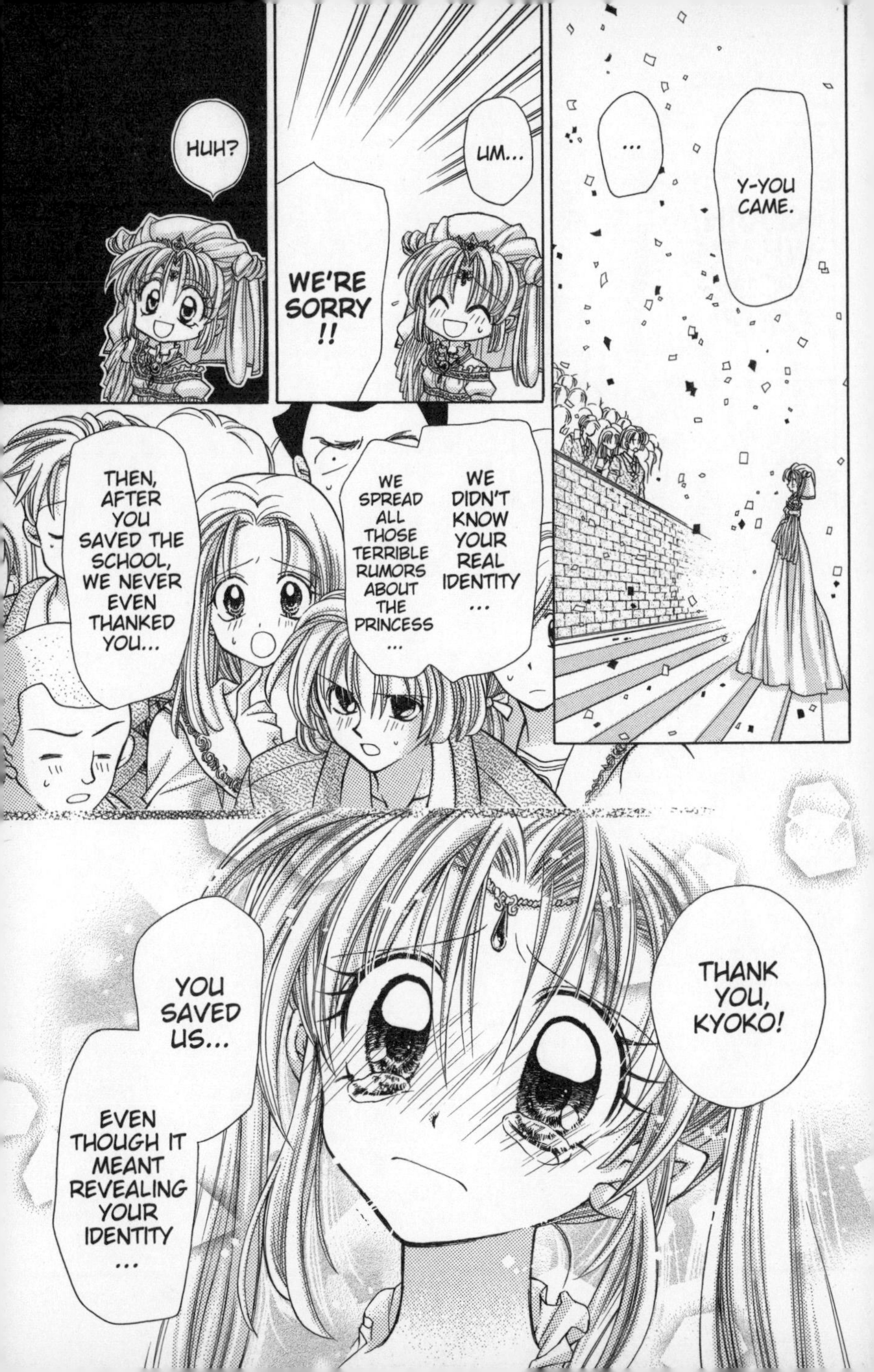
Y-YOU CAME.
...
UM...
WE'RE SORRY !!
HUH?
WE DIDN'T KNOW YOUR REAL IDENTITY ...
WE SPREAD ALL THOSE TERRIBLE RUMORS ABOUT THE PRINCESS ...
THEN, AFTER YOU SAVED THE SCHOOL, WE NEVER EVEN THANKED YOU...
THANK YOU, KYOKO!
YOU SAVED US...
EVEN THOUGH IT MEANT REVEALING YOUR IDENTITY ...

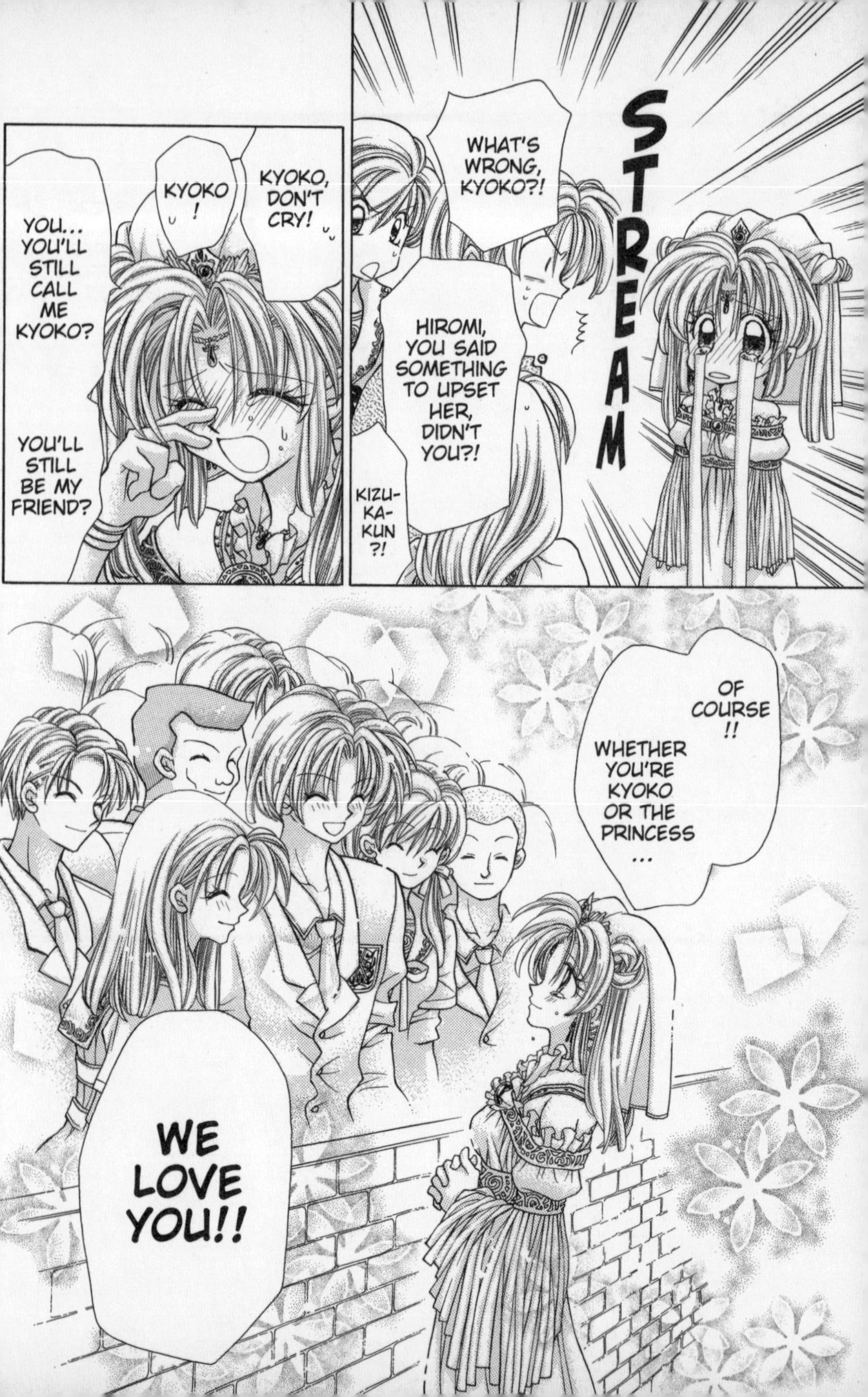
STREAM
WHAT'S WRONG, KYOKO?!
HIROMI, YOU SAID SOMETHING TO UPSET HER, DIDN'T YOU?!
KIZU-KA-KUN?!
KYOKO, DON'T CRY!
KYOKO!
YOU... YOU'LL STILL CALL ME KYOKO?
YOU'LL STILL BE MY FRIEND?
OF COURSE!!
WHETHER YOU'RE KYOKO OR THE PRINCESS...
WE LOVE YOU!!

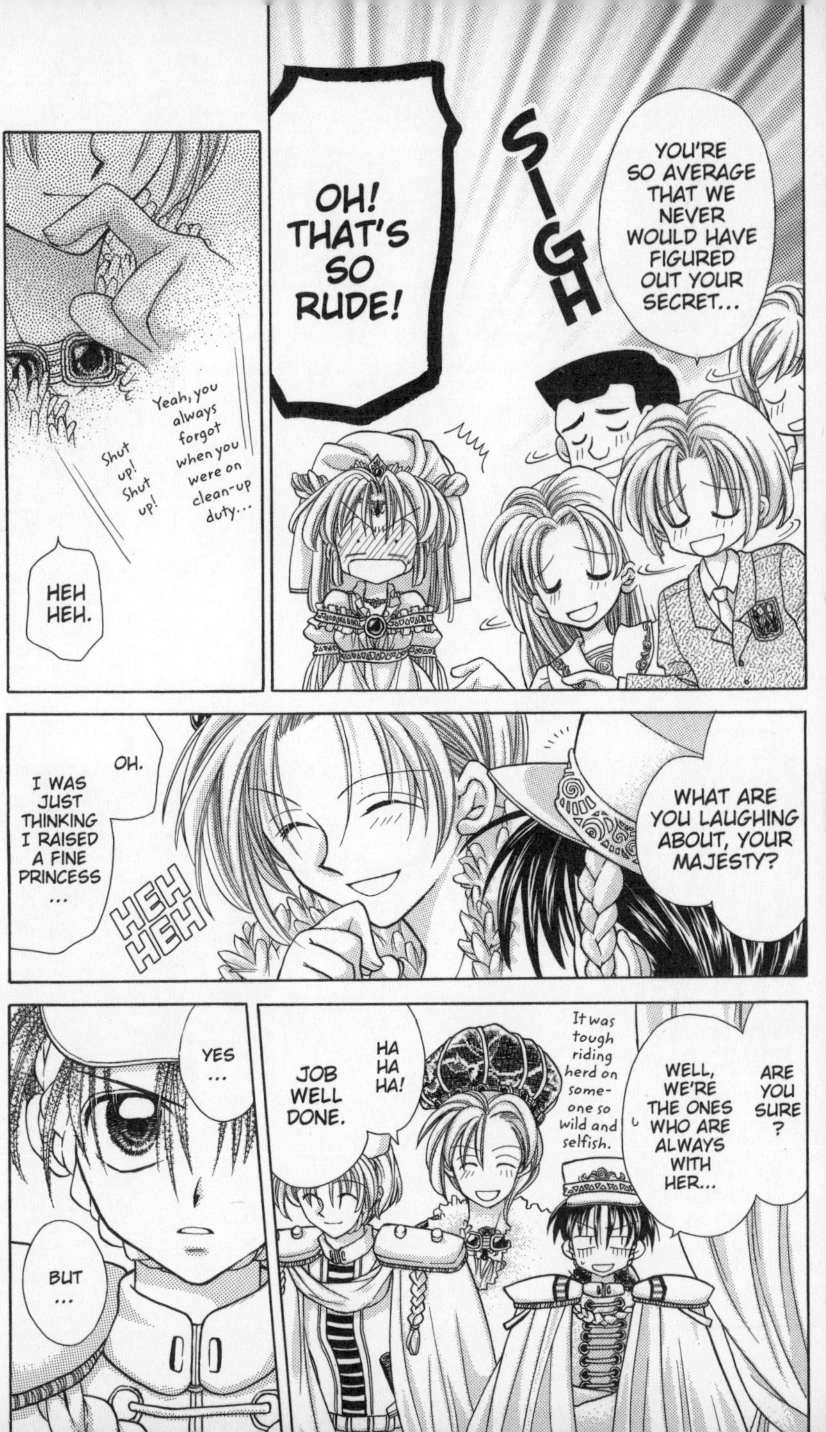
YOU'RE SO AVERAGE THAT WE NEVER WOULD HAVE FIGURED OUT YOUR SECRET...
SIGH
OH! THAT'S SO RUDE!
Yeah, you always forgot when you were on clean-up duty...
Shut up! Shut up!
HEH HEH.
WHAT ARE YOU LAUGHING ABOUT, YOUR MAJESTY?
OH.
I WAS JUST THINKING I RAISED A FINE PRINCESS...
HEH HEH
ARE YOU SURE?
WELL, WE'RE THE ONES WHO ARE ALWAYS WITH HER...
It was tough riding herd on someone so wild and selfish.
HA HA HA!
JOB WELL DONE.
YES...
BUT...

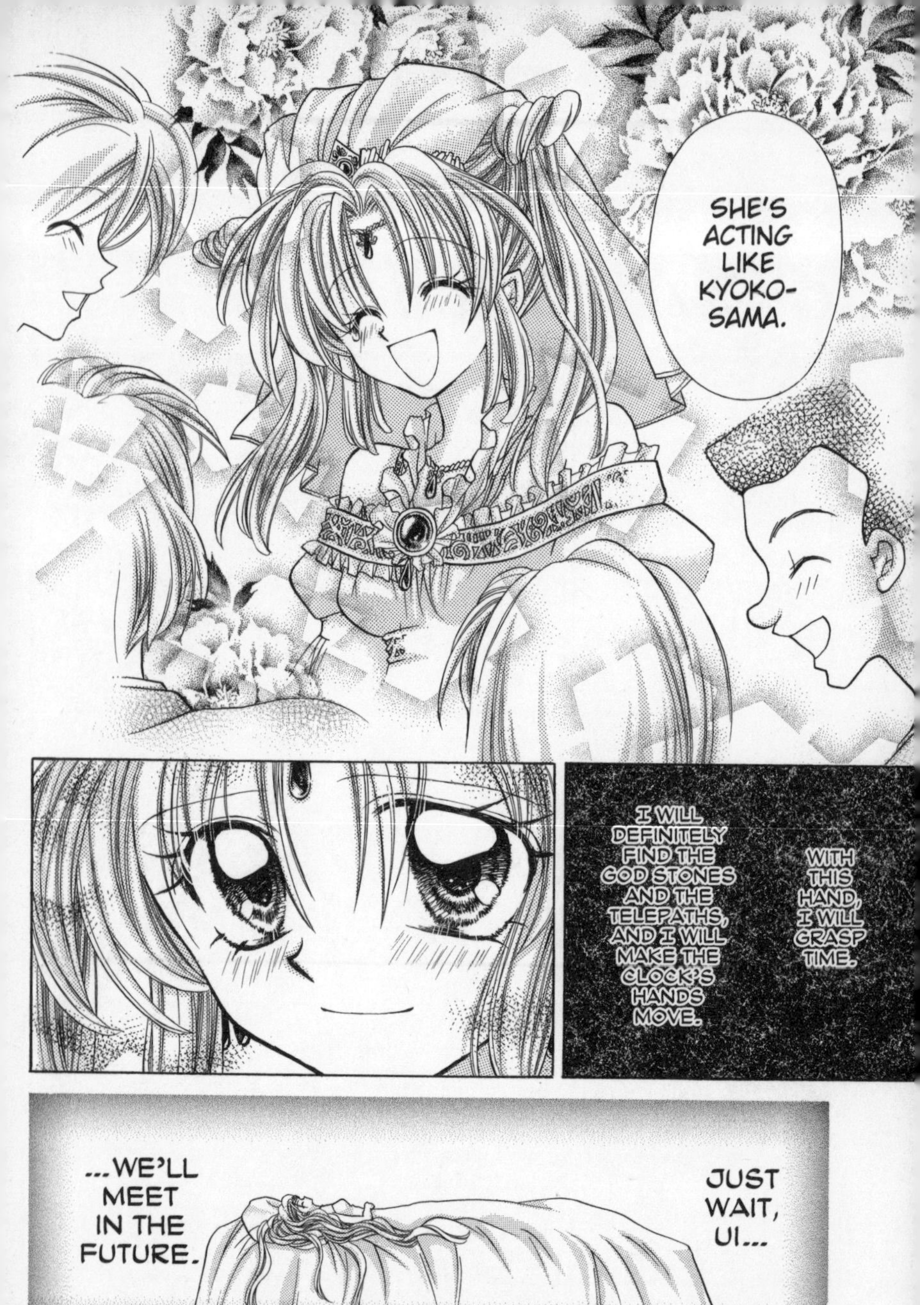
SHE'S ACTING LIKE KYOKO-SAMA.
I WILL DEFINITELY FIND THE GOD STONES AND THE TELEPATHS, AND I WILL MAKE THE CLOCK'S HANDS MOVE.
WITH THIS HAND, I WILL GRASP TIME.
JUST WAIT, UI...
...WE'LL MEET IN THE FUTURE.

CHAPTER 1/END

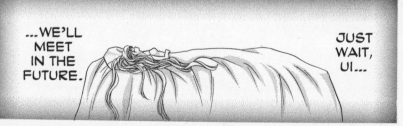

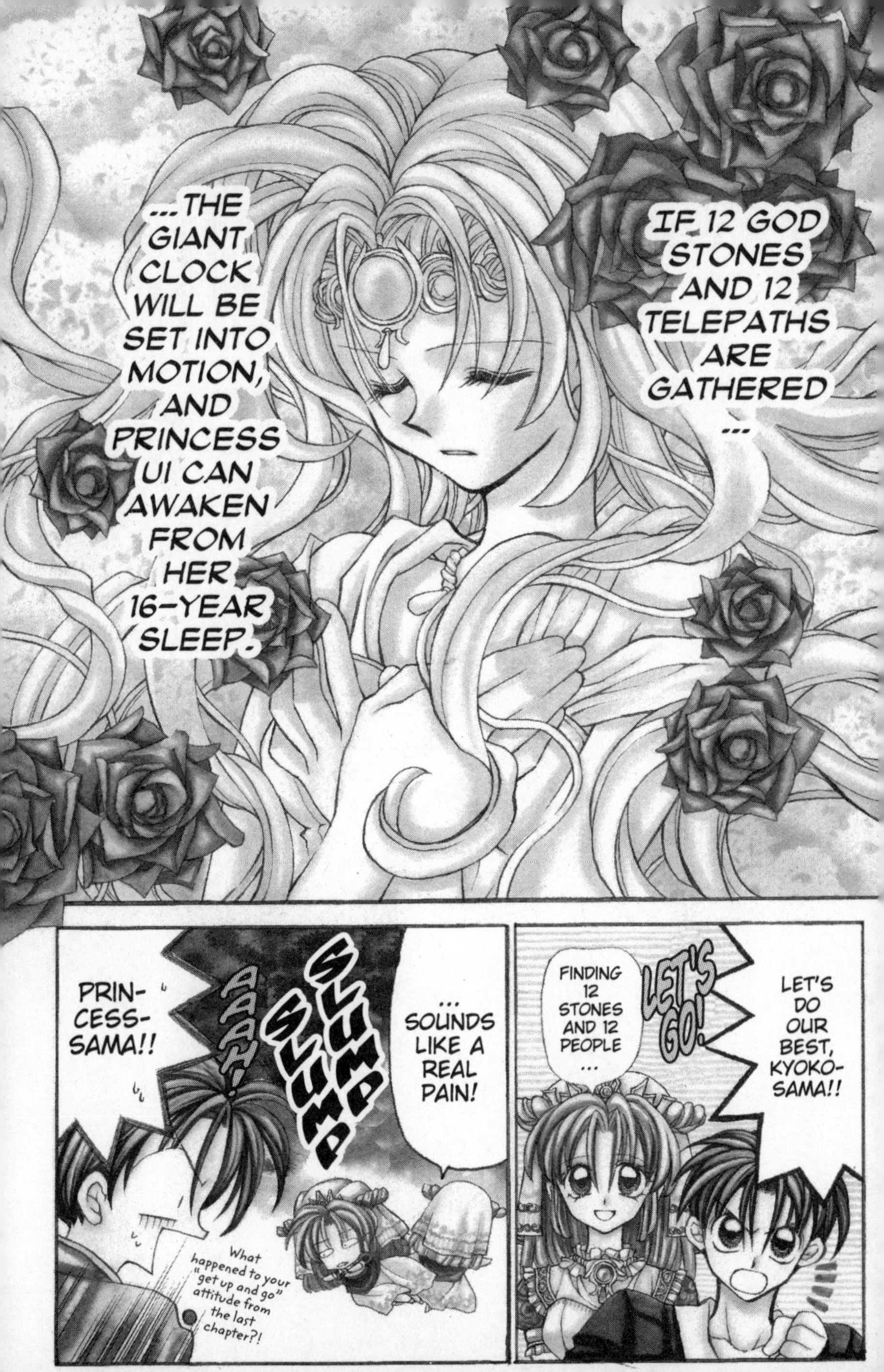
IF 12 GOD STONES AND 12 TELEPATHS ARE GATHERED ...
...THE GIANT CLOCK WILL BE SET INTO MOTION, AND PRINCESS UI CAN AWAKEN FROM HER 16-YEAR SLEEP.
LET'S DO OUR BEST, KYOKO-SAMA!!
LET'S GO!
FINDING 12 STONES AND 12 PEOPLE ...
... SOUNDS LIKE A REAL PAIN!
SLUMP SLUMP
AAAH
PRIN-CESS-SAMA!!
What happened to your "get up and go" attitude from the last chapter?!

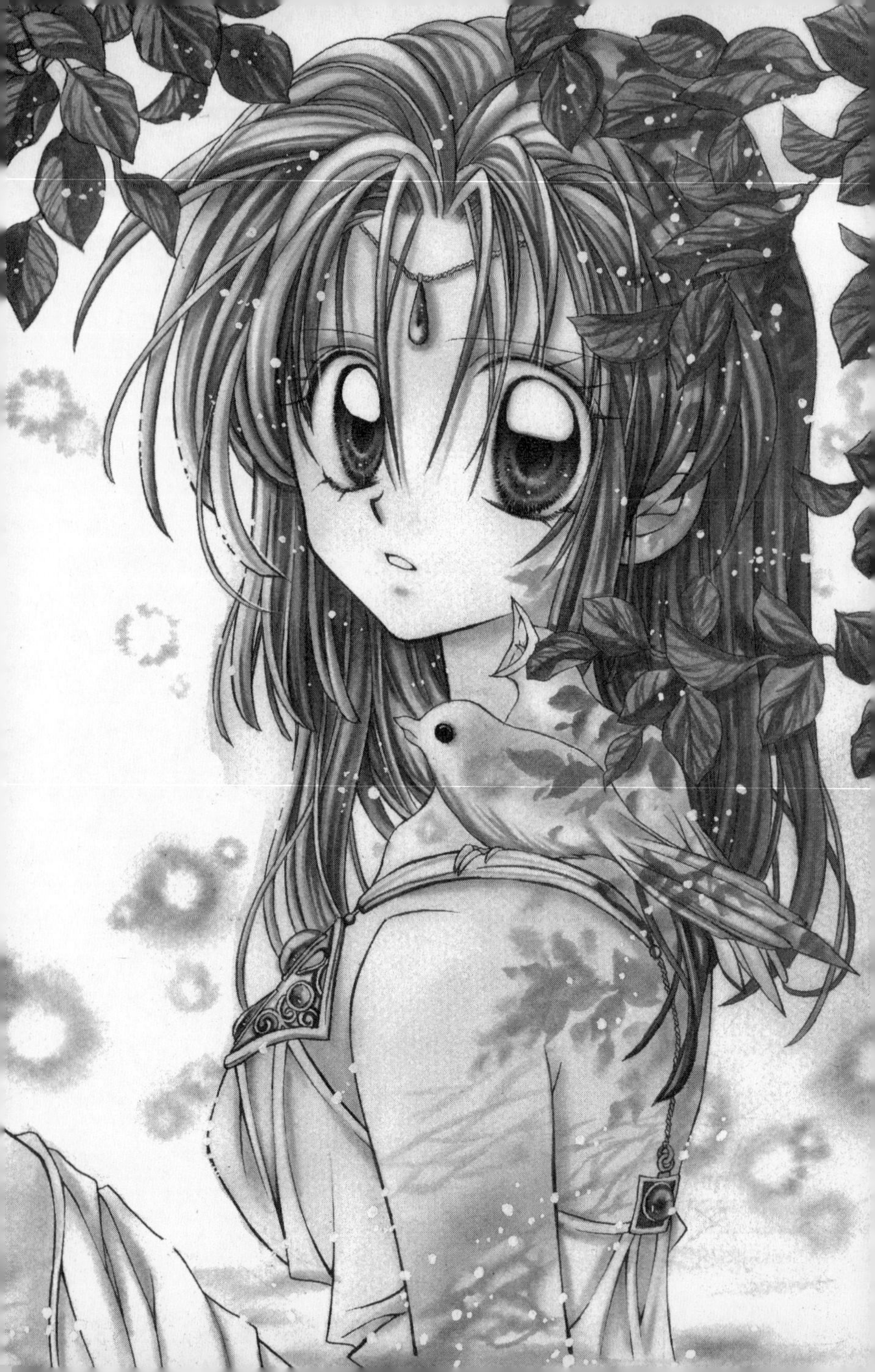

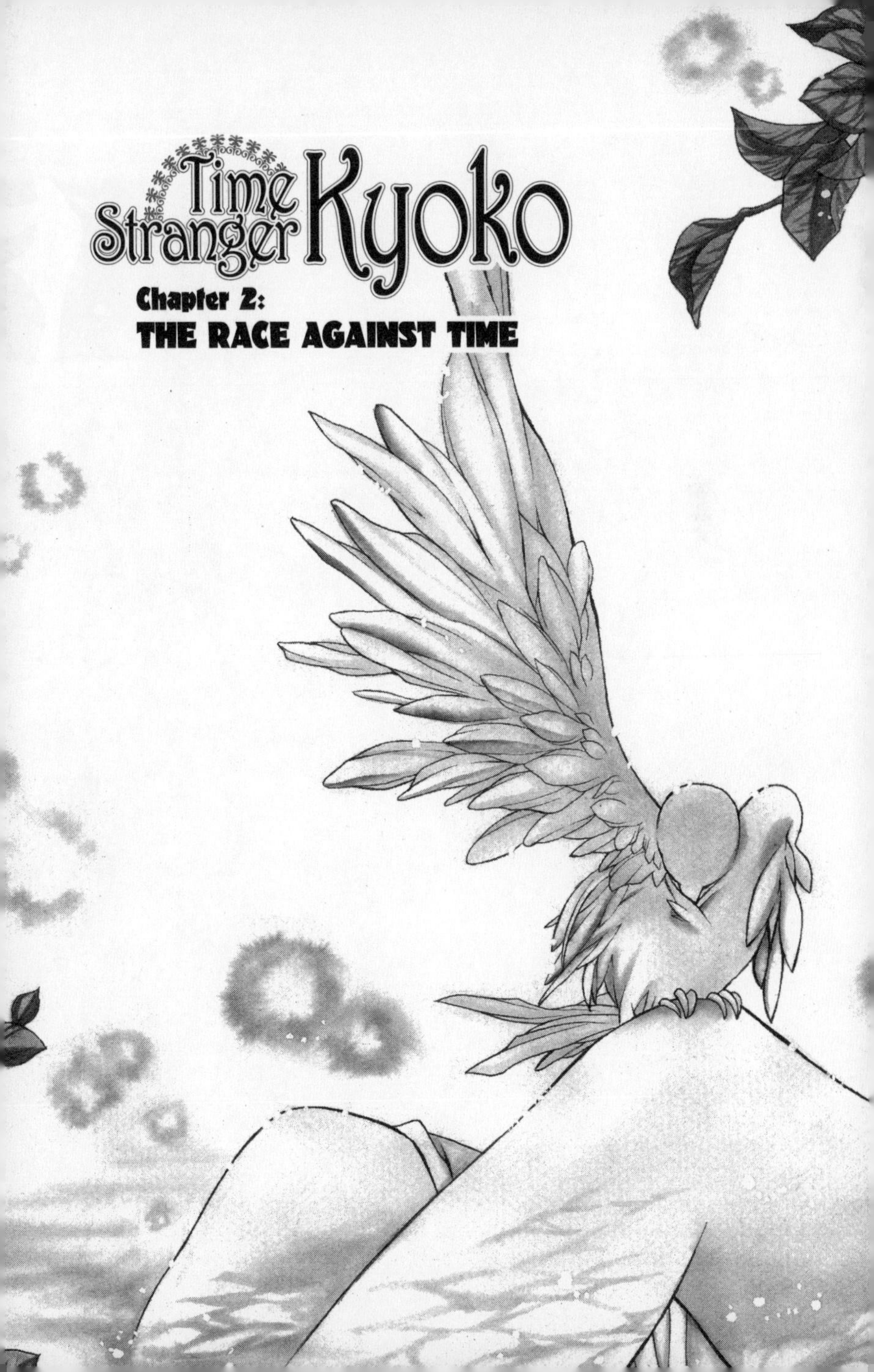
Time Stranger Kyoko
Chapter 2:
THE RACE AGAINST TIME

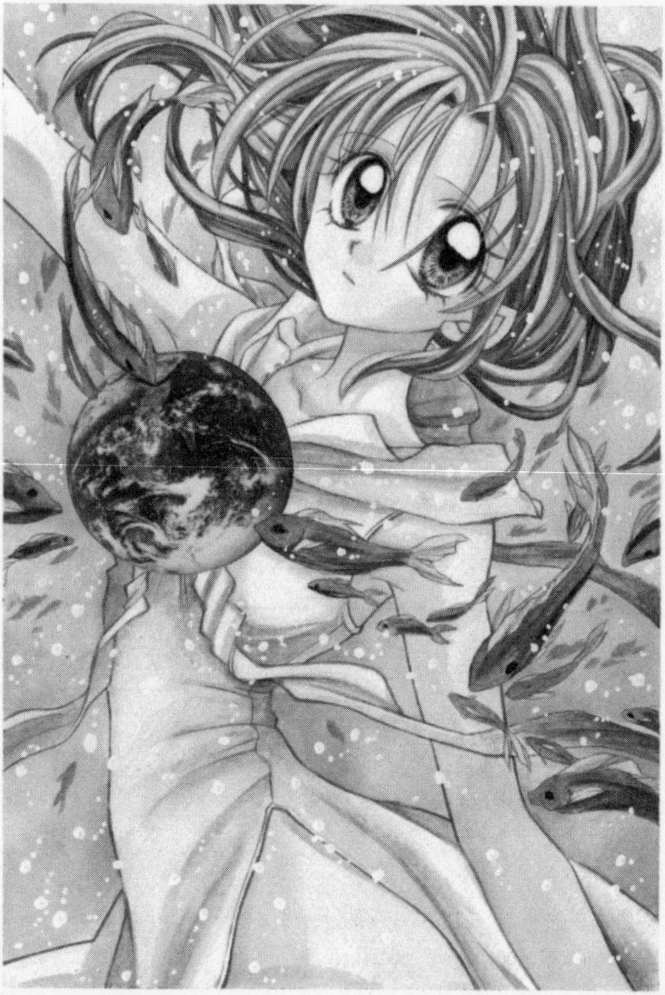

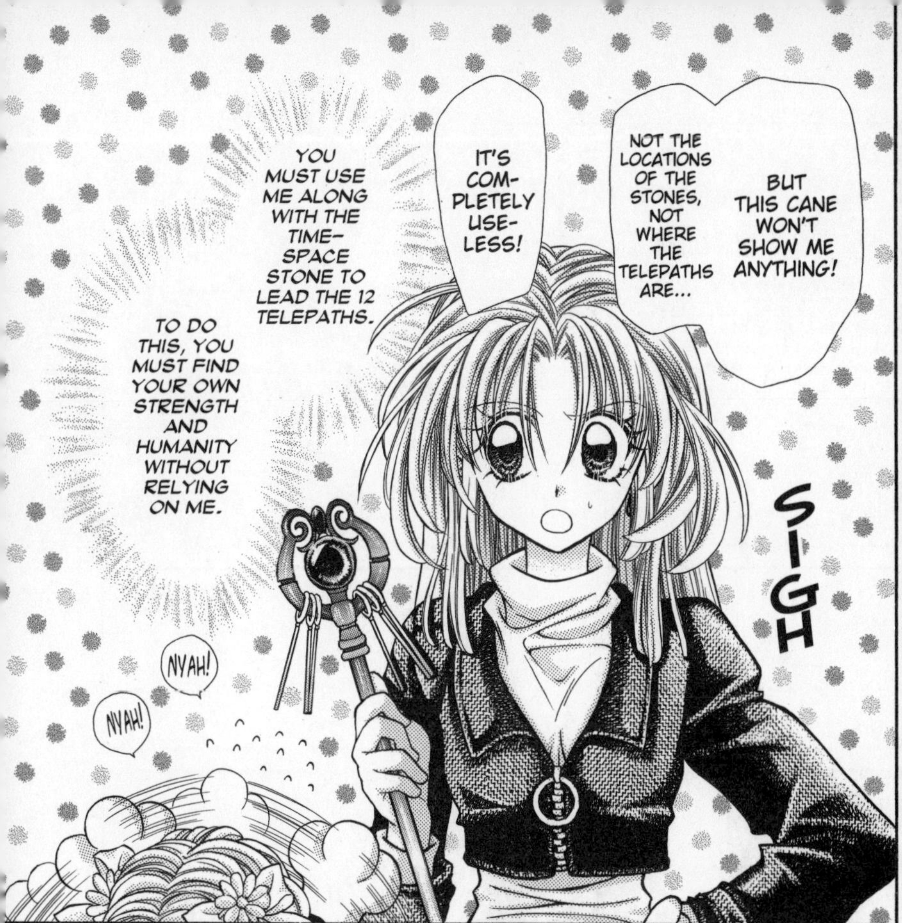
BUT THIS CANE WON'T SHOW ME ANYTHING!
NOT THE LOCATIONS OF THE STONES, NOT WHERE THE TELEPATHS ARE...
IT'S COM-PLETELY USE-LESS!
SIGH
YOU MUST USE ME ALONG WITH THE TIME-SPACE STONE TO LEAD THE 12 TELEPATHS.
TO DO THIS, YOU MUST FIND YOUR OWN STRENGTH AND HUMANITY WITHOUT RELYING ON ME.
NYAH!
NYAH!

CHAPTER 1: THERE IS BUT ONE PAST; THE FUTURE IS IN YOUR HEART

(LEAD-IN) PRINCESS KYOKO. 16 YEARS OLD. A DREAMLIKE ADVENTURE IS ABOUT TO BEGIN!

IT ALL STARTS IN CHAPTER 1. IT WAS MY FIRST SERIALIZED MANGA IN ABOUT TWO AND A HALF YEARS. I WAS IN THE MIDST OF A SLUMP THAT STARTED AROUND THE SECOND OR THIRD CHAPTER OF THE PREVIOUS SERIES. (I RECOVERED FROM THAT SLUMP JUST RECENTLY.) BUT I MANAGED TO COME UP WITH AN OPENING ILLUSTRATION. I GOT THE IDEA FROM A CD JACKET OF MY FAVORITE MUSICIAN, AND I USED A DESIGN THAT INCORPORATES A PHOTO. CG IS ALL THE RAGE NOW, BUT I STILL LIKE ANTIQUES AND ANALOG, AND I'LL ALWAYS (?) HAND-COLOR MY ILLUSTRATIONS. EVEN THE THIRTIETH CENTURY THAT I DRAW HAS AN ANTIQUE DESIGN.

CHAPTER 2: THE RACE AGAINST TIME

(LEAD-IN) GAZING AT TOMORROW

THE TITLE PAGE... ♪ I GOT IT DONE SOMEHOW (THE ILLUSTRATION AS WELL AS THE STORY), EVEN THOUGH I WAS IN THE MIDST OF A SLUMP. THERE WASN'T MUCH COMPOSITION, BUT THE READERS SEEM TO LIKE IT. I REALLY CAN'T DRAW BIRDS WELL, CAN I? (OR ANIMALS IN GENERAL, FOR THAT MATTER.) I TRIED TO IMAGINE THINGS FROM SAKATAKI'S POINT OF VIEW. HE'S COME TO THE LAKE IN SEARCH OF THE PRINCESS... AT LEAST THAT'S THE FEELING I WAS GOING FOR. THIS CHAPTER RAN IN THE SEPTEMBER ISSUE OF THE MAGAZINE, BUT I DREW IT IN JULY—SMACK IN THE MIDDLE OF SUMMER. I TRIED TO CONVEY THE BRIGHT, DRY DAYS OF FALL, BUT... THE STORY IS ABOUT KYOKO TRYING TO FIND THE POWER TO TRAVEL TO THE PAST. I THINK I FINALLY GOT A GRIP ON THE CHARACTERS IN THIS CHAPTER.

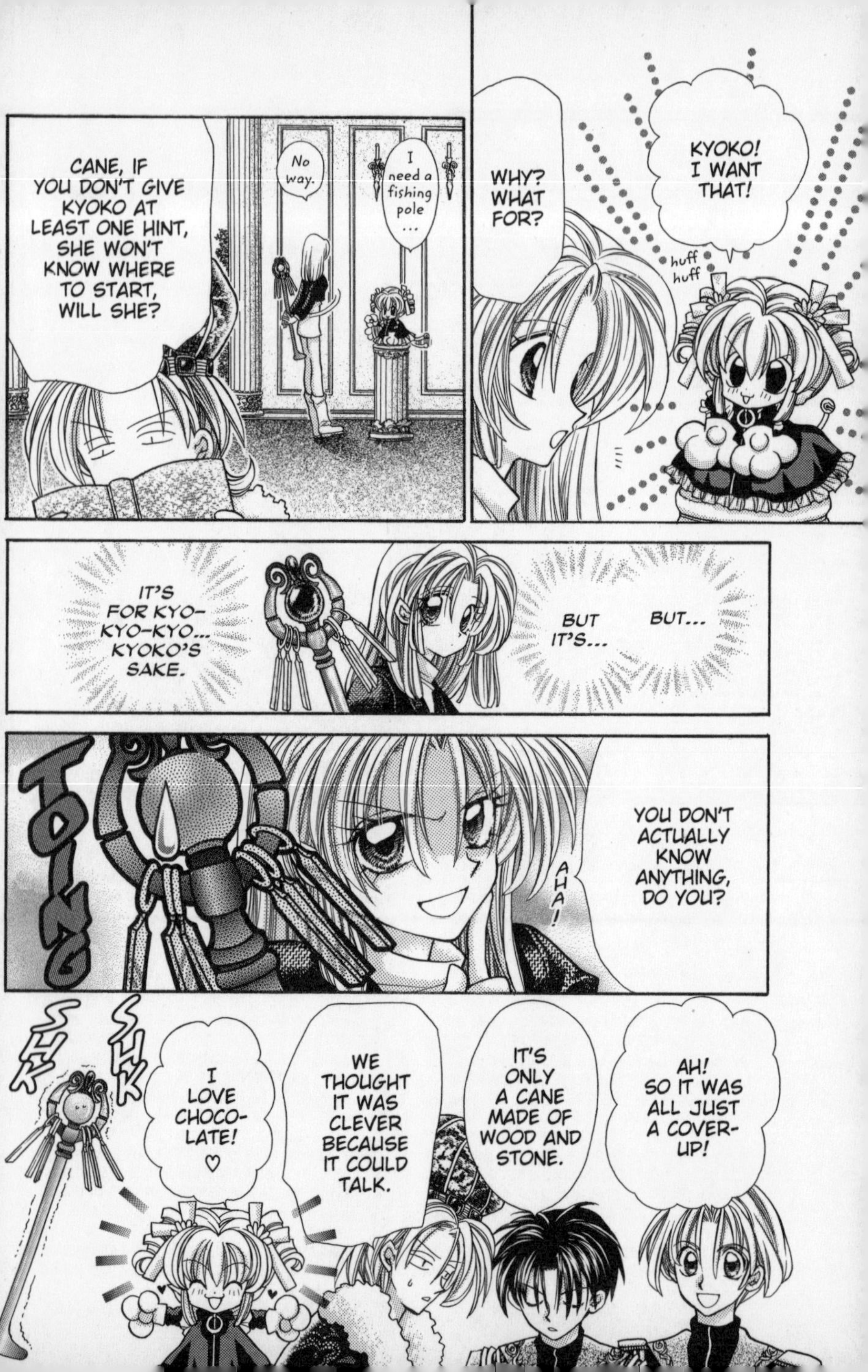

KYOKO! I WANT THAT!
huff huff
WHY? WHAT FOR?
I need a fishing pole ...
No way.
CANE, IF YOU DON'T GIVE KYOKO AT LEAST ONE HINT, SHE WON'T KNOW WHERE TO START, WILL SHE?
BUT...
BUT IT'S...
IT'S FOR KYO-KYO-KYO... KYOKO'S SAKE.
YOU DON'T ACTUALLY KNOW ANYTHING, DO YOU?
AHA!
TOING
AH! SO IT WAS ALL JUST A COVER-UP!
IT'S ONLY A CANE MADE OF WOOD AND STONE.
WE THOUGHT IT WAS CLEVER BECAUSE IT COULD TALK.
I LOVE CHOCO-LATE! ♡
SHK
SHK

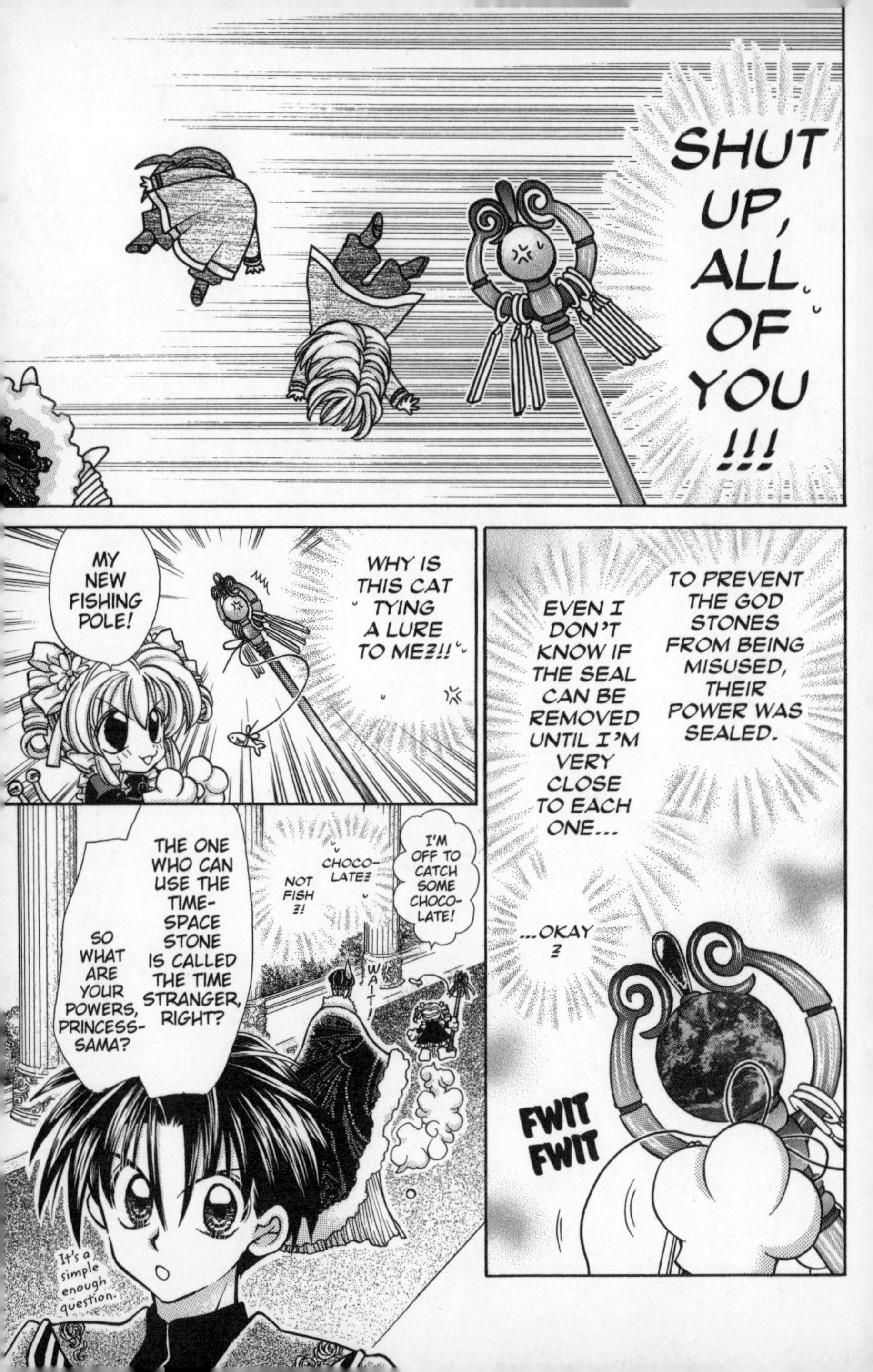
SHUT UP, ALL OF YOU!!!
TO PREVENT THE GOD STONES FROM BEING MISUSED, THEIR POWER WAS SEALED.
EVEN I DON'T KNOW IF THE SEAL CAN BE REMOVED UNTIL I'M VERY CLOSE TO EACH ONE...
...OKAY?
FWIT FWIT
WHY IS THIS CAT TYING A LURE TO ME?!!
MY NEW FISHING POLE!
I'M OFF TO CATCH SOME CHOCOLATE!
CHOCOLATE?
NOT FISH?!
WAIT!
THE ONE WHO CAN USE THE TIME-SPACE STONE IS CALLED THE TIME STRANGER, RIGHT?
SO WHAT ARE YOUR POWERS, PRINCESS-SAMA?
It's a simple enough question.

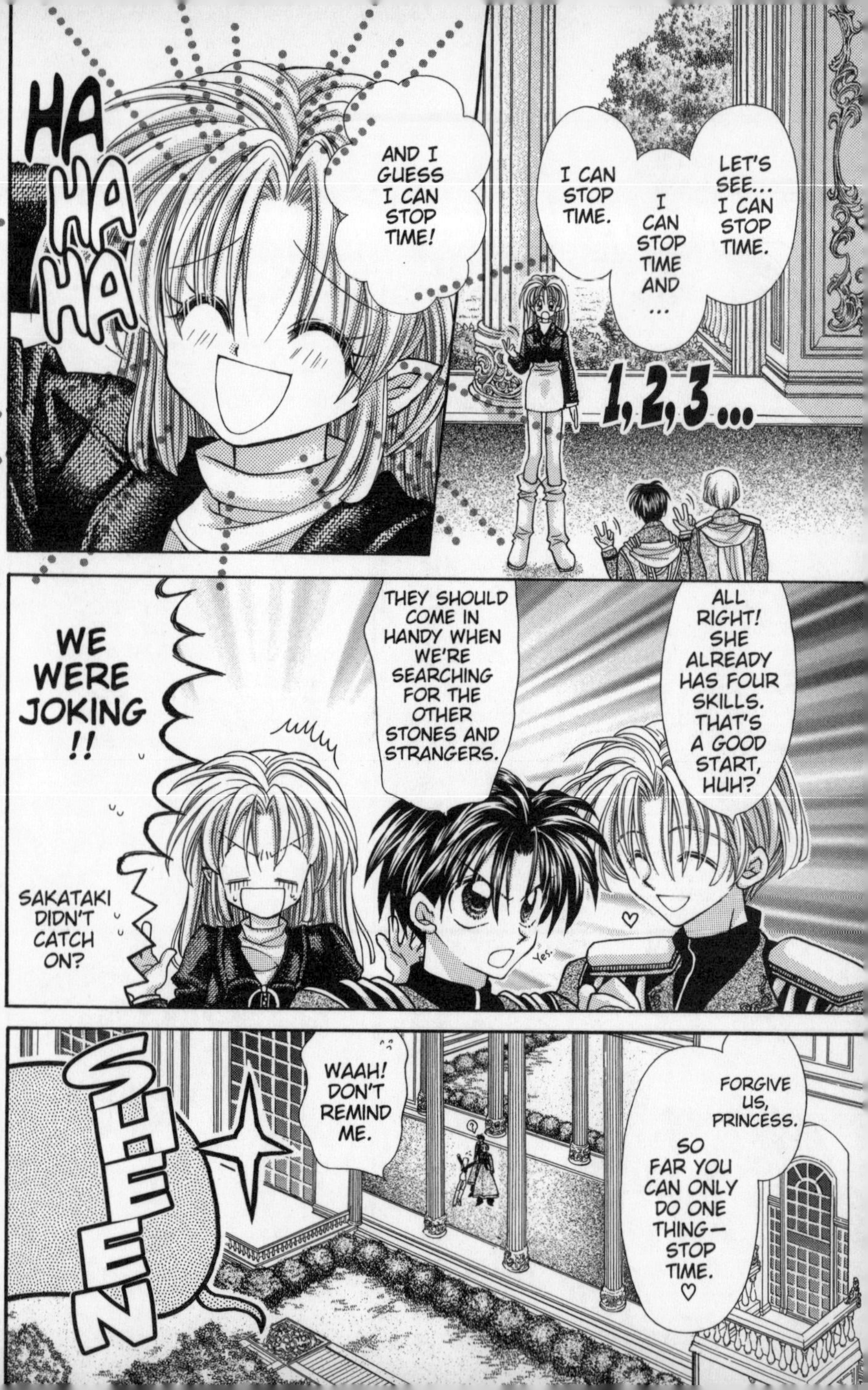
LET'S SEE... I CAN STOP TIME.
I CAN STOP TIME AND ...
I CAN STOP TIME.
1, 2, 3...
HA HA HA HA
AND I GUESS I CAN STOP TIME!
ALL RIGHT! SHE ALREADY HAS FOUR SKILLS. THAT'S A GOOD START, HUH?
THEY SHOULD COME IN HANDY WHEN WE'RE SEARCHING FOR THE OTHER STONES AND STRANGERS.
Yes.
WE WERE JOKING!!
SAKATAKI DIDN'T CATCH ON?
FORGIVE US, PRINCESS.
SO FAR YOU CAN ONLY DO ONE THING—STOP TIME. ♡
WAAH! DON'T REMIND ME.
SHEEN

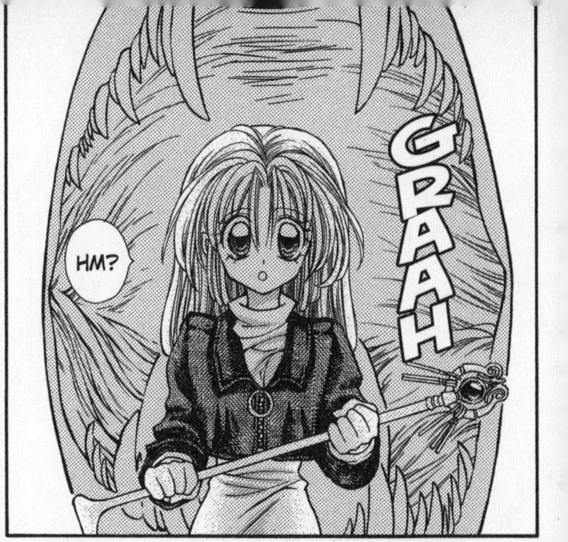
GRAAH
HM?

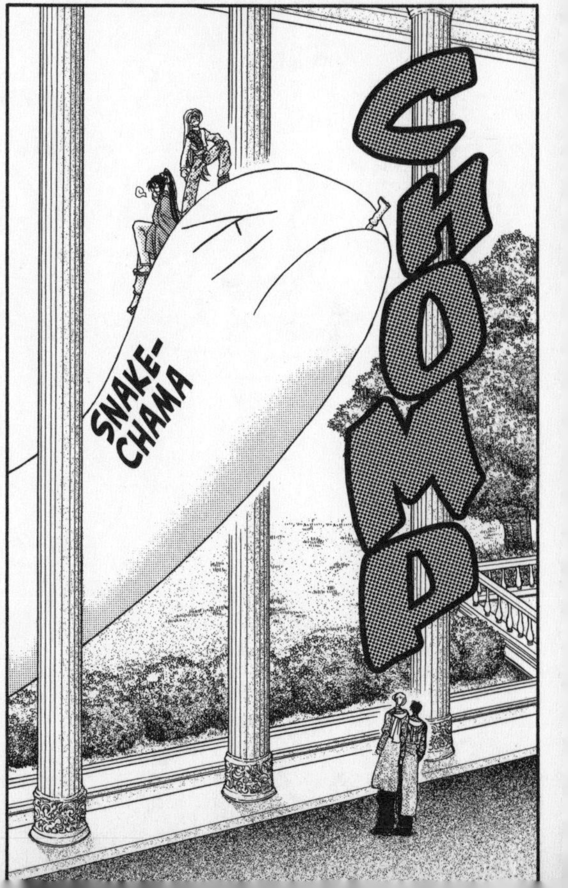
CHOMP
SNAKE-CHAMA

ZEALOUS, PURE, SERIOUS, STRAITLACED, AND SINGLE-MINDED!!

SAKATAKI JIN

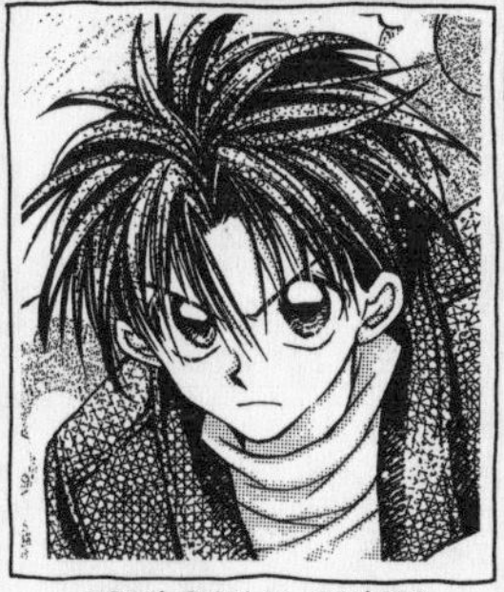

BORN JULY 21, CANCER, BLOOD-TYPE A, CRYSTAL STRANGER → STANDS AT 7:00

(?)

HIS STRAIGHTFORWARD GAZE HAS GARNERED POPULARITY. I WANTED TO CREATE A CHARACTER WHO IS A HERO AMONG HEROES, BUT HE TURNED OUT WAY MORE SERIOUS THAN I HAD PLANNED. SOMEHOW HE TURNED OUT TO BE A STRAITLACED GUY WHO DOESN'T EVEN GET JOKES. Oops.~

I'VE HEARD THAT PEOPLE WHO SERVE OTHERS ARE HAPPIEST WHEN THEIR MASTERS ACT RESPONSIBLY, SO SAKATAKI IS HAPPIEST WHEN KYOKO-CHAN IS ACTING NOBLE. (HE FINDS HER SELFISHNESS TO BE A PAIN.) ← But the truth is Kyoko-chan acts selfishly only with Sakataki...

SAKATAKI IS A PRINCE OF THE DRAGON TRIBE KIRITO WHO WAS DESTINED TO BECOME THE CHIEF. HE HAS AN OLDER BROTHER NAMED HIZUKI. HIS VILLAGE WAS DESTROYED BY SOMEONE OR SOMETHING UNKNOWN, AND ONLY SAKATAKI AND HIZUKI SURVIVED. THEY WERE TAKEN IN BY THE ROYAL FAMILY, AND HE IS NOW 17. HE IS KYOKO-CHAN'S BODYGUARD.

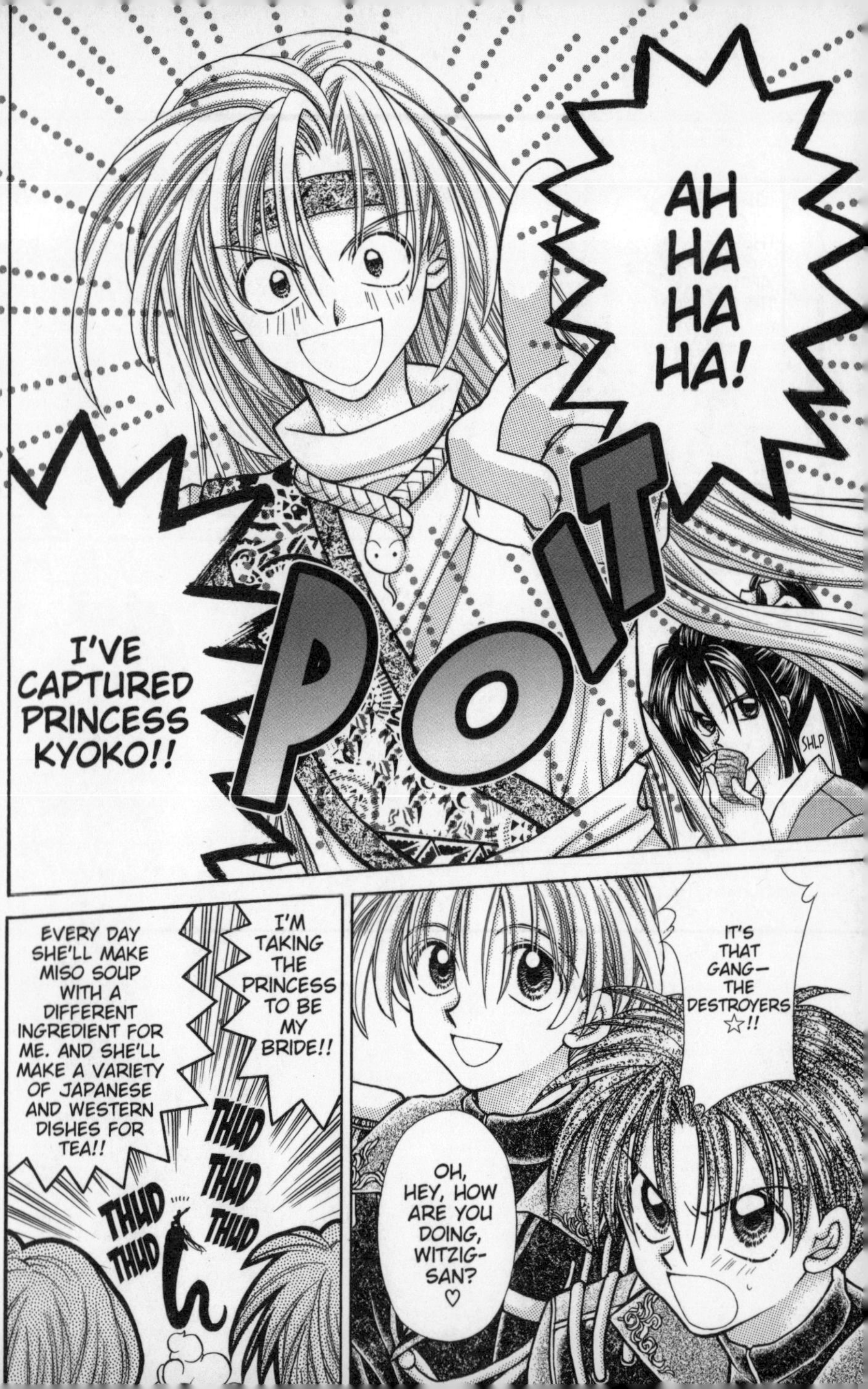
AH HA HA HA!
POIT
SHLP
I'VE CAPTURED PRINCESS KYOKO!!
IT'S THAT GANG— THE DESTROYERS☆!!
OH, HEY, HOW ARE YOU DOING, WITZIG-SAN? ♡
I'M TAKING THE PRINCESS TO BE MY BRIDE!!
EVERY DAY SHE'LL MAKE MISO SOUP WITH A DIFFERENT INGREDIENT FOR ME. AND SHE'LL MAKE A VARIETY OF JAPANESE AND WESTERN DISHES FOR TEA!!
THUD THUD THUD
THUD THUD

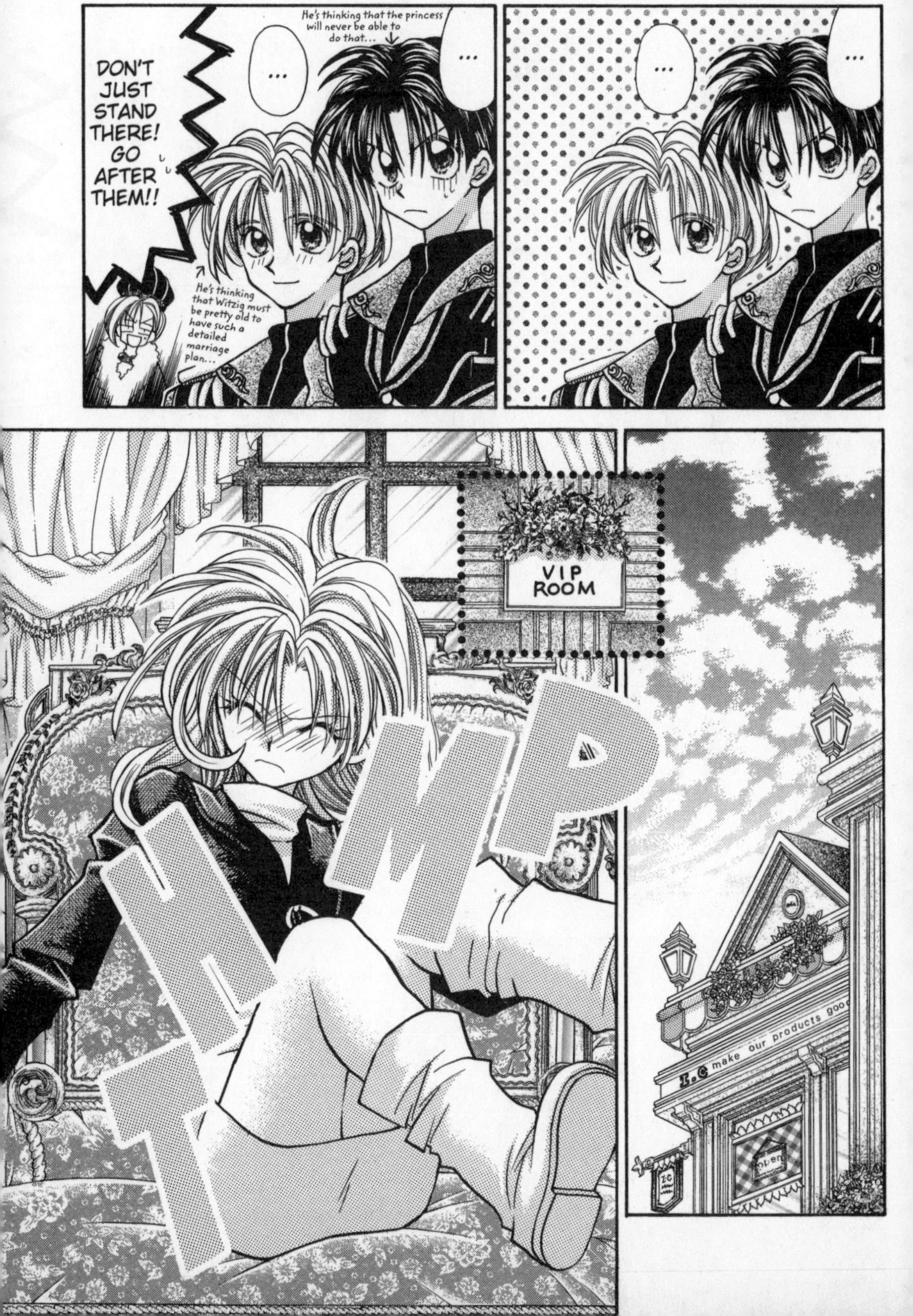
...
...
...
He's thinking that the princess will never be able to do that...
...
DON'T JUST STAND THERE! GO AFTER THEM!!
He's thinking that Witzig must be pretty old to have such a detailed marriage plan...
make our products goo
open
VIP ROOM
THMP

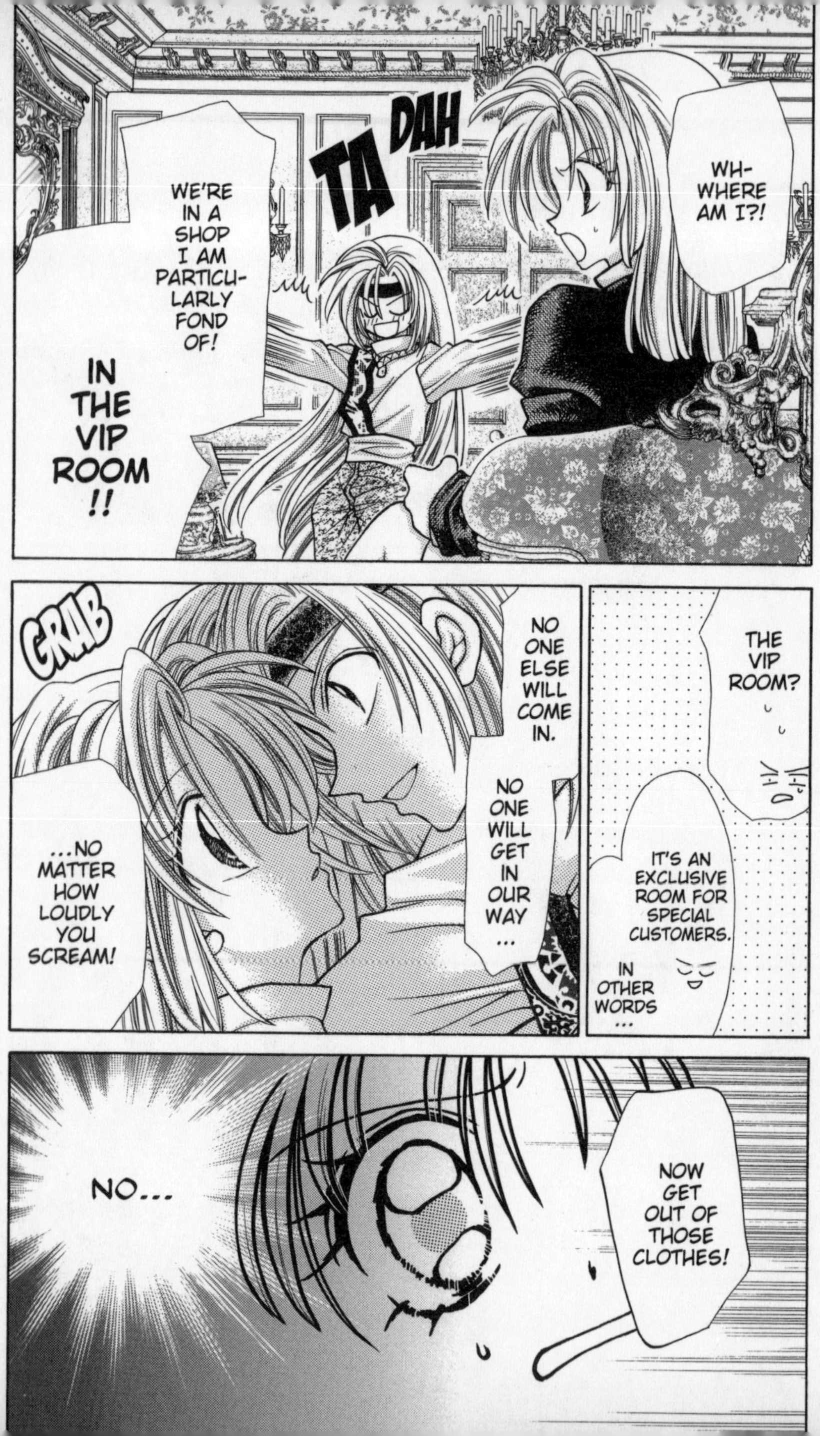
WH- WHERE AM I?!
TA DAH
WE'RE IN A SHOP I AM PARTICULARLY FOND OF!
IN THE VIP ROOM!!
THE VIP ROOM?
IT'S AN EXCLUSIVE ROOM FOR SPECIAL CUSTOMERS.
IN OTHER WORDS...
NO ONE ELSE WILL COME IN.
NO ONE WILL GET IN OUR WAY...
GRAB
...NO MATTER HOW LOUDLY YOU SCREAM!
NOW GET OUT OF THOSE CLOTHES!
NO...

A DIVINE, COOL ONII-CHAN.

HIZUKI JIN

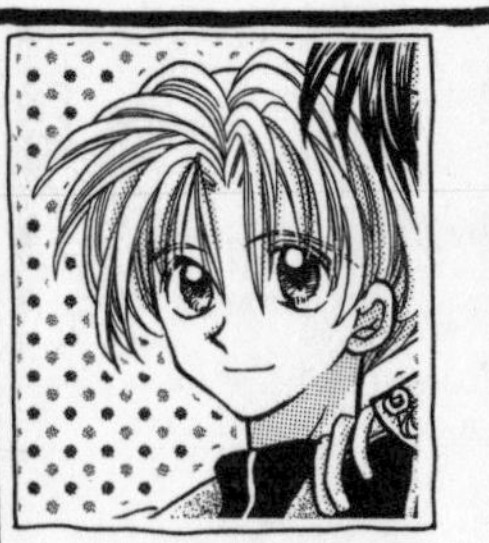

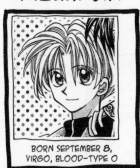

BORN SEPTEMBER 8, VIRGO, BLOOD-TYPE O

HE IS SAKATAKI'S OLDER BROTHER AS WELL AS BODYGUARD TO KYOKO. HE PRETTY MUCH DOES HIS OWN THING, BUT HE IS ALWAYS READY TO GET IN ON A JOKE.

ALTHOUGH HE'S SAKATAKI'S OLDER BROTHER, SAKATAKI WAS THE ONE APPOINTED FUTURE CHIEF OF THE DRAGON TRIBE. THAT MAKES HIZUKI SOMETHING OF A MYSTERY.

HE'S FAIRLY OPTIMISTIC AND LIKES TO ENJOY LIFE. HE ALSO LIKES SLIGHTLY JUICY PROPOSITIONS. ON THE OTHER HAND, HE'S KIND OF VAGUE, AND THAT MAKES HIM HARD TO READ.

I THINK THERE IS A LOT TO LEARN ABOUT HIM, BUT I WANT TO WRITE ABOUT IT ALL AT ONE TIME, SO PLEASE BEAR WITH ME! YOU'RE NOT BUYING THAT, ARE YOU? OKAY, I GUESS I'LL REVEAL THINGS ABOUT HIM LITTLE BY LITTLE!

HIZUKI IS 22. HE IS MISCHIEVOUS AND HAS DROOPING EYES.

HIS HOBBY IS GOING TO HOT-WATER SPRINGS! HIS FAVORITE BURIAL MOUNDS ARE LARGE KEYHOLE-SHAPED TOMBS!!

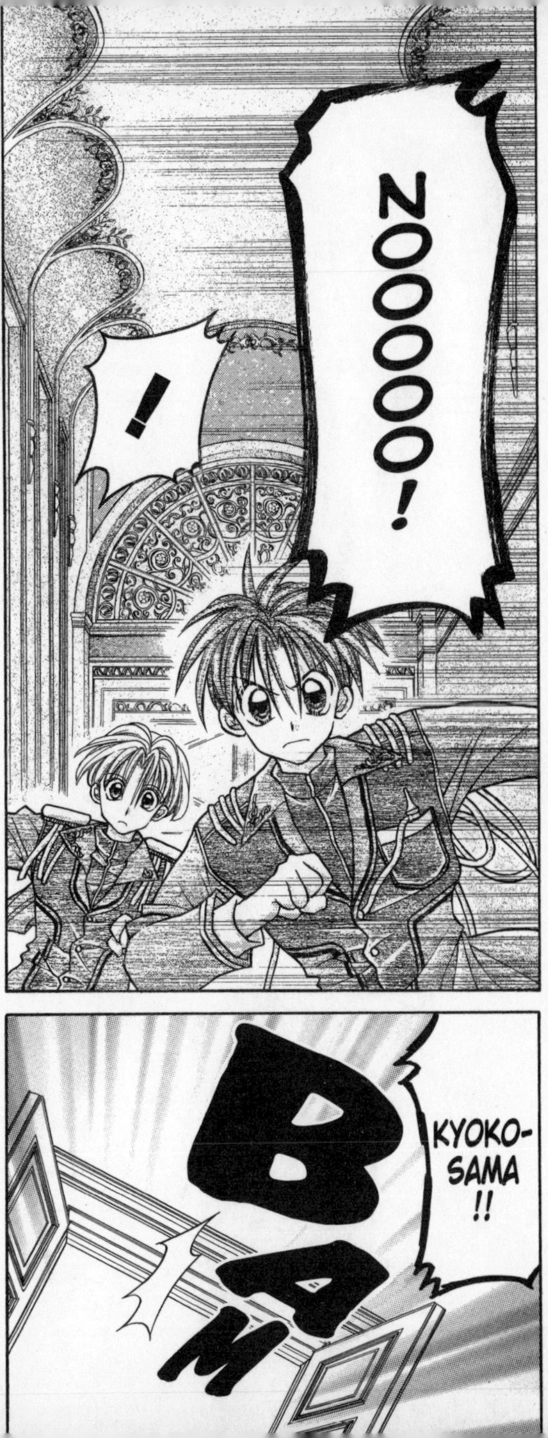
NOOOOO!
!
KYOKO-SAMA!!
BAM

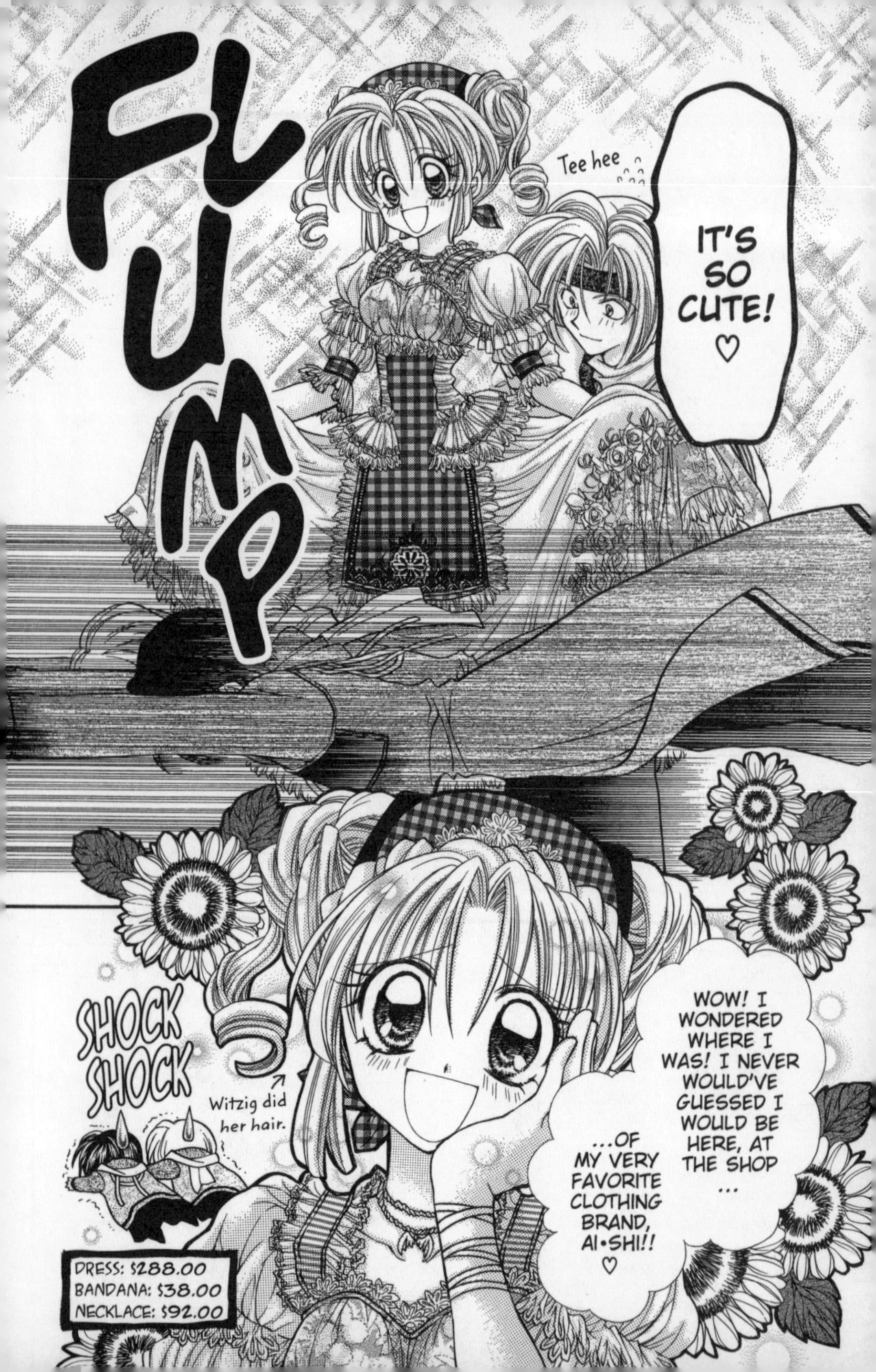
IT'S SO CUTE! ♡
Tee hee
FLUMP
WOW! I WONDERED WHERE I WAS! I NEVER WOULD'VE GUESSED I WOULD BE HERE, AT THE SHOP ...
...OF MY VERY FAVORITE CLOTHING BRAND, AI•SHI!! ♡
Witzig did her hair.
SHOCK SHOCK
DRESS: $288.00
BANDANA: $38.00
NECKLACE: $92.00

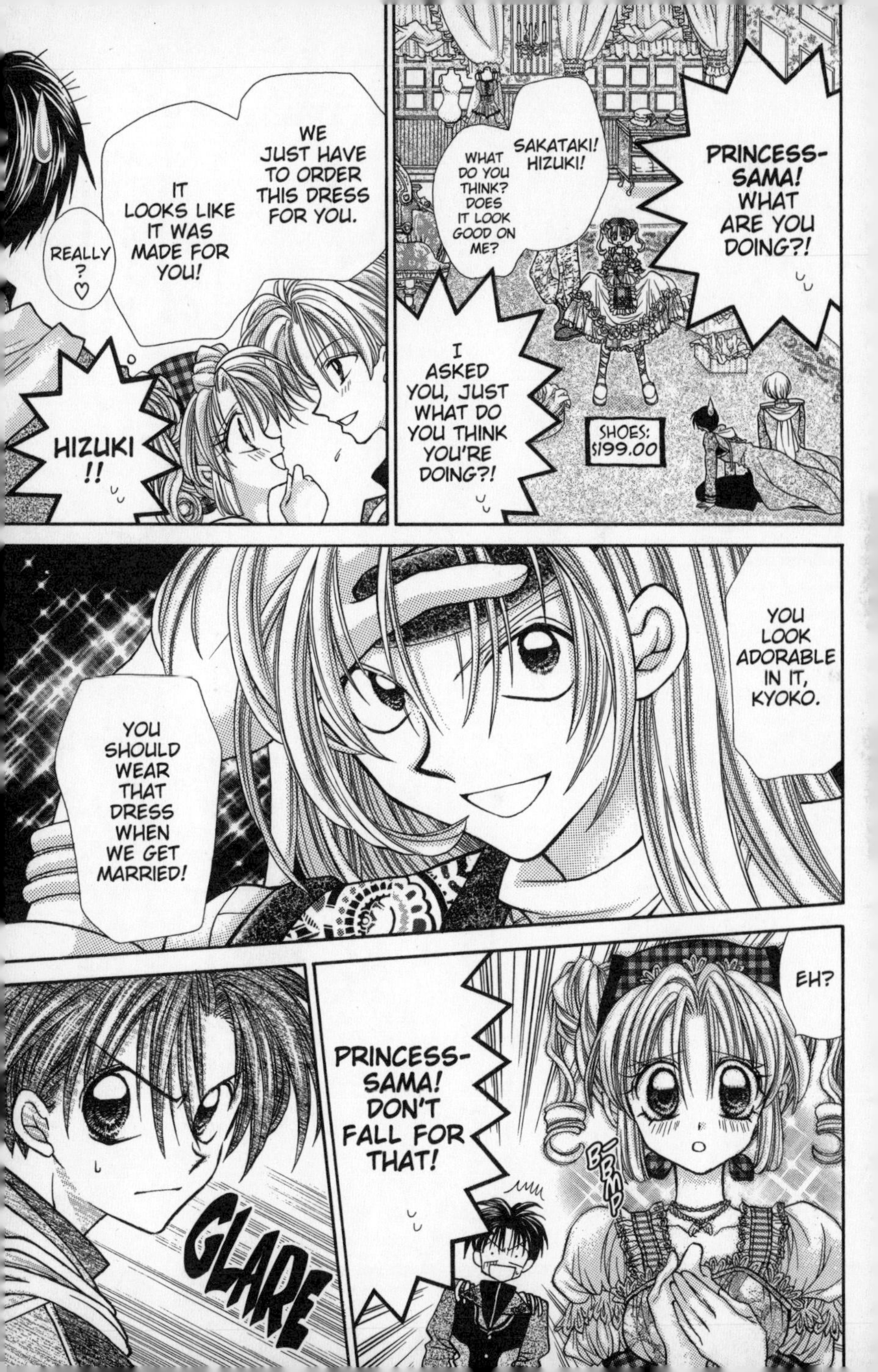
PRINCESS-SAMA! WHAT ARE YOU DOING?!
SAKATAKI! HIZUKI!
WHAT DO YOU THINK? DOES IT LOOK GOOD ON ME?
I ASKED YOU, JUST WHAT DO YOU THINK YOU'RE DOING?!
SHOES: $199.00
WE JUST HAVE TO ORDER THIS DRESS FOR YOU.
IT LOOKS LIKE IT WAS MADE FOR YOU!
REALLY? ♡
HIZUKI!!
YOU LOOK ADORABLE IN IT, KYOKO.
YOU SHOULD WEAR THAT DRESS WHEN WE GET MARRIED!
EH?
PRINCESS-SAMA! DON'T FALL FOR THAT!
B-BMP
GLARE

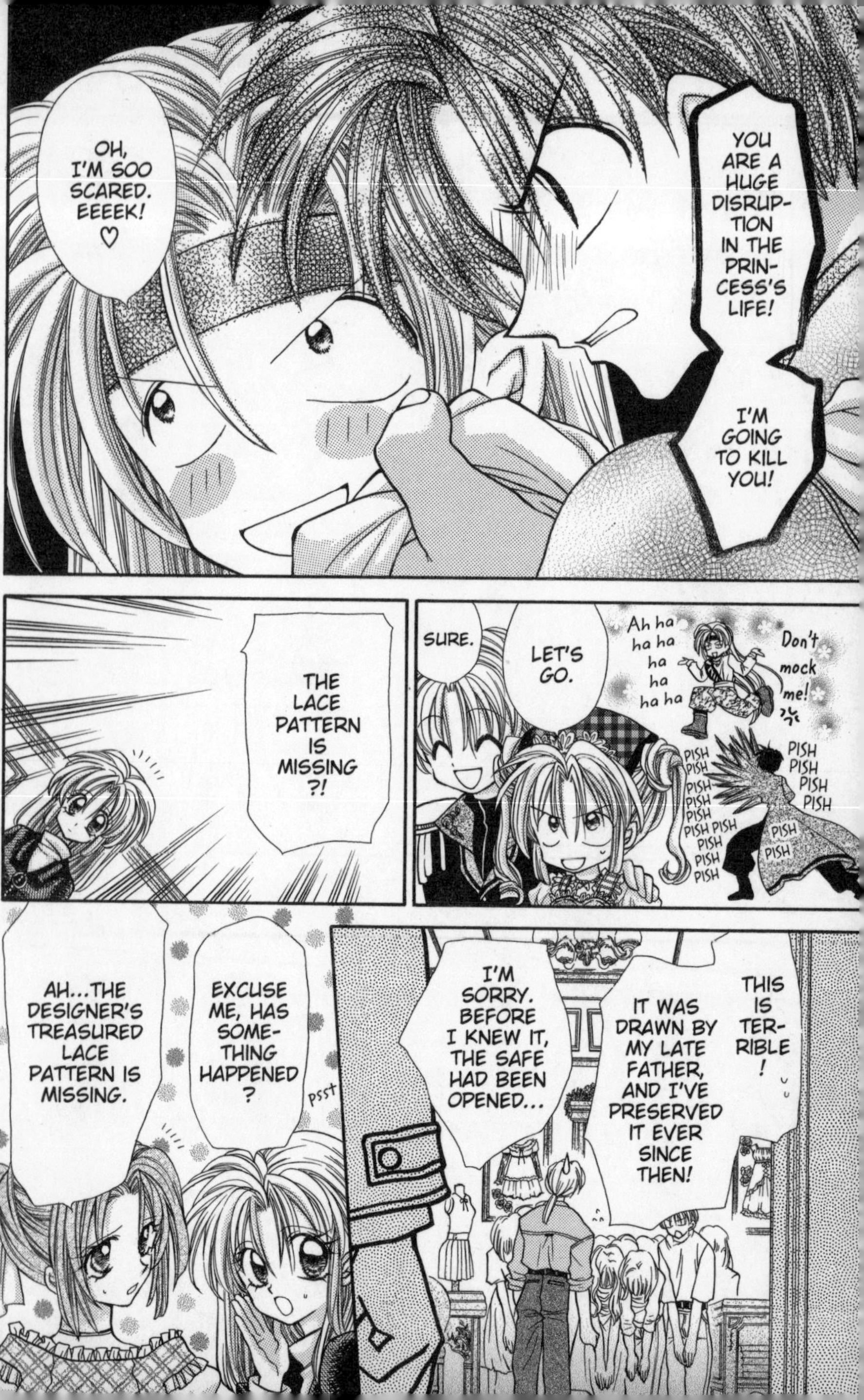
YOU ARE A HUGE DISRUPTION IN THE PRINCESS'S LIFE!
I'M GOING TO KILL YOU!
OH, I'M SOO SCARED. EEEEK! ♡
Don't mock me!
Ah ha ha ha ha ha ha ha ha
LET'S GO.
SURE.
PISH PISH PISH PISH
PISH PISH PISH PISH PISH PISH PISH PISH PISH PISH PISH PISH
THE LACE PATTERN IS MISSING?!
THIS IS TERRIBLE!
IT WAS DRAWN BY MY LATE FATHER, AND I'VE PRESERVED IT EVER SINCE THEN!
I'M SORRY. BEFORE I KNEW IT, THE SAFE HAD BEEN OPENED...
EXCUSE ME, HAS SOMETHING HAPPENED?
psst
AH...THE DESIGNER'S TREASURED LACE PATTERN IS MISSING.

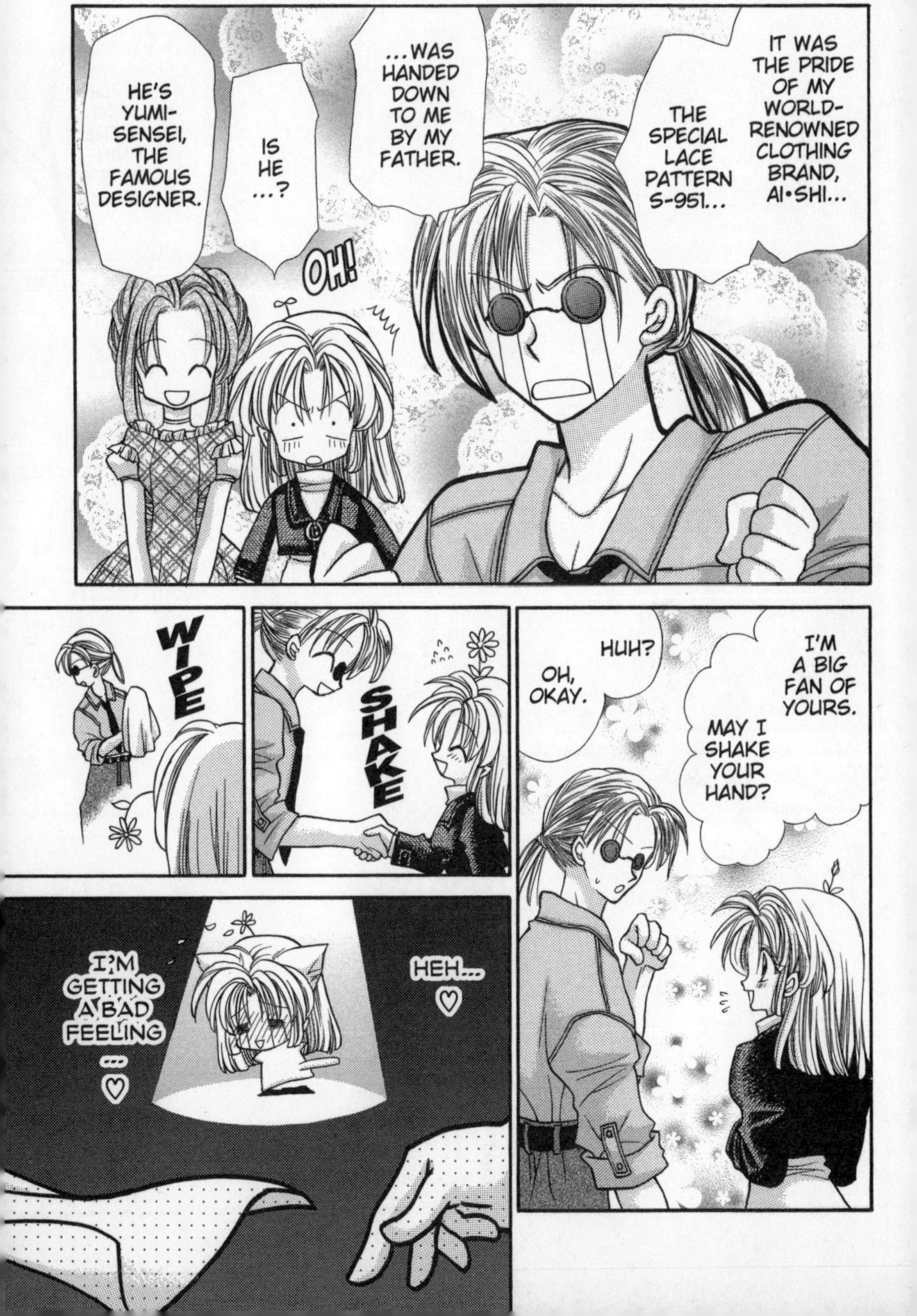
IT WAS THE PRIDE OF MY WORLD-RENOWNED CLOTHING BRAND, AI•SHI...
THE SPECIAL LACE PATTERN S-951...
...WAS HANDED DOWN TO ME BY MY FATHER.
IS HE ...?
HE'S YUMI-SENSEI, THE FAMOUS DESIGNER.
OH!
I'M A BIG FAN OF YOURS.
MAY I SHAKE YOUR HAND?
HUH?
OH, OKAY.
SHAKE
WIPE
HEH... ♡
I'M GETTING A BAD FEELING ... ♡

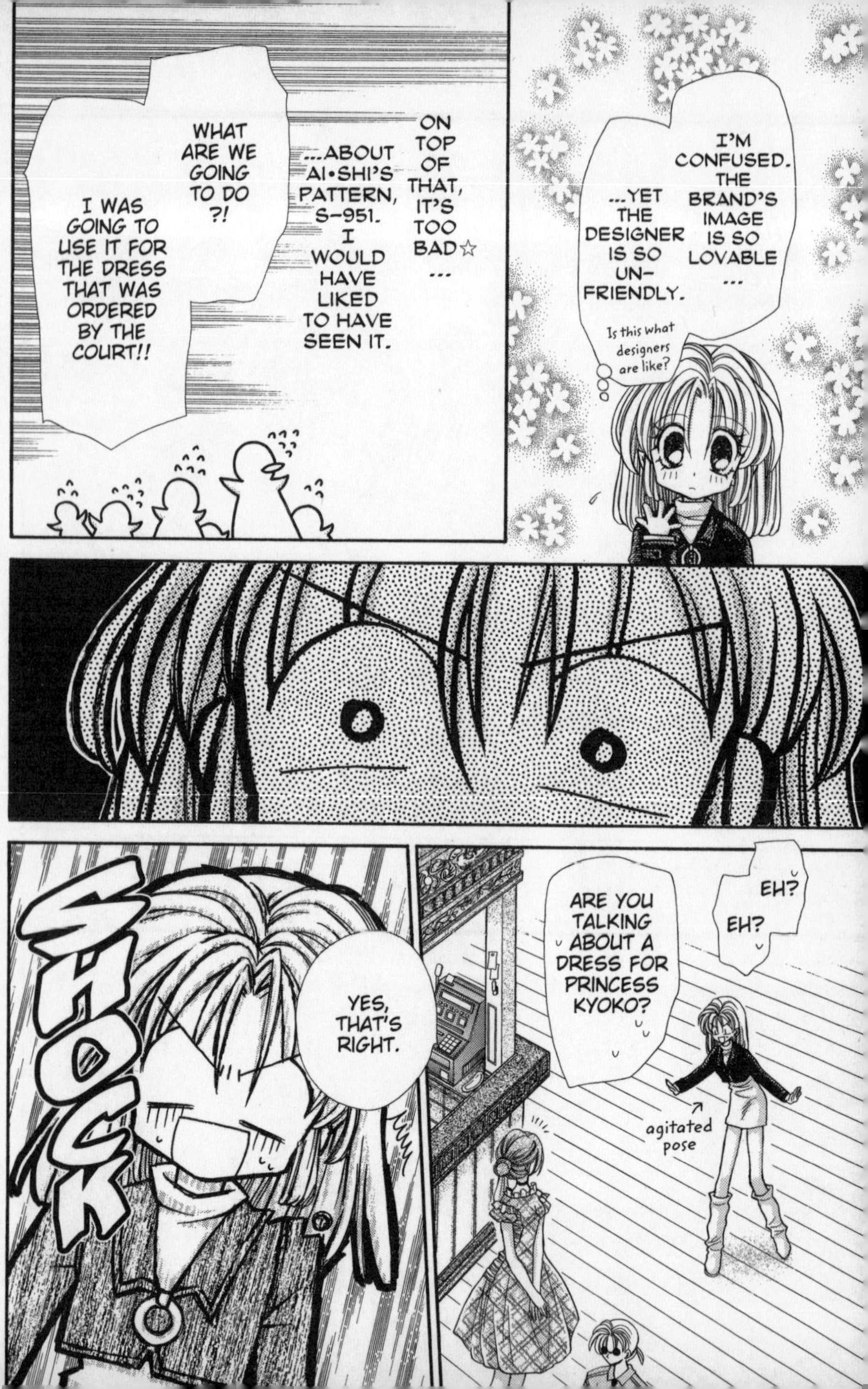
I'M CONFUSED. THE BRAND'S IMAGE IS SO LOVABLE...
...YET THE DESIGNER IS SO UN-FRIENDLY.
Is this what designers are like?
ON TOP OF THAT, IT'S TOO BAD☆...
...ABOUT AI•SHI'S PATTERN, S-951. I WOULD HAVE LIKED TO HAVE SEEN IT.
WHAT ARE WE GOING TO DO?!
I WAS GOING TO USE IT FOR THE DRESS THAT WAS ORDERED BY THE COURT!!
EH?
EH?
ARE YOU TALKING ABOUT A DRESS FOR PRINCESS KYOKO?
agitated pose
YES, THAT'S RIGHT.
SHOCK

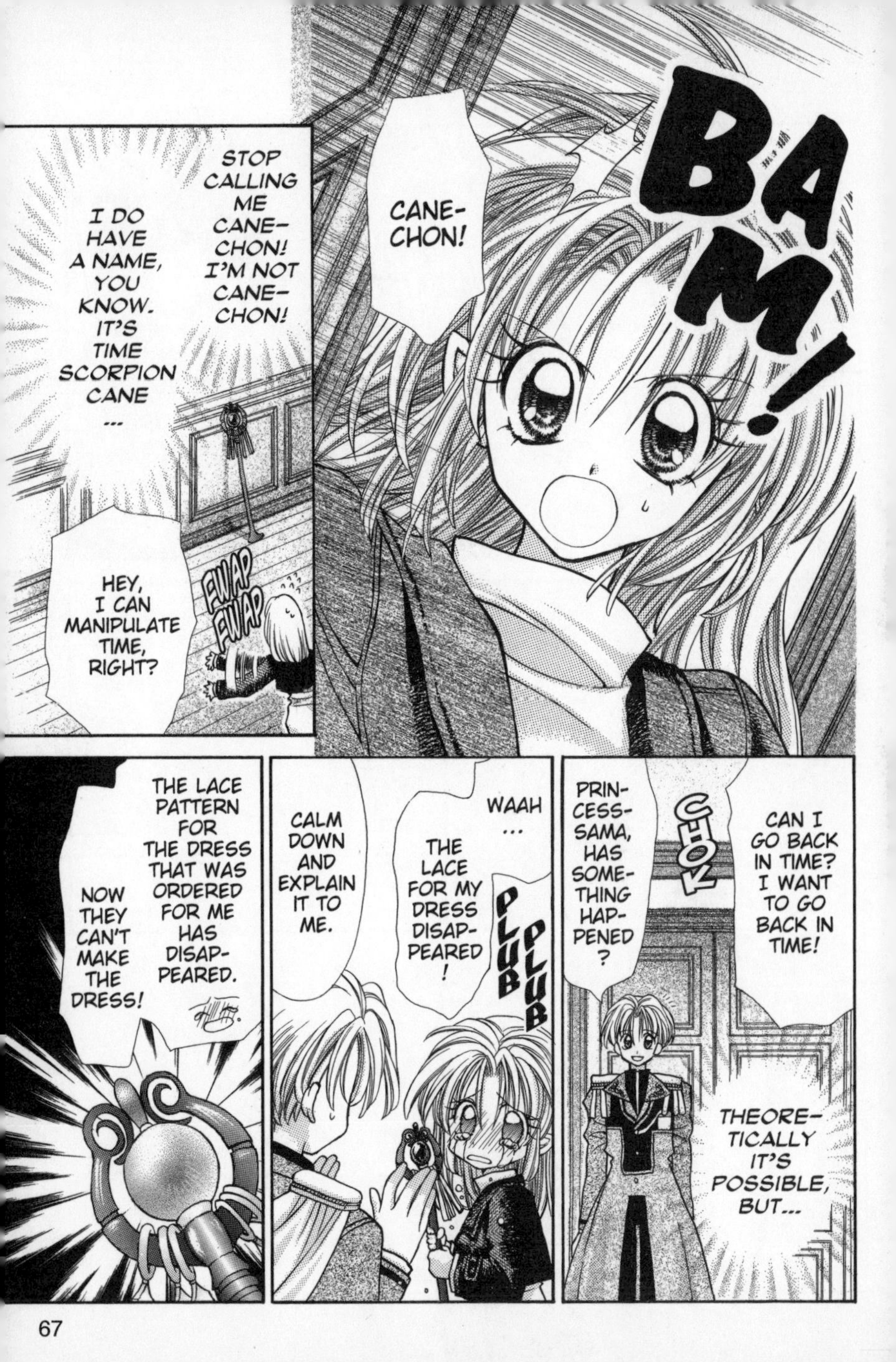
BAM!
CANE-CHON!
STOP CALLING ME CANE-CHON! I'M NOT CANE-CHON!
I DO HAVE A NAME, YOU KNOW. IT'S TIME SCORPION CANE ...
FWAP FWAP
HEY, I CAN MANIPULATE TIME, RIGHT?
CHOK
CAN I GO BACK IN TIME? I WANT TO GO BACK IN TIME!
PRIN-CESS-SAMA, HAS SOME-THING HAP-PENED?
THEORE-TICALLY IT'S POSSIBLE, BUT...
WAAH ...
THE LACE FOR MY DRESS DISAP-PEARED!
PLUB PLUB
CALM DOWN AND EXPLAIN IT TO ME.
THE LACE PATTERN FOR THE DRESS THAT WAS ORDERED FOR ME HAS DISAP-PEARED.
NOW THEY CAN'T MAKE THE DRESS!

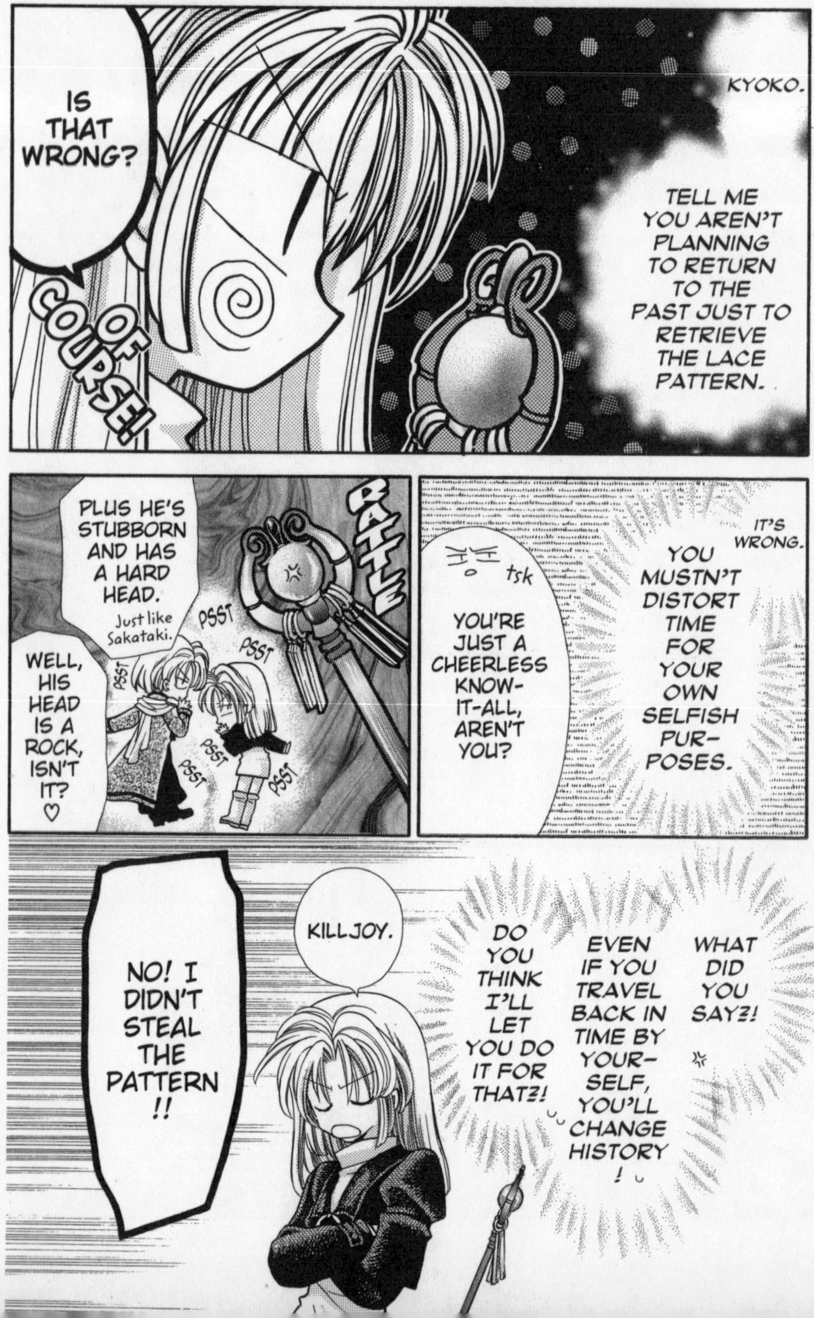
KYOKO.
TELL ME YOU AREN'T PLANNING TO RETURN TO THE PAST JUST TO RETRIEVE THE LACE PATTERN.
IS THAT WRONG?
OF COURSE!
IT'S WRONG.
YOU MUSTN'T DISTORT TIME FOR YOUR OWN SELFISH PURPOSES.
tsk
YOU'RE JUST A CHEERLESS KNOW-IT-ALL, AREN'T YOU?
RATTLE
PLUS HE'S STUBBORN AND HAS A HARD HEAD.
Just like Sakataki.
PSST PSST PSST PSST PSST PSST
WELL, HIS HEAD IS A ROCK, ISN'T IT? ♡
WHAT DID YOU SAY?!
EVEN IF YOU TRAVEL BACK IN TIME BY YOURSELF, YOU'LL CHANGE HISTORY!
DO YOU THINK I'LL LET YOU DO IT FOR THAT?!
KILLJOY.
NO! I DIDN'T STEAL THE PATTERN!!

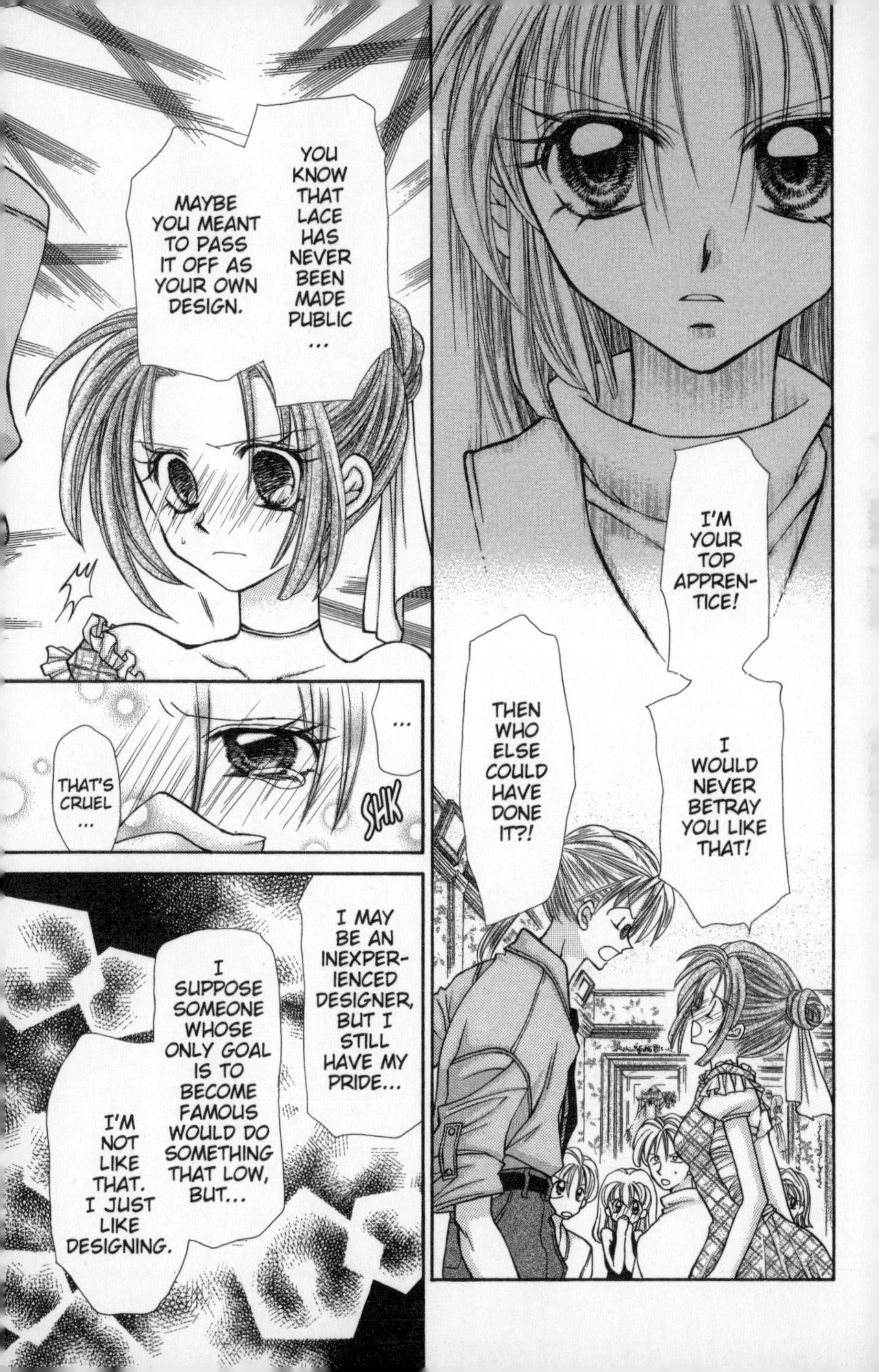
I'M YOUR TOP APPRENTICE!
I WOULD NEVER BETRAY YOU LIKE THAT!
THEN WHO ELSE COULD HAVE DONE IT?!
YOU KNOW THAT LACE HAS NEVER BEEN MADE PUBLIC...
MAYBE YOU MEANT TO PASS IT OFF AS YOUR OWN DESIGN.
...
SHK
THAT'S CRUEL...
I MAY BE AN INEXPERIENCED DESIGNER, BUT I STILL HAVE MY PRIDE...
I SUPPOSE SOMEONE WHOSE ONLY GOAL IS TO BECOME FAMOUS WOULD DO SOMETHING THAT LOW, BUT...
I'M NOT LIKE THAT. I JUST LIKE DESIGNING.

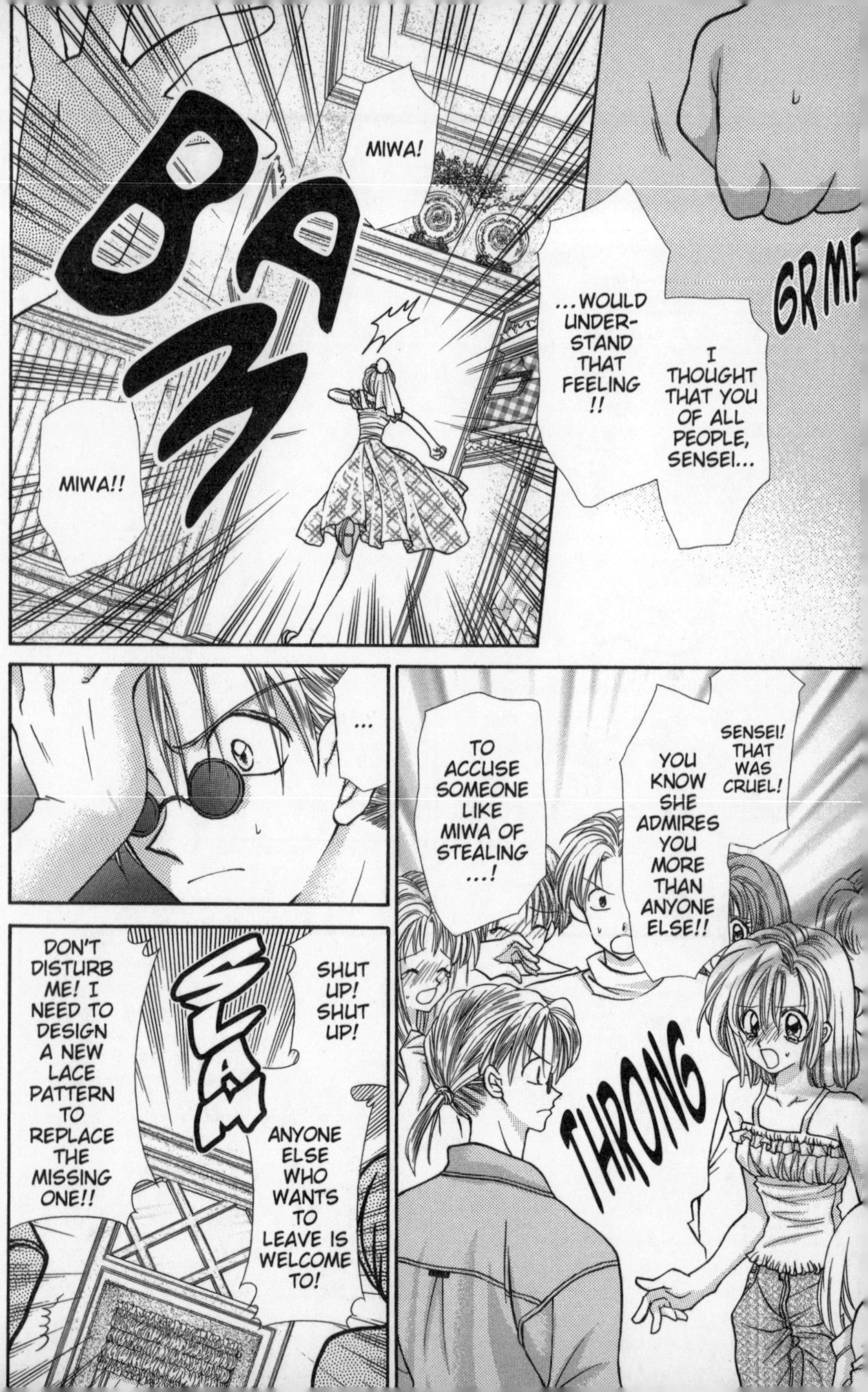
GRMF
I THOUGHT THAT YOU OF ALL PEOPLE, SENSEI...
...WOULD UNDER-STAND THAT FEELING!!
BAM
MIWA!
MIWA!!
SENSEI! THAT WAS CRUEL!
YOU KNOW SHE ADMIRES YOU MORE THAN ANYONE ELSE!!
TO ACCUSE SOMEONE LIKE MIWA OF STEALING...!
THRONG
...
SHUT UP! SHUT UP!
SLAM
ANYONE ELSE WHO WANTS TO LEAVE IS WELCOME TO!
DON'T DISTURB ME! I NEED TO DESIGN A NEW LACE PATTERN TO REPLACE THE MISSING ONE!!

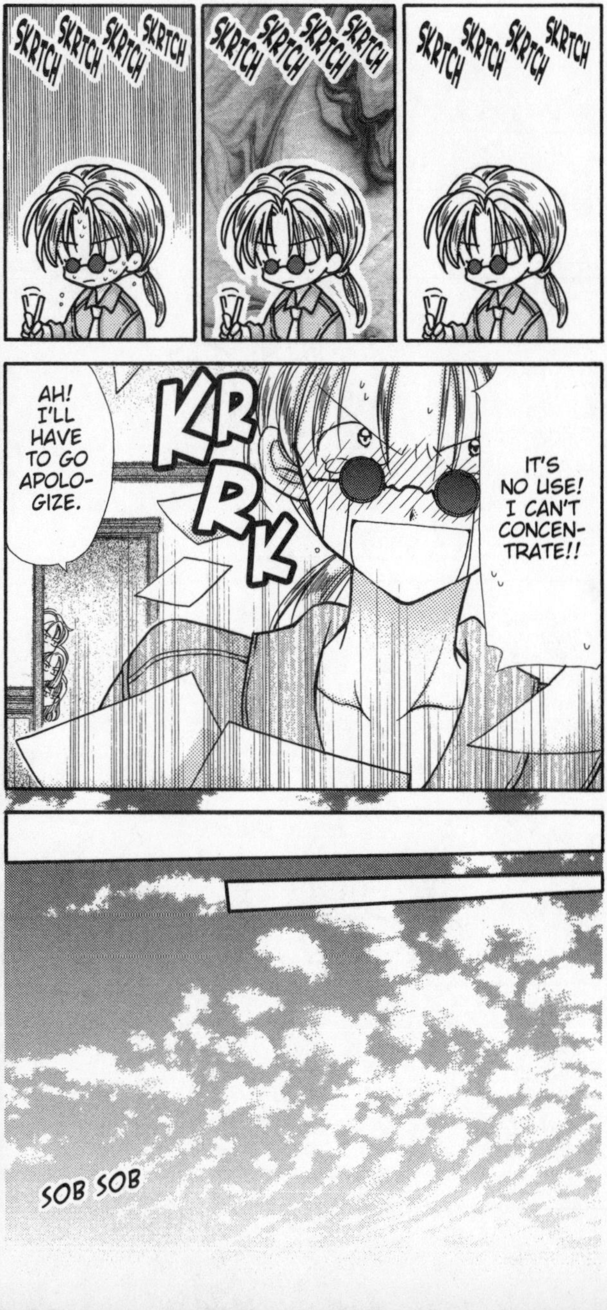
SKRTCH SKRTCH SKRTCH SKRTCH
SKRTCH SKRTCH SKRTCH SKRTCH
SKRTCH SKRTCH SKRTCH SKRTCH
IT'S NO USE! I CAN'T CONCENTRATE!!
KRRK
AH! I'LL HAVE TO GO APOLOGIZE.
SOB SOB

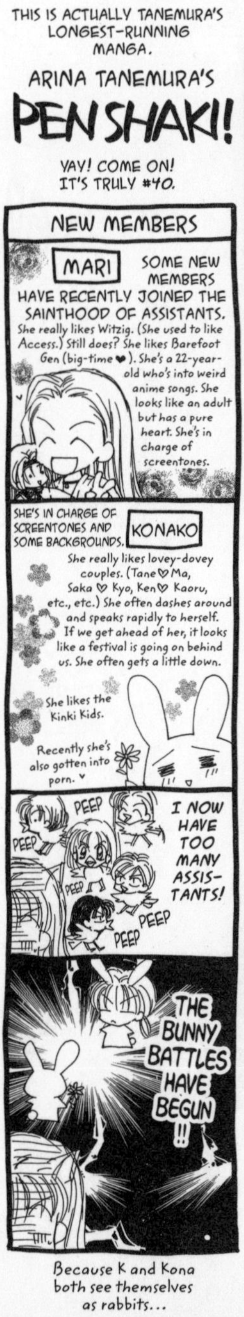
THIS IS ACTUALLY TANEMURA'S LONGEST-RUNNING MANGA.
ARINA TANEMURA'S
PEN SHAKI!
YAY! COME ON! IT'S TRULY #40.
NEW MEMBERS
MARI
SOME NEW MEMBERS HAVE RECENTLY JOINED THE SAINTHOOD OF ASSISTANTS.
She really likes Witzig. (She used to like Access.) Still does? She likes Barefoot Gen (big-time ♥). She's a 22-year-old who's into weird anime songs. She looks like an adult but has a pure heart. She's in charge of screentones.
KONAKO
SHE'S IN CHARGE OF SCREENTONES AND SOME BACKGROUNDS.
She really likes lovey-dovey couples. (Tane ♡ Ma, Saka ♡ Kyo, Ken ♡ Kaoru, etc., etc.) She often dashes around and speaks rapidly to herself. If we get ahead of her, it looks like a festival is going on behind us. She often gets a little down.
She likes the Kinki Kids.
Recently she's also gotten into porn. ♥
I NOW HAVE TOO MANY ASSISTANTS!
PEEP
PEEP
PEEP
PEEP
PEEP
THE BUNNY BATTLES HAVE BEGUN!!
Because K and Kona both see themselves as rabbits...

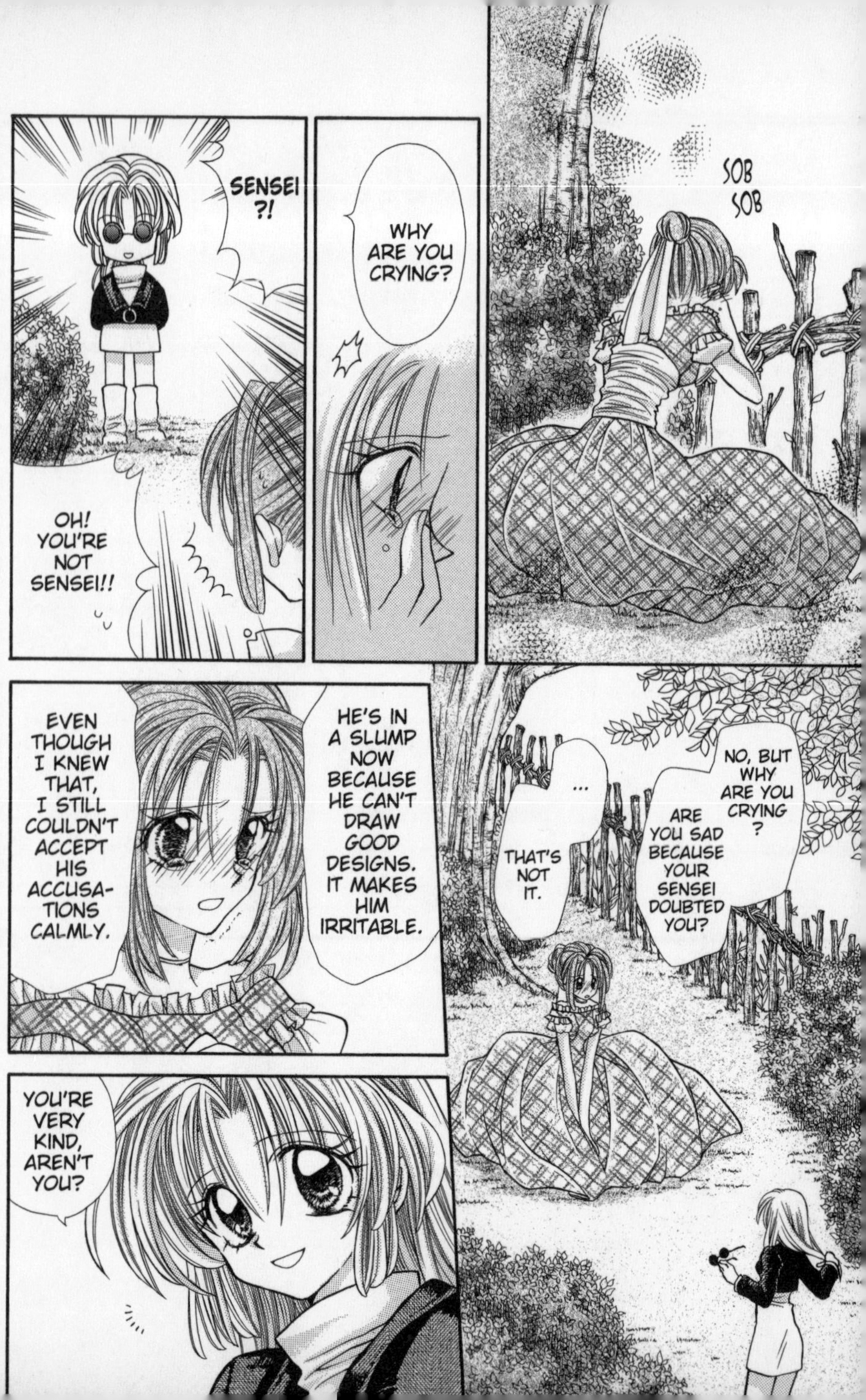
SOB SOB
WHY ARE YOU CRYING?
SENSEI ?!
OH! YOU'RE NOT SENSEI!!
NO, BUT WHY ARE YOU CRYING ?
ARE YOU SAD BECAUSE YOUR SENSEI DOUBTED YOU?
...
THAT'S NOT IT.
HE'S IN A SLUMP NOW BECAUSE HE CAN'T DRAW GOOD DESIGNS. IT MAKES HIM IRRITABLE.
EVEN THOUGH I KNEW THAT, I STILL COULDN'T ACCEPT HIS ACCUSA-TIONS CALMLY.
YOU'RE VERY KIND, AREN'T YOU?

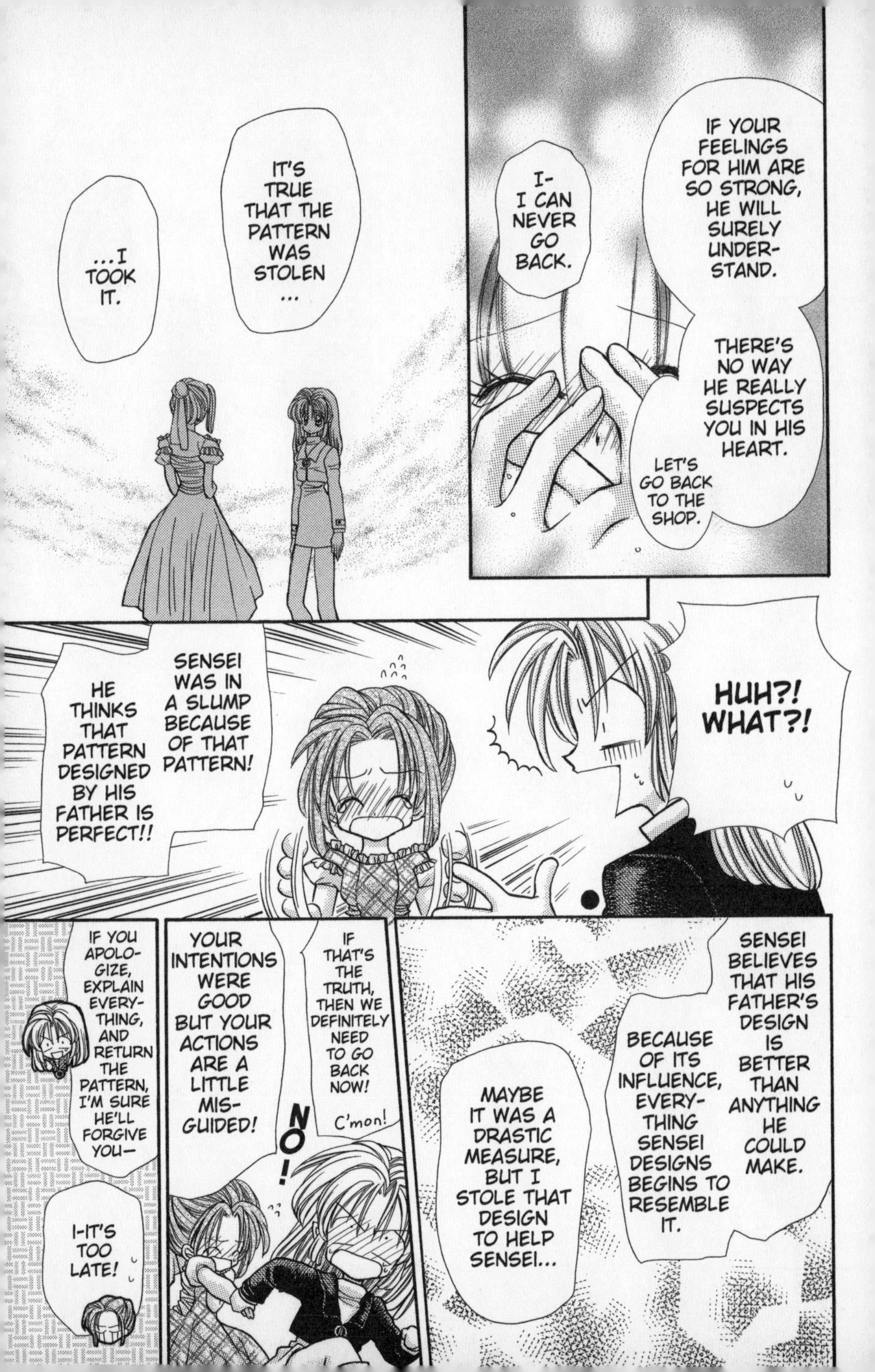
IF YOUR FEELINGS FOR HIM ARE SO STRONG, HE WILL SURELY UNDER-STAND.
I- I CAN NEVER GO BACK.
THERE'S NO WAY HE REALLY SUSPECTS YOU IN HIS HEART.
LET'S GO BACK TO THE SHOP.
IT'S TRUE THAT THE PATTERN WAS STOLEN...
...I TOOK IT.
HUH?! WHAT?!
SENSEI WAS IN A SLUMP BECAUSE OF THAT PATTERN!
HE THINKS THAT PATTERN DESIGNED BY HIS FATHER IS PERFECT!!
SENSEI BELIEVES THAT HIS FATHER'S DESIGN IS BETTER THAN ANYTHING HE COULD MAKE.
BECAUSE OF ITS INFLUENCE, EVERY-THING SENSEI DESIGNS BEGINS TO RESEMBLE IT.
MAYBE IT WAS A DRASTIC MEASURE, BUT I STOLE THAT DESIGN TO HELP SENSEI...
IF THAT'S THE TRUTH, THEN WE DEFINITELY NEED TO GO BACK NOW!
C'mon!
YOUR INTENTIONS WERE GOOD BUT YOUR ACTIONS ARE A LITTLE MIS-GUIDED!
NO!
IF YOU APOLO-GIZE, EXPLAIN EVERY-THING, AND RETURN THE PATTERN, I'M SURE HE'LL FORGIVE YOU—
I-IT'S TOO LATE!

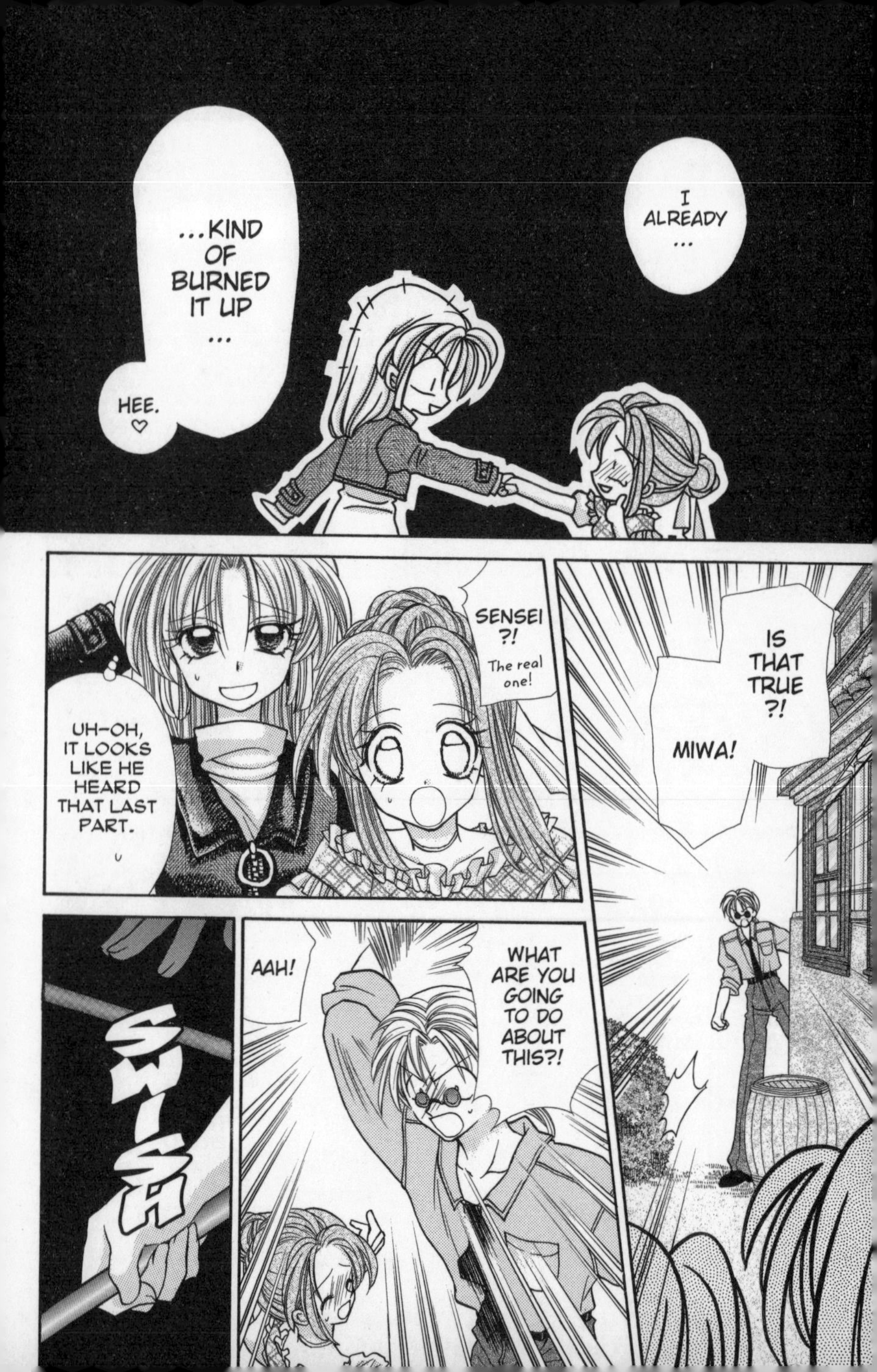
I ALREADY ...
...KIND OF BURNED IT UP ...
HEE. ♡
IS THAT TRUE?!
MIWA!
SENSEI?!
The real one!
UH-OH, IT LOOKS LIKE HE HEARD THAT LAST PART.
WHAT ARE YOU GOING TO DO ABOUT THIS?!
AAH!
SWISH

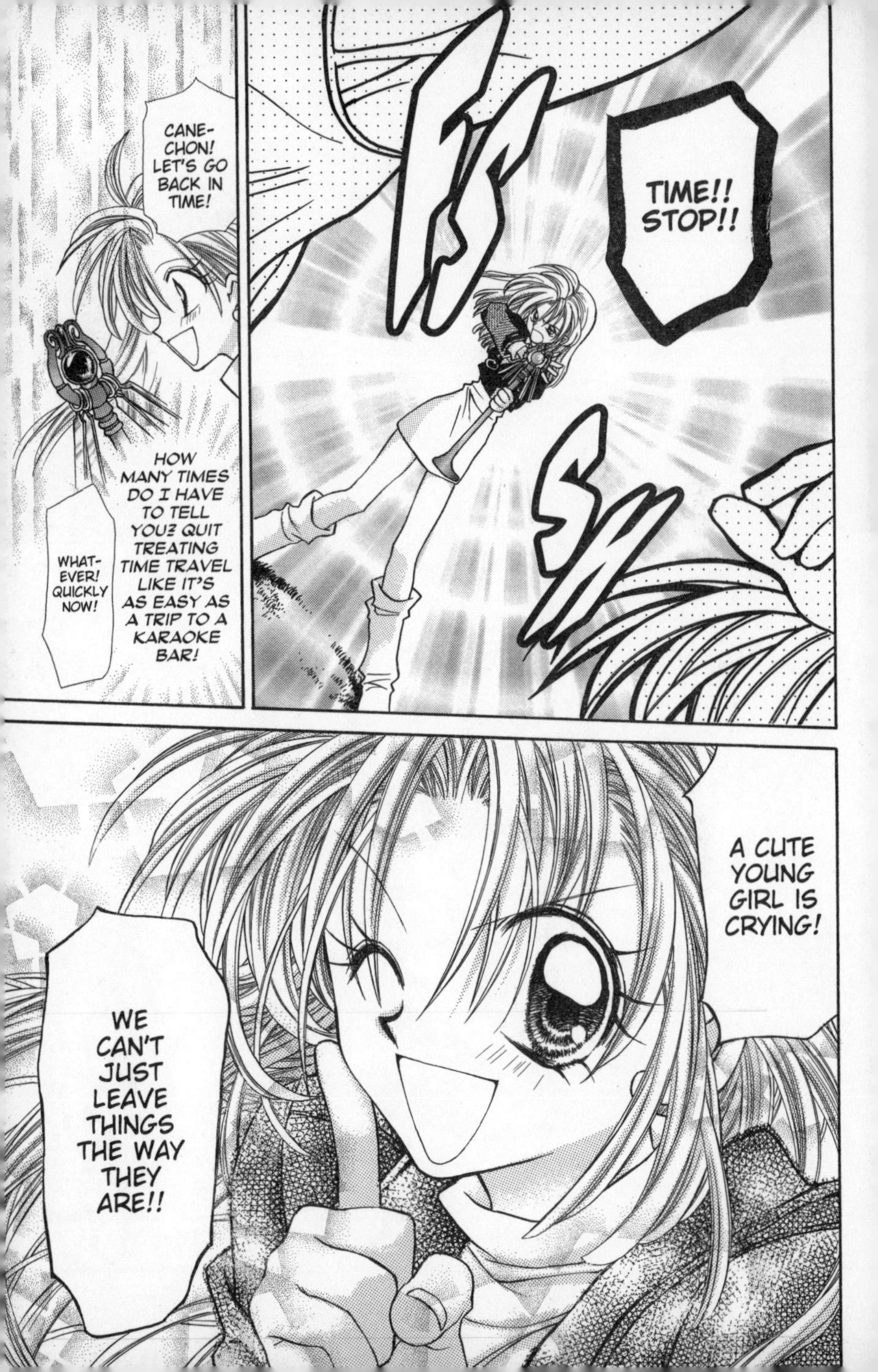
TIME!! STOP!!
CANE-CHON! LET'S GO BACK IN TIME!
HOW MANY TIMES DO I HAVE TO TELL YOU? QUIT TREATING TIME TRAVEL LIKE IT'S AS EASY AS A TRIP TO A KARAOKE BAR!
WHAT-EVER! QUICKLY NOW!
A CUTE YOUNG GIRL IS CRYING!
WE CAN'T JUST LEAVE THINGS THE WAY THEY ARE!!

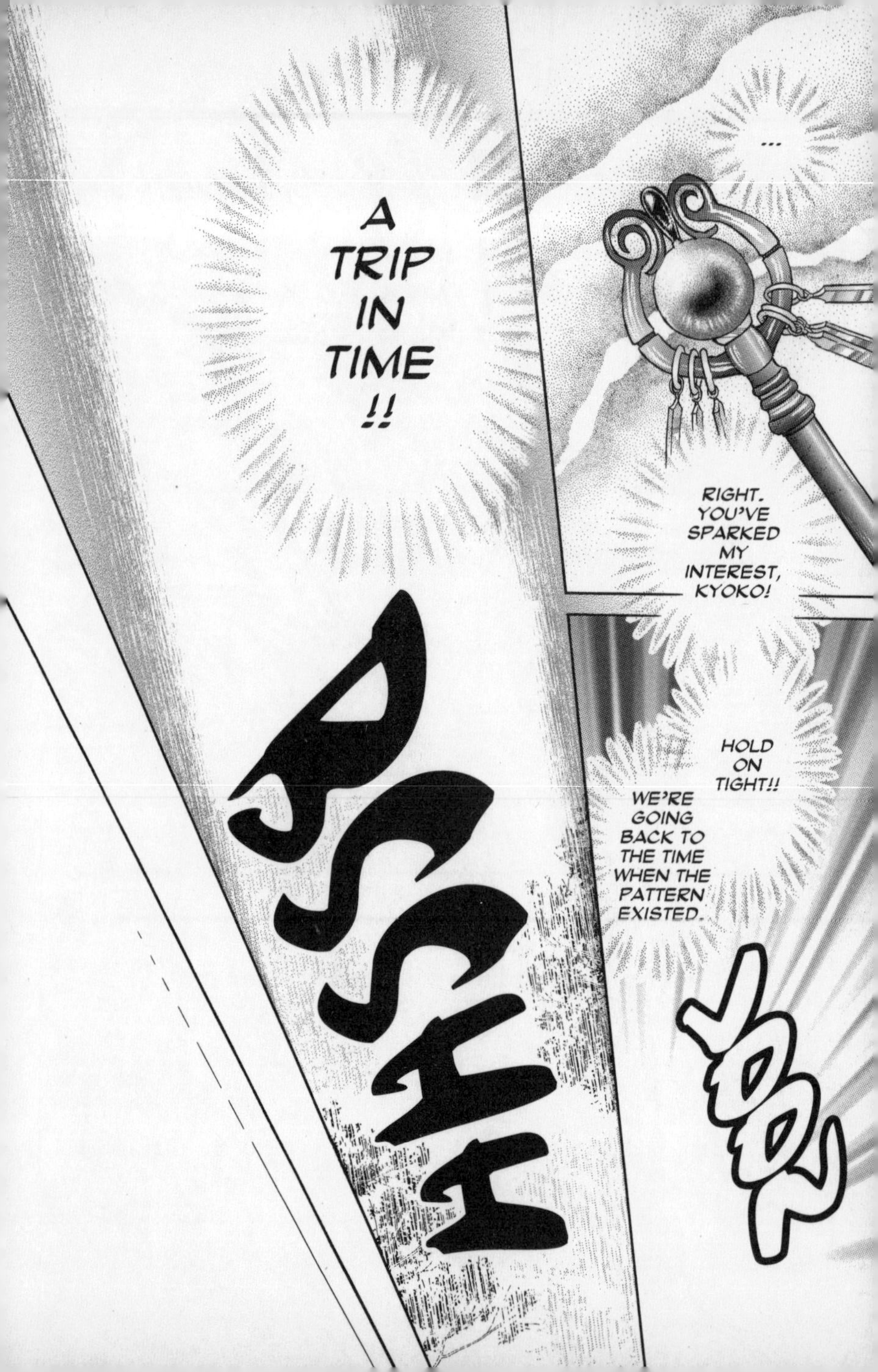
...
RIGHT. YOU'VE SPARKED MY INTEREST, KYOKO!
HOLD ON TIGHT!!
WE'RE GOING BACK TO THE TIME WHEN THE PATTERN EXISTED.
ZOOT
A TRIP IN TIME!!
BSSHH

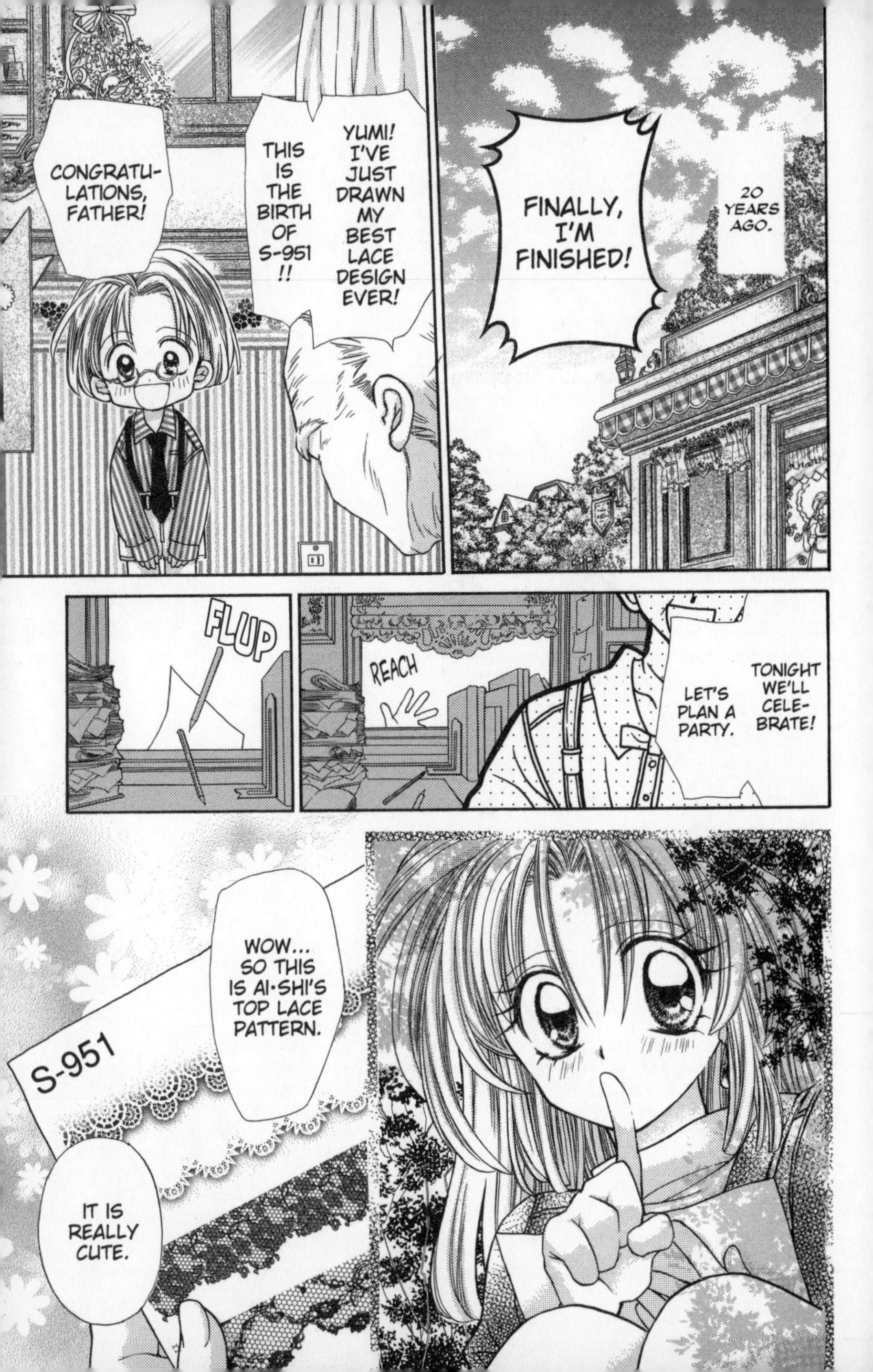
20 YEARS AGO.
FINALLY, I'M FINISHED!
YUMI! I'VE JUST DRAWN MY BEST LACE DESIGN EVER!
THIS IS THE BIRTH OF S-951 !!
CONGRATULATIONS, FATHER!
TONIGHT WE'LL CELEBRATE!
LET'S PLAN A PARTY.
REACH
FLUP
WOW... SO THIS IS AI·SHI'S TOP LACE PATTERN.
S-951
IT IS REALLY CUTE.

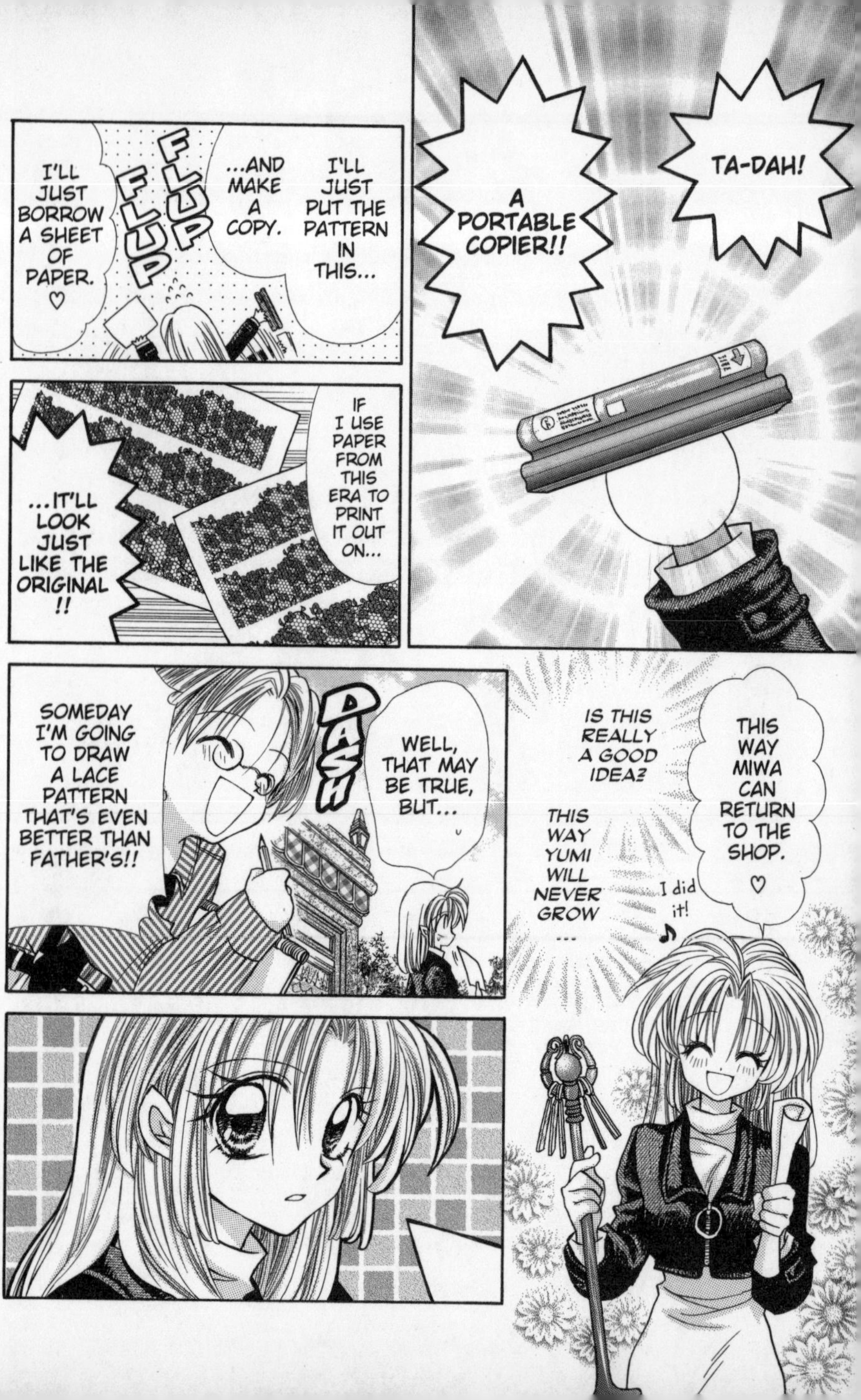
TA-DAH!
A PORTABLE COPIER!!
I'LL JUST PUT THE PATTERN IN THIS...
...AND MAKE A COPY.
FLUP FLUP
I'LL JUST BORROW A SHEET OF PAPER. ♡
IF I USE PAPER FROM THIS ERA TO PRINT IT OUT ON...
...IT'LL LOOK JUST LIKE THE ORIGINAL!!
THIS WAY MIWA CAN RETURN TO THE SHOP. ♡
I did it! ♪
IS THIS REALLY A GOOD IDEA?
THIS WAY YUMI WILL NEVER GROW...
WELL, THAT MAY BE TRUE, BUT...
DASH
SOMEDAY I'M GOING TO DRAW A LACE PATTERN THAT'S EVEN BETTER THAN FATHER'S!!

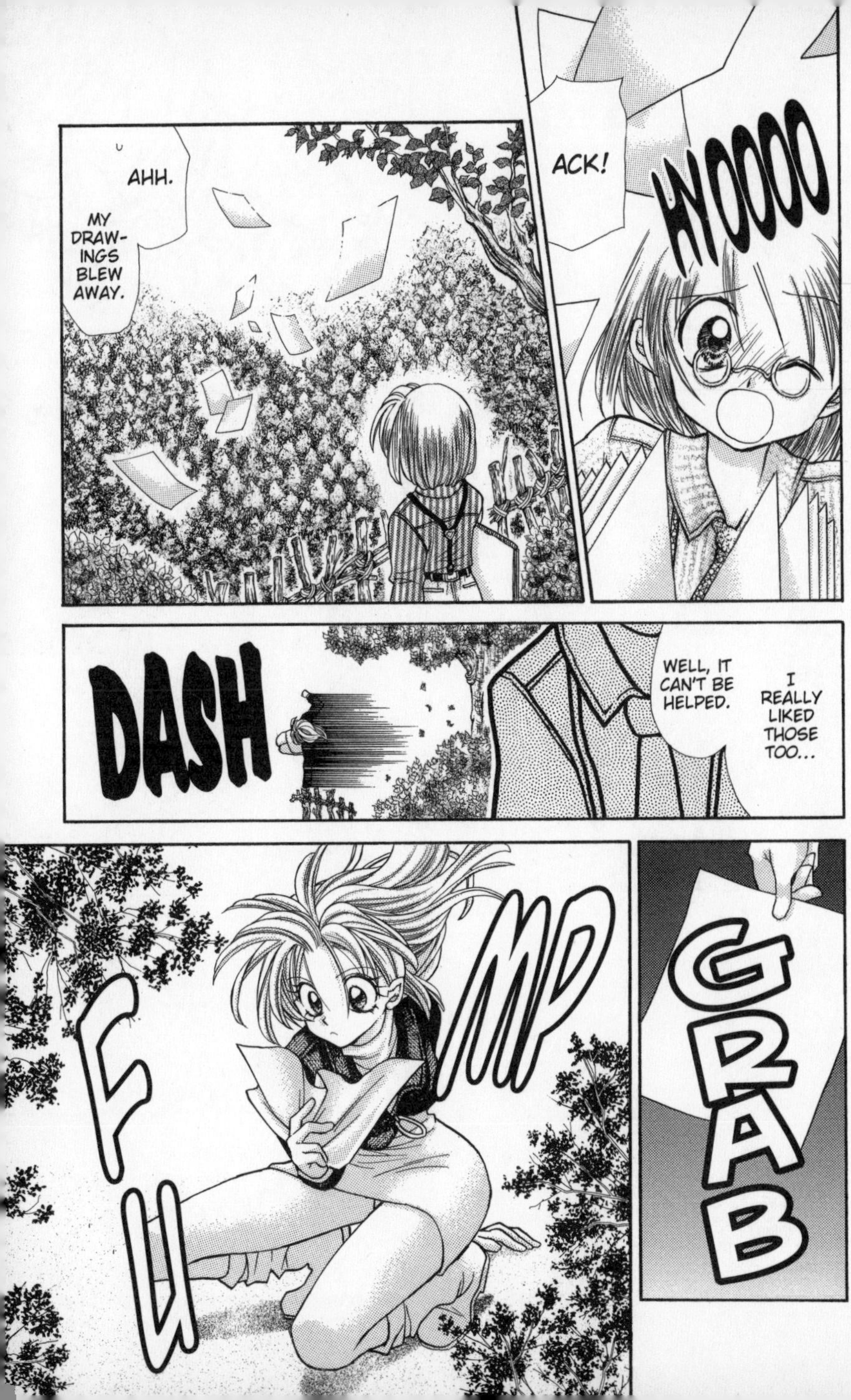
ACK!
HYOOOO
AHH.
MY DRAWINGS BLEW AWAY.
I REALLY LIKED THOSE TOO...
WELL, IT CAN'T BE HELPED.
DASH
GRAB
FUMP

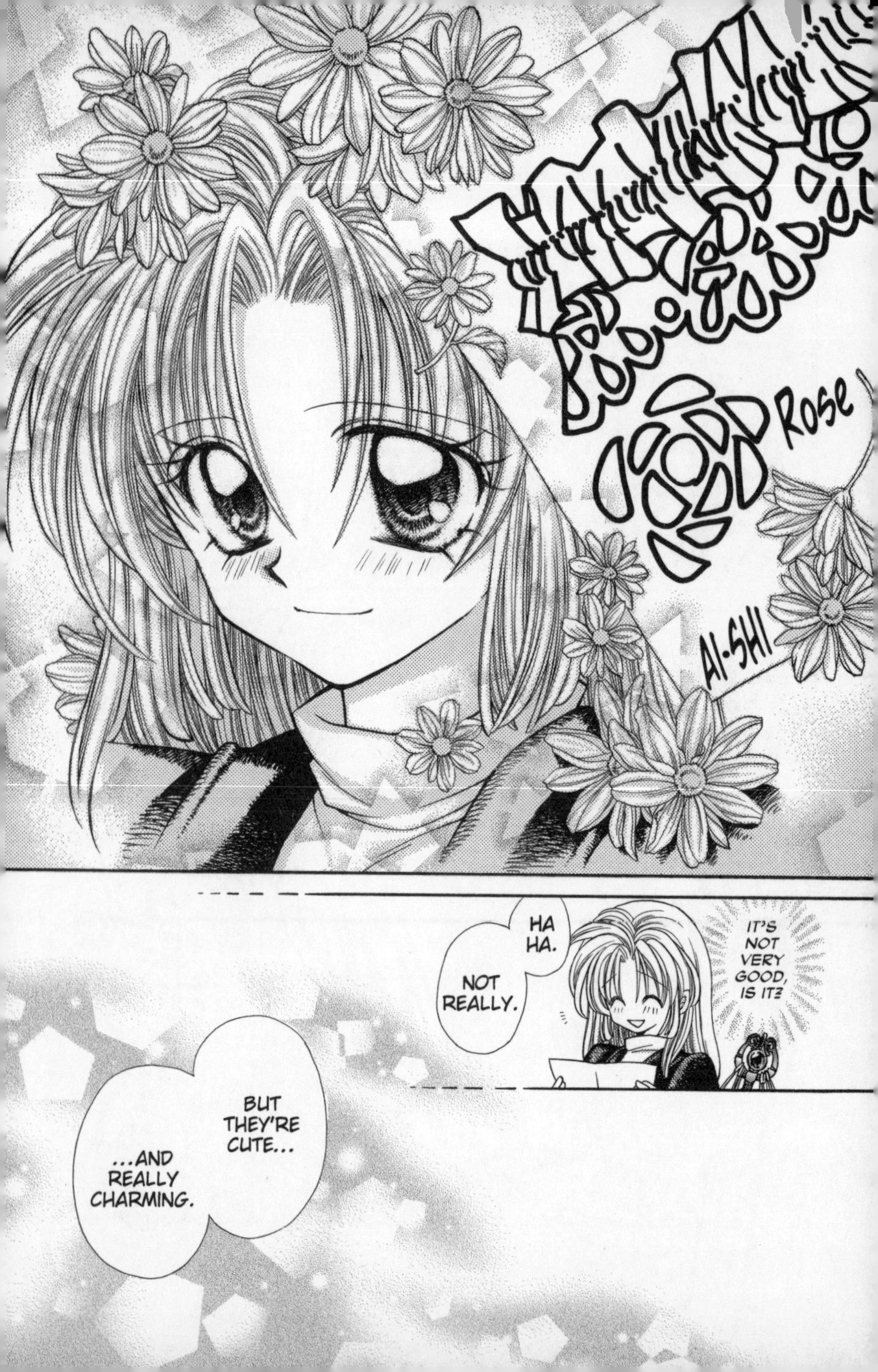
Rose
AI-SHI
IT'S NOT VERY GOOD, IS IT?
HA HA. NOT REALLY.
BUT THEY'RE CUTE...
...AND REALLY CHARMING.

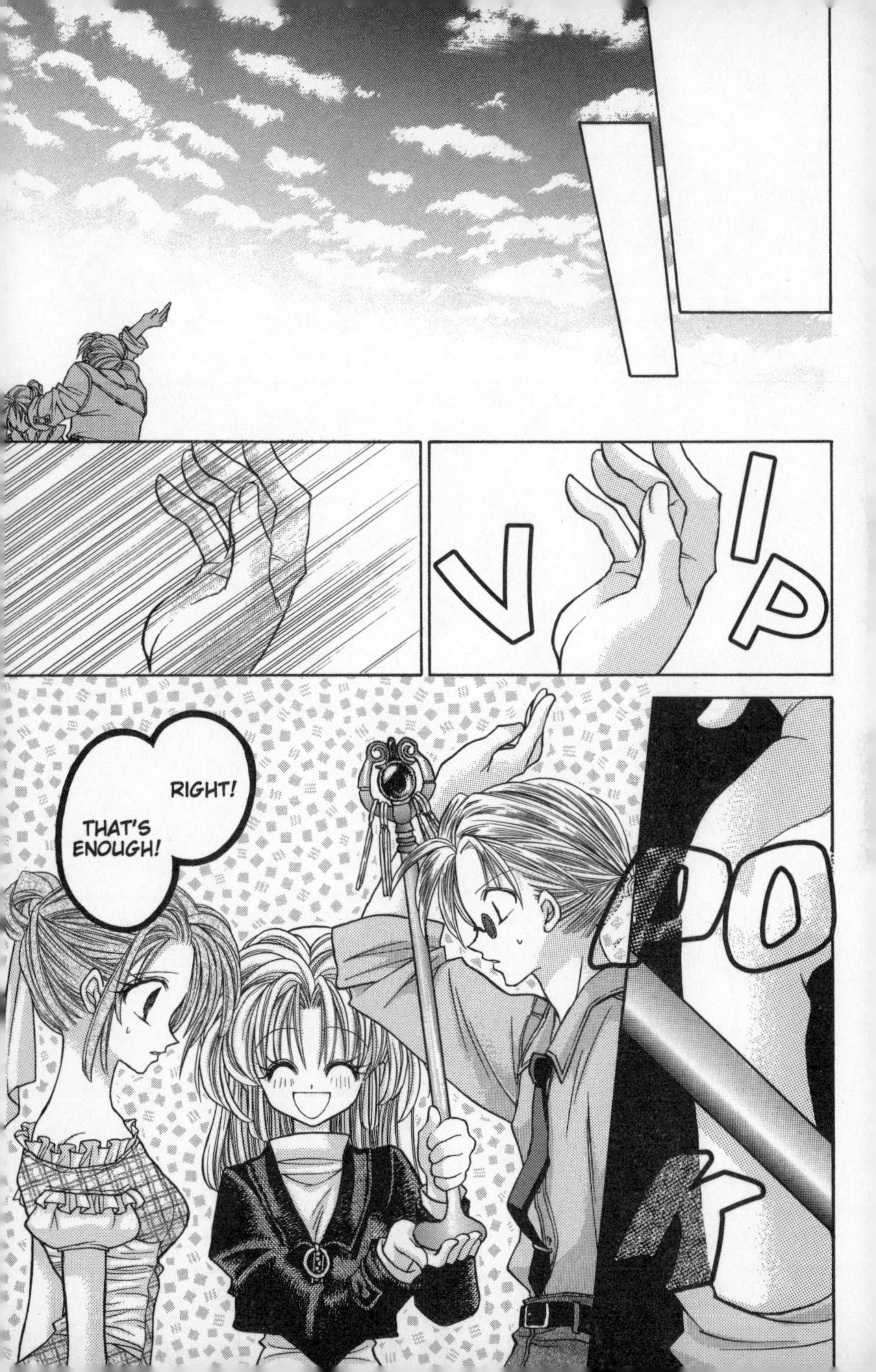
VIP
RIGHT!
THAT'S ENOUGH!

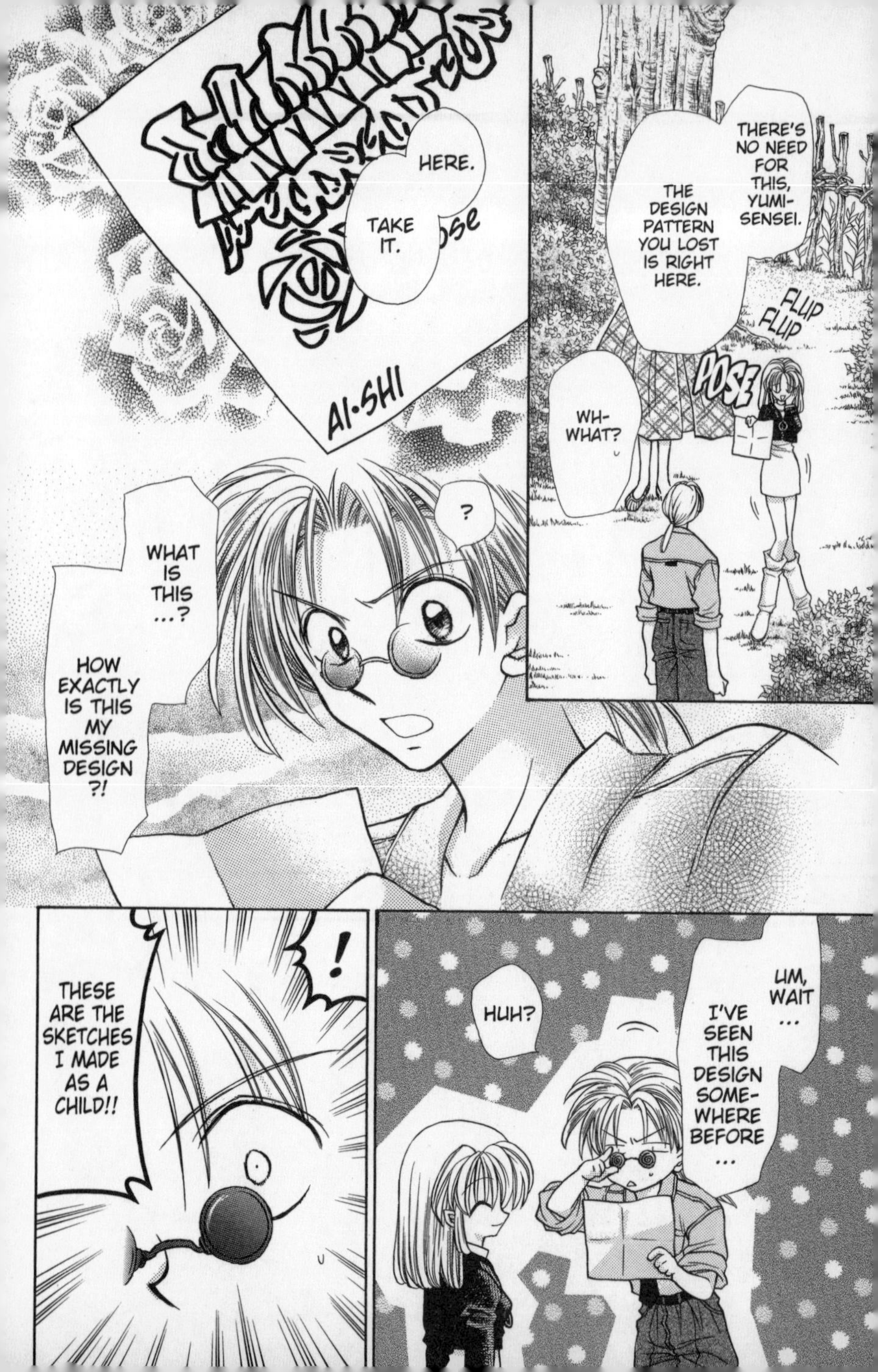
THERE'S NO NEED FOR THIS, YUMI-SENSEI.
THE DESIGN PATTERN YOU LOST IS RIGHT HERE.
FLUP FLUP
POSE
WH-WHAT?
HERE.
TAKE IT.
AI·SHI
?
WHAT IS THIS ...?
HOW EXACTLY IS THIS MY MISSING DESIGN?!
UM, WAIT ...
I'VE SEEN THIS DESIGN SOMEWHERE BEFORE ...
HUH?
!
THESE ARE THE SKETCHES I MADE AS A CHILD!!

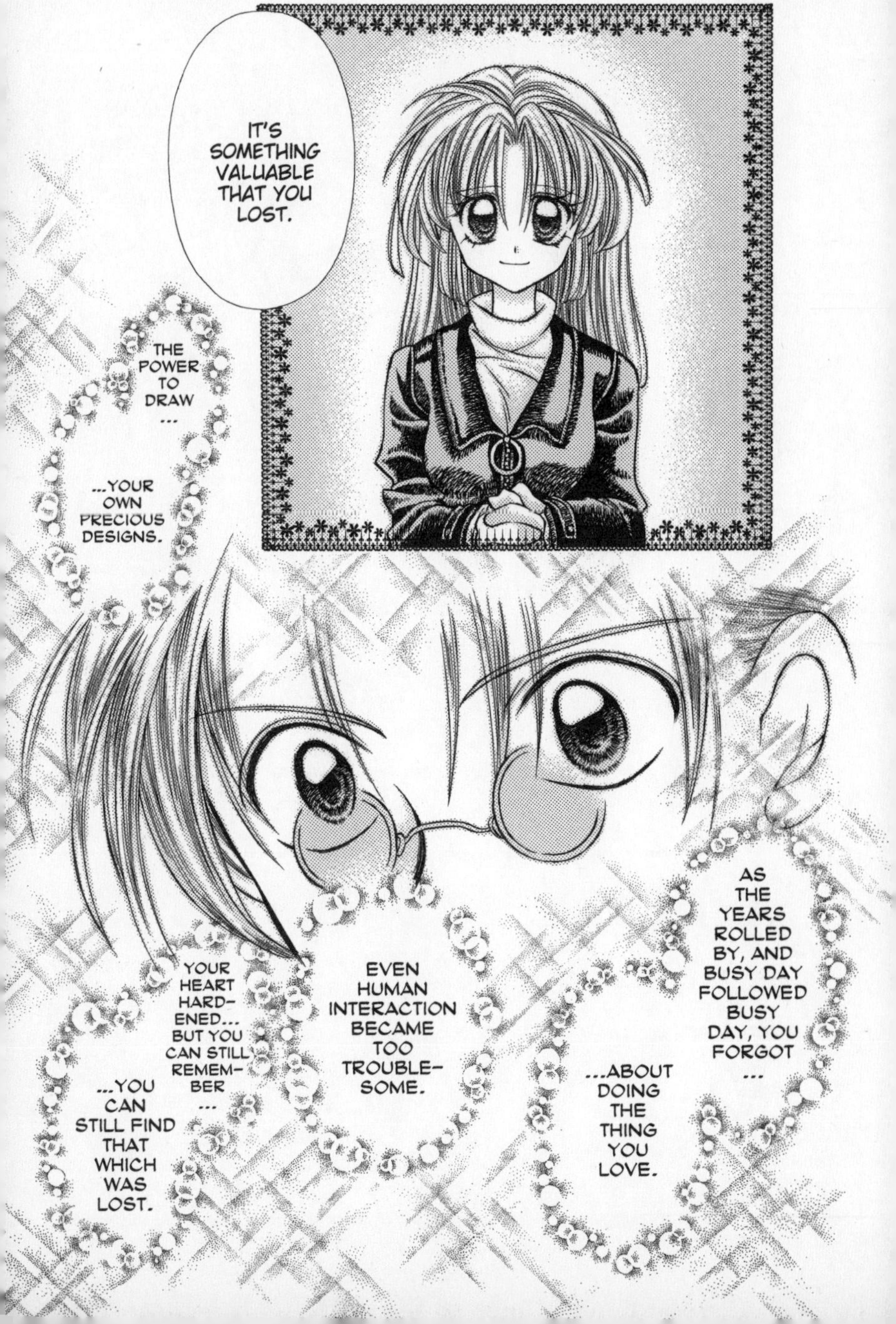
IT'S SOMETHING VALUABLE THAT YOU LOST.
THE POWER TO DRAW ...
...YOUR OWN PRECIOUS DESIGNS.
AS THE YEARS ROLLED BY, AND BUSY DAY FOLLOWED BUSY DAY, YOU FORGOT ...
...ABOUT DOING THE THING YOU LOVE.
EVEN HUMAN INTERACTION BECAME TOO TROUBLE-SOME.
YOUR HEART HARD-ENED... BUT YOU CAN STILL REMEM-BER ...
...YOU CAN STILL FIND THAT WHICH WAS LOST.

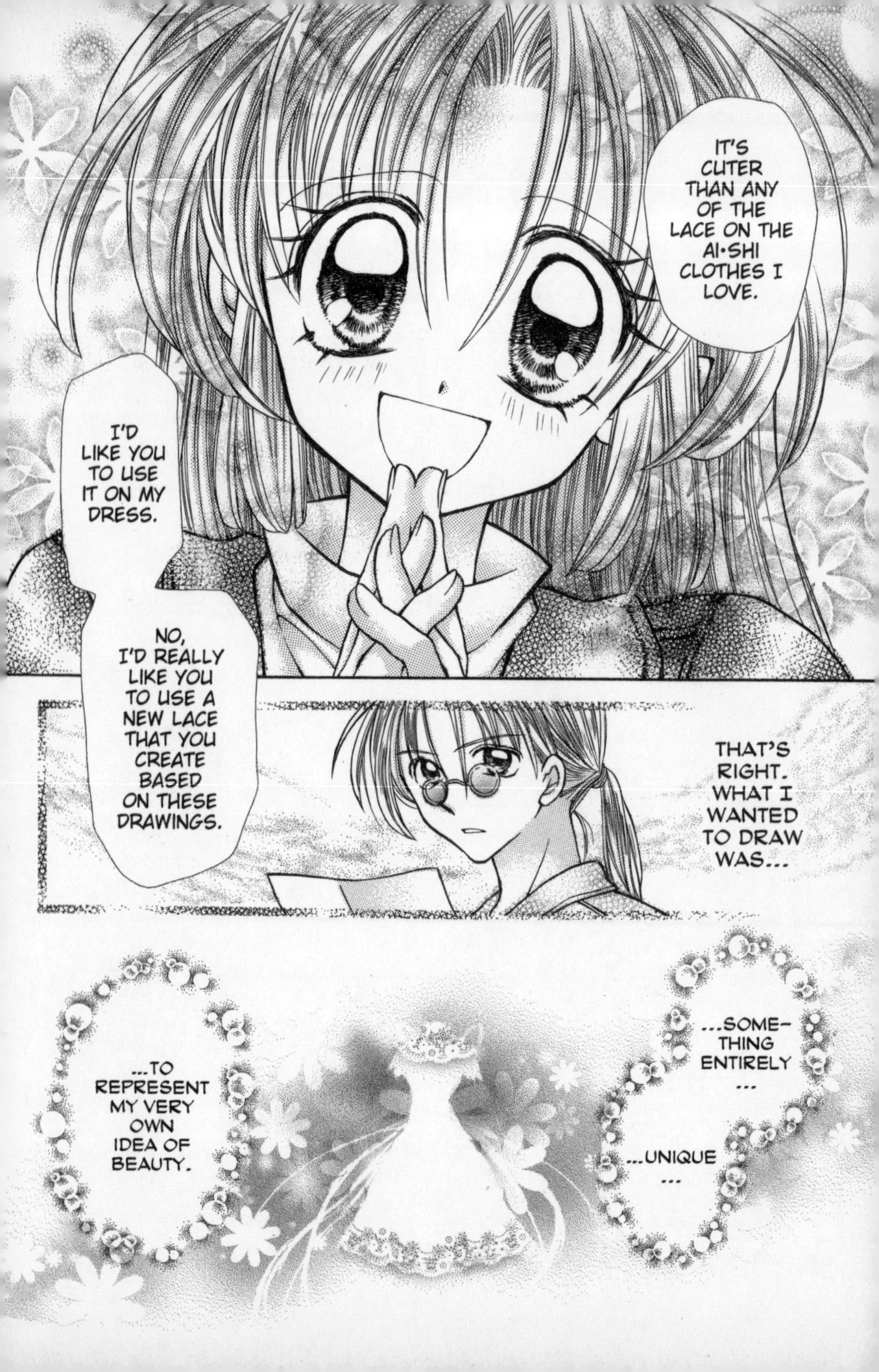
IT'S CUTER THAN ANY OF THE LACE ON THE AI•SHI CLOTHES I LOVE.
I'D LIKE YOU TO USE IT ON MY DRESS.
NO, I'D REALLY LIKE YOU TO USE A NEW LACE THAT YOU CREATE BASED ON THESE DRAWINGS.
THAT'S RIGHT. WHAT I WANTED TO DRAW WAS...
...SOME-THING ENTIRELY ...
...UNIQUE ...
...TO REPRESENT MY VERY OWN IDEA OF BEAUTY.

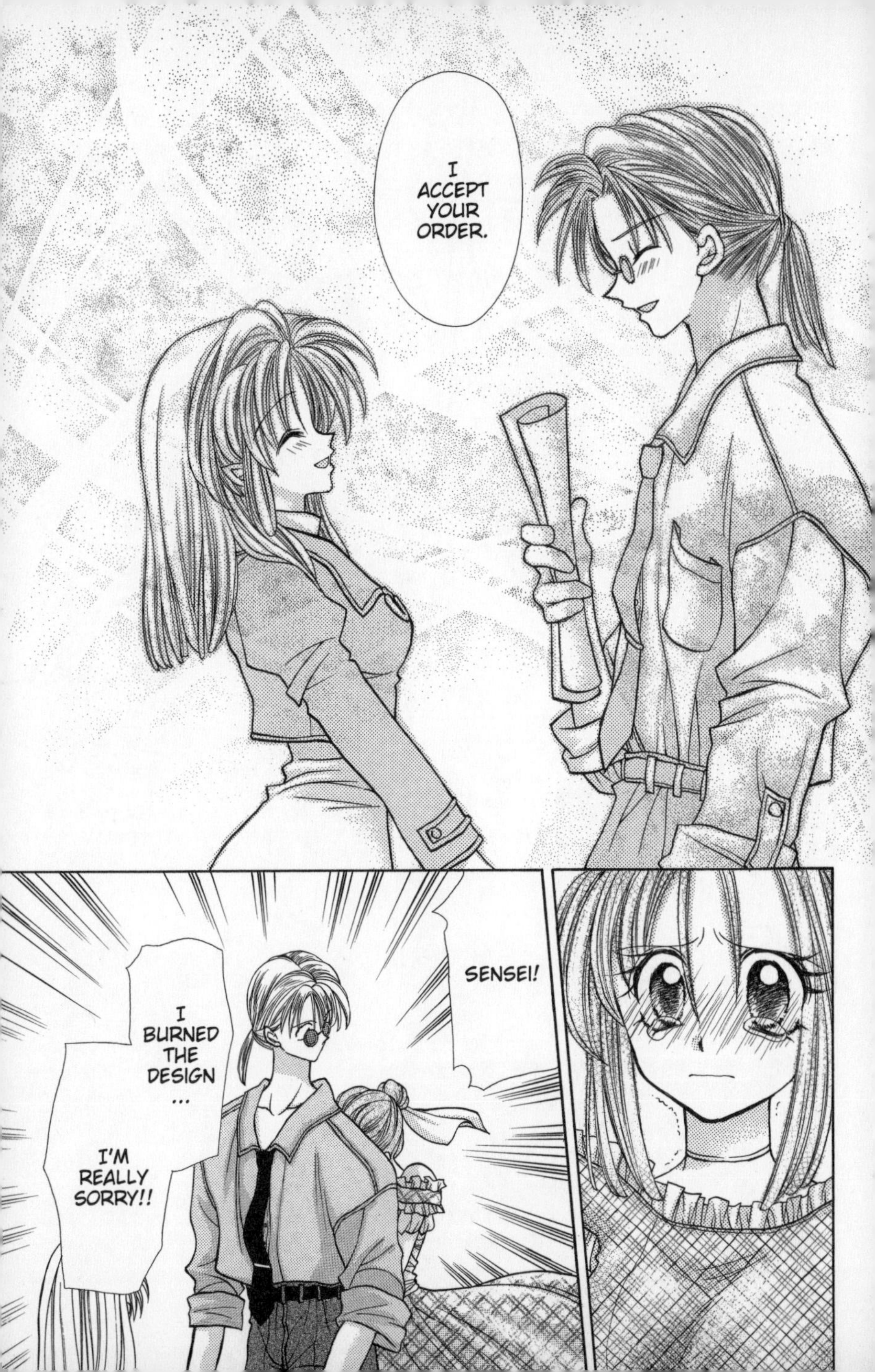
I ACCEPT YOUR ORDER.
SENSEI!
I BURNED THE DESIGN ...
I'M REALLY SORRY!!

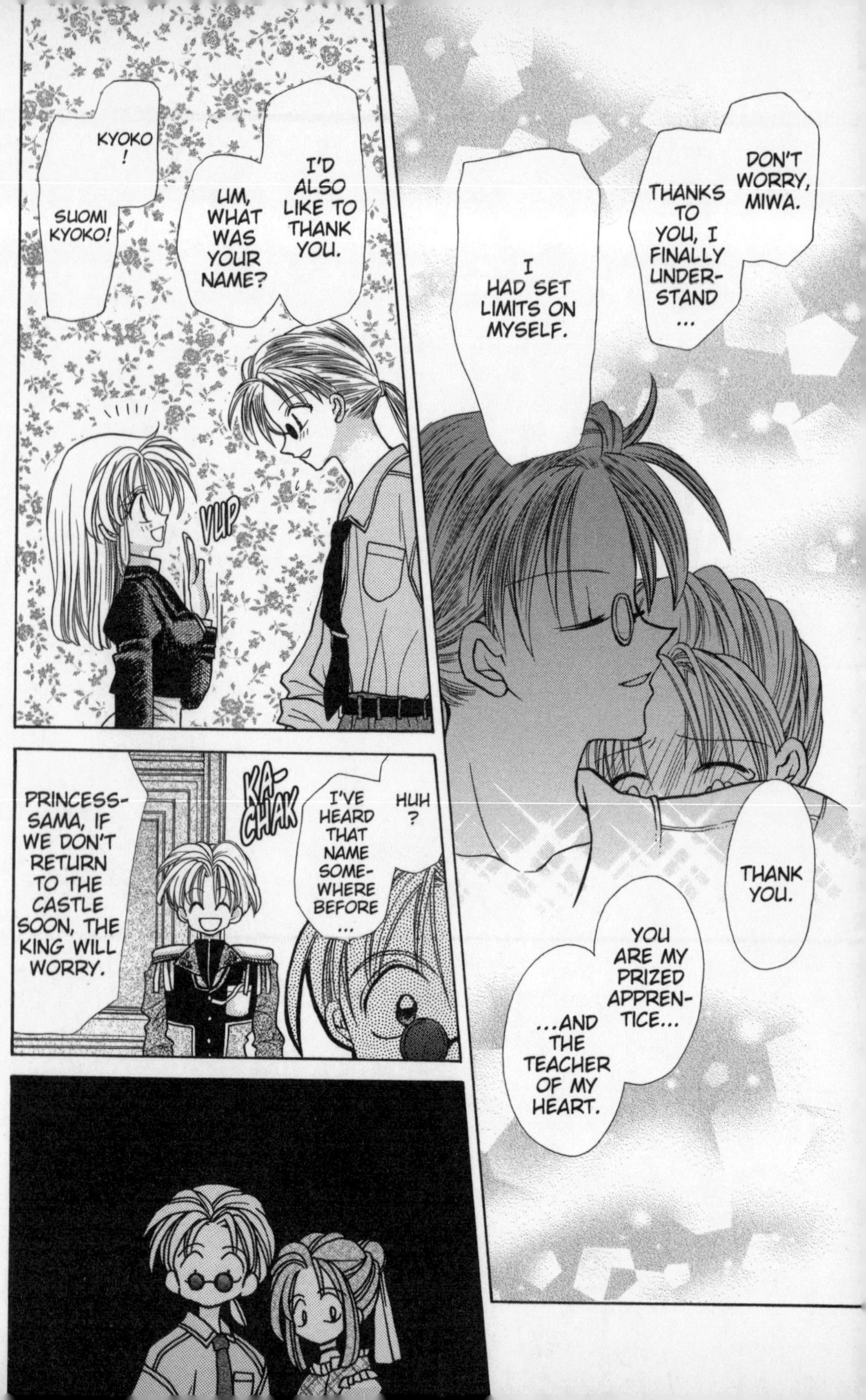
DON'T WORRY, MIWA.
THANKS TO YOU, I FINALLY UNDER-STAND ...
I HAD SET LIMITS ON MYSELF.
THANK YOU.
YOU ARE MY PRIZED APPREN-TICE...
...AND THE TEACHER OF MY HEART.
I'D ALSO LIKE TO THANK YOU.
UM, WHAT WAS YOUR NAME?
KYOKO !
SUOMI KYOKO!
VLIP
HUH ?
I'VE HEARD THAT NAME SOME-WHERE BEFORE ...
KA-CHAK
PRINCESS-SAMA, IF WE DON'T RETURN TO THE CASTLE SOON, THE KING WILL WORRY.

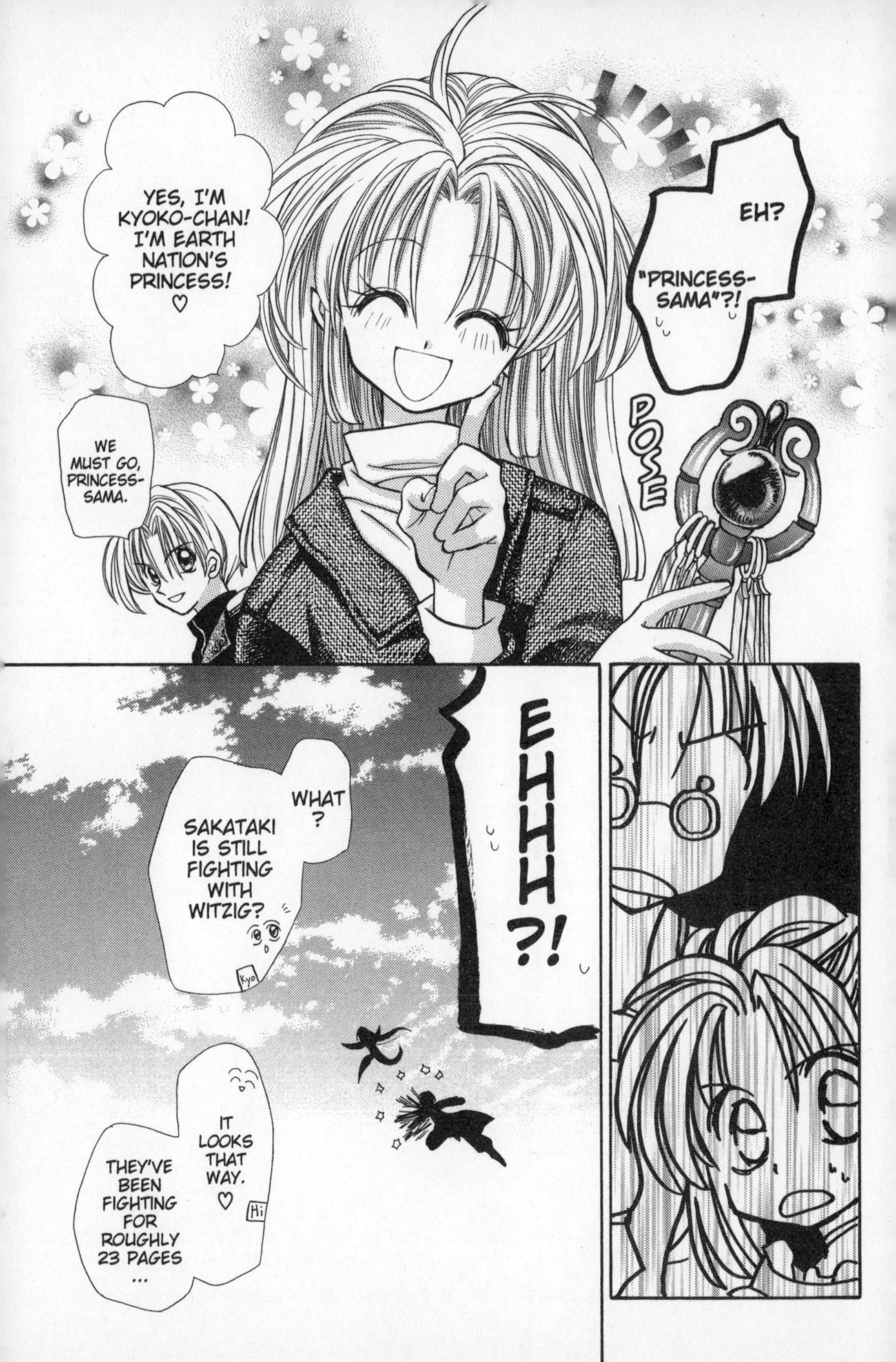
EH?
"PRINCESS-SAMA"?!
POSE
YES, I'M KYOKO-CHAN! I'M EARTH NATION'S PRINCESS! ♡
WE MUST GO, PRINCESS-SAMA.
EHHH?!
WHAT?
SAKATAKI IS STILL FIGHTING WITH WITZIG?
Kyo
IT LOOKS THAT WAY. ♡
Hi
THEY'VE BEEN FIGHTING FOR ROUGHLY 23 PAGES ...

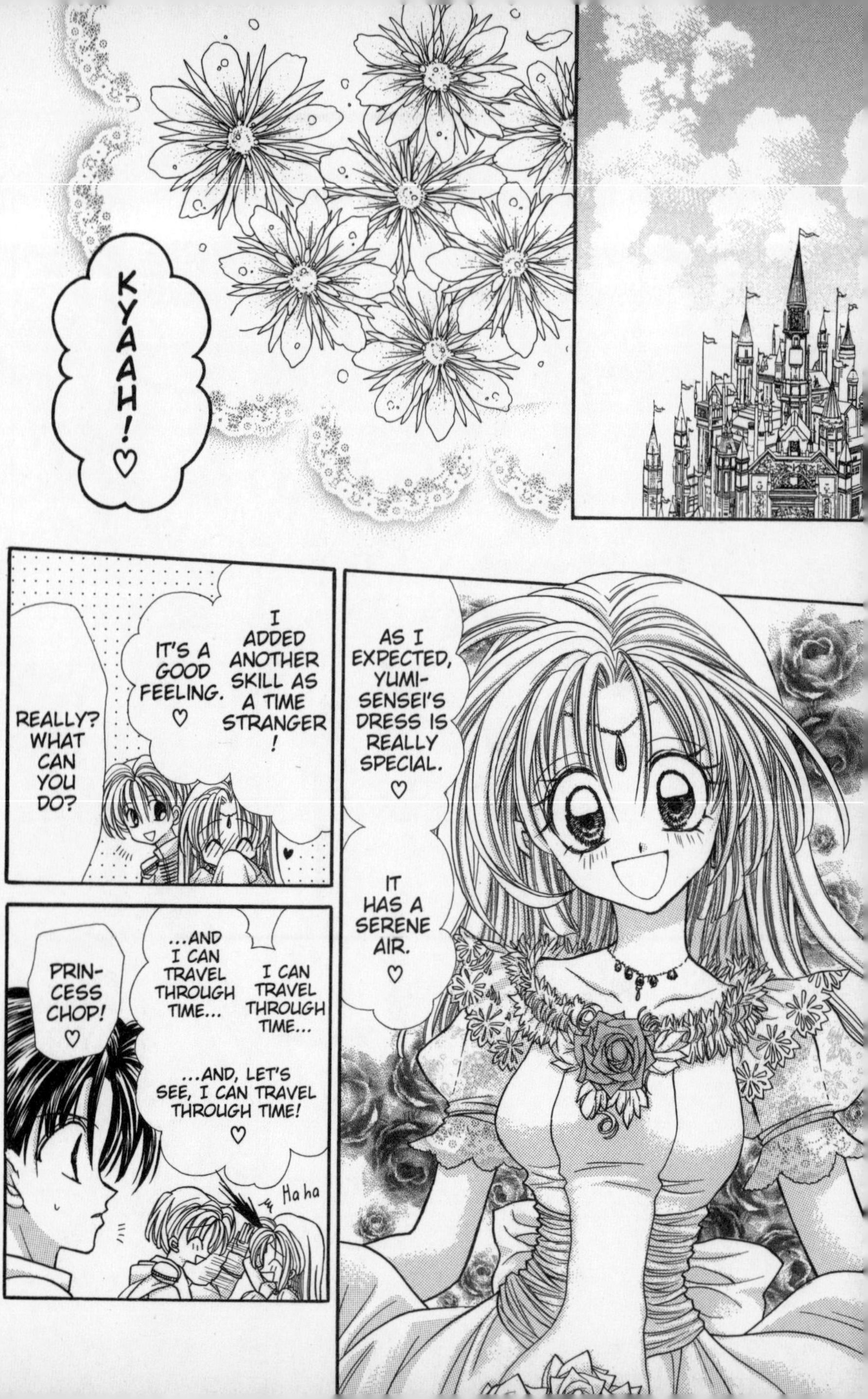

KYAAH! ♡
AS I EXPECTED, YUMI-SENSEI'S DRESS IS REALLY SPECIAL. ♡
IT HAS A SERENE AIR. ♡
I ADDED ANOTHER SKILL AS A TIME STRANGER!
IT'S A GOOD FEELING. ♡
REALLY? WHAT CAN YOU DO?
I CAN TRAVEL THROUGH TIME...
...AND I CAN TRAVEL THROUGH TIME...
...AND, LET'S SEE, I CAN TRAVEL THROUGH TIME! ♡
PRIN-CESS CHOP! ♡
Ha ha

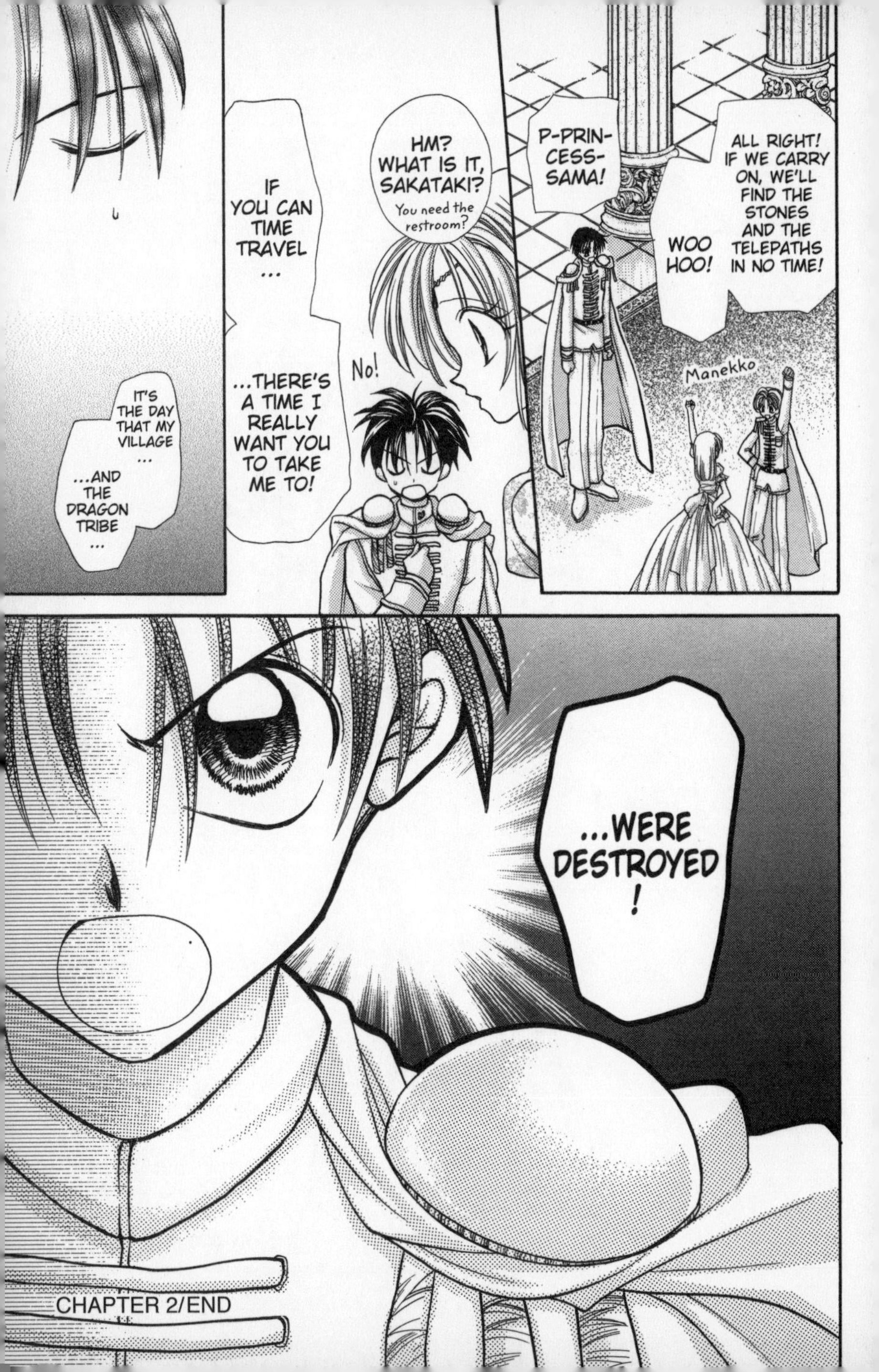
ALL RIGHT! IF WE CARRY ON, WE'LL FIND THE STONES AND THE TELEPATHS IN NO TIME!
P-PRINCESS-SAMA!
WOO HOO!
Manekko
HM? WHAT IS IT, SAKATAKI?
You need the restroom?
IF YOU CAN TIME TRAVEL...
No!
...THERE'S A TIME I REALLY WANT YOU TO TAKE ME TO!
IT'S THE DAY THAT MY VILLAGE...
...AND THE DRAGON TRIBE...
...WERE DESTROYED!
CHAPTER 2/END

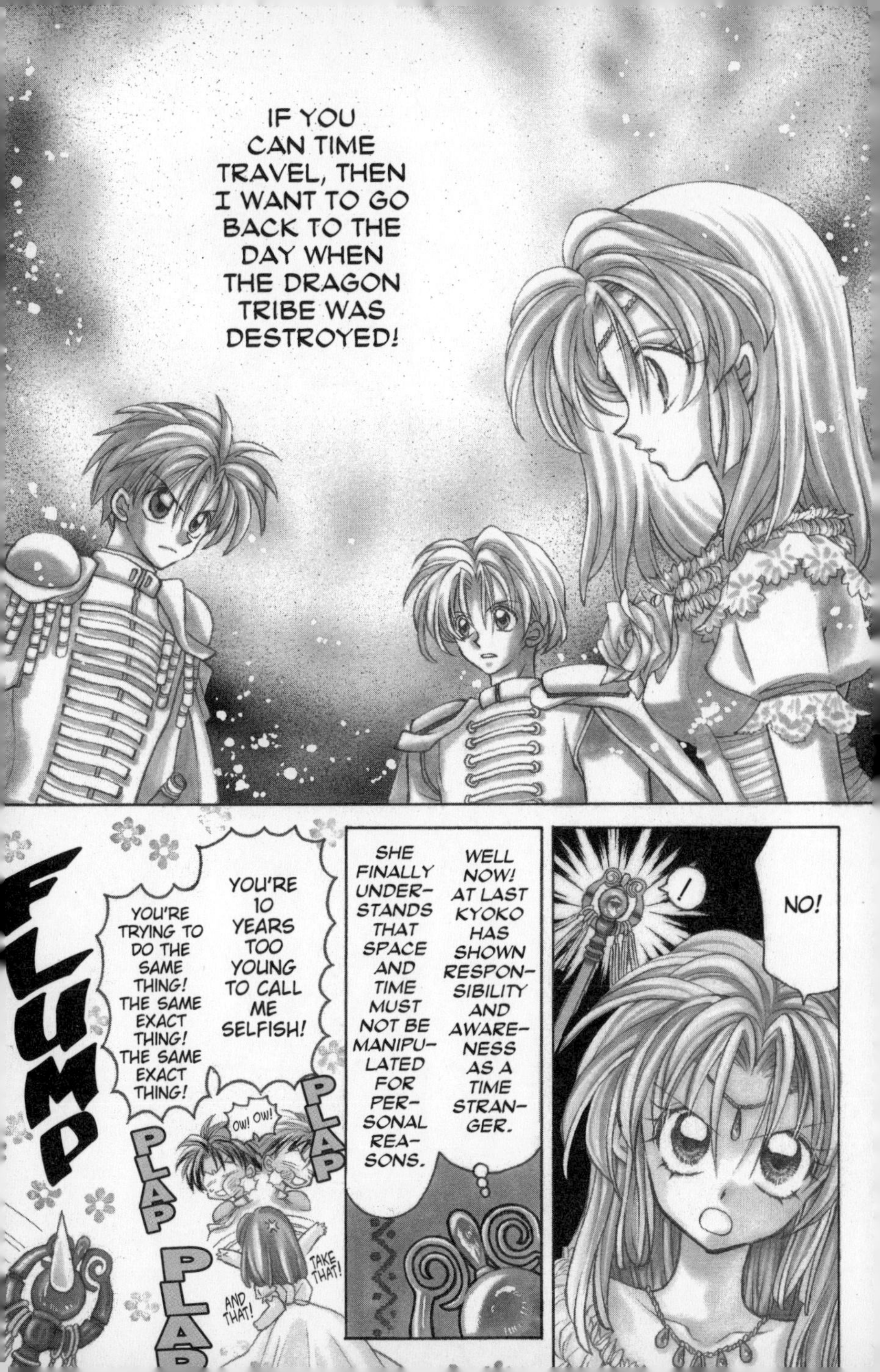
IF YOU CAN TIME TRAVEL, THEN I WANT TO GO BACK TO THE DAY WHEN THE DRAGON TRIBE WAS DESTROYED!
NO!
!
WELL NOW! AT LAST KYOKO HAS SHOWN RESPON-SIBILITY AND AWARE-NESS AS A TIME STRAN-GER.
SHE FINALLY UNDER-STANDS THAT SPACE AND TIME MUST NOT BE MANIPU-LATED FOR PER-SONAL REA-SONS.
YOU'RE 10 YEARS TOO YOUNG TO CALL ME SELFISH!
YOU'RE TRYING TO DO THE SAME THING! THE SAME EXACT THING! THE SAME EXACT THING!
PLAP
OW! OW!
FLUMP
PLAP PLAP
TAKE THAT!
AND THAT!
PLAP

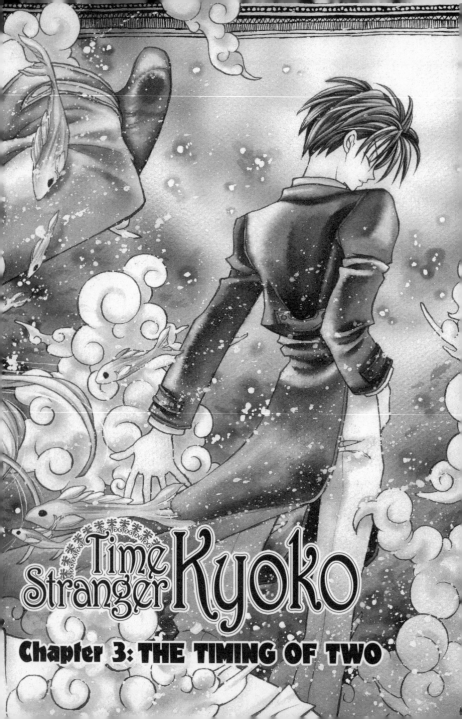

Time Stranger Kyoko

Chapter 3: THE TIMING OF TWO

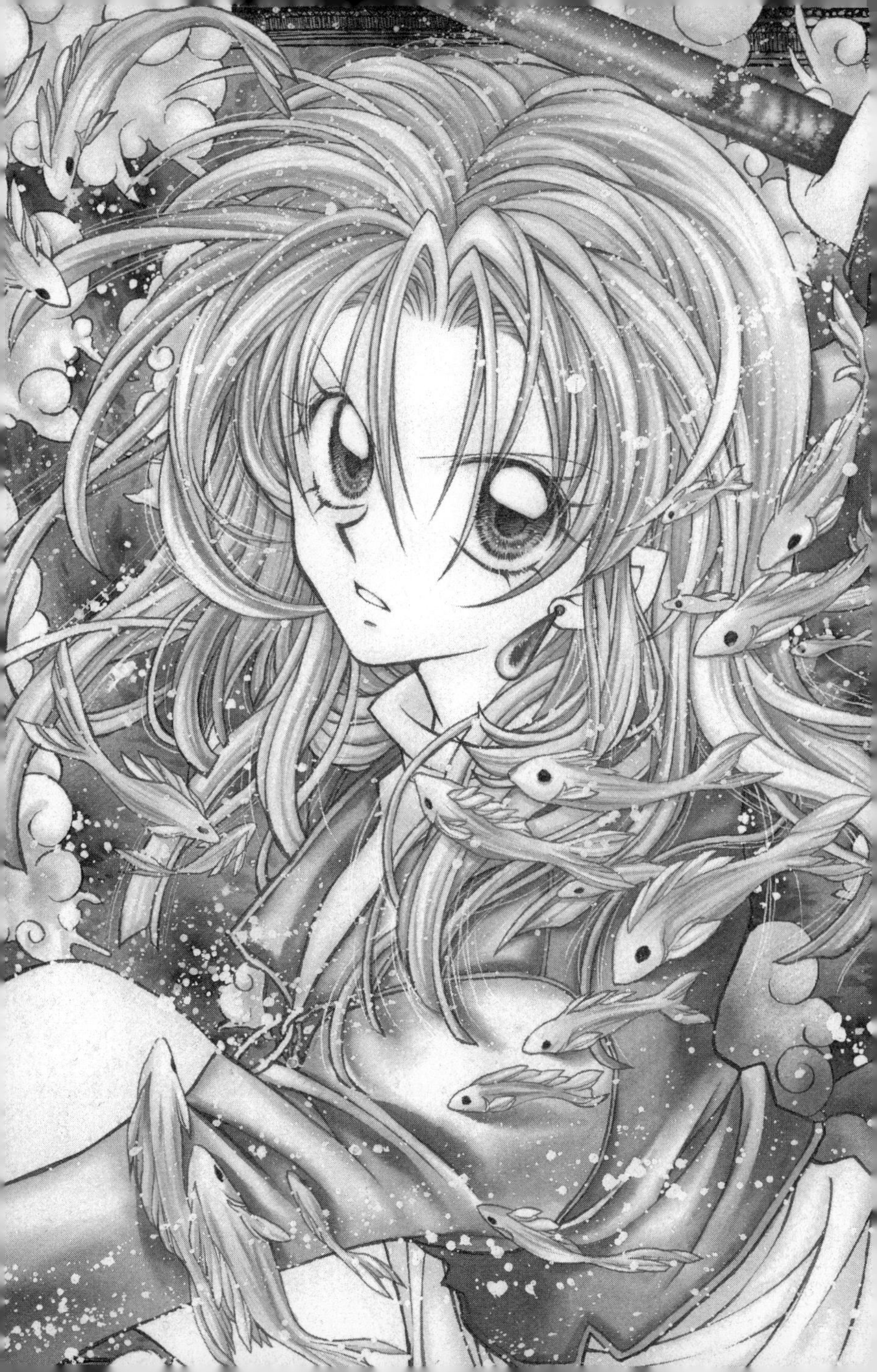

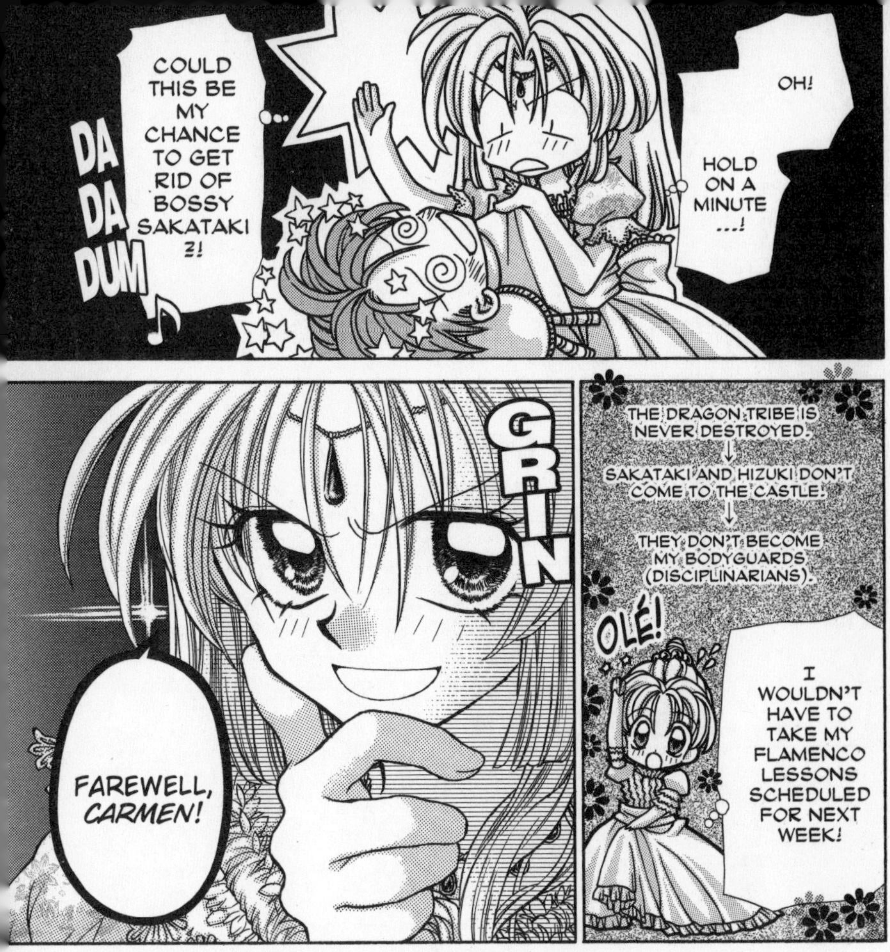
OH!
HOLD ON A MINUTE...!
COULD THIS BE MY CHANCE TO GET RID OF BOSSY SAKATAKI?!
DA DA DUM
THE DRAGON TRIBE IS NEVER DESTROYED.
↓
SAKATAKI AND HIZUKI DON'T COME TO THE CASTLE.
↓
THEY DON'T BECOME MY BODYGUARDS (DISCIPLINARIANS).
OLÉ!
I WOULDN'T HAVE TO TAKE MY FLAMENCO LESSONS SCHEDULED FOR NEXT WEEK!
GRIN
FAREWELL, CARMEN!

CHAPTER 3: THE TIMING OF TWO (LEAD-IN) THE JOURNEY BEGINS TOGETHER...!

I REALLY LIKE THIS TITLE PAGE ILLUSTRATION. WHEN I DREW IT, I BOUGHT NEW COLOR INKS AND REDID ALL THE COLORS FOR VARIOUS REASONS. THAT IS WHY THE COLORS ARE SO GORGEOUS. ◇ I HEARD THAT "NEW INKS PROVIDE THE BEST COLOR." I THOUGHT THAT WAS JUST FOR BLACK AND WHITE INKS, BUT IT HOLDS TRUE FOR COLORS TOO. I CHANGED MY BRUSHES AS WELL, AND THE LONGER HAIRS ALLOWED ME TO PAINT MORE BEAUTIFULLY AND SKILLFULLY. I WAS VERY HAPPY WITH THEM. I LIKE KYOKO-CHAN'S VALIANT EXPRESSION. IT IS EXACTLY WHAT I HAD ENVISIONED.

AS FOR THE STORY, IT'S ABOUT SAKATAKI GOING BACK TO THE DAY HIS VILLAGE WAS DESTROYED. SAKATAKI'S POPULARITY EXPLODED WITH THIS CHAPTER. EVERYONE WAS SAYING, "ISN'T HE COOL?" OR "ISN'T HE WEAK?" AND SO ON. GEEZ. (BY THE WAY, THE POPULARITY RANKING IN THE OFFICE WAS #1: WITZIG, #2: SAKATAKI, #3: HIZUKI!)

IT'S ALSO THE FIRST CHAPTER IN WHICH A TELEPATH (STRANGER) IS DISCOVERED. THE LAST PAGE MADE A LOT OF MY FRIENDS BURST OUT LAUGHING. IT WAS A LITTLE BIT AGONIZING? (WHY?!) IS IT THAT FUNNY?! WELL, I GUESS I CAN TAKE IT. I LIKE TAKESHIBA. IT WAS ALSO A LOT OF FUN TO DRAW SAKATAKI (AGE 5) AND HIZUKI (AGE 13).

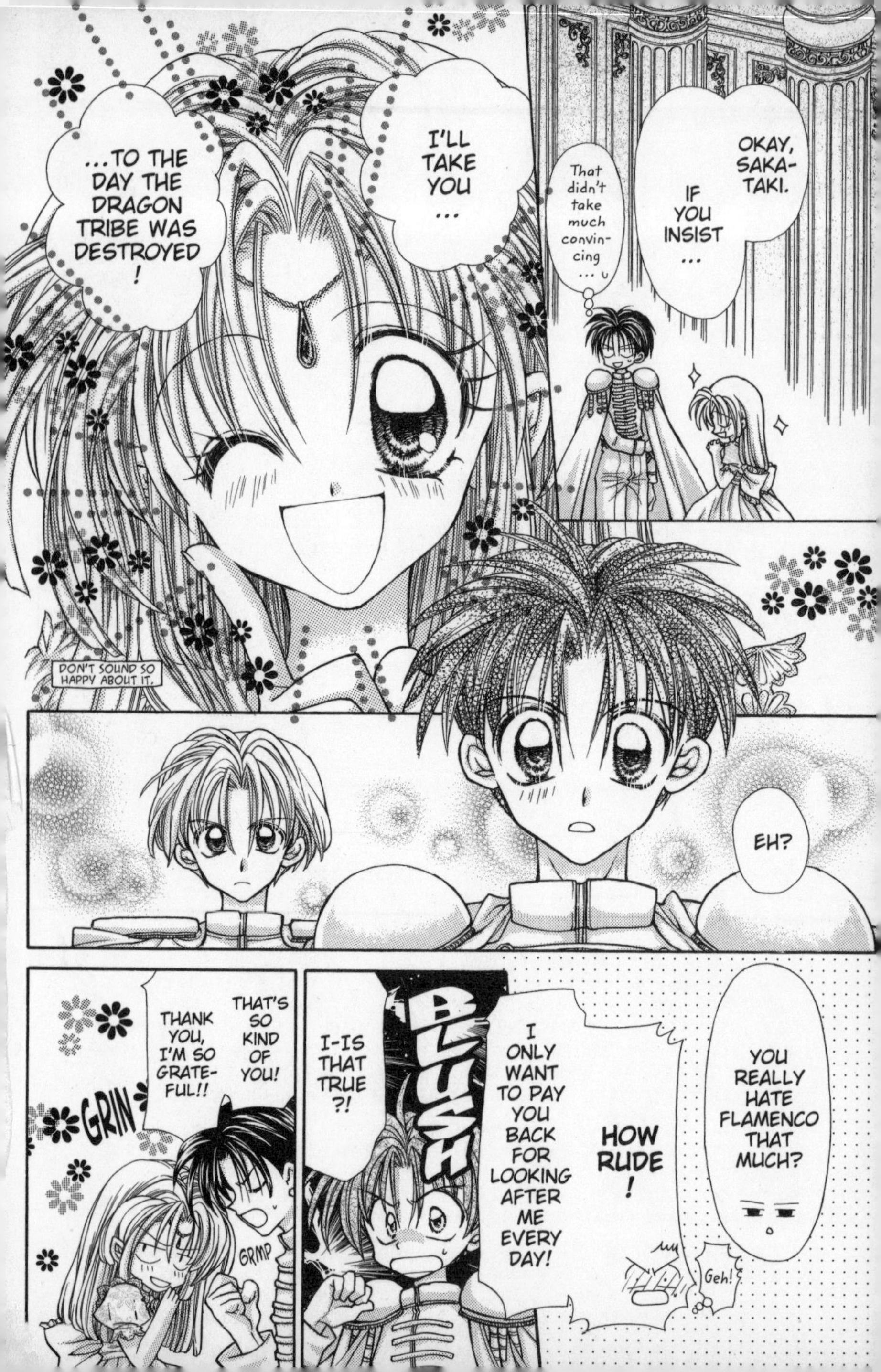
OKAY, SAKA-TAKI.
IF YOU INSIST ...
That didn't take much convincing ...
I'LL TAKE YOU ...
...TO THE DAY THE DRAGON TRIBE WAS DESTROYED!
DON'T SOUND SO HAPPY ABOUT IT.
EH?
YOU REALLY HATE FLAMENCO THAT MUCH?
Geh!
HOW RUDE!
I ONLY WANT TO PAY YOU BACK FOR LOOKING AFTER ME EVERY DAY!
BLUSH
I-IS THAT TRUE?!
THAT'S SO KIND OF YOU!
THANK YOU, I'M SO GRATE-FUL!!
GRIN
GRMP

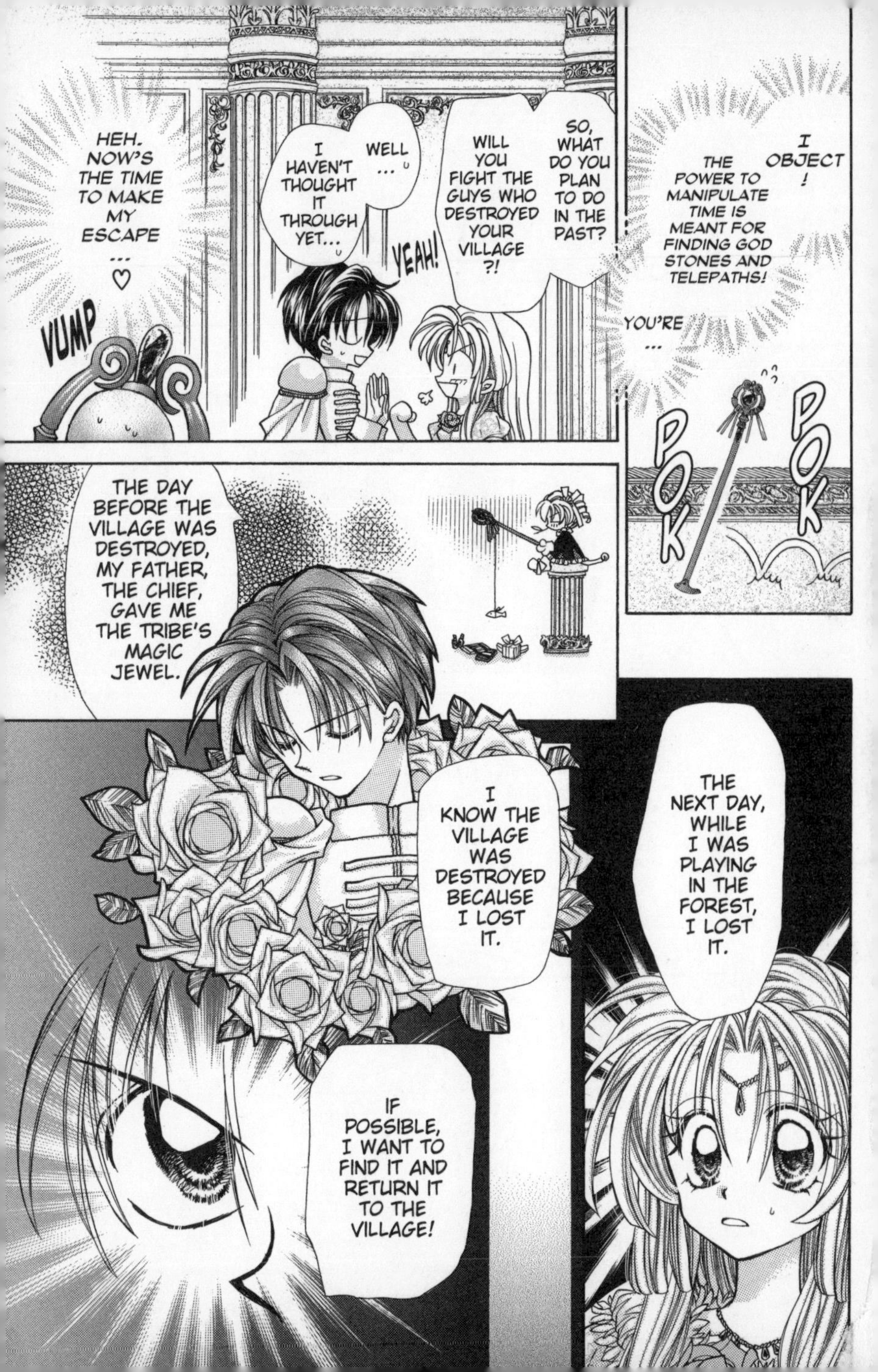
I OBJECT!
THE POWER TO MANIPULATE TIME IS MEANT FOR FINDING GOD STONES AND TELEPATHS!
YOU'RE ...
POK POK
SO, WHAT DO YOU PLAN TO DO IN THE PAST?
WILL YOU FIGHT THE GUYS WHO DESTROYED YOUR VILLAGE?!
YEAH!
WELL ...
I HAVEN'T THOUGHT IT THROUGH YET...
HEH. NOW'S THE TIME TO MAKE MY ESCAPE ... ♡
VUMP
THE DAY BEFORE THE VILLAGE WAS DESTROYED, MY FATHER, THE CHIEF, GAVE ME THE TRIBE'S MAGIC JEWEL.
THE NEXT DAY, WHILE I WAS PLAYING IN THE FOREST, I LOST IT.
I KNOW THE VILLAGE WAS DESTROYED BECAUSE I LOST IT.
IF POSSIBLE, I WANT TO FIND IT AND RETURN IT TO THE VILLAGE!

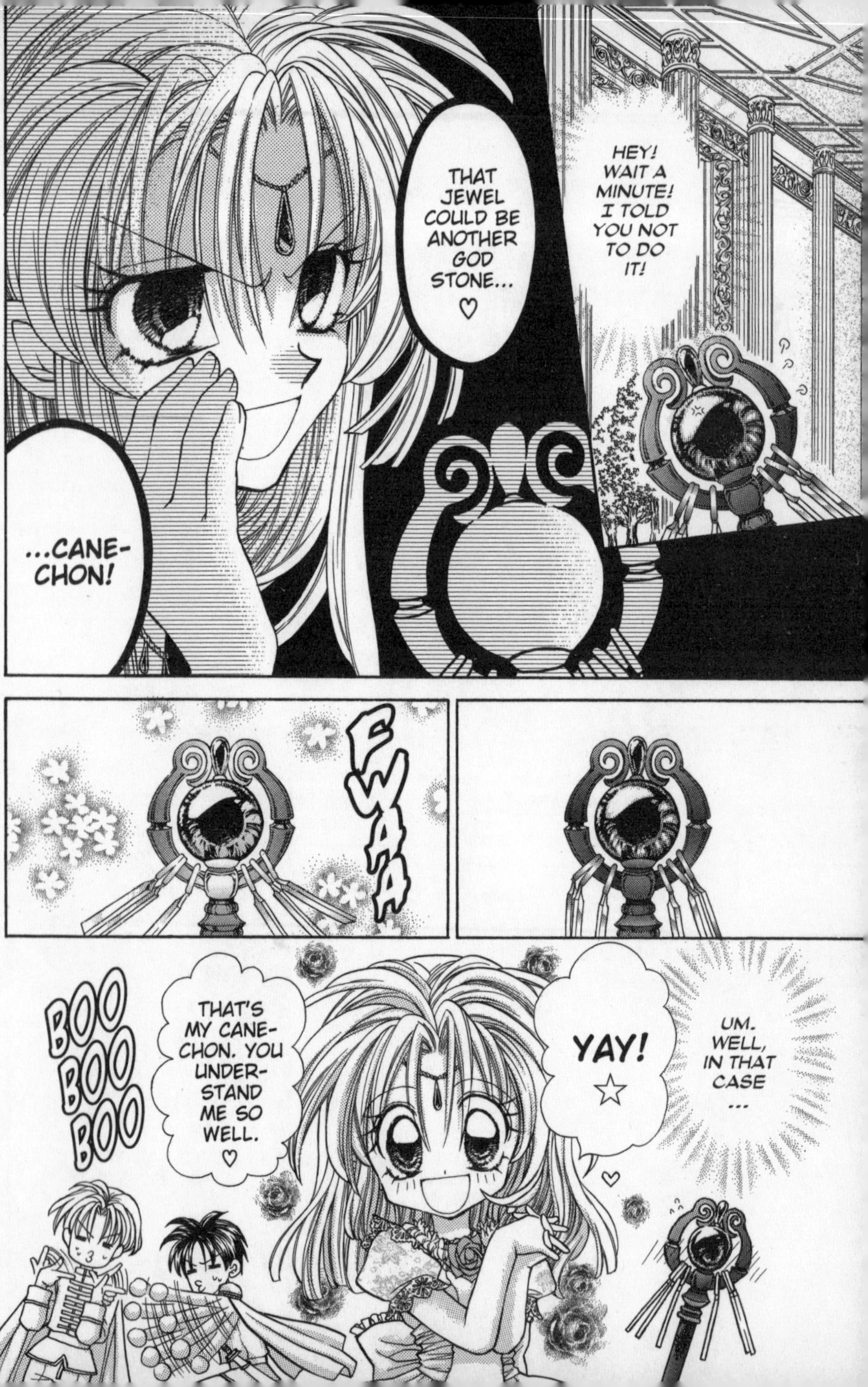
HEY! WAIT A MINUTE! I TOLD YOU NOT TO DO IT!
THAT JEWEL COULD BE ANOTHER GOD STONE... ♡
...CANE-CHON!
EWAA
UM. WELL, IN THAT CASE ...
YAY! ☆
THAT'S MY CANE-CHON. YOU UNDER-STAND ME SO WELL. ♡
BOO BOO BOO

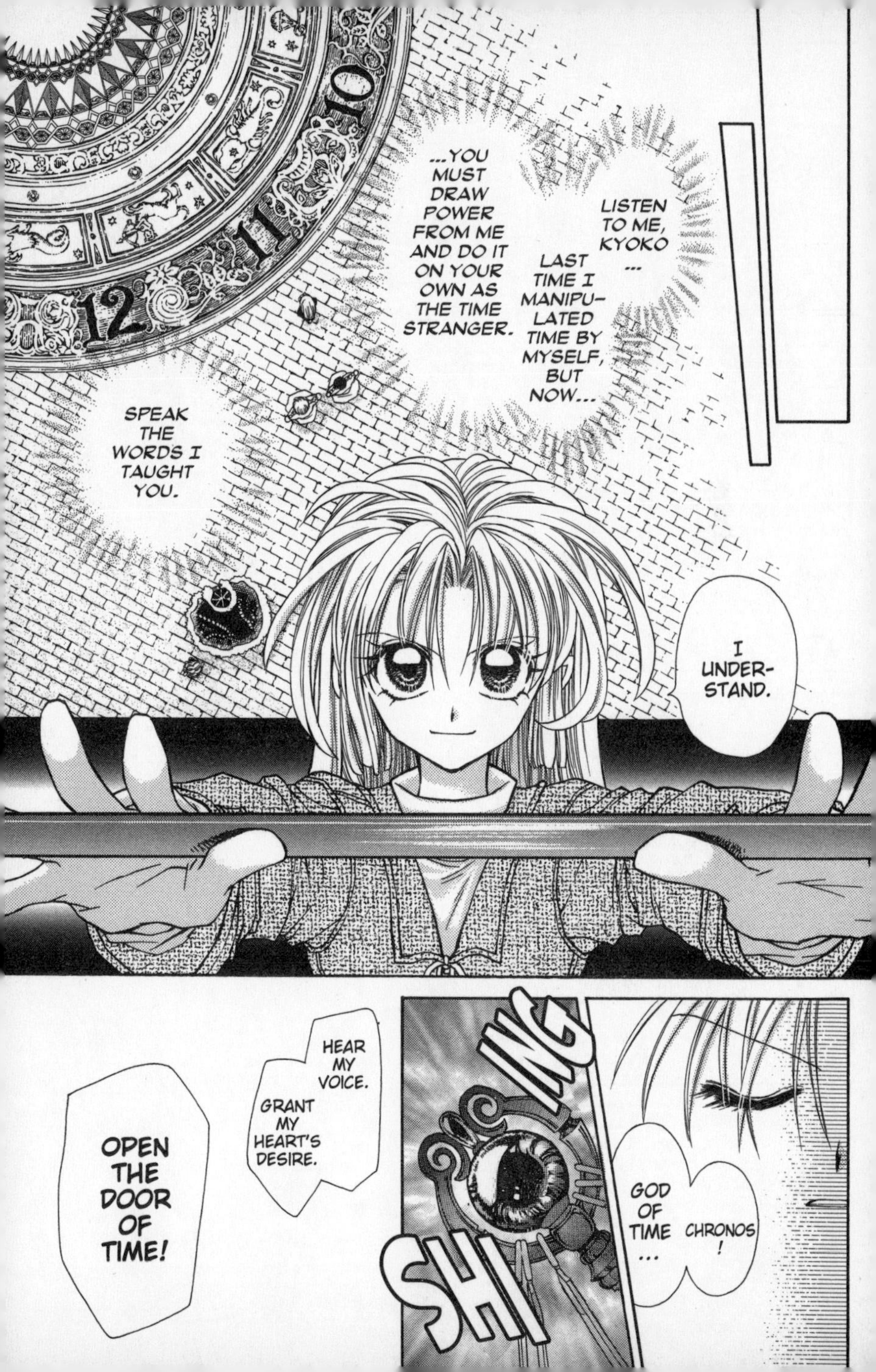
LISTEN TO ME, KYOKO...
LAST TIME I MANIPULATED TIME BY MYSELF, BUT NOW...
...YOU MUST DRAW POWER FROM ME AND DO IT ON YOUR OWN AS THE TIME STRANGER.
SPEAK THE WORDS I TAUGHT YOU.
I UNDERSTAND.
GOD OF TIME...
CHRONOS!
SHING
HEAR MY VOICE.
GRANT MY HEART'S DESIRE.
OPEN THE DOOR OF TIME!

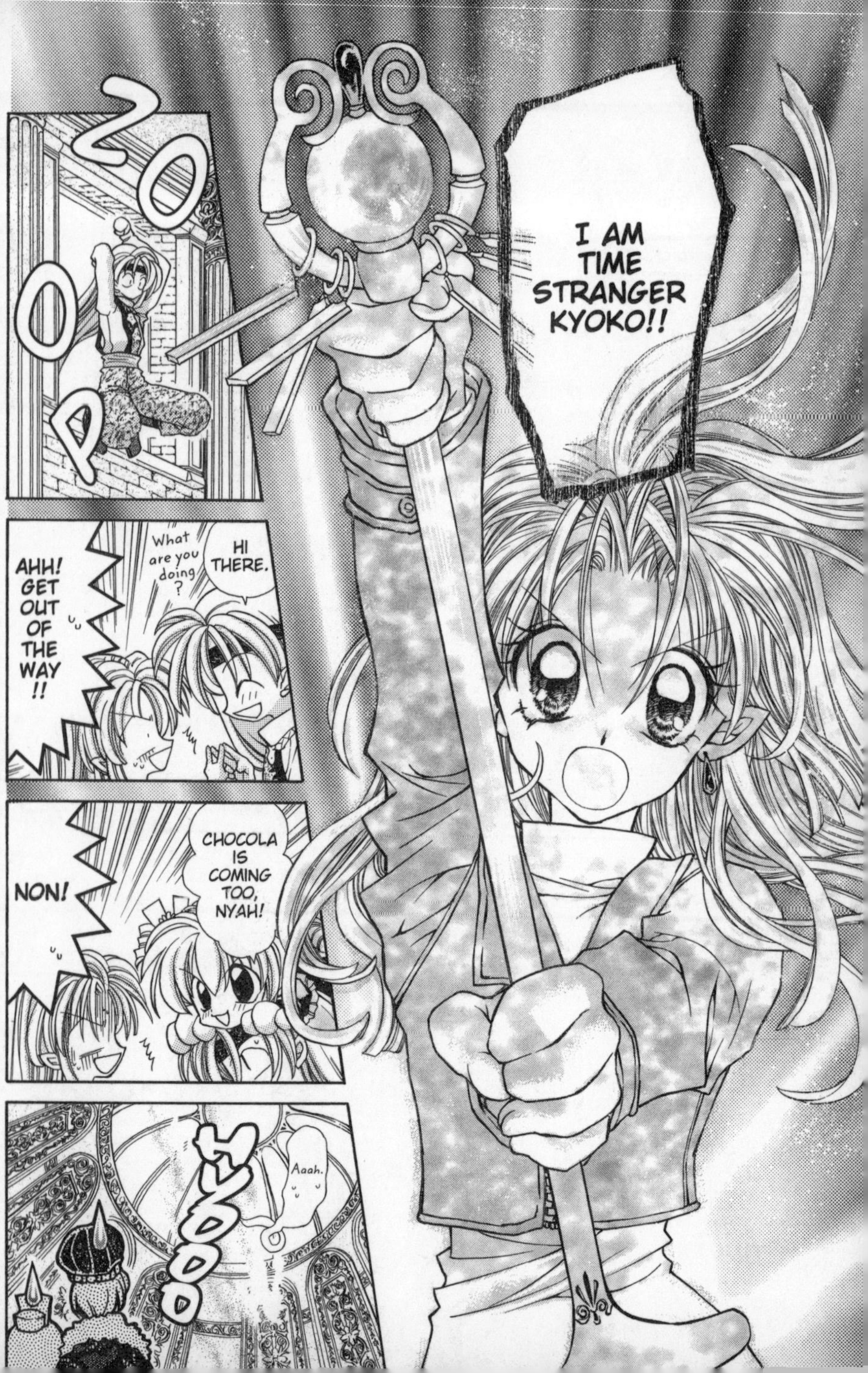
I AM TIME STRANGER KYOKO!!
ZOOP
HI THERE.
What are you doing?
AHH! GET OUT OF THE WAY!!
CHOCOLA IS COMING TOO, NYAH!
NON!
HYOOO
Aaah.

ARINA TANEMURA'S

PACHIN TO KISHAN

IT'S SOMEHOW ALREADY #41.

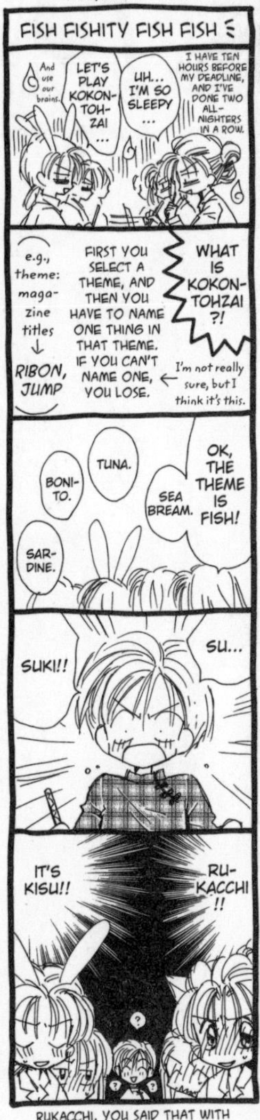

FISH FISHITY FISH FISH
I HAVE TEN HOURS BEFORE MY DEADLINE, AND I'VE DONE TWO ALL-NIGHTERS IN A ROW.
UH... I'M SO SLEEPY ...
LET'S PLAY KOKON-TOHZAI ...
And use our brains.
WHAT IS KOKON-TOHZAI ?!
FIRST YOU SELECT A THEME, AND THEN YOU HAVE TO NAME ONE THING IN THAT THEME. IF YOU CAN'T NAME ONE, YOU LOSE.
e.g., theme: magazine titles ↓ RIBON, JUMP
I'm not really sure, but I think it's this.
OK, THE THEME IS FISH!
SEA BREAM.
TUNA.
BONITO.
SARDINE.
SU...
SUKI!!
RU-KACCHI !!
IT'S KISU!!

RUKACCHI, YOU SAID THAT WITH SUCH FERVOR...I'M SOMEHOW EMBARRASSED. I GUESS I'M STILL A SHY MAIDEN. /////

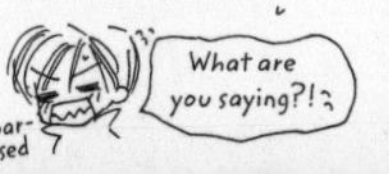

What are you saying?!
embarrassed

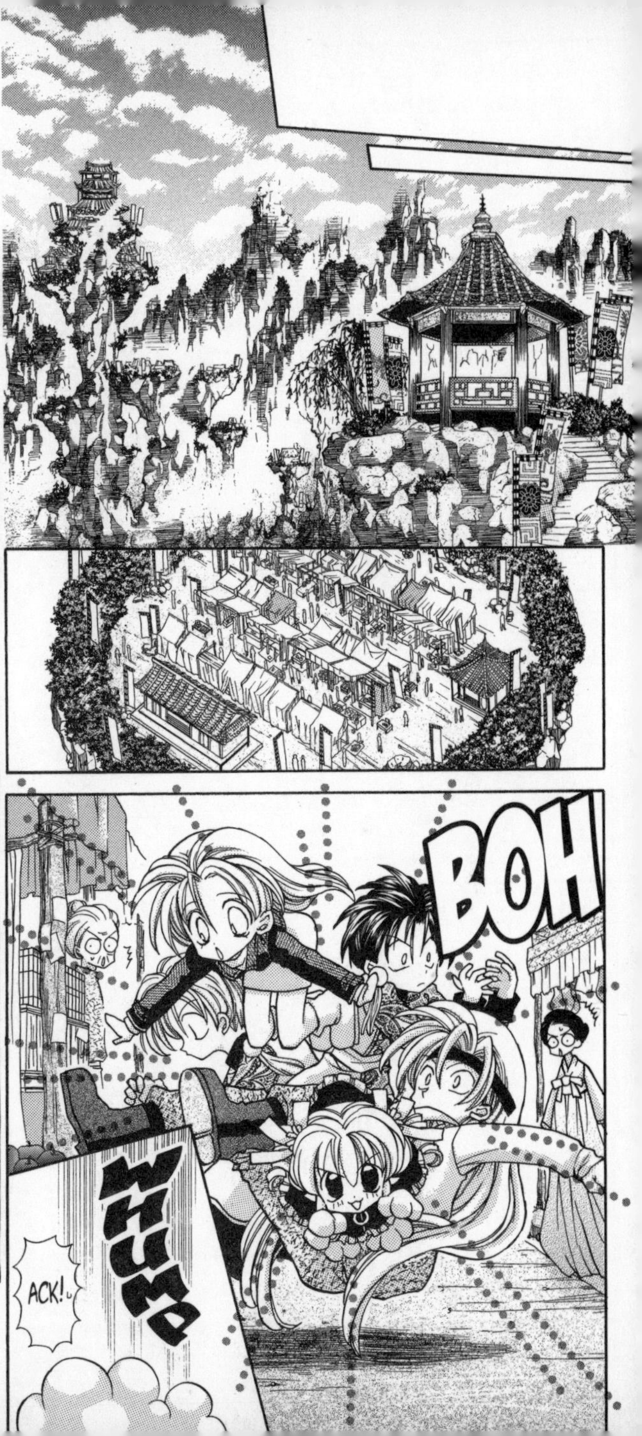

BOH
ACK!
WHUMP

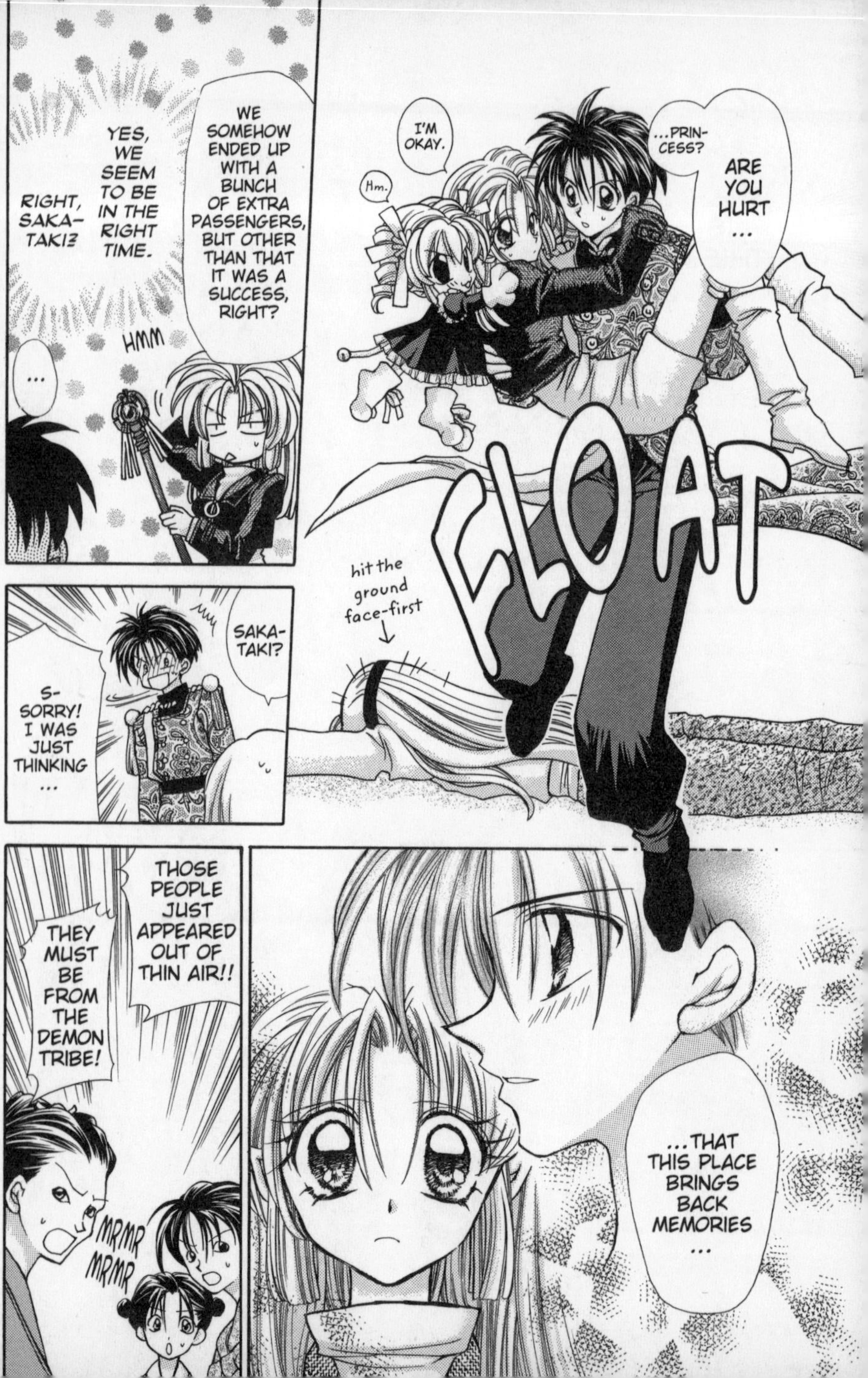
...PRIN-CESS?
ARE YOU HURT ...
I'M OKAY.
Hm.
FLOAT
hit the ground face-first
WE SOMEHOW ENDED UP WITH A BUNCH OF EXTRA PASSENGERS, BUT OTHER THAN THAT IT WAS A SUCCESS, RIGHT?
YES, WE SEEM TO BE IN THE RIGHT TIME.
RIGHT, SAKA-TAKI?
HMM
...
SAKA-TAKI?
S-SORRY! I WAS JUST THINKING ...
...THAT THIS PLACE BRINGS BACK MEMORIES ...
THOSE PEOPLE JUST APPEARED OUT OF THIN AIR!!
THEY MUST BE FROM THE DEMON TRIBE!
MRMR MRMR

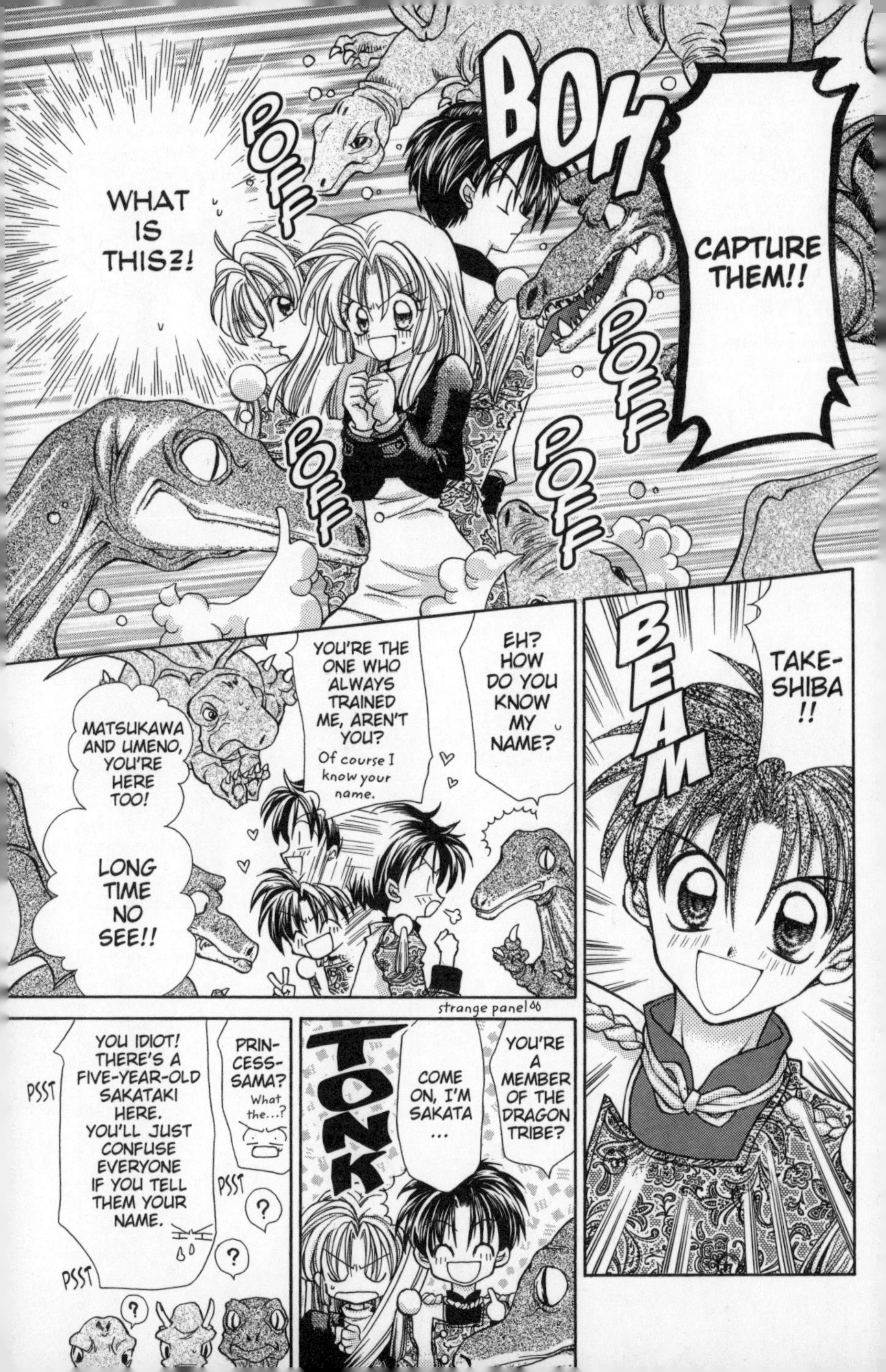
CAPTURE THEM!!
BOH
POFF
POFF
POFF
POFF
WHAT IS THIS?!
TAKE-SHIBA!!
BEAM
EH? HOW DO YOU KNOW MY NAME?
YOU'RE THE ONE WHO ALWAYS TRAINED ME, AREN'T YOU?
Of course I know your name.
MATSUKAWA AND UMENO, YOU'RE HERE TOO!
LONG TIME NO SEE!!
strange panel
YOU'RE A MEMBER OF THE DRAGON TRIBE?
COME ON, I'M SAKATA...
TONK
PRIN-CESS-SAMA?
What the...?
YOU IDIOT! THERE'S A FIVE-YEAR-OLD SAKATAKI HERE. YOU'LL JUST CONFUSE EVERYONE IF YOU TELL THEM YOUR NAME.
PSST
PSST
PSST
?
?
?

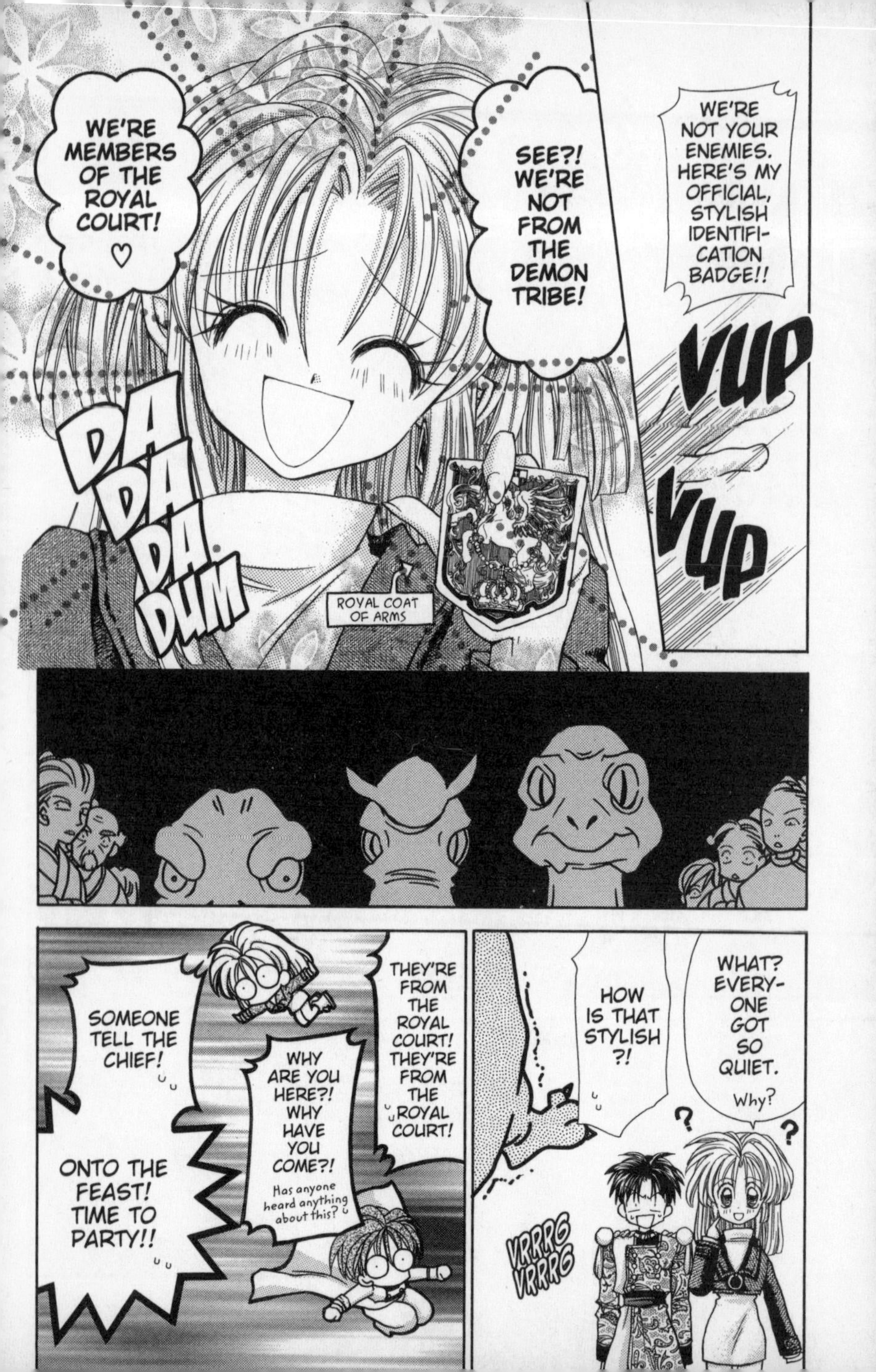
WE'RE NOT YOUR ENEMIES. HERE'S MY OFFICIAL, STYLISH IDENTIFICATION BADGE!!
VUP
VUP
SEE?! WE'RE NOT FROM THE DEMON TRIBE!
WE'RE MEMBERS OF THE ROYAL COURT! ♡
DA DA DA DUM
ROYAL COAT OF ARMS
WHAT? EVERYONE GOT SO QUIET.
Why?
HOW IS THAT STYLISH?!
VRRRG VRRRG
THEY'RE FROM THE ROYAL COURT! THEY'RE FROM THE ROYAL COURT!
WHY ARE YOU HERE?! WHY HAVE YOU COME?!
Has anyone heard anything about this?
SOMEONE TELL THE CHIEF!
ONTO THE FEAST! TIME TO PARTY!!

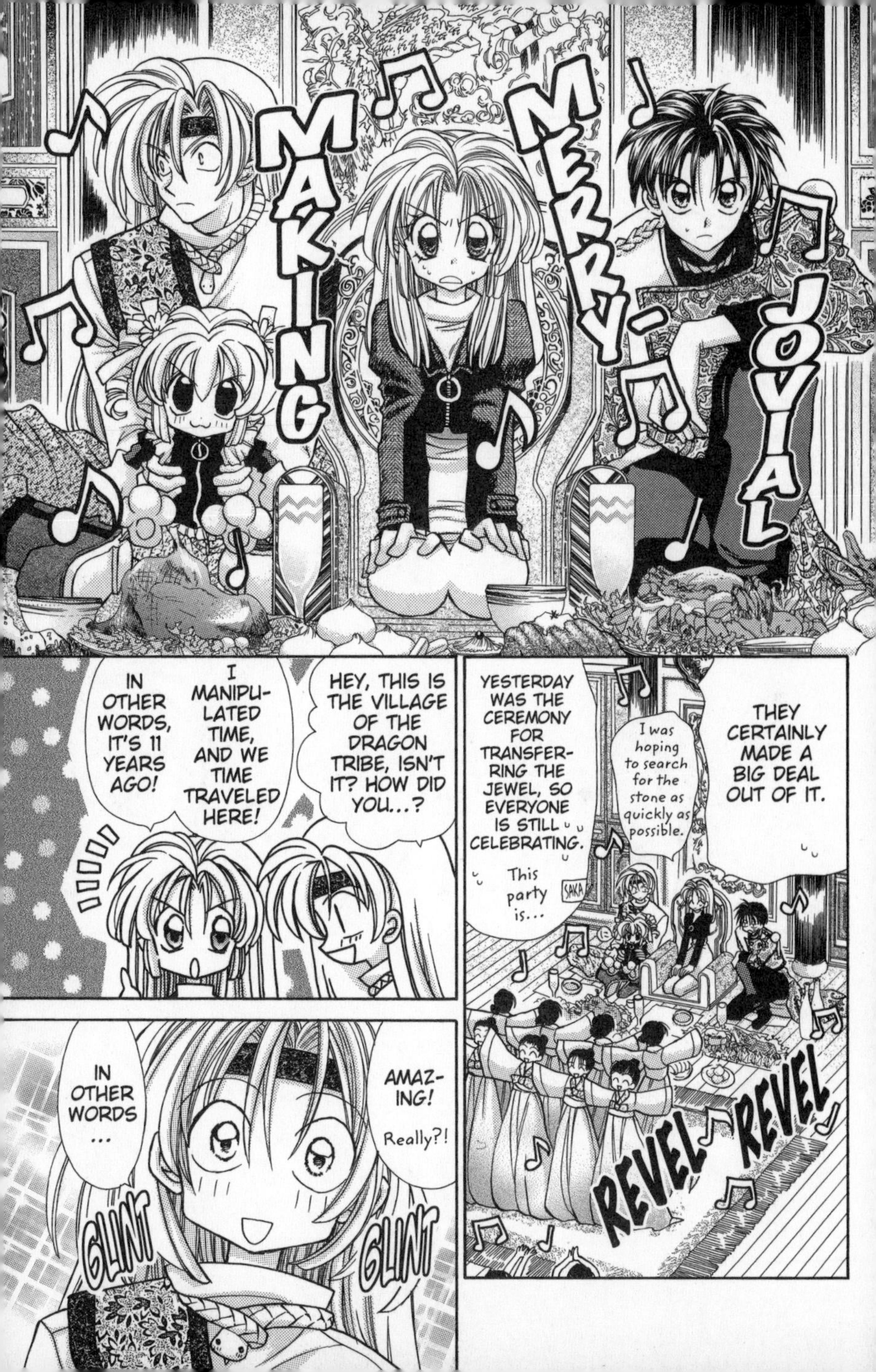
MAKING
MERRY-
JOVIAL
THEY CERTAINLY MADE A BIG DEAL OUT OF IT.
I was hoping to search for the stone as quickly as possible.
YESTERDAY WAS THE CEREMONY FOR TRANSFER-RING THE JEWEL, SO EVERYONE IS STILL CELEBRATING.
This party is...
SAKA
REVEL REVEL
HEY, THIS IS THE VILLAGE OF THE DRAGON TRIBE, ISN'T IT? HOW DID YOU...?
I MANIPU-LATED TIME, AND WE TIME TRAVELED HERE!
IN OTHER WORDS, IT'S 11 YEARS AGO!
AMAZ-ING!
Really?!
IN OTHER WORDS...
GLINT
GLINT

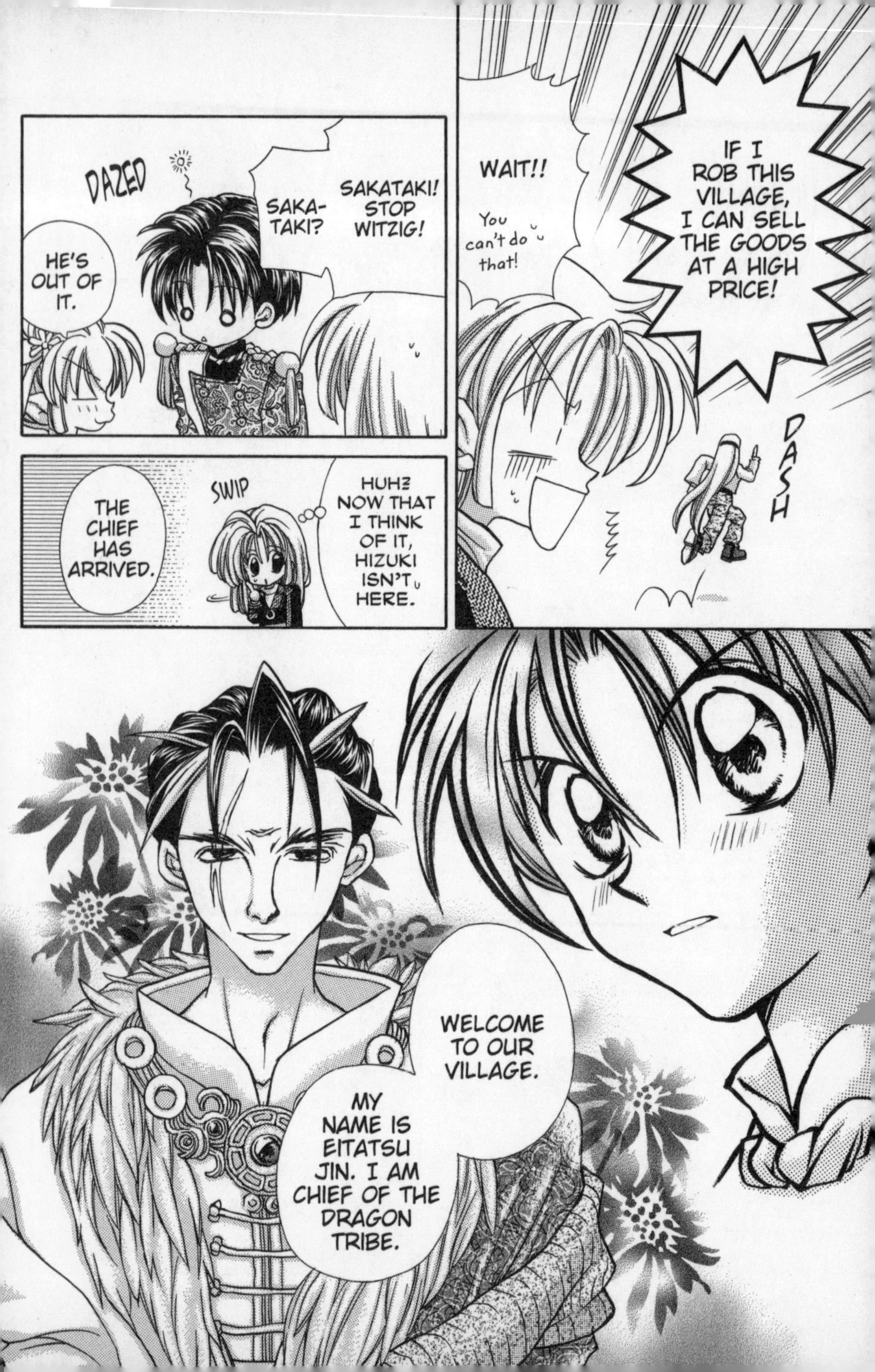
IF I ROB THIS VILLAGE, I CAN SELL THE GOODS AT A HIGH PRICE!
WAIT!!
You can't do that!
DASH
SAKATAKI! STOP WITZIG!
SAKA-TAKI?
DAZED
HE'S OUT OF IT.
HUH? NOW THAT I THINK OF IT, HIZUKI ISN'T HERE.
SWIP
THE CHIEF HAS ARRIVED.
WELCOME TO OUR VILLAGE.
MY NAME IS EITATSU JIN. I AM CHIEF OF THE DRAGON TRIBE.

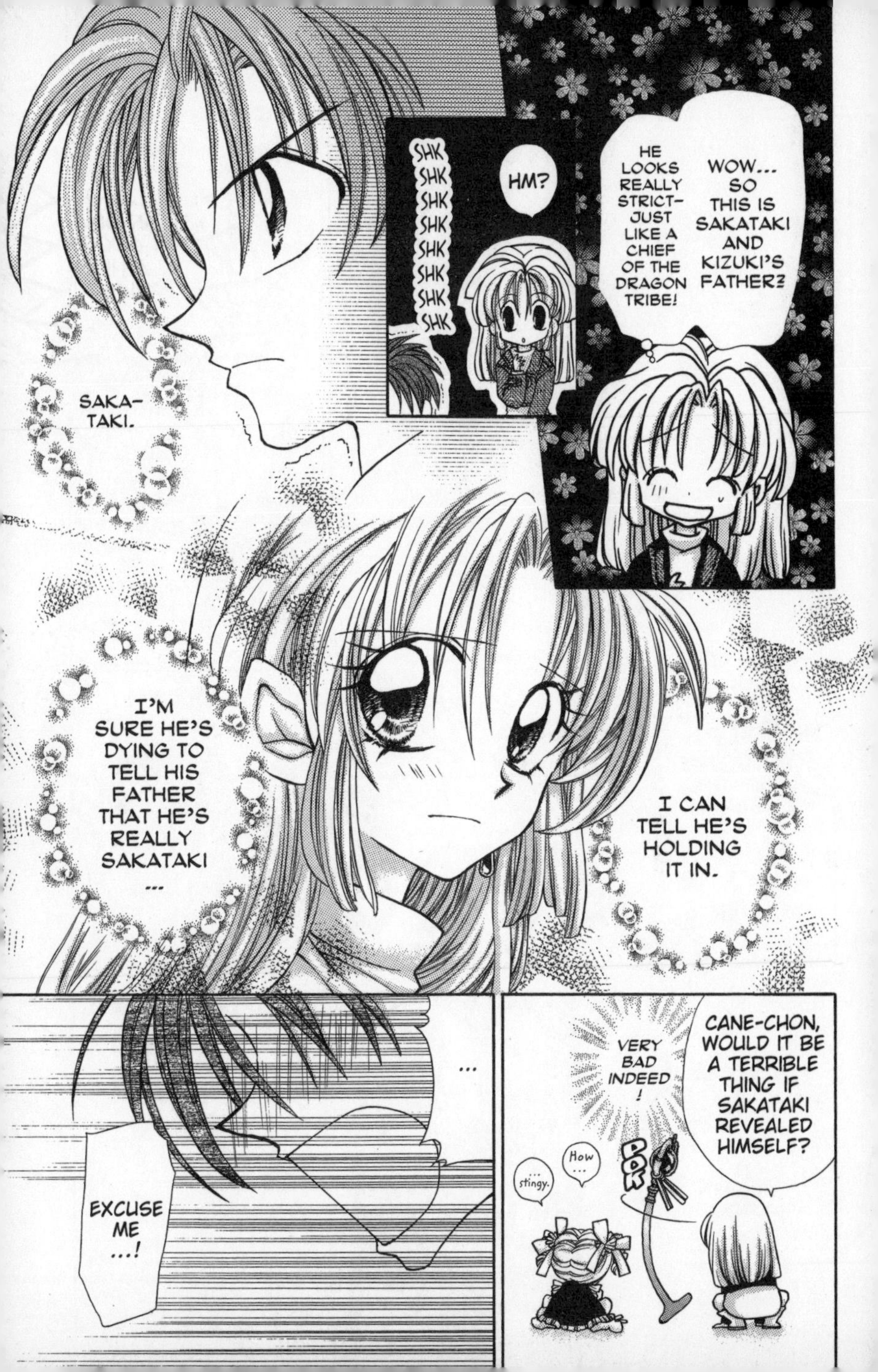
WOW... SO THIS IS SAKATAKI AND KIZUKI'S FATHER?
HE LOOKS REALLY STRICT—JUST LIKE A CHIEF OF THE DRAGON TRIBE!
HM?
SHK SHK SHK SHK SHK SHK SHK SHK
SAKA-TAKI.
I CAN TELL HE'S HOLDING IT IN.
I'M SURE HE'S DYING TO TELL HIS FATHER THAT HE'S REALLY SAKATAKI ...
CANE-CHON, WOULD IT BE A TERRIBLE THING IF SAKATAKI REVEALED HIMSELF?
VERY BAD INDEED!
DOK
How ...
... stingy.
...
EXCUSE ME ...!

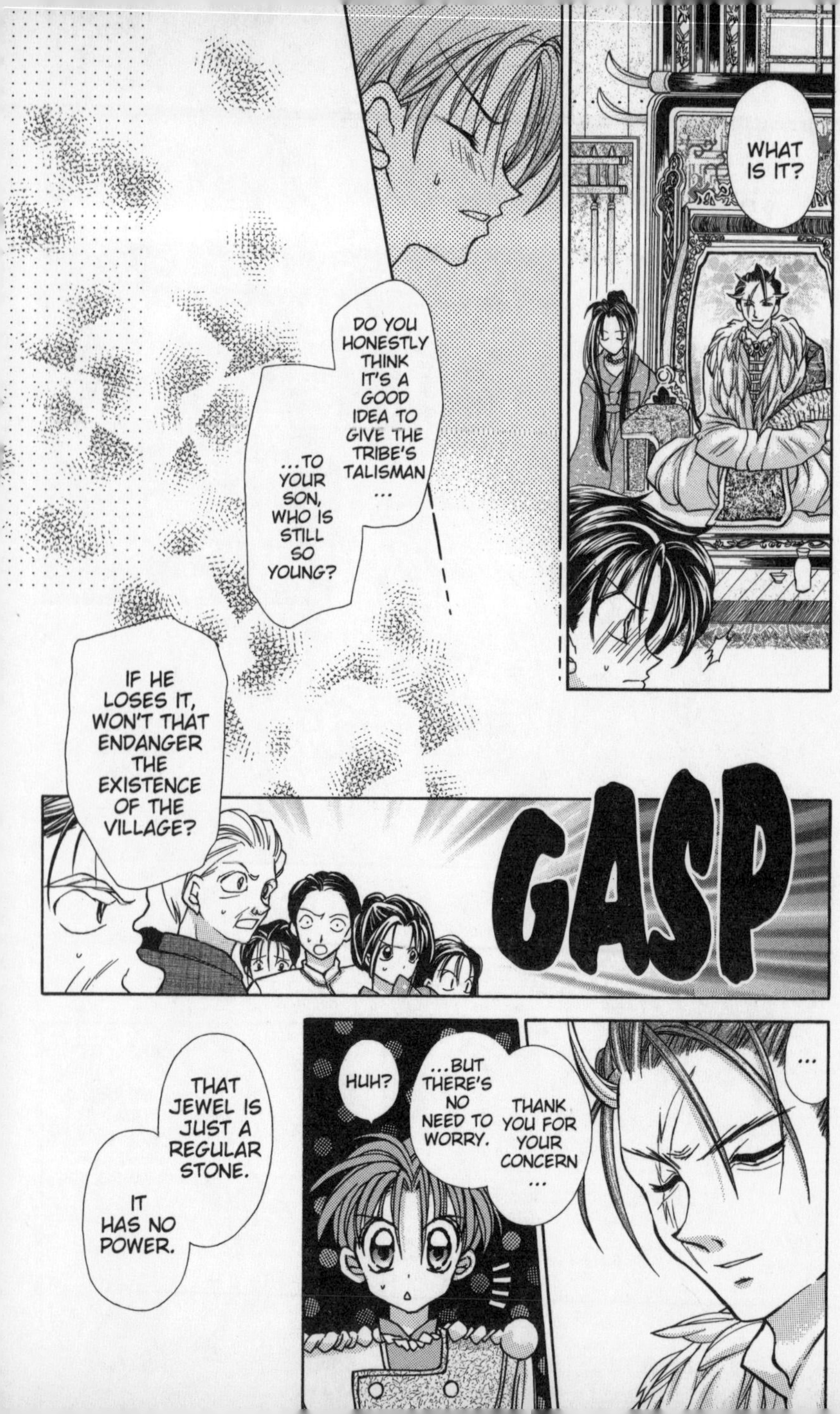
WHAT IS IT?
DO YOU HONESTLY THINK IT'S A GOOD IDEA TO GIVE THE TRIBE'S TALISMAN...
...TO YOUR SON, WHO IS STILL SO YOUNG?
IF HE LOSES IT, WON'T THAT ENDANGER THE EXISTENCE OF THE VILLAGE?
GASP
...
THANK YOU FOR YOUR CONCERN...
...BUT THERE'S NO NEED TO WORRY.
HUH?
THAT JEWEL IS JUST A REGULAR STONE.
IT HAS NO POWER.

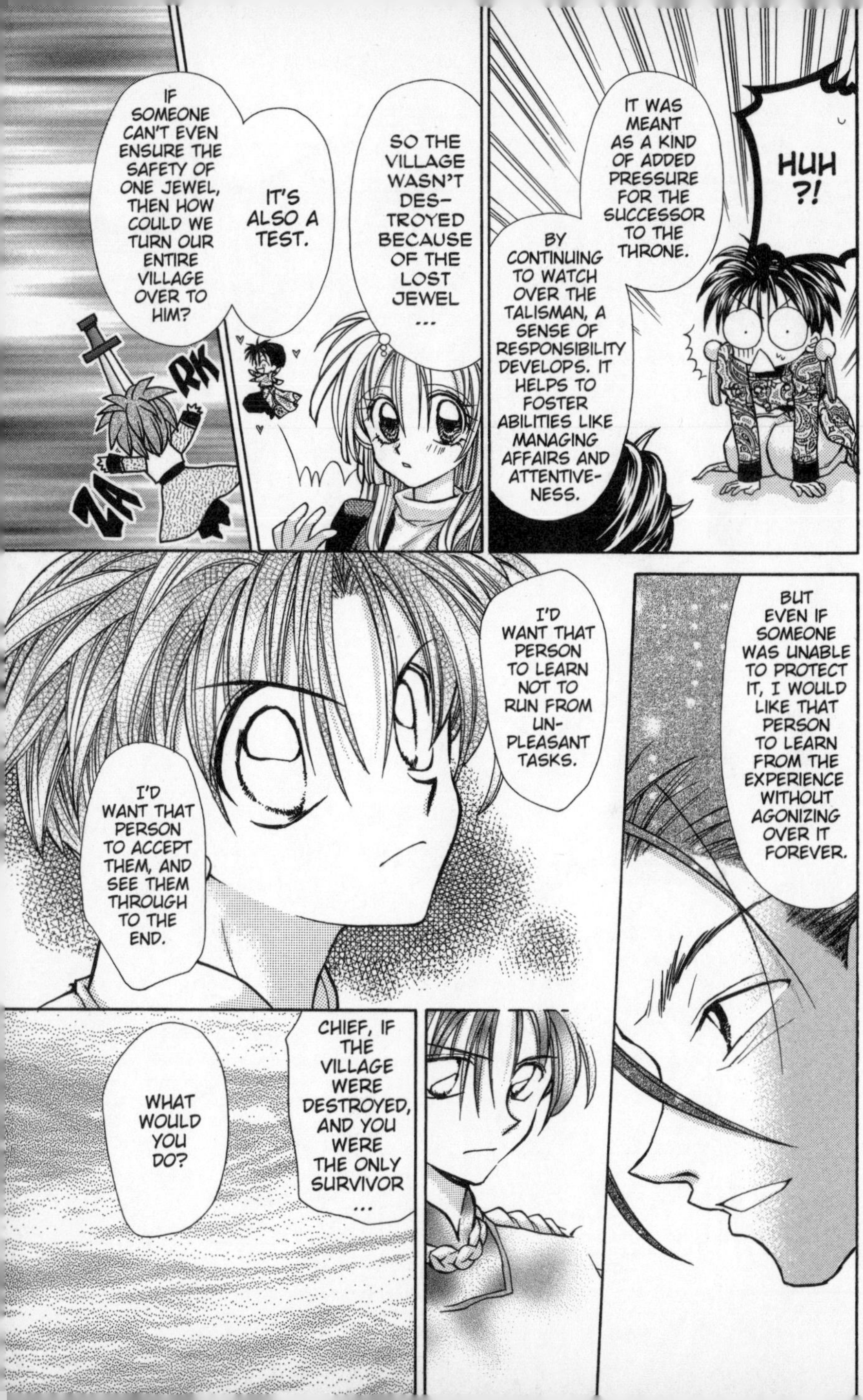
HUH ?!
IT WAS MEANT AS A KIND OF ADDED PRESSURE FOR THE SUCCESSOR TO THE THRONE.
BY CONTINUING TO WATCH OVER THE TALISMAN, A SENSE OF RESPONSIBILITY DEVELOPS. IT HELPS TO FOSTER ABILITIES LIKE MANAGING AFFAIRS AND ATTENTIVE-NESS.
SO THE VILLAGE WASN'T DES-TROYED BECAUSE OF THE LOST JEWEL ...
IT'S ALSO A TEST.
IF SOMEONE CAN'T EVEN ENSURE THE SAFETY OF ONE JEWEL, THEN HOW COULD WE TURN OUR ENTIRE VILLAGE OVER TO HIM?
ZA RK
BUT EVEN IF SOMEONE WAS UNABLE TO PROTECT IT, I WOULD LIKE THAT PERSON TO LEARN FROM THE EXPERIENCE WITHOUT AGONIZING OVER IT FOREVER.
I'D WANT THAT PERSON TO LEARN NOT TO RUN FROM UN-PLEASANT TASKS.
I'D WANT THAT PERSON TO ACCEPT THEM, AND SEE THEM THROUGH TO THE END.
CHIEF, IF THE VILLAGE WERE DESTROYED, AND YOU WERE THE ONLY SURVIVOR ...
WHAT WOULD YOU DO?

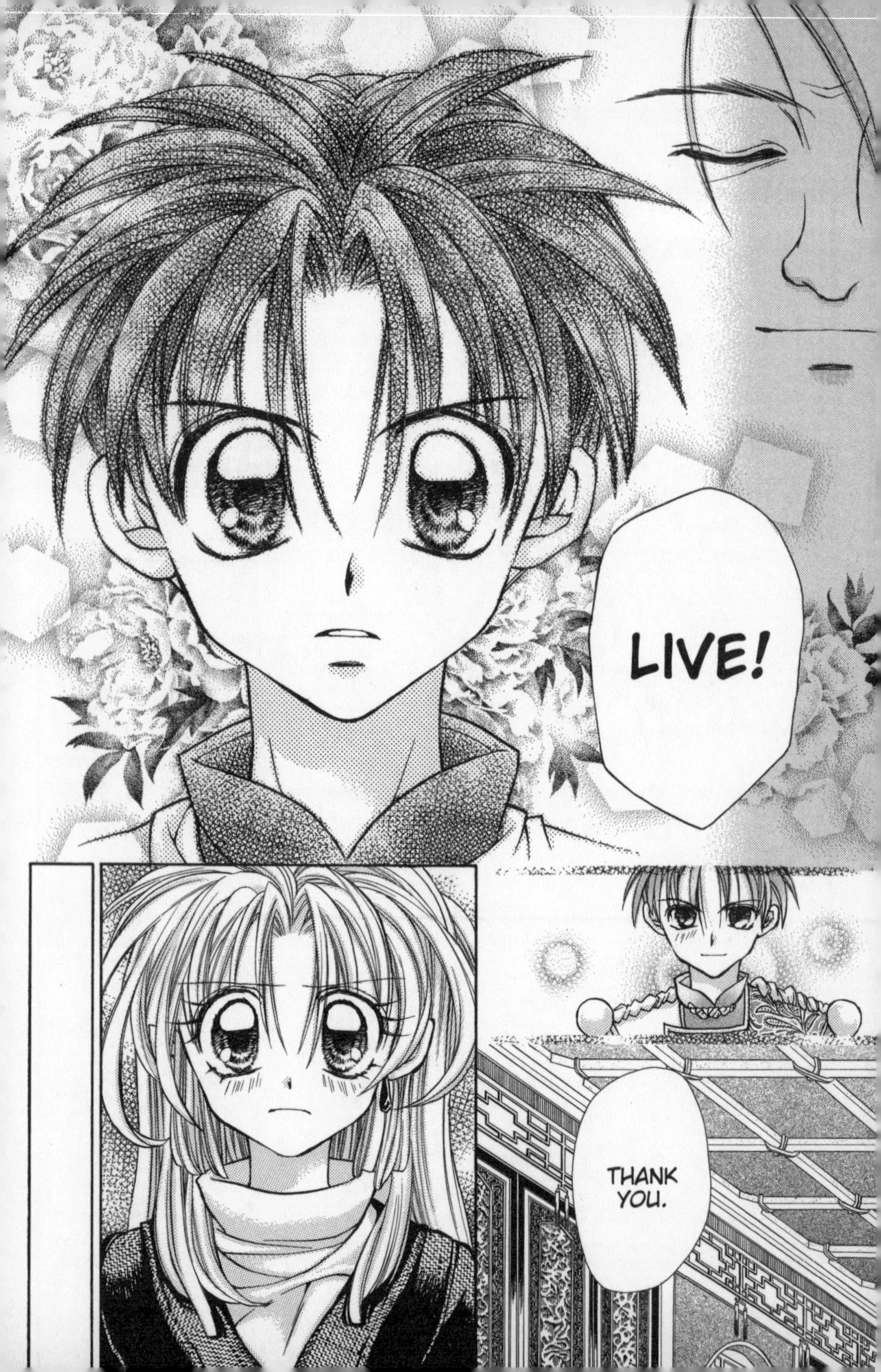
LIVE!
THANK YOU.

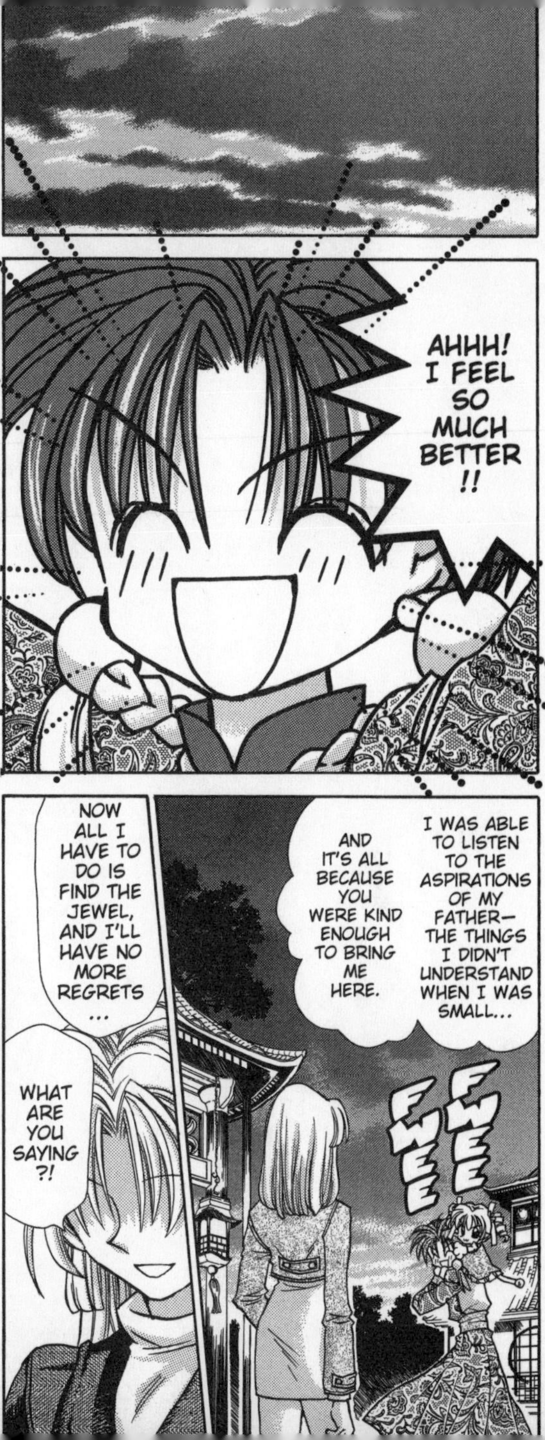
AHHH! I FEEL SO MUCH BETTER !!
I WAS ABLE TO LISTEN TO THE ASPIRATIONS OF MY FATHER— THE THINGS I DIDN'T UNDERSTAND WHEN I WAS SMALL...
AND IT'S ALL BECAUSE YOU WERE KIND ENOUGH TO BRING ME HERE.
NOW ALL I HAVE TO DO IS FIND THE JEWEL, AND I'LL HAVE NO MORE REGRETS ...
WHAT ARE YOU SAYING ?!
FWEE
FWEE

THIS TOTALLY LAID-BACK GUY IS THE KING?!

KING OF EARTH NATION

KING

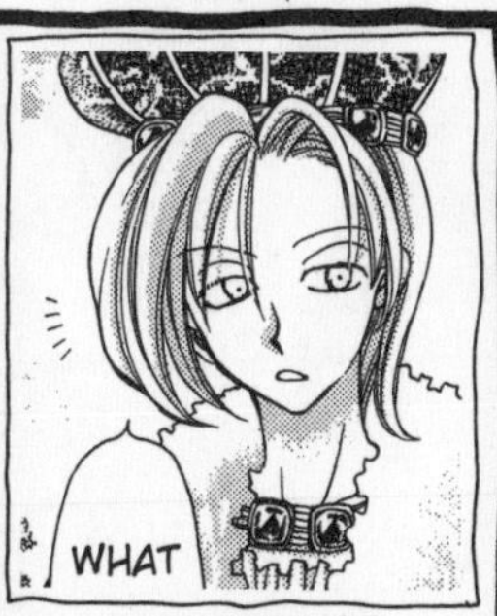
WHAT

BORN APRIL 28, TAURUS, BLOOD-TYPE O

HE'S AN ALBINO WITH WHITE HAIR, EYES, AND SKIN. HE IS THE KING OF EARTH, AND HE LOVES CHOCOLA VERY MUCH. HE'S ACTUALLY 40 YEARS OLD, BUT THROUGH SURGERY HE MAINTAINS AN ETERNALLY YOUTHFUL APPEARANCE.

A SHADOW LEAD CHARACTER?! ♥ AN ANDROID WHO LOVES THE KING.

CHOCOLA

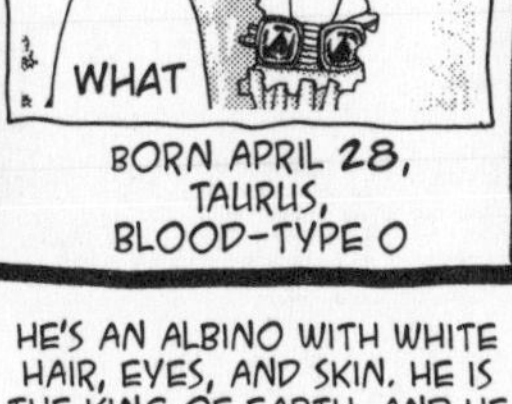

PHOTO TAKEN ON DEC. 24...

SHE'S THE MASCOT OF THIS MANGA. THE TRUTH IS THAT SHE MIGHT BE THE MOST POPULAR WITH THE FANS. SHE CONSIDERS HERSELF THE KING'S LOVER, AND CALLS HIM "KING." SHE OFTEN SAYS "NYAH" AT THE END OF HER SENTENCES. ♪

REAL NAME: CHOCORINA MIZO ♪

SHE LOVES CHOCOLATE. (SHE NEEDS FIVE BARS A DAY TO POWER HER.) ♥

SHE ALSO GLOMPS ON KYOKO-CHAN A LOT.

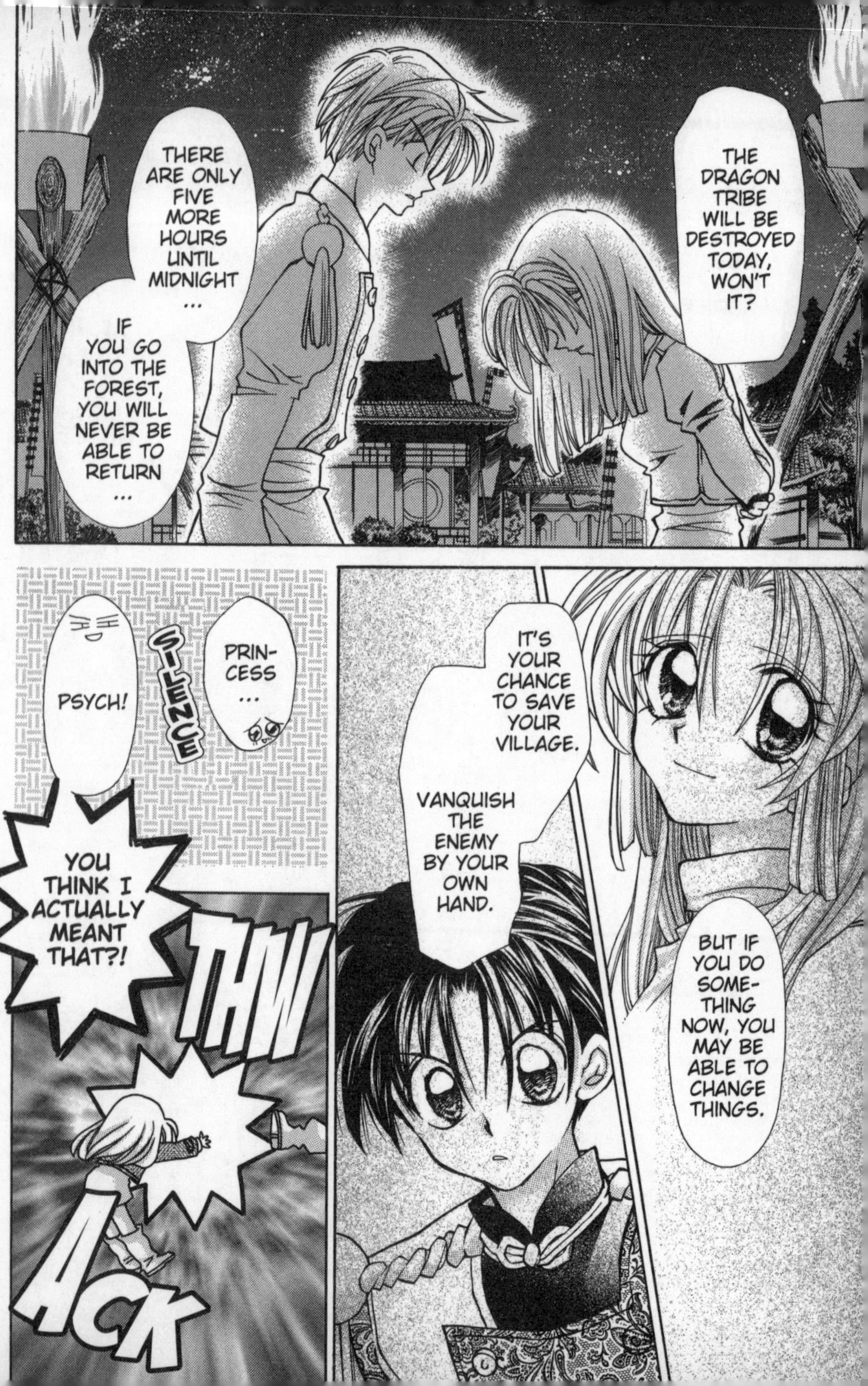
THE DRAGON TRIBE WILL BE DESTROYED TODAY, WON'T IT?
THERE ARE ONLY FIVE MORE HOURS UNTIL MIDNIGHT ...
IF YOU GO INTO THE FOREST, YOU WILL NEVER BE ABLE TO RETURN ...
IT'S YOUR CHANCE TO SAVE YOUR VILLAGE.
VANQUISH THE ENEMY BY YOUR OWN HAND.
BUT IF YOU DO SOMETHING NOW, YOU MAY BE ABLE TO CHANGE THINGS.
PRINCESS ...
SILENCE
PSYCH!
YOU THINK I ACTUALLY MEANT THAT?!
THWACK

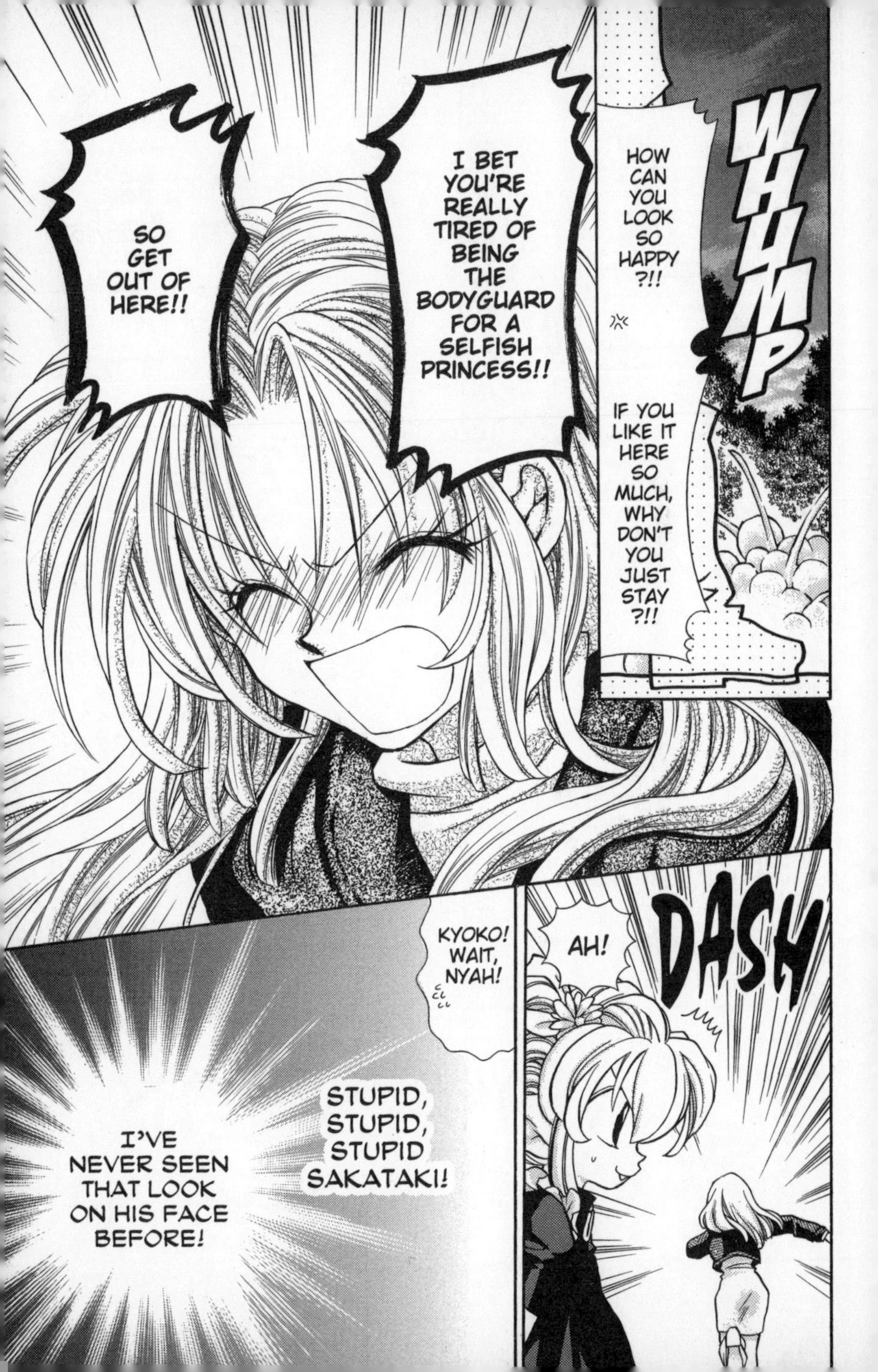
HOW CAN YOU LOOK SO HAPPY?!!
WHUMP
IF YOU LIKE IT HERE SO MUCH, WHY DON'T YOU JUST STAY?!!
I BET YOU'RE REALLY TIRED OF BEING THE BODYGUARD FOR A SELFISH PRINCESS!!
SO GET OUT OF HERE!!
DASH
AH!
KYOKO! WAIT, NYAH!
STUPID, STUPID, STUPID SAKATAKI!
I'VE NEVER SEEN THAT LOOK ON HIS FACE BEFORE!

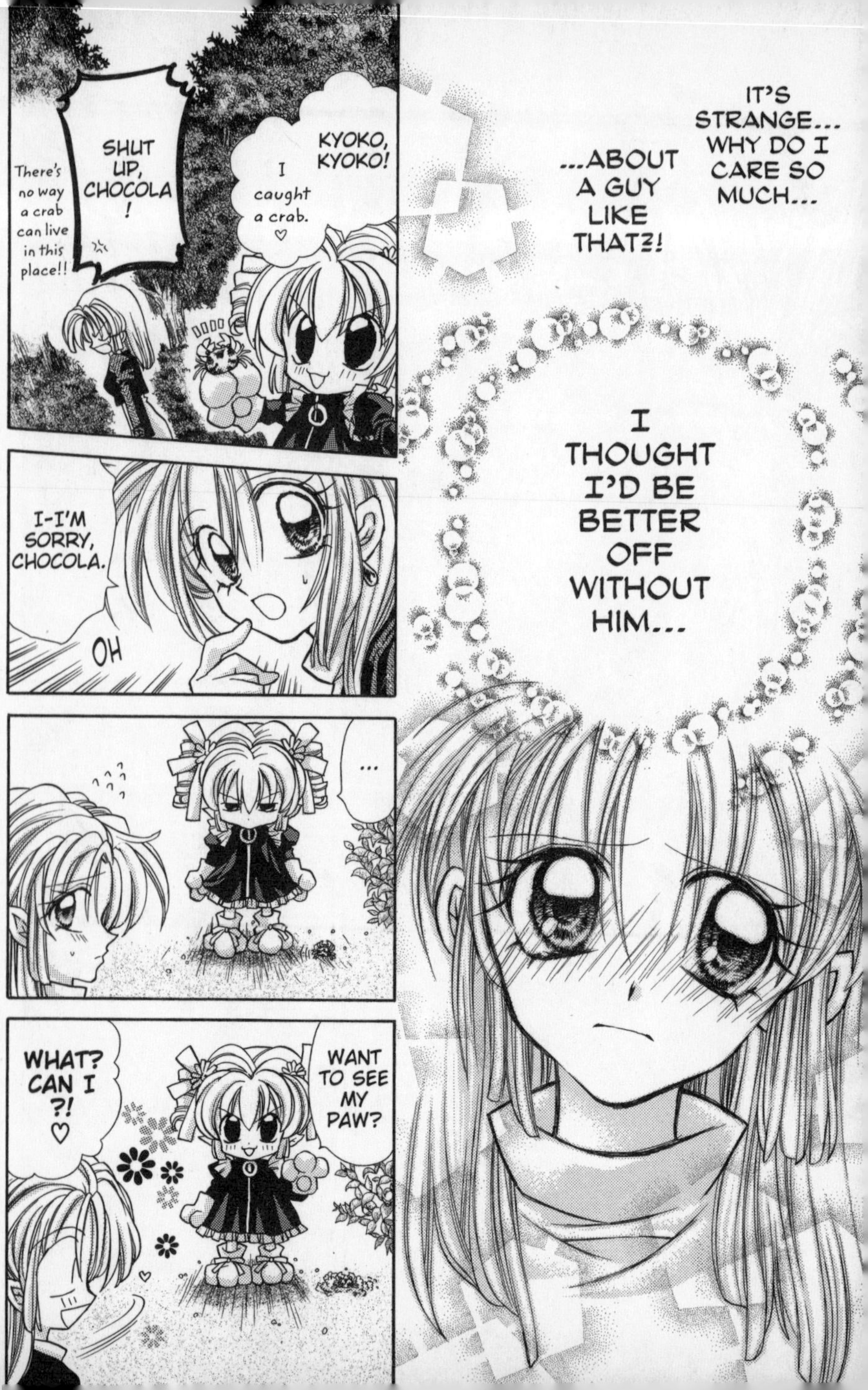
IT'S STRANGE... WHY DO I CARE SO MUCH...
...ABOUT A GUY LIKE THAT?!
I THOUGHT I'D BE BETTER OFF WITHOUT HIM...
KYOKO, KYOKO!
I caught a crab. ♡
SHUT UP, CHOCOLA!
There's no way a crab can live in this place!!
I-I'M SORRY, CHOCOLA.
OH
...
WANT TO SEE MY PAW?
WHAT? CAN I ?! ♡

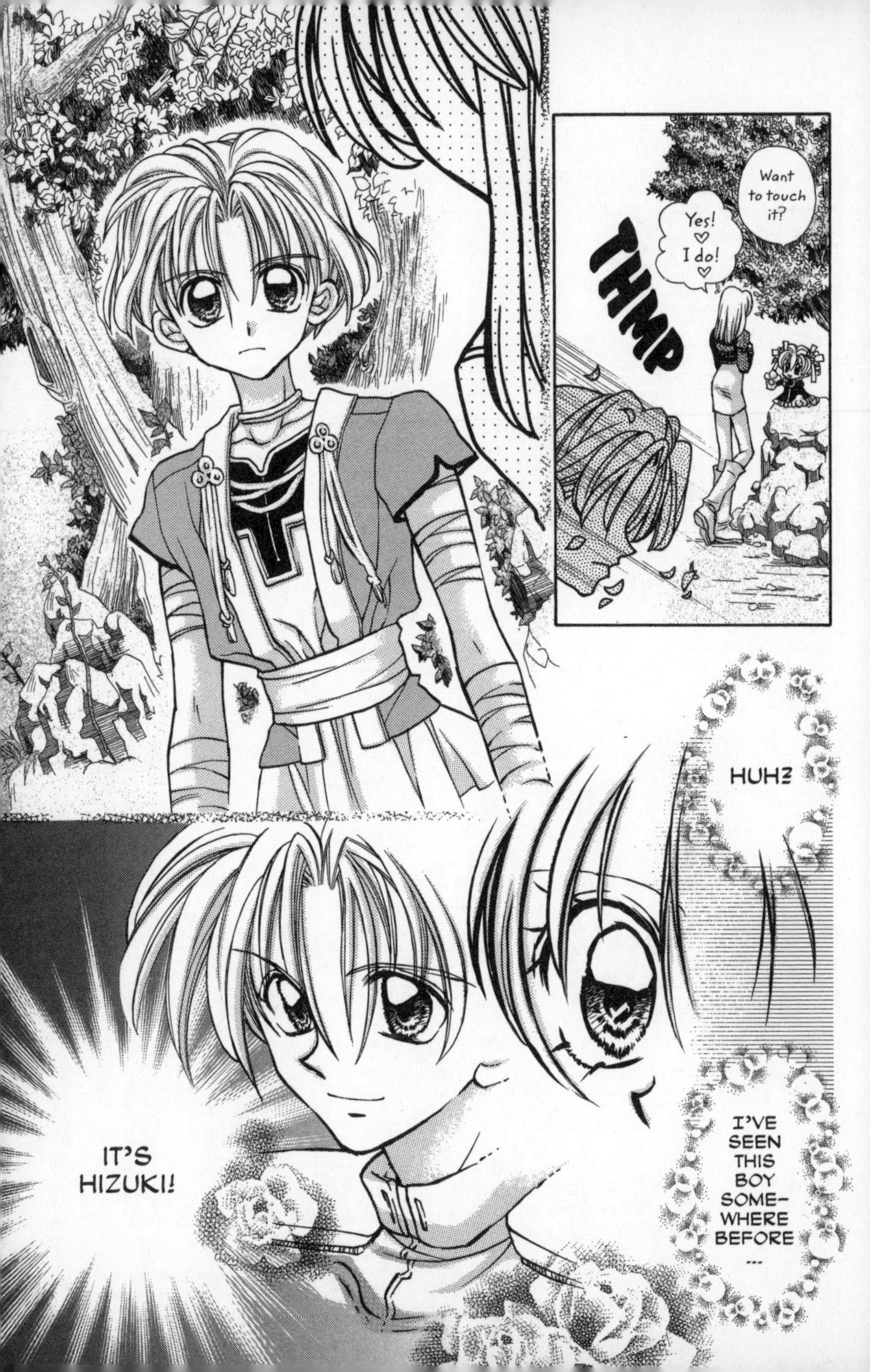
Want to touch it?
Yes! ♡ I do! ♡
THUMP
HUH?
I'VE SEEN THIS BOY SOME-WHERE BEFORE ...
IT'S HIZUKI!

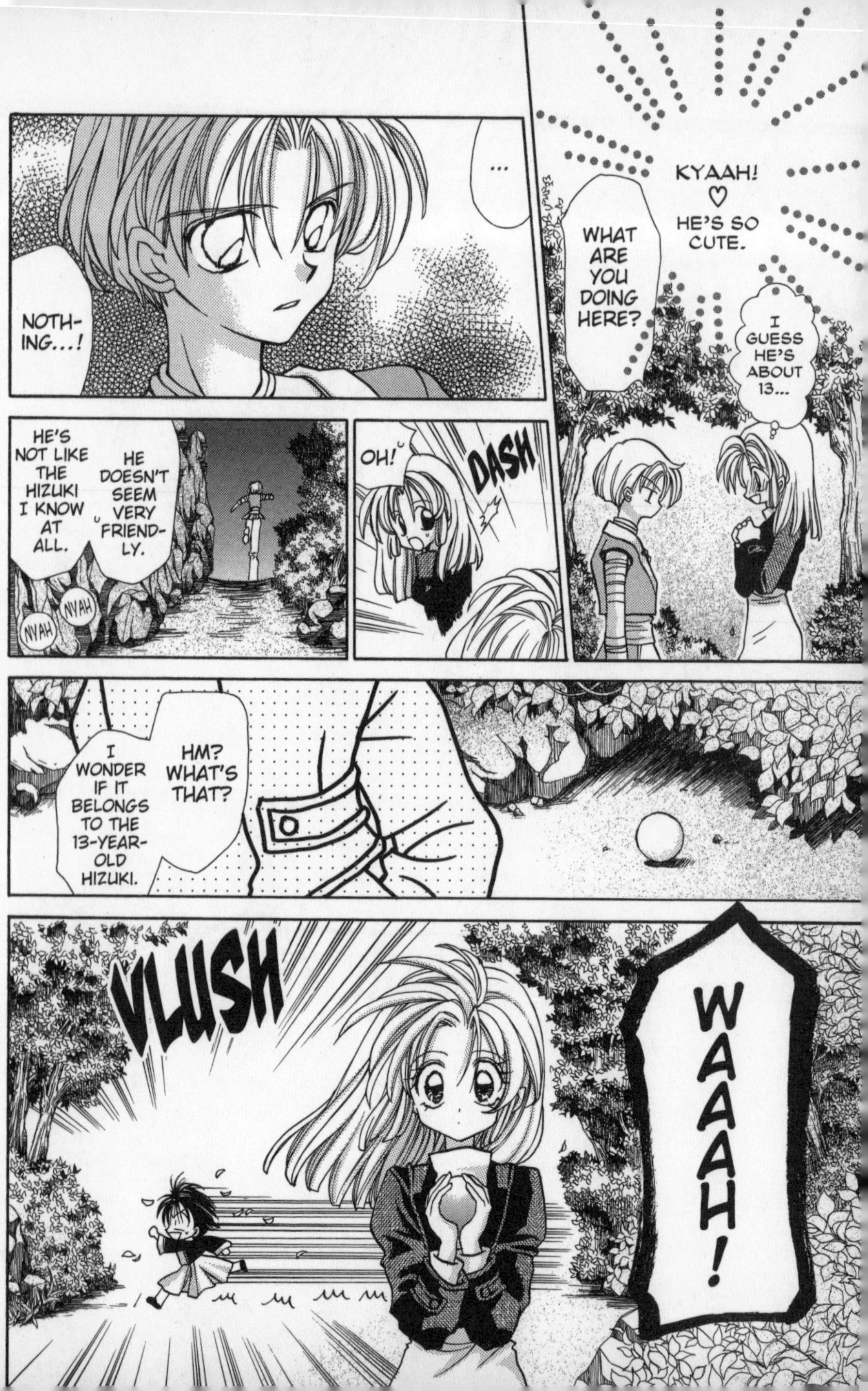
KYAAH! ♡ HE'S SO CUTE.
WHAT ARE YOU DOING HERE?
I GUESS HE'S ABOUT 13...
...
NOTHING...!
OH!
DASH
HE DOESN'T SEEM VERY FRIENDLY.
HE'S NOT LIKE THE HIZUKI I KNOW AT ALL.
NVAH
NVAH
HM? WHAT'S THAT?
I WONDER IF IT BELONGS TO THE 13-YEAR-OLD HIZUKI.
WAAAH!
VLUSH

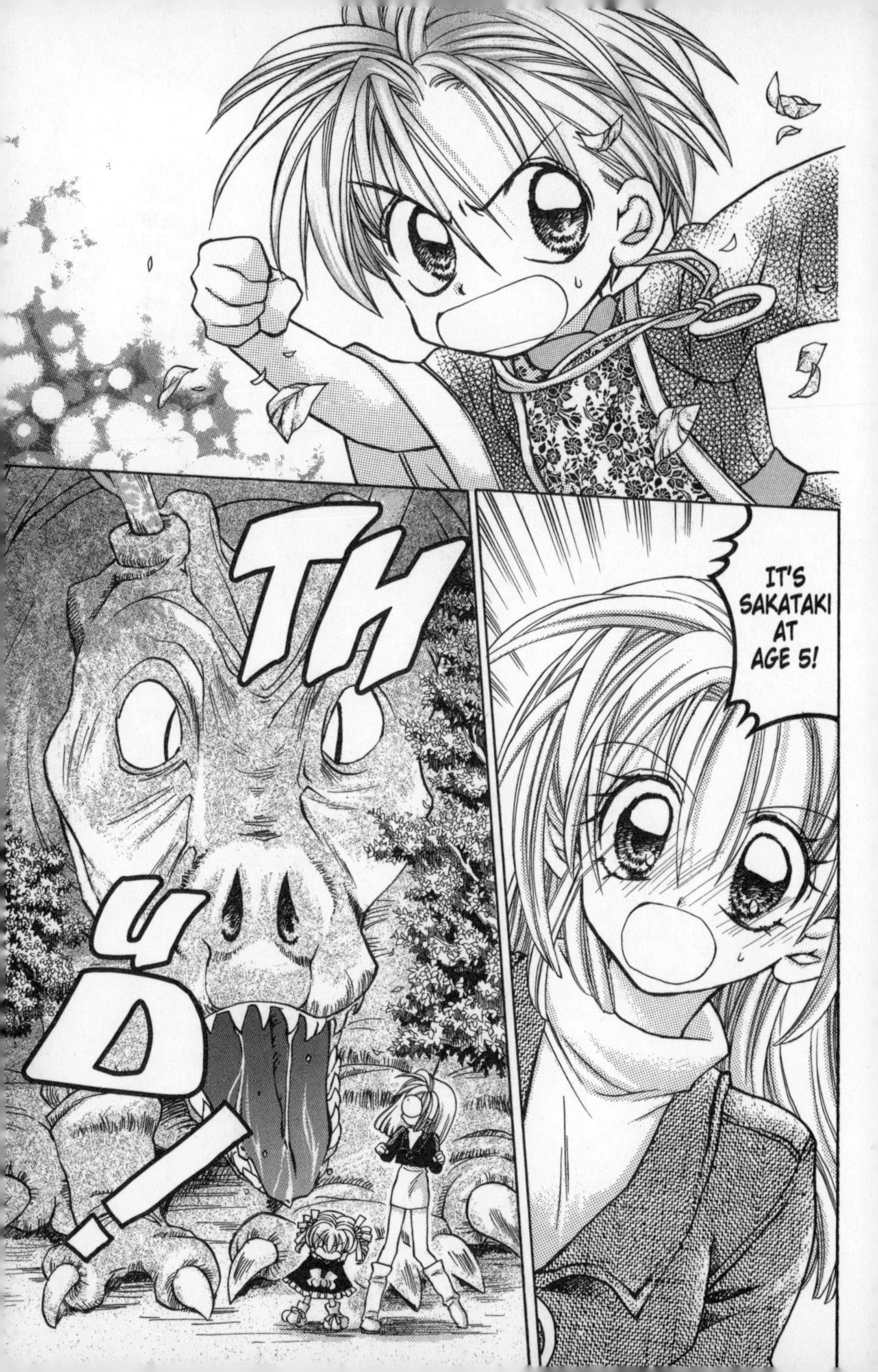
IT'S SAKATAKI AT AGE 5!
THUD!

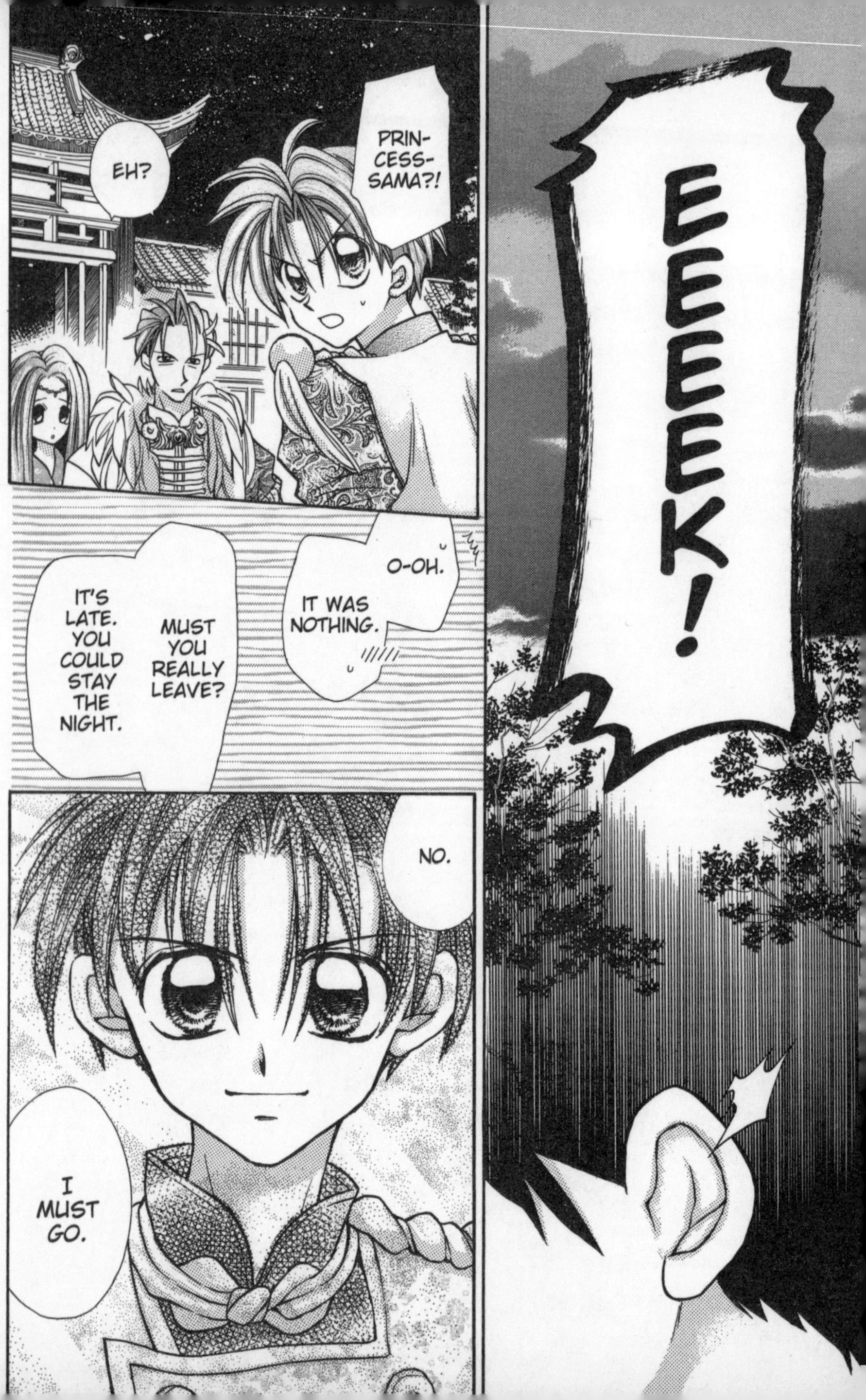
EEEEK!
PRIN-CESS-SAMA?!
EH?
O-OH.
IT WAS NOTHING.
MUST YOU REALLY LEAVE?
IT'S LATE. YOU COULD STAY THE NIGHT.
NO.
I MUST GO.

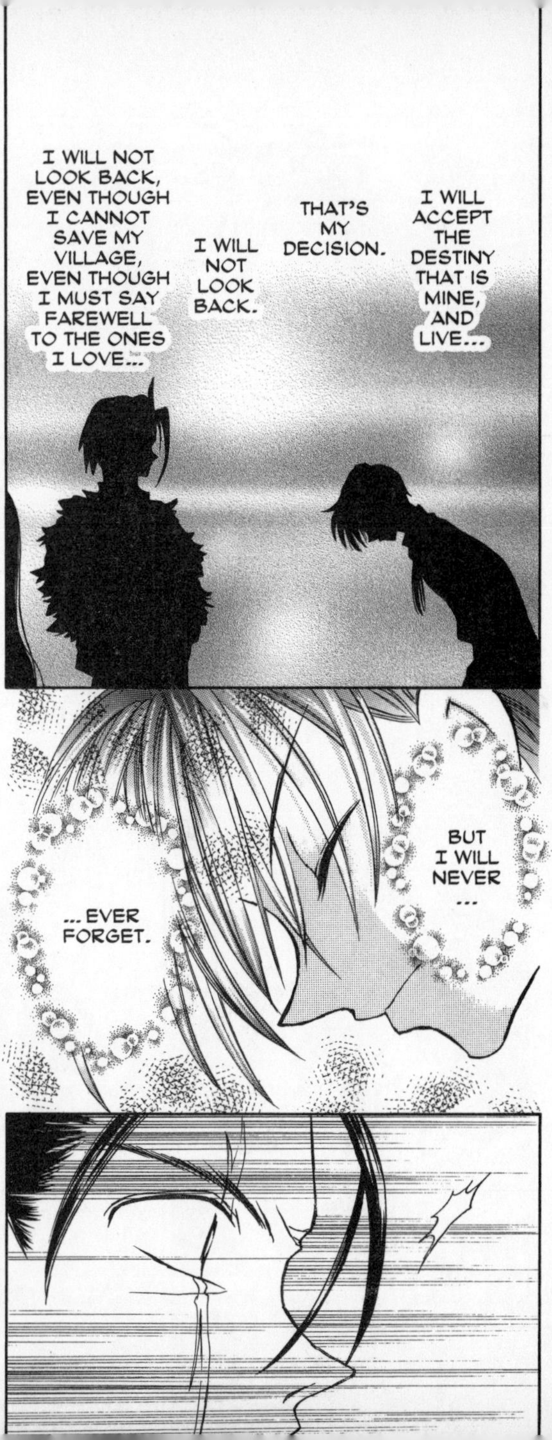
I WILL ACCEPT THE DESTINY THAT IS MINE, AND LIVE...
THAT'S MY DECISION.
I WILL NOT LOOK BACK.
I WILL NOT LOOK BACK, EVEN THOUGH I CANNOT SAVE MY VILLAGE, EVEN THOUGH I MUST SAY FAREWELL TO THE ONES I LOVE...
BUT I WILL NEVER ...
... EVER FORGET.

APPEARING THEN DISAPPEARING?! A KICK-BUTT GANG LEADER! ☆

THE DESTROYERS ☆

WITZIG, THE LEADER

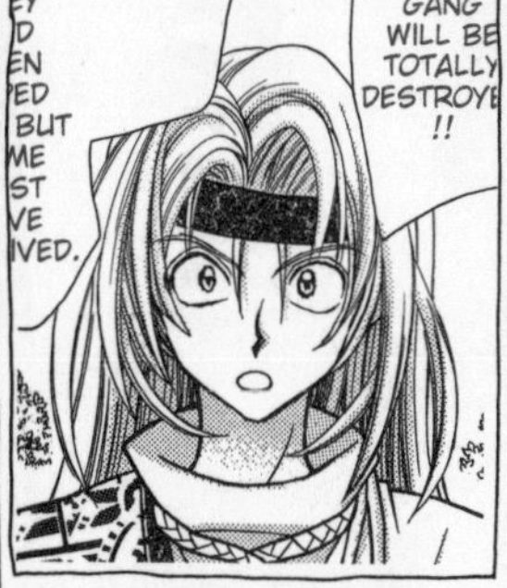

BORN JANUARY 18, CAPRICORN, BLOOD-TYPE O

AT FIRST, I WAS JUST DOODLING AND DIDN'T HAVE ANYTHING IN MIND WHEN I DREW THE THIEVES, BUT NOW I REALLY, REALLY LIKE THEM. THE GANG IS MADE UP OF 46 MEMBERS, INCLUDING WITZIG. THEY HAVE A SAFEHOUSE SURPRISINGLY NEAR THE CASTLE. WITZIG AND GINGA'S RELATIONSHIP IS... ↙

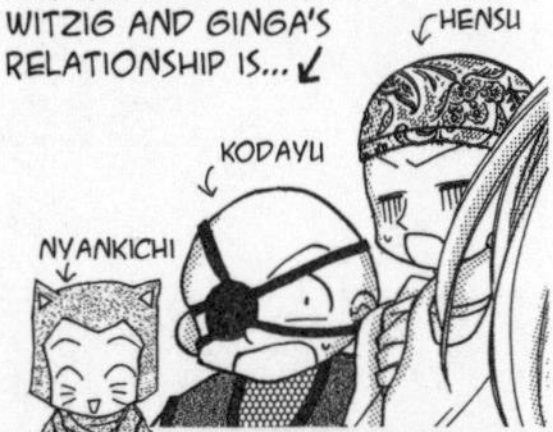
HENSU
KODAYU
NYANKICHI

GINGA SOHBA, SECOND-IN-COMMAND

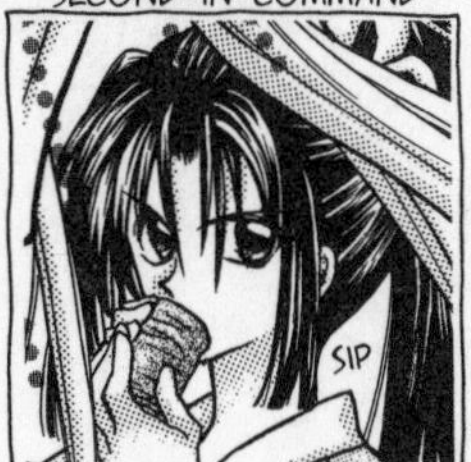
SIP

BORN JUNE 3, GEMINI, BLOOD-TYPE B

↗ ...REVEALED IN THE NEXT VOLUME, I THINK. (IT'S ALREADY BEEN RUN IN THE MAGAZINE.) THERE'S BEEN A RAGING WAR OF WORDS BETWEEN FANS AS TO GINGA'S GENDER, BUT HE'S A GUY.

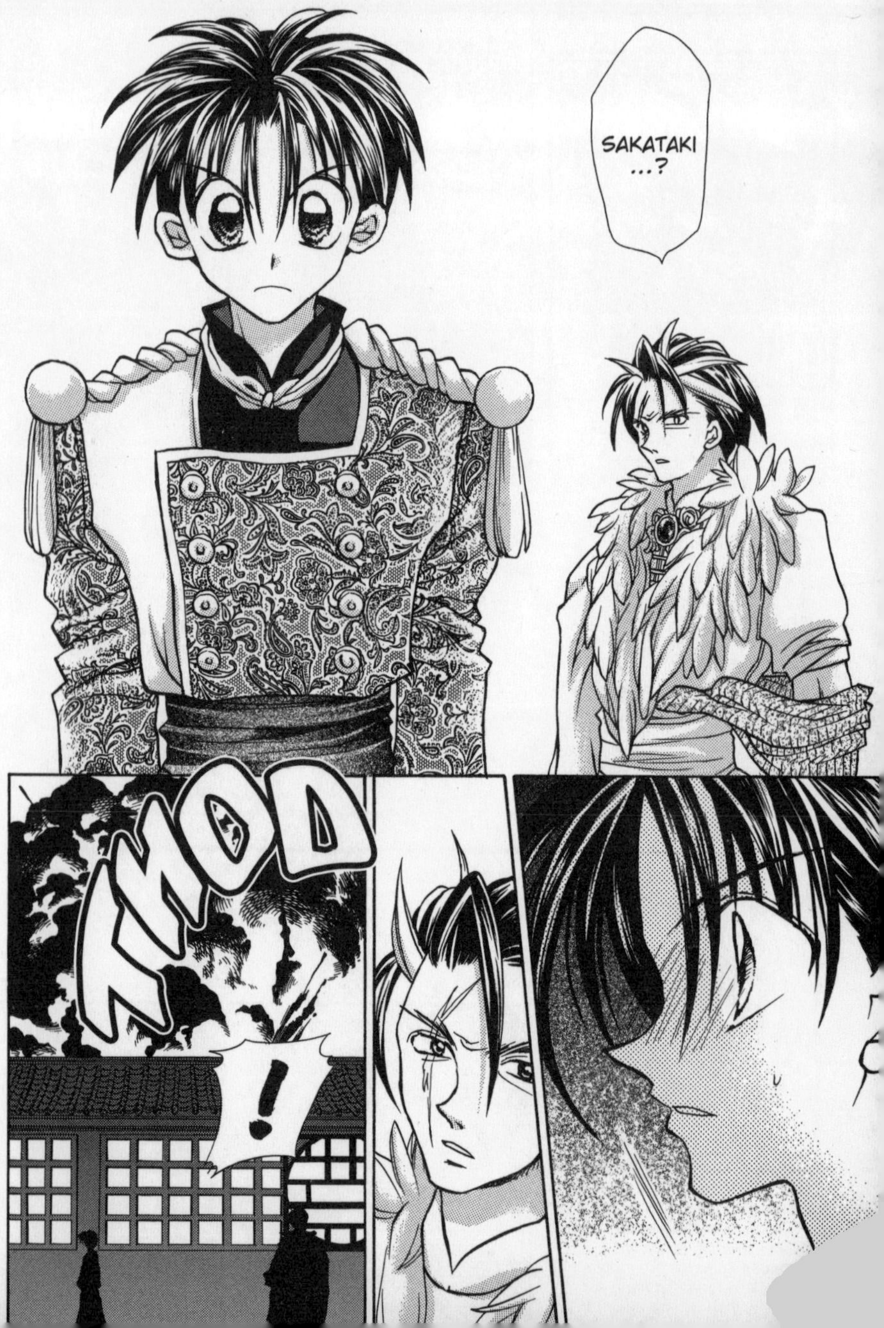
SAKATAKI ...?
THOD
!

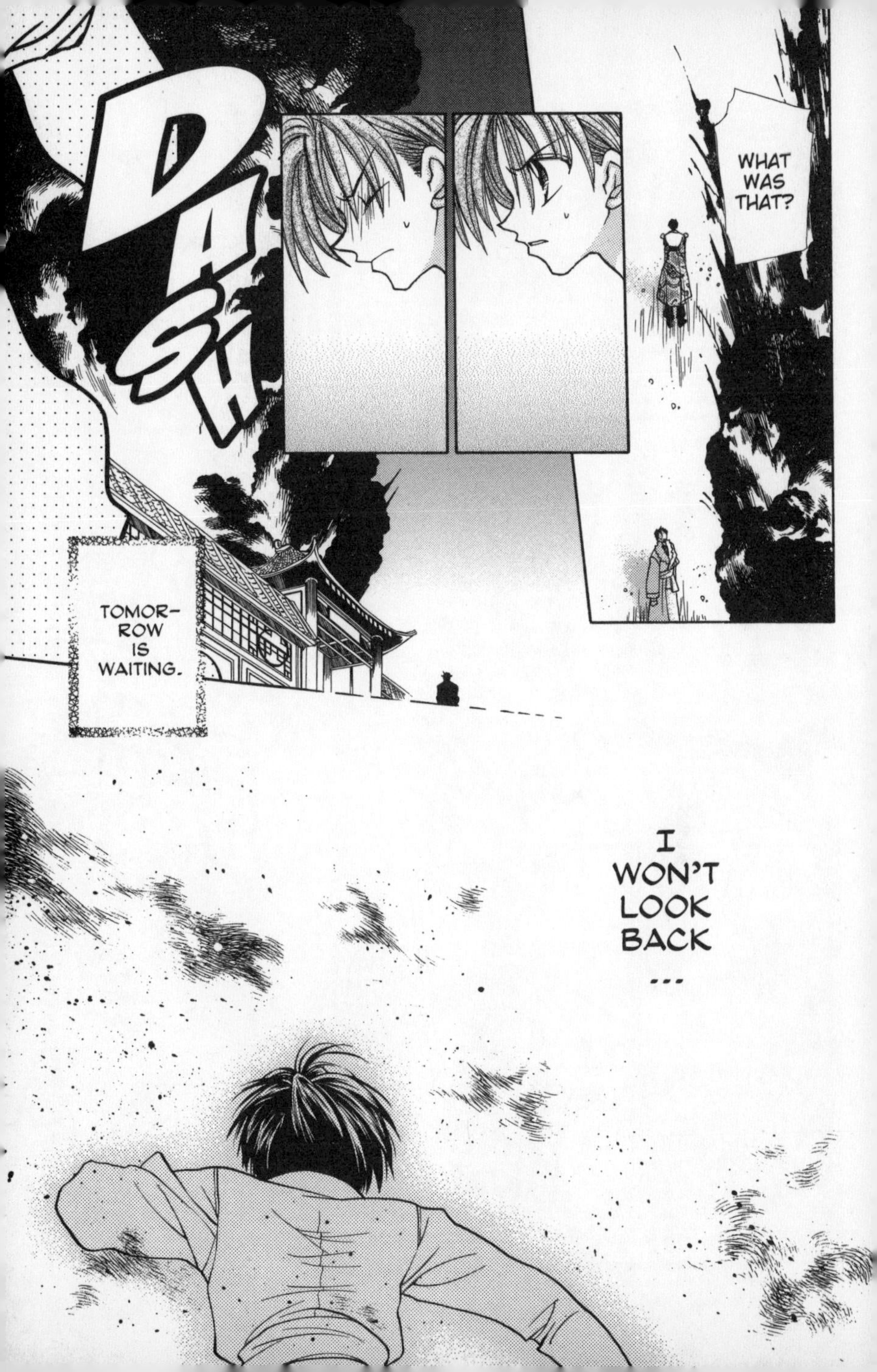
WHAT WAS THAT?
DASH
TOMOR-ROW IS WAITING.
I WON'T LOOK BACK ...

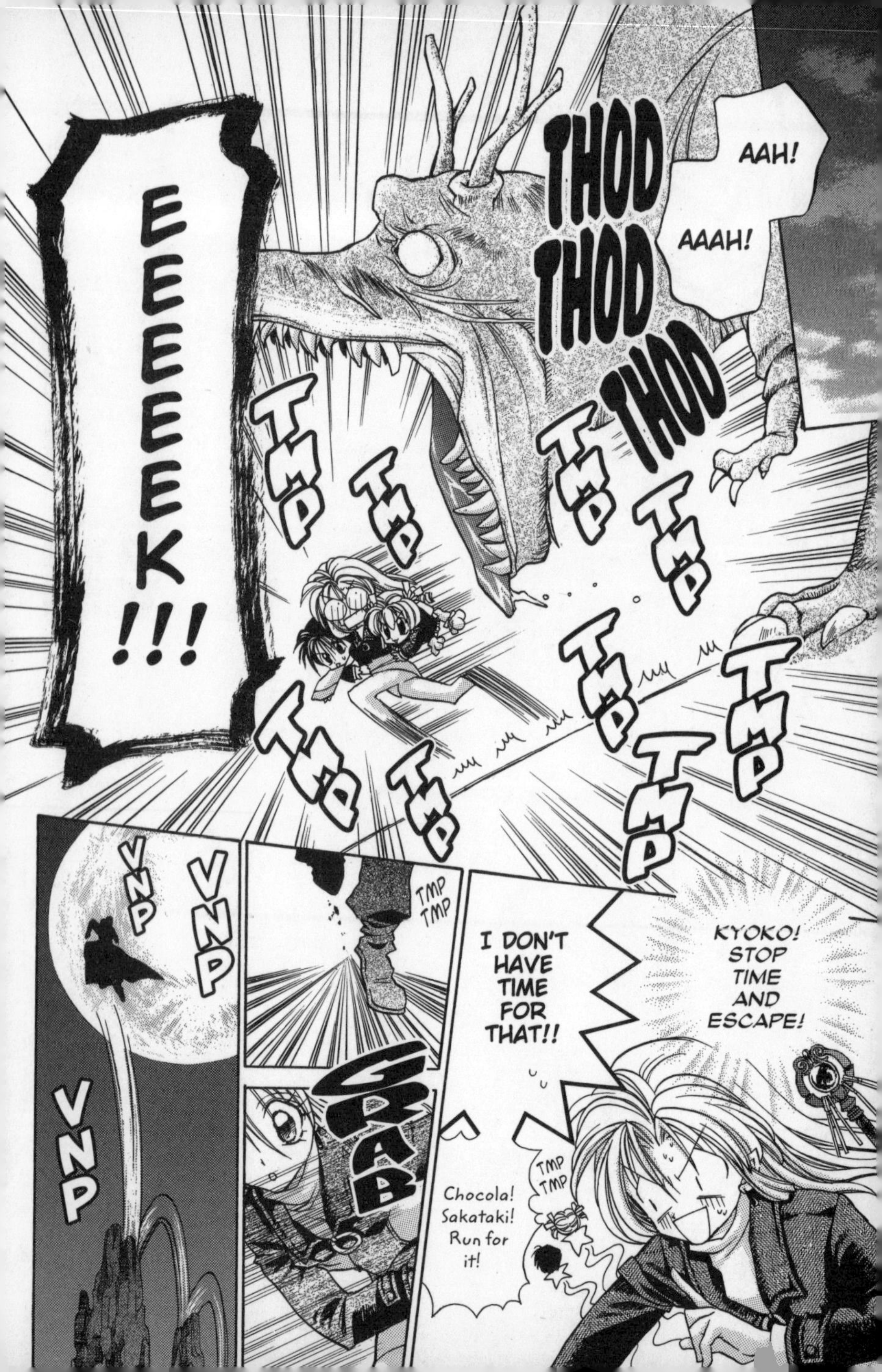
AAH!
AAAH!
THOD
THOD
THOD
THOD
TMP
TMP
TMP
TMP
TMP
TMP
TMP
TMP
TMP
EEEEEK!!!
KYOKO! STOP TIME AND ESCAPE!
I DON'T HAVE TIME FOR THAT!!
TMP TMP
Chocola! Sakataki! Run for it!
TMP TMP
GRAB
VNP
VNP
VNP

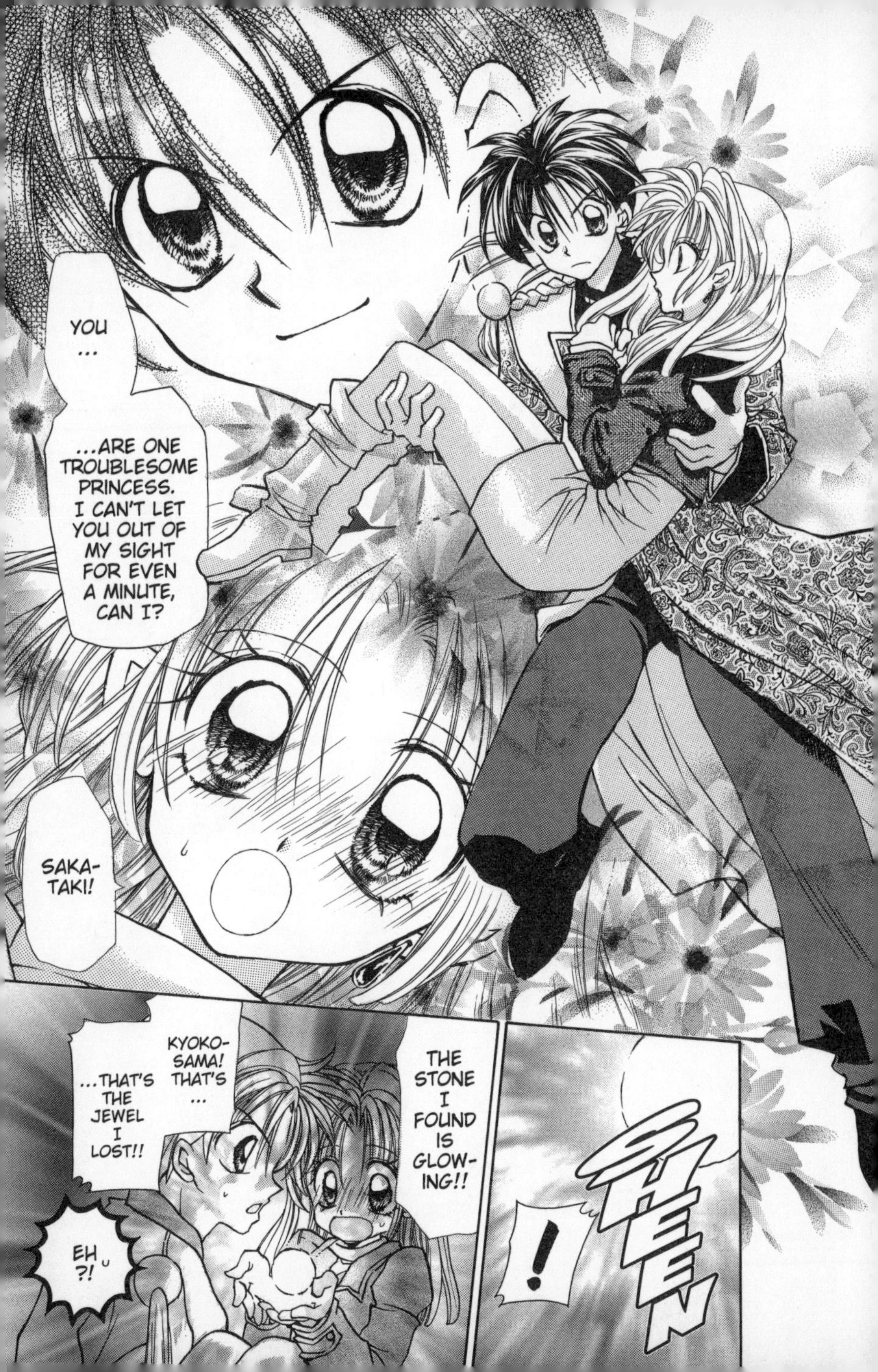
YOU ...
...ARE ONE TROUBLESOME PRINCESS. I CAN'T LET YOU OUT OF MY SIGHT FOR EVEN A MINUTE, CAN I?
SAKA-TAKI!
SHEEN
!
THE STONE I FOUND IS GLOWING!!
KYOKO-SAMA! THAT'S ...
...THAT'S THE JEWEL I LOST!!
EH ?!

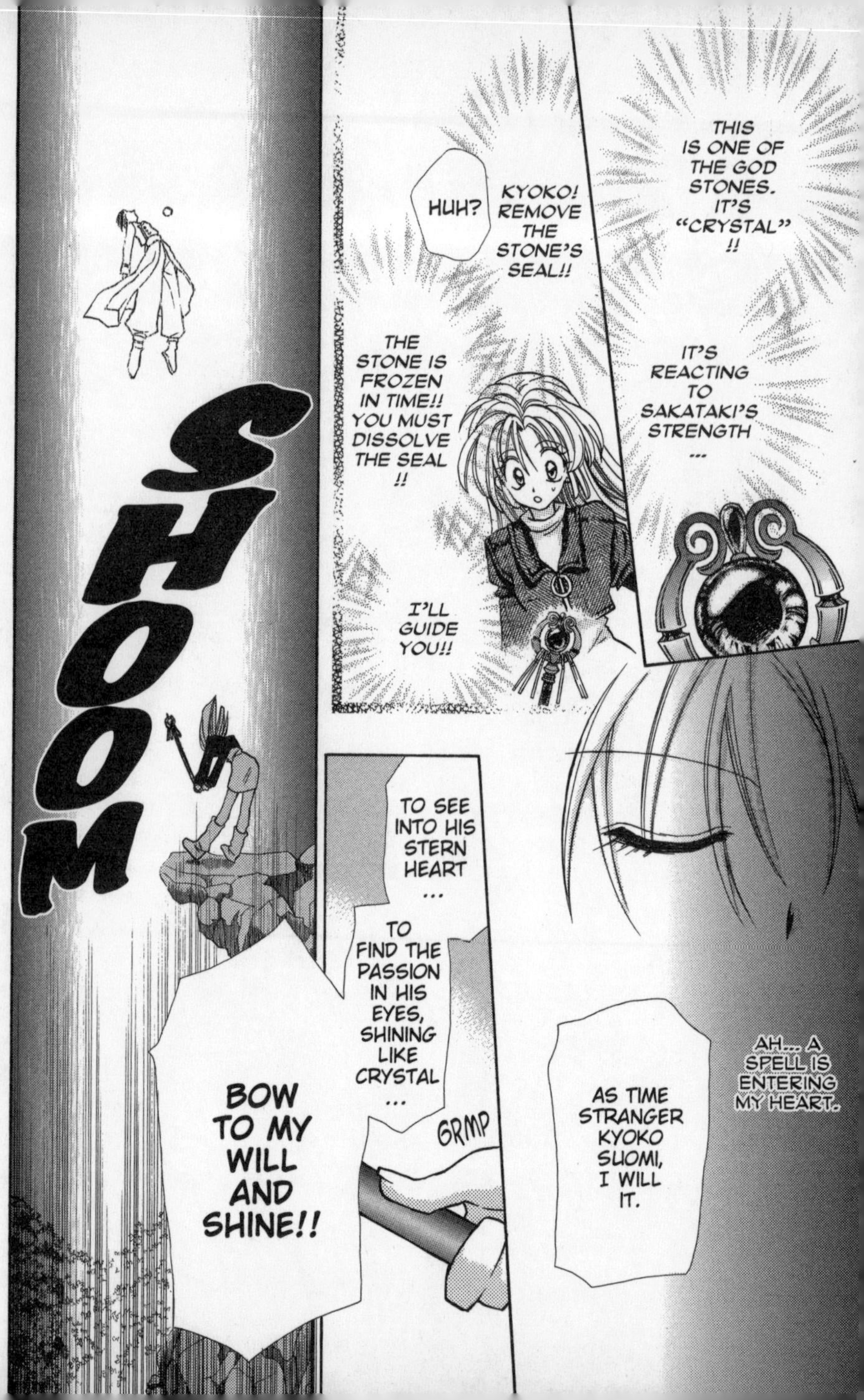
THIS IS ONE OF THE GOD STONES. IT'S "CRYSTAL" !!
IT'S REACTING TO SAKATAKI'S STRENGTH ...
KYOKO! REMOVE THE STONE'S SEAL!!
HUH?
THE STONE IS FROZEN IN TIME!! YOU MUST DISSOLVE THE SEAL !!
I'LL GUIDE YOU!!
AH... A SPELL IS ENTERING MY HEART.
AS TIME STRANGER KYOKO SUOMI, I WILL IT.
TO SEE INTO HIS STERN HEART ...
TO FIND THE PASSION IN HIS EYES, SHINING LIKE CRYSTAL ...
GRMP
SHOOM
BOW TO MY WILL AND SHINE!!

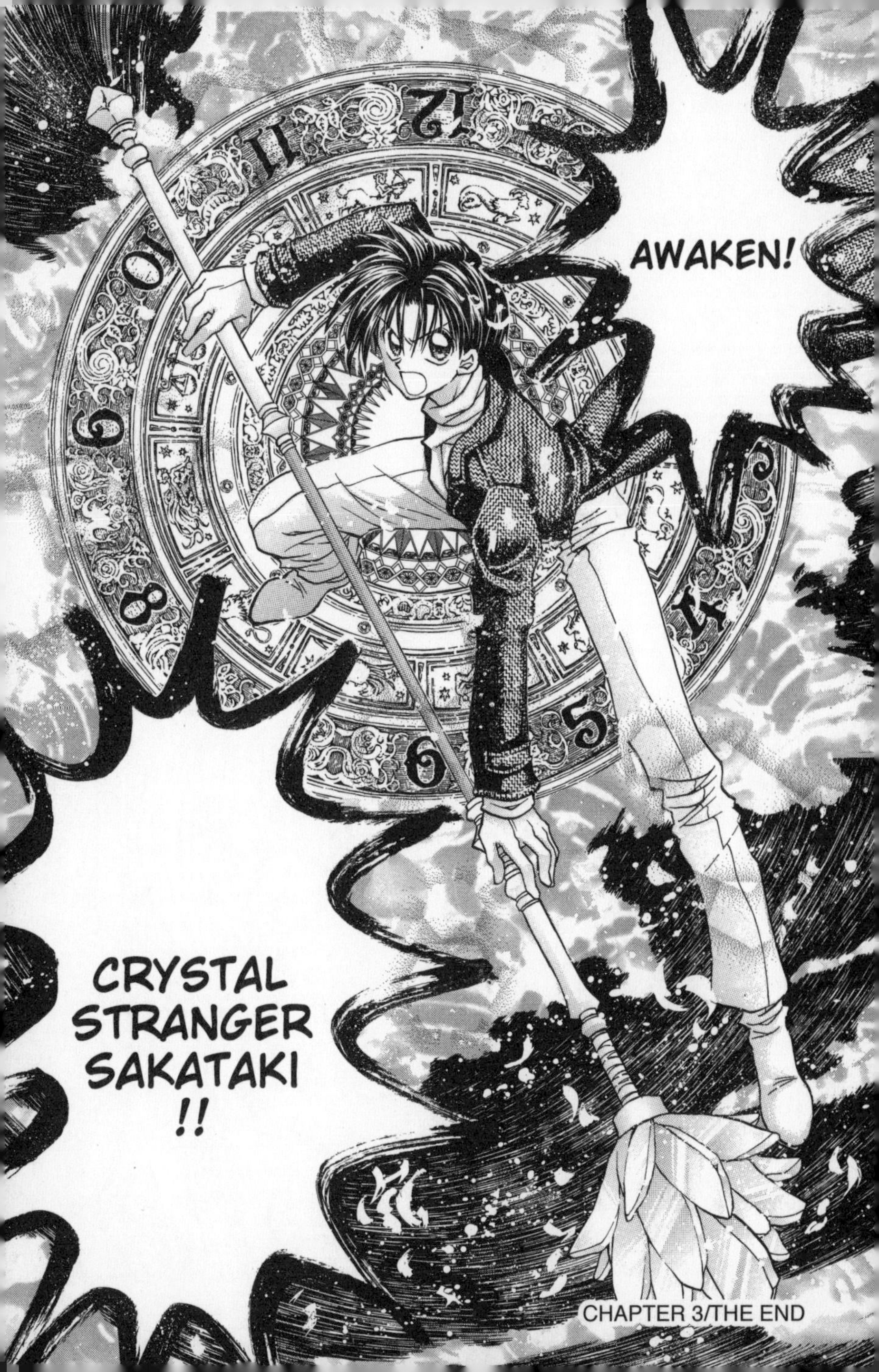
AWAKEN!
CRYSTAL STRANGER SAKATAKI !!
CHAPTER 3/THE END

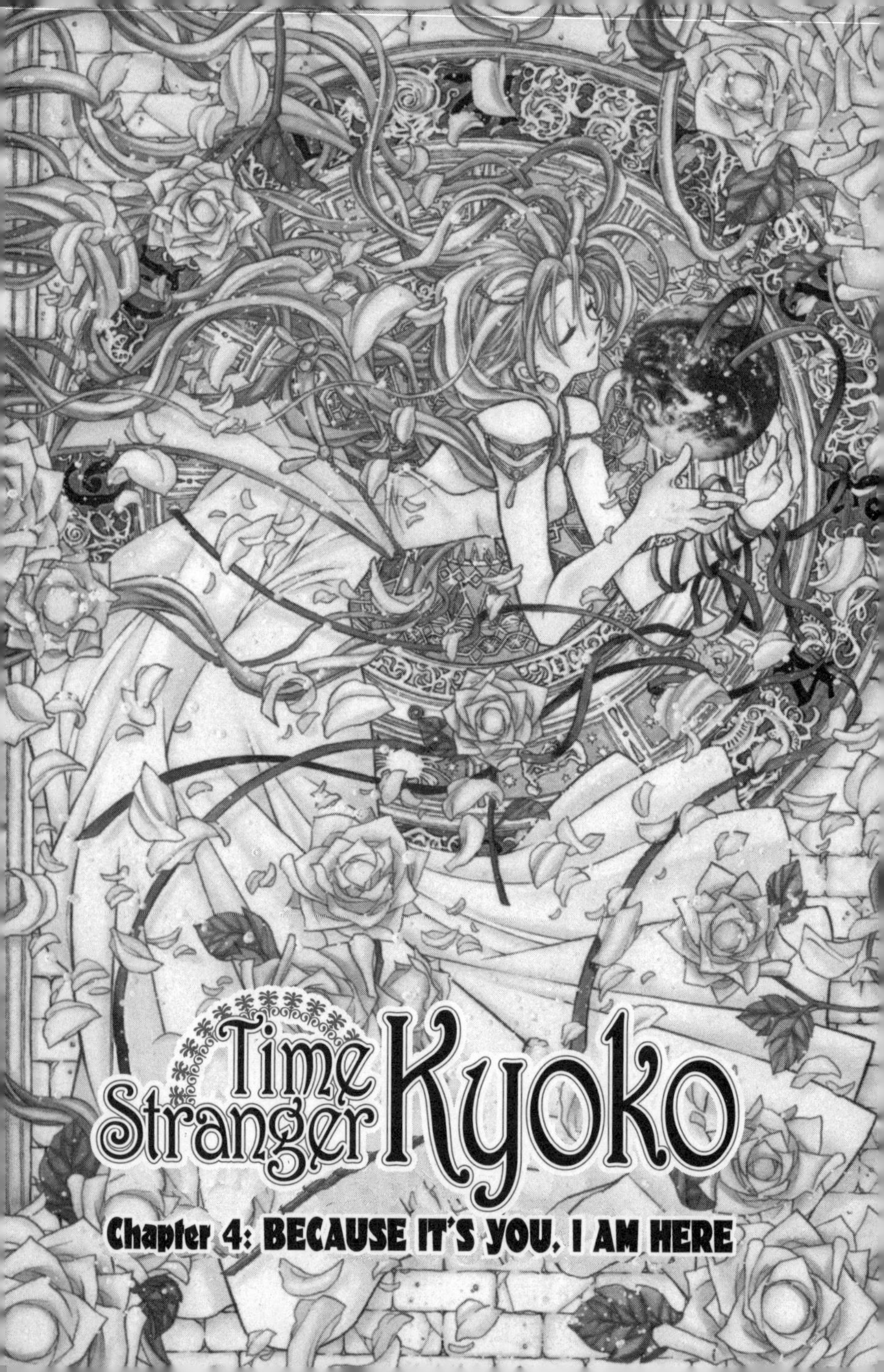
Time Stranger Kyoko
Chapter 4: BECAUSE IT'S YOU, I AM HERE

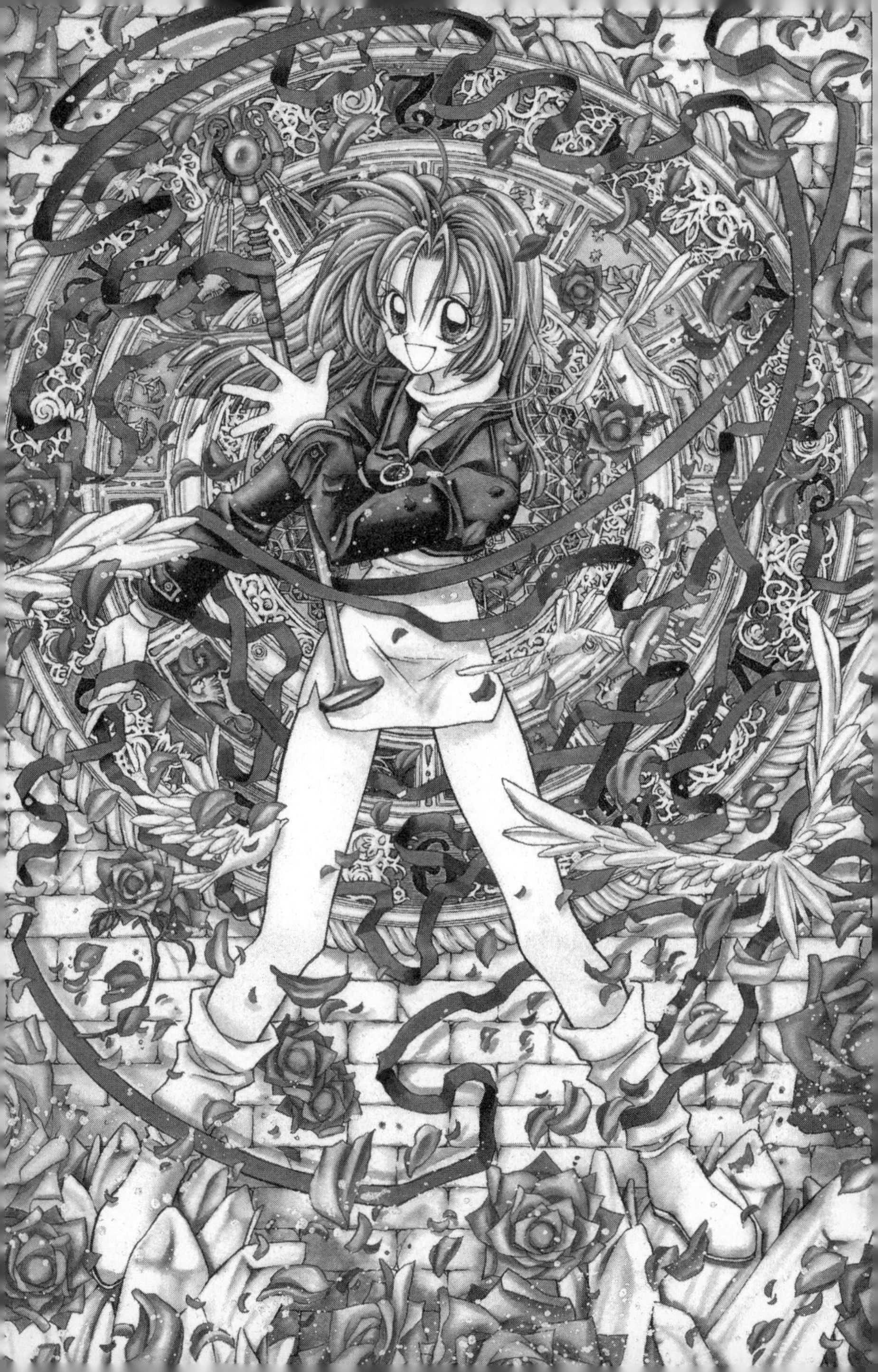

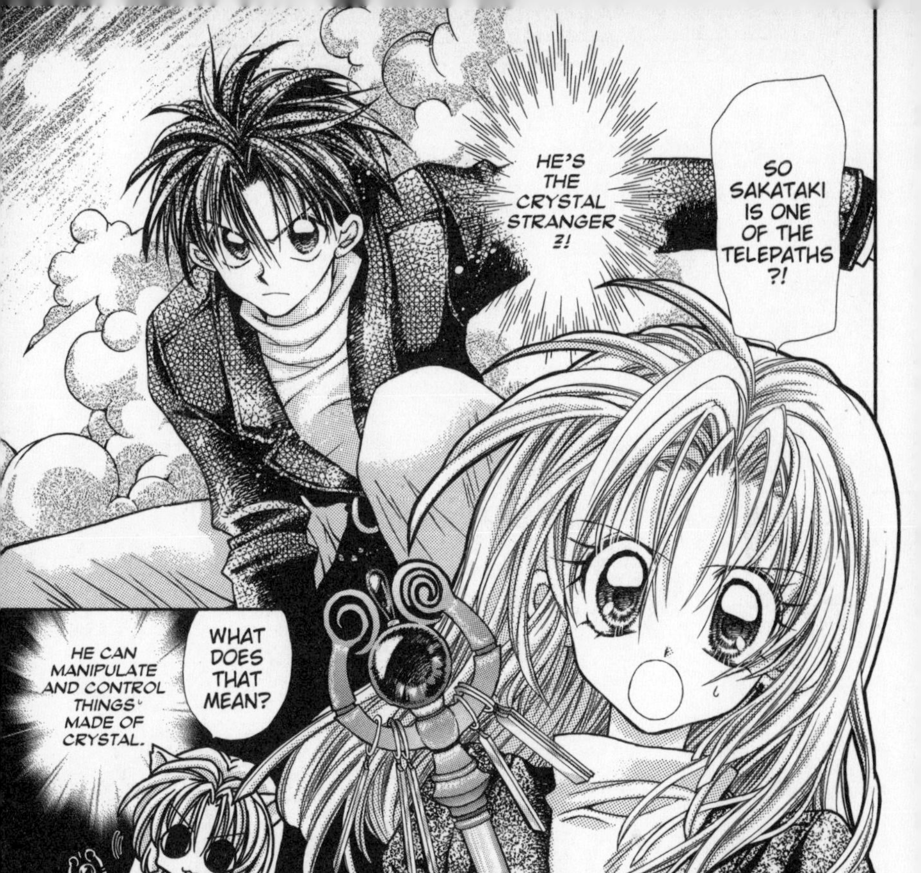
SO SAKATAKI IS ONE OF THE TELEPATHS ?!
HE'S THE CRYSTAL STRANGER ?!
WHAT DOES THAT MEAN?
HE CAN MANIPULATE AND CONTROL THINGS MADE OF CRYSTAL.

CHAPTER 4: BECAUSE IT'S YOU, I AM HERE (LEAD-IN) IT'S ALL WITHIN THE BONDS OF TIME!

THE RESPONSE TO THE CHAPTER TITLE ILLUSTRATION WAS REALLY PHENOMENAL. IT WAS REALLY DIFFICULT TO DRAW TOO. THE PRELIMINARY SKETCH WAS FINISHED RELATIVELY QUICKLY, BUT IT TOOK TEN HOURS PER PAGE (X 3 PAGES) TO INK IT... (I TRACED THE CLOCKS IN THE BACKGROUND FROM RUKACCHI'S DRAWING, BUT THEN I INKED THEM MYSELF, ONE BY ONE). COLORING ALSO TOOK ABOUT EIGHT HOURS PER PAGE. HONESTLY, IT WAS SUPER-DIFFICULT. FOR SOME REASON, I SUDDENLY SAID TO MYSELF ONE DAY, "THERE ARE MANY, MANY PEOPLE WHO DRAW REALLY WELL (BETTER THAN I CAN)." I KNEW MY DRAWINGS WERE NOT VERY POWERFUL, BUT I THOUGHT THAT IF I TRIED REALLY HARD, I COULD IMPROVE. I KNEW IT WOULDN'T HAPPEN OVERNIGHT, THOUGH. THAT BEING THE CASE, I DECIDED TO DRAW A PICTURE SO ELABORATE THAT EVEN THE MOST SKILLED ARTIST WOULD HAVE HAD A DIFFICULT TIME DRAWING IT! (THE PROBLEM IS THAT A MANGAKA DOESN'T REALLY HAVE THAT KIND OF TIME. WHEN IT TOOK ME ABOUT A WEEK TO DRAW THREE PAGES, I GOT YELLED AT ← BY MY EDITOR.) I ACTUALLY WANTED TO SPEND MORE THAN A WEEK DRAWING ONE PAGE. THE HIGHLIGHT (?) OF THIS VOLUME IS THE DRAGONS! IT WAS SO MUCH FUN INKING THEM!! ALSO, THERE WAS THE FIRST MYSTERY SURROUNDING HIZUKI. PERSONALLY, I REALLY LIKED THE PART WHERE CHOCOLA WAS (SEEMINGLY) DEPRESSED AFTER KYOKO TOOK HER ANGER OUT ON HER. THAT SCENE INCREASED CHOCOLA'S POPULARITY. IT WAS A DREAM FOR ME TO DRAW CHOCOLA, SO HER POPULARITY REALLY MADE ME HAPPY.

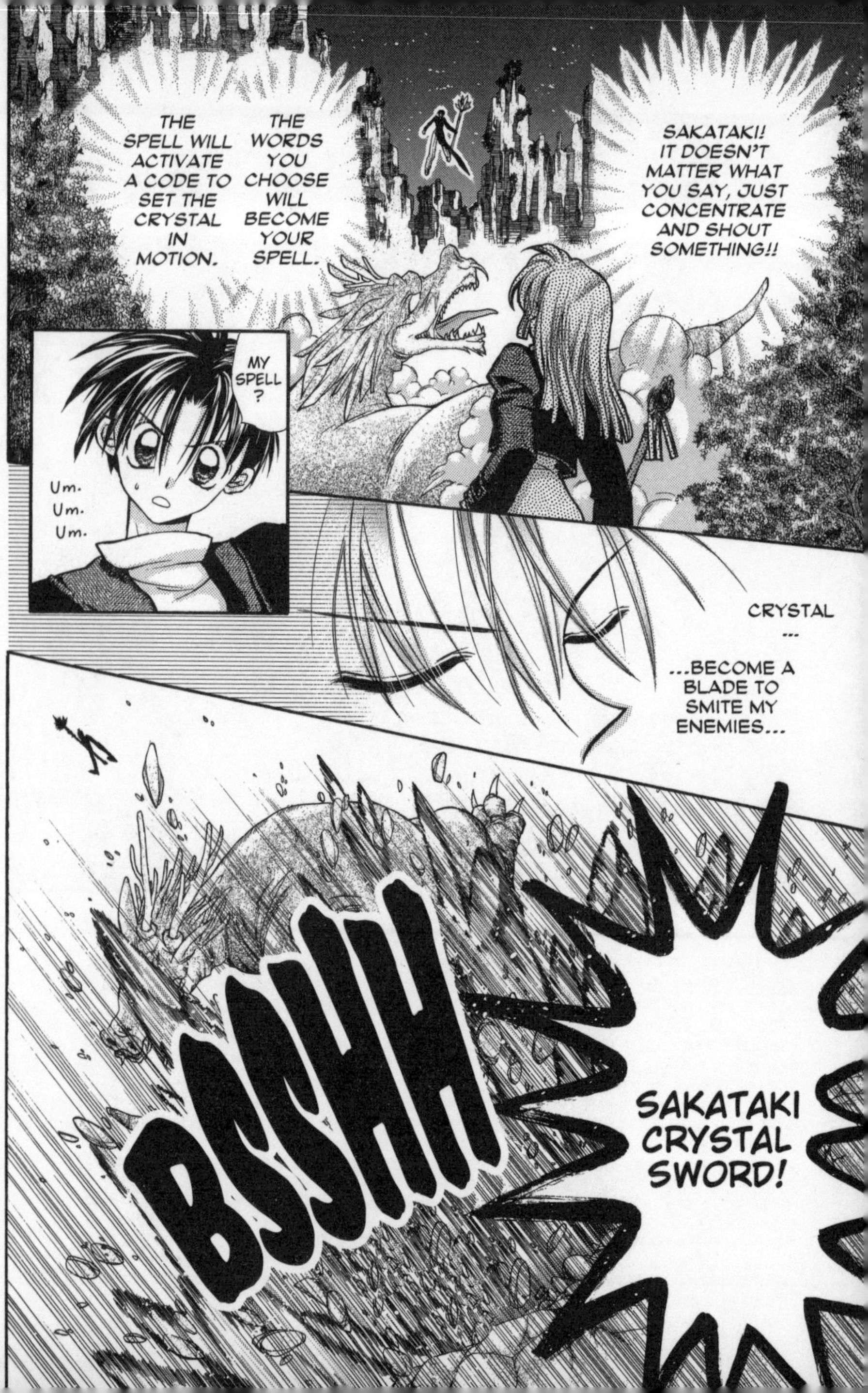
SAKATAKI! IT DOESN'T MATTER WHAT YOU SAY, JUST CONCENTRATE AND SHOUT SOMETHING!!
THE WORDS YOU CHOOSE WILL BECOME YOUR SPELL.
THE SPELL WILL ACTIVATE A CODE TO SET THE CRYSTAL IN MOTION.
MY SPELL?
Um. Um. Um.
CRYSTAL ...
...BECOME A BLADE TO SMITE MY ENEMIES...
SAKATAKI CRYSTAL SWORD!
BSSHH

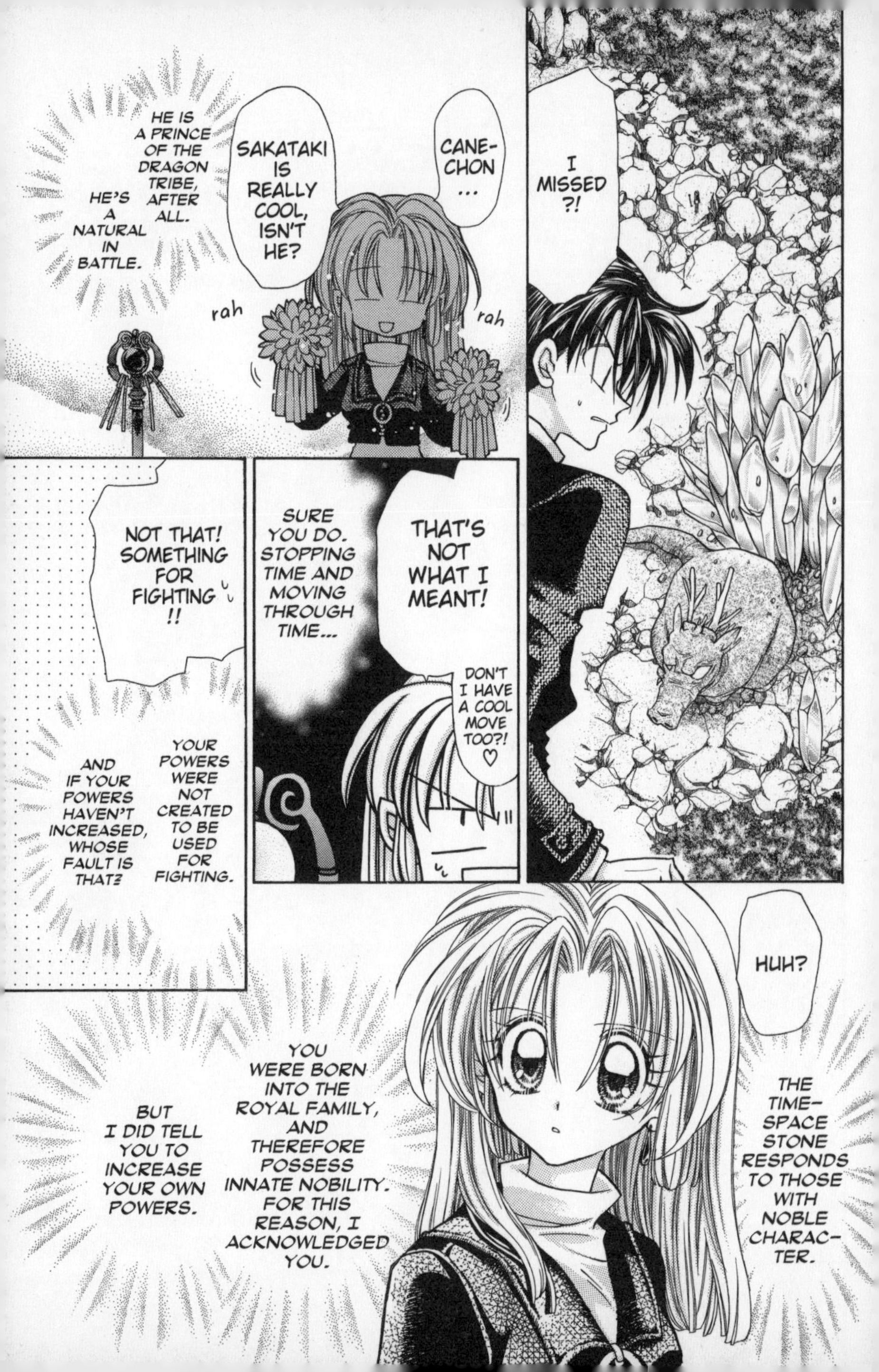
I MISSED ?!
CANE-CHON ...
SAKATAKI IS REALLY COOL, ISN'T HE?
HE IS A PRINCE OF THE DRAGON TRIBE, AFTER ALL.
HE'S A NATURAL IN BATTLE.
rah
rah
DON'T I HAVE A COOL MOVE TOO?! ♡
SURE YOU DO. STOPPING TIME AND MOVING THROUGH TIME...
THAT'S NOT WHAT I MEANT!
NOT THAT! SOMETHING FOR FIGHTING !!
YOUR POWERS WERE NOT CREATED TO BE USED FOR FIGHTING.
AND IF YOUR POWERS HAVEN'T INCREASED, WHOSE FAULT IS THAT?
HUH?
THE TIME-SPACE STONE RESPONDS TO THOSE WITH NOBLE CHARACTER.
YOU WERE BORN INTO THE ROYAL FAMILY, AND THEREFORE POSSESS INNATE NOBILITY. FOR THIS REASON, I ACKNOWLEDGED YOU.
BUT I DID TELL YOU TO INCREASE YOUR OWN POWERS.

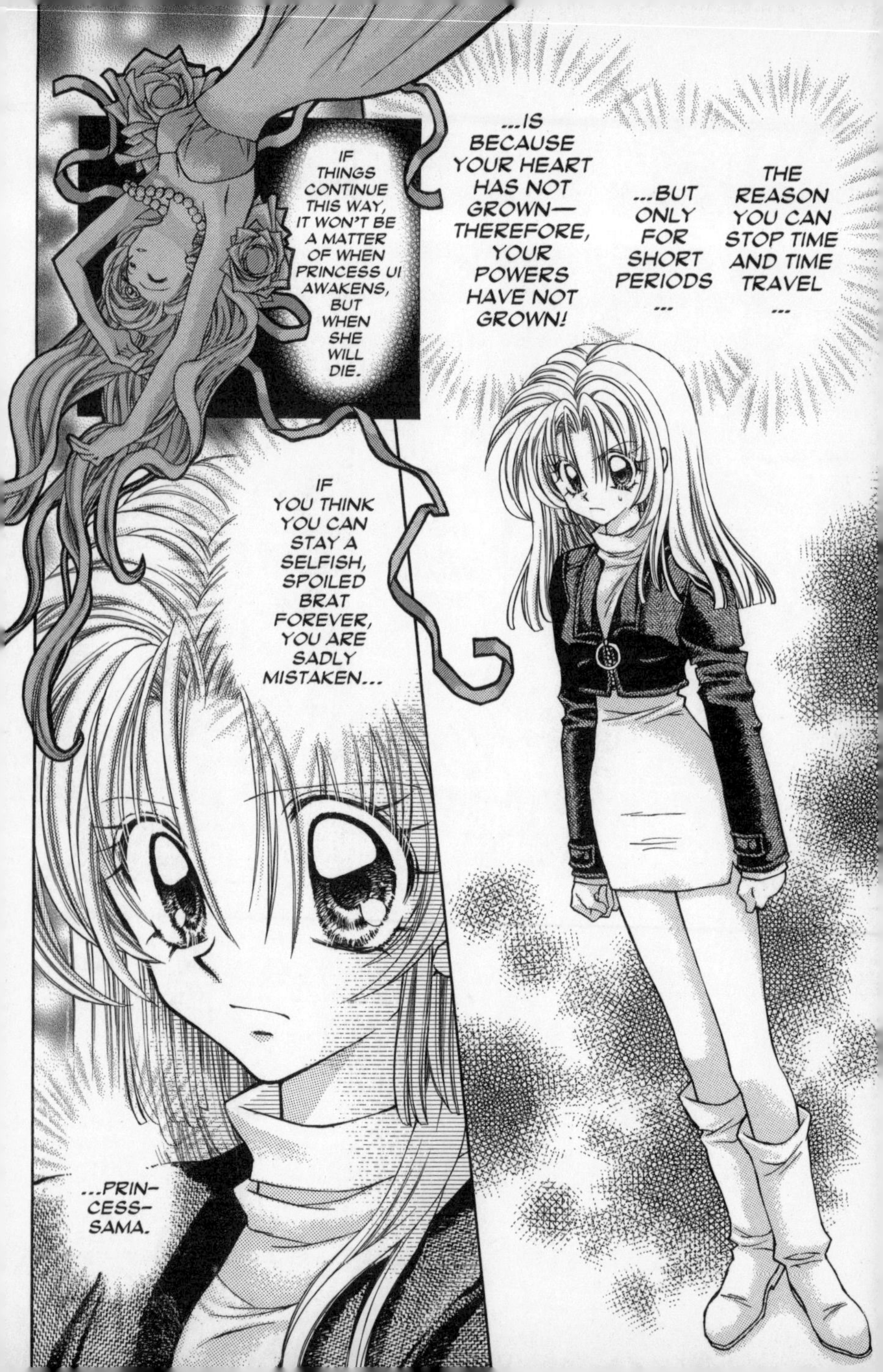
THE REASON YOU CAN STOP TIME AND TIME TRAVEL ...
...BUT ONLY FOR SHORT PERIODS ...
...IS BECAUSE YOUR HEART HAS NOT GROWN— THEREFORE, YOUR POWERS HAVE NOT GROWN!
IF THINGS CONTINUE THIS WAY, IT WON'T BE A MATTER OF WHEN PRINCESS UI AWAKENS, BUT WHEN SHE WILL DIE.
IF YOU THINK YOU CAN STAY A SELFISH, SPOILED BRAT FOREVER, YOU ARE SADLY MISTAKEN...
...PRIN-CESS-SAMA.

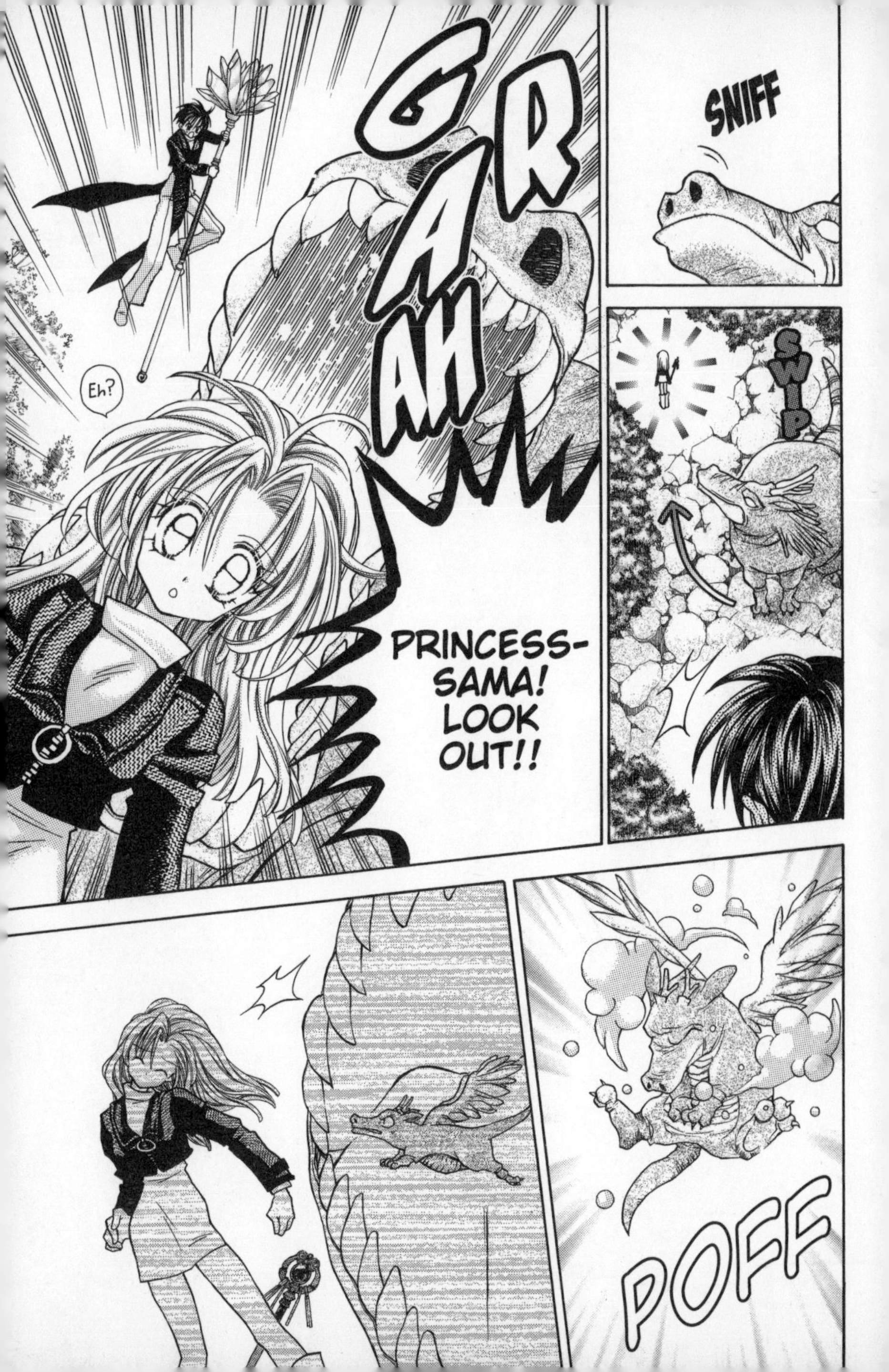
SNIFF
SWIP
GRAAH
PRINCESS-SAMA! LOOK OUT!!
Eh?
POFF

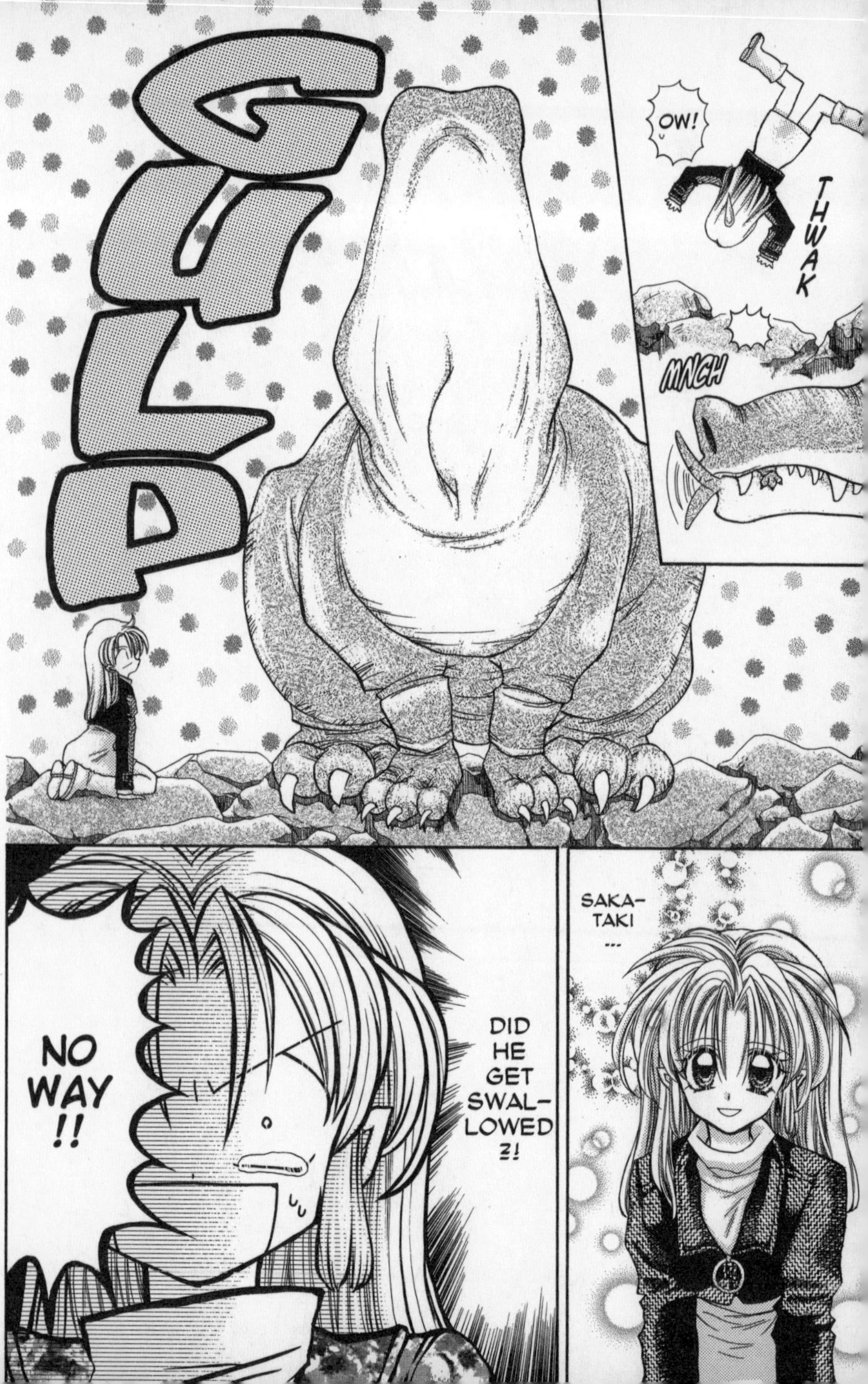
OW!
THWAK
MNCH
GULP
SAKA-TAKI ...
DID HE GET SWAL-LOWED ?!
NO WAY !!

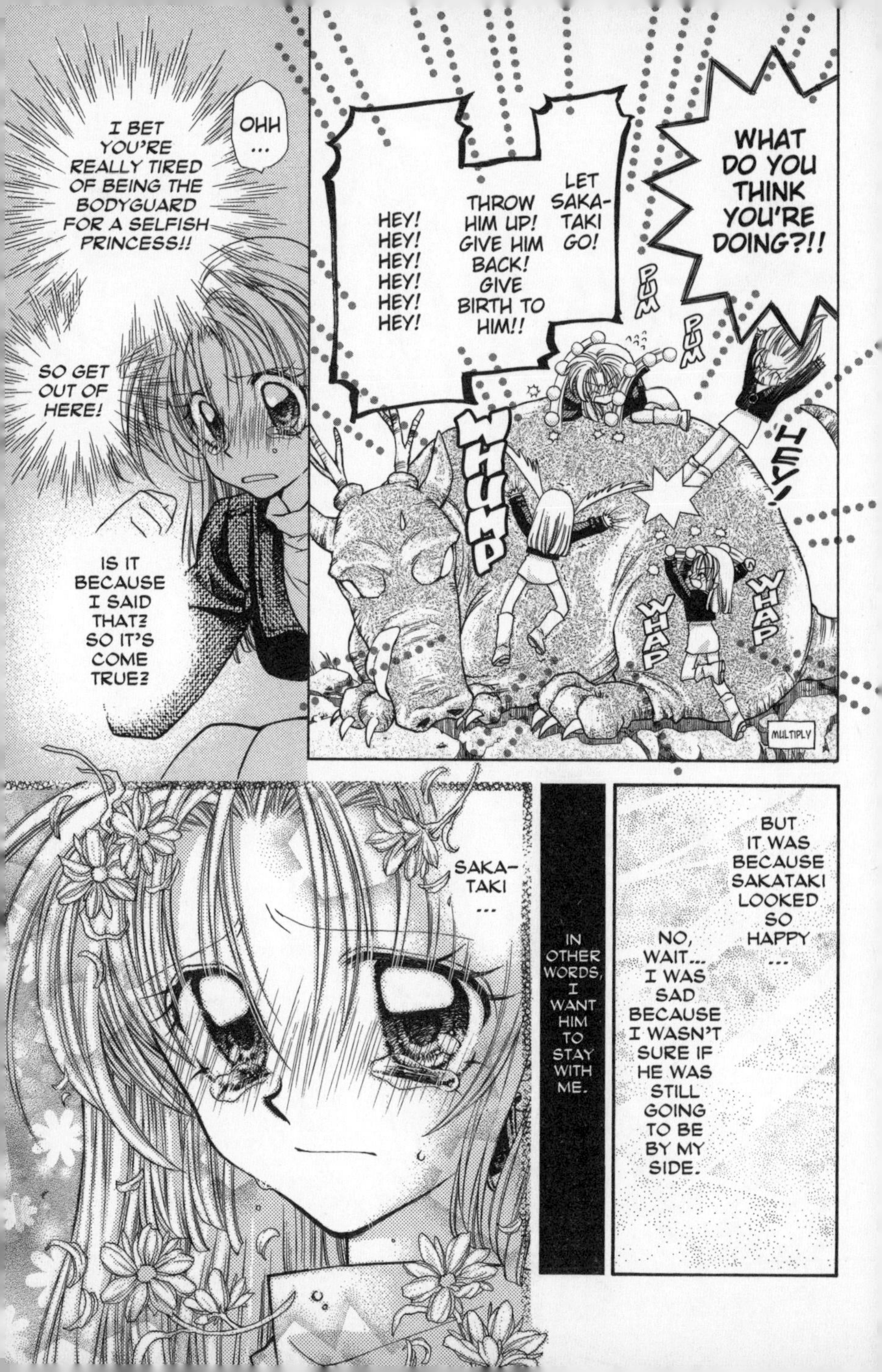
WHAT DO YOU THINK YOU'RE DOING?!!
PUM PUM
HEY!
LET SAKA-TAKI GO!
THROW HIM UP! GIVE HIM BACK! GIVE BIRTH TO HIM!!
HEY! HEY! HEY! HEY! HEY! HEY!
WHUMP
WHAP WHAP
MULTIPLY
OHH ...
I BET YOU'RE REALLY TIRED OF BEING THE BODYGUARD FOR A SELFISH PRINCESS!!
SO GET OUT OF HERE!
IS IT BECAUSE I SAID THAT? SO IT'S COME TRUE?
BUT IT WAS BECAUSE SAKATAKI LOOKED SO HAPPY ...
NO, WAIT... I WAS SAD BECAUSE I WASN'T SURE IF HE WAS STILL GOING TO BE BY MY SIDE.
IN OTHER WORDS, I WANT HIM TO STAY WITH ME.
SAKA-TAKI ...

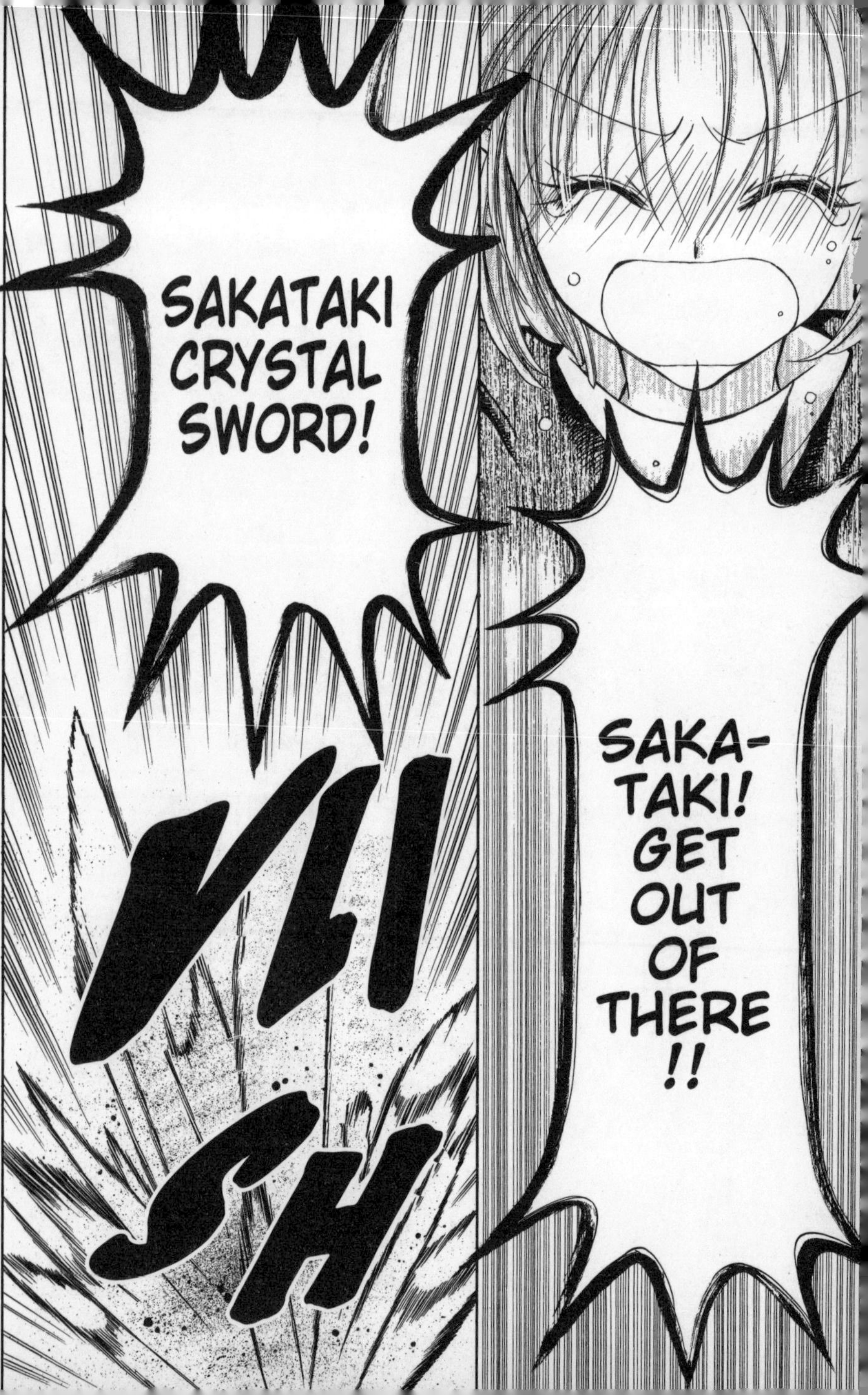
SAKA-TAKI! GET OUT OF THERE!!
SAKATAKI CRYSTAL SWORD!

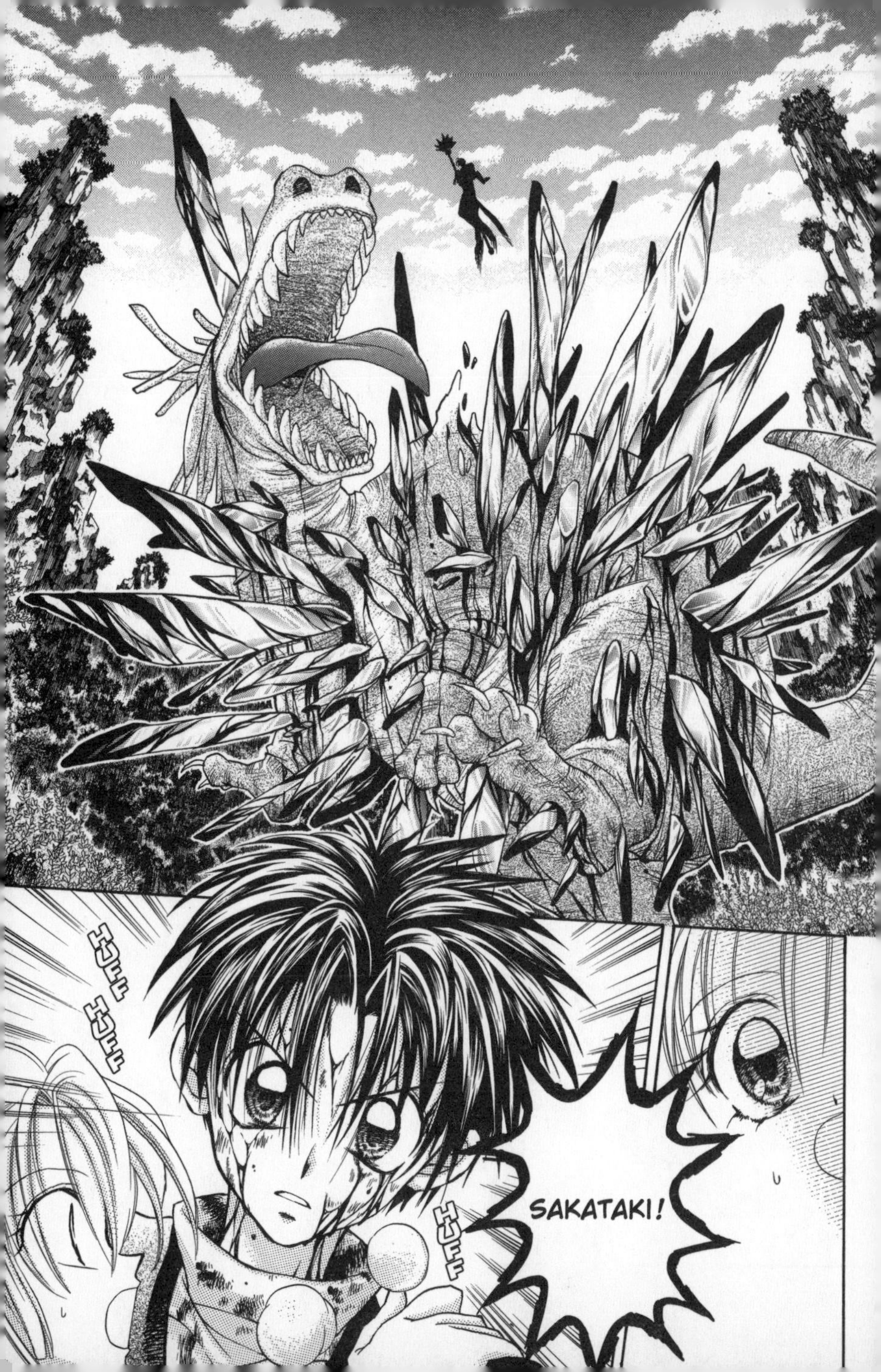
HUFF
HUFF
HUFF
SAKATAKI!

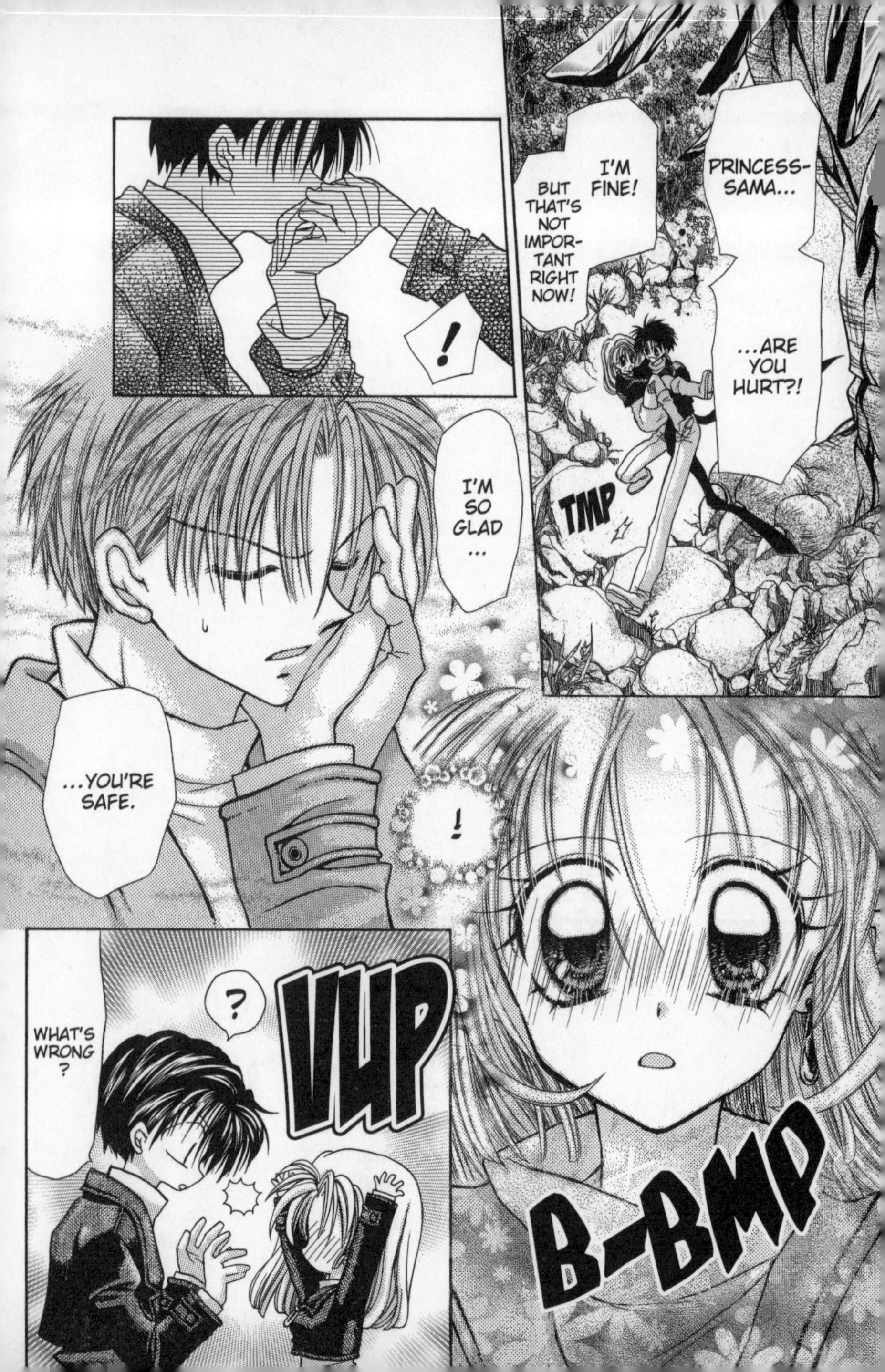
PRINCESS-SAMA...
...ARE YOU HURT?!
I'M FINE!
BUT THAT'S NOT IMPORTANT RIGHT NOW!
TMP
!
I'M SO GLAD...
...YOU'RE SAFE.
!
B-BMP
VMP
?
WHAT'S WRONG?

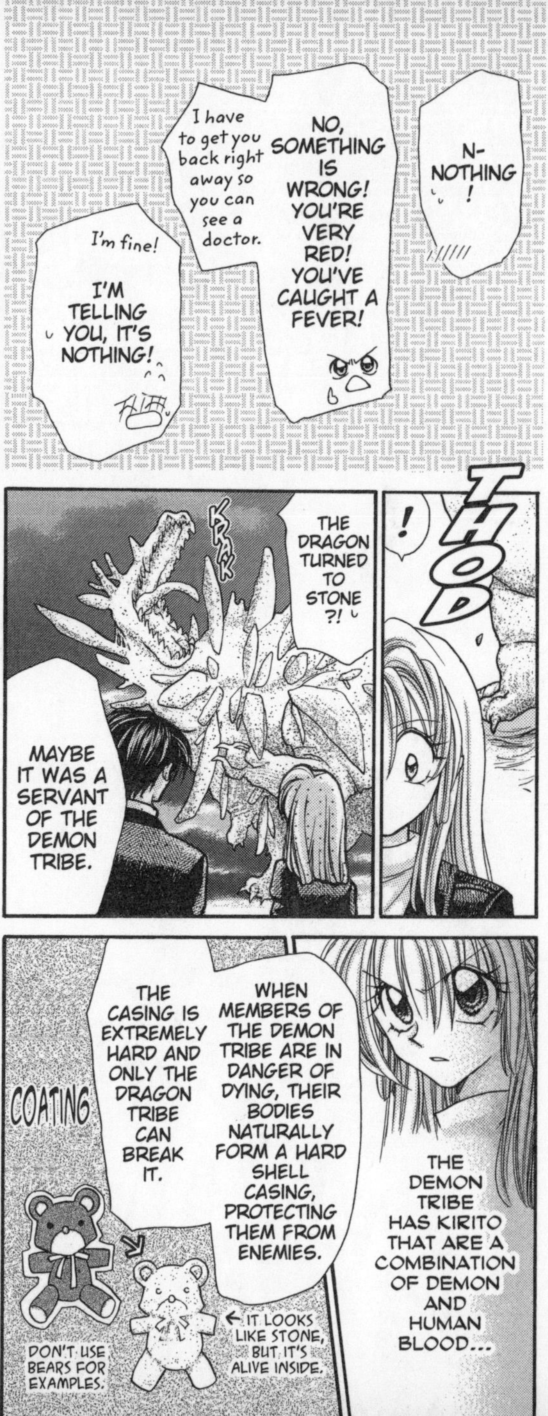
N-NOTHING!
NO, SOMETHING IS WRONG! YOU'RE VERY RED! YOU'VE CAUGHT A FEVER!
I have to get you back right away so you can see a doctor.
I'm fine!
I'M TELLING YOU, IT'S NOTHING!
THOD
!
THE DRAGON TURNED TO STONE?!
KRAK
MAYBE IT WAS A SERVANT OF THE DEMON TRIBE.
THE DEMON TRIBE HAS KIRITO THAT ARE A COMBINATION OF DEMON AND HUMAN BLOOD...
WHEN MEMBERS OF THE DEMON TRIBE ARE IN DANGER OF DYING, THEIR BODIES NATURALLY FORM A HARD SHELL CASING, PROTECTING THEM FROM ENEMIES.
THE CASING IS EXTREMELY HARD AND ONLY THE DRAGON TRIBE CAN BREAK IT.
COATING
← IT LOOKS LIKE STONE, BUT IT'S ALIVE INSIDE.
DON'T USE BEARS FOR EXAMPLES.

A PRINCESS WHO SLEEPS FROM MORNING UNTIL NIGHT. ♥

PRINCESS UI

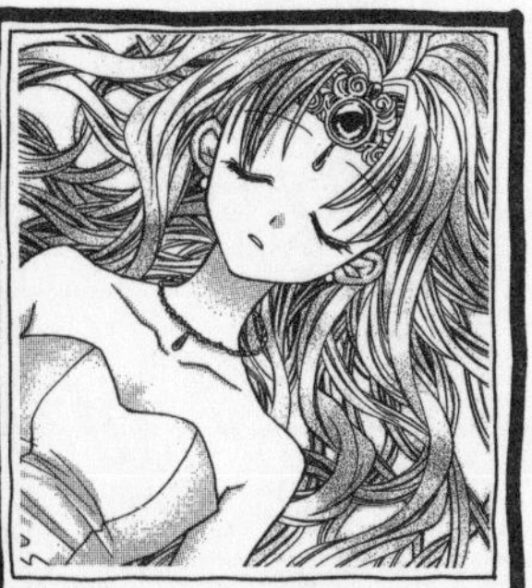

BORN JUNE 10, GEMINI, BLOOD-TYPE A

UI IS KYOKO'S YOUNGER TWIN SISTER. SHE HAS BEEN ASLEEP SINCE THE MOMENT SHE WAS BORN. SHE'S 16. EVERYTHING ABOUT HER IS A MYSTERY. HER PERSONALITY IS UNKNOWN.

SNAKE-CHAMA

THIS IS WITZIG'S PET SNAKE, SNAKE-CHAMA. WHEN WITZIG LEFT HIS VILLAGE SOME YEARS AGO, IT SEEMS THAT HE BROUGHT THE SNAKE WITH HIM. THE SNAKE APPARENTLY HAS A LOVER, BUT FOR THE ABOVE-MENTIONED REASON, IT IS CURRENTLY A LONG-DISTANCE LOVE AFFAIR.

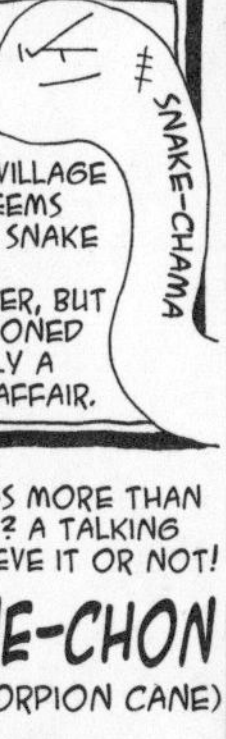
SNAKE-CHAMA

WHAT NAGS MORE THAN SAKATAKI? A TALKING CANE, BELIEVE IT OR NOT!

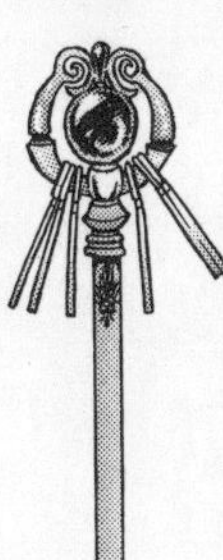

←CANE-CHON

(TIME SCORPION CANE)

EVEN THOUGH THIS CANE HAS A VERY GRAND NAME BECAUSE OF KYOKO (?), HE HAS BEEN SADDLED WITH AN UNDIGNIFIED NICKNAME.

THE CANE IS THE FORM THAT THE TIME-SPACE STONE TOOK WHEN ITS SEAL WAS REMOVED. IT IS USUALLY STORED INSIDE AN EARRING. (IT'S THE SAME FOR STRANGERS OTHER THAN KYOKO.)

MY EDITOR ALWAYS CALLS HIM GRANDPA.

Some nicknames are more fitting than others.

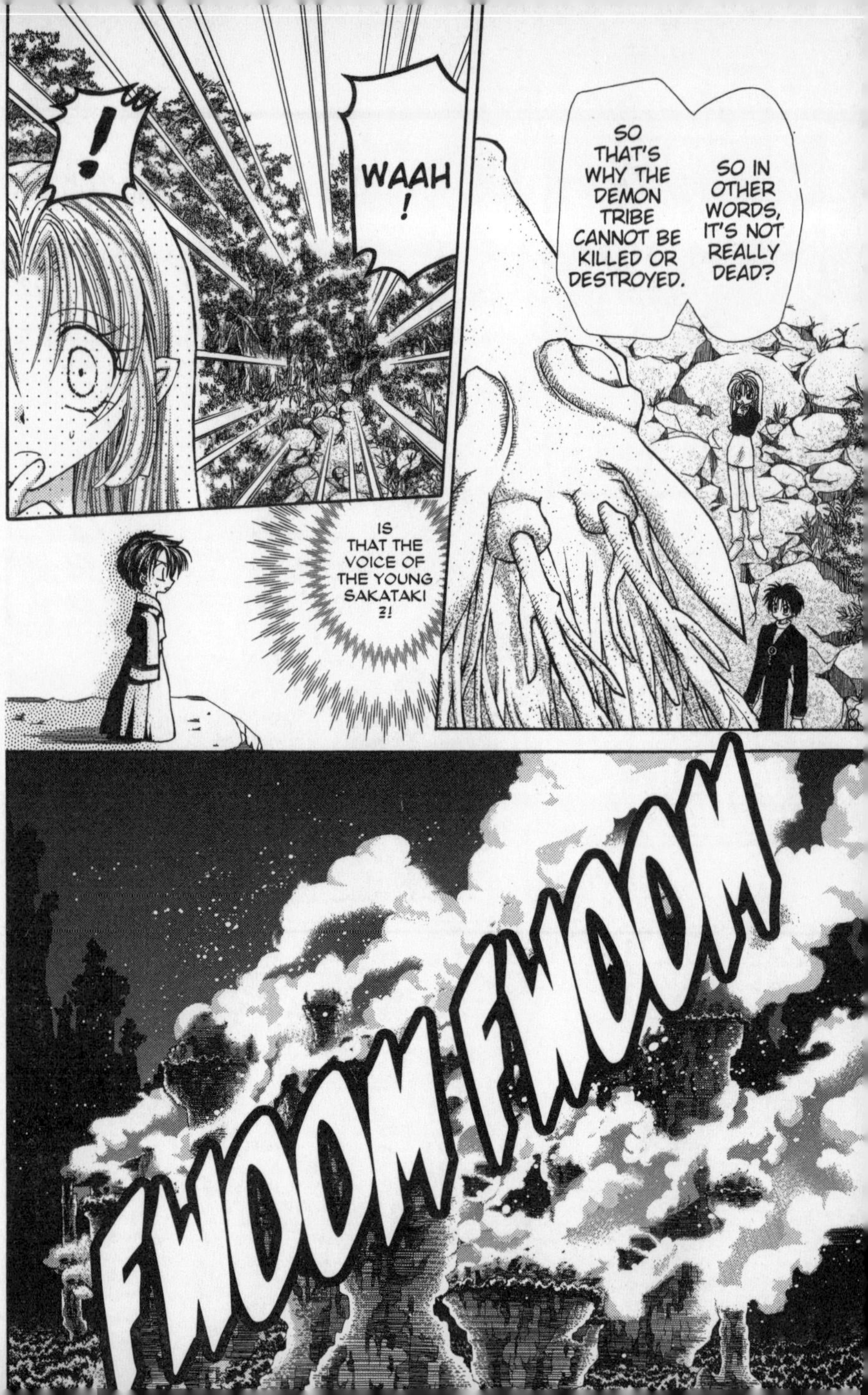
SO IN OTHER WORDS, IT'S NOT REALLY DEAD?
SO THAT'S WHY THE DEMON TRIBE CANNOT BE KILLED OR DESTROYED.
WAAH!
!
IS THAT THE VOICE OF THE YOUNG SAKATAKI ?!
FWOOM FWOOM

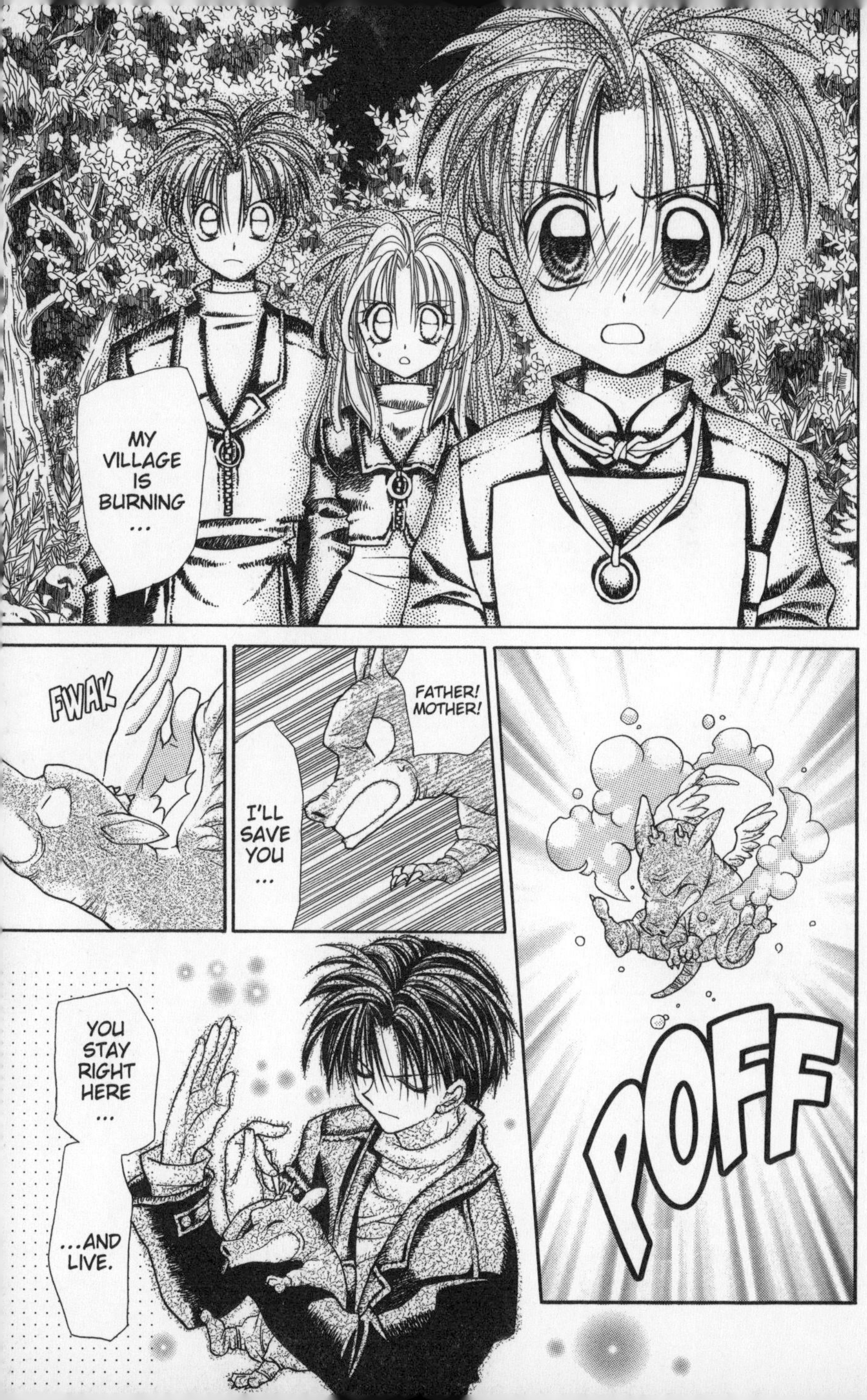
MY VILLAGE IS BURNING...
POFF
FATHER! MOTHER!
I'LL SAVE YOU...
FWAK
YOU STAY RIGHT HERE...
...AND LIVE.

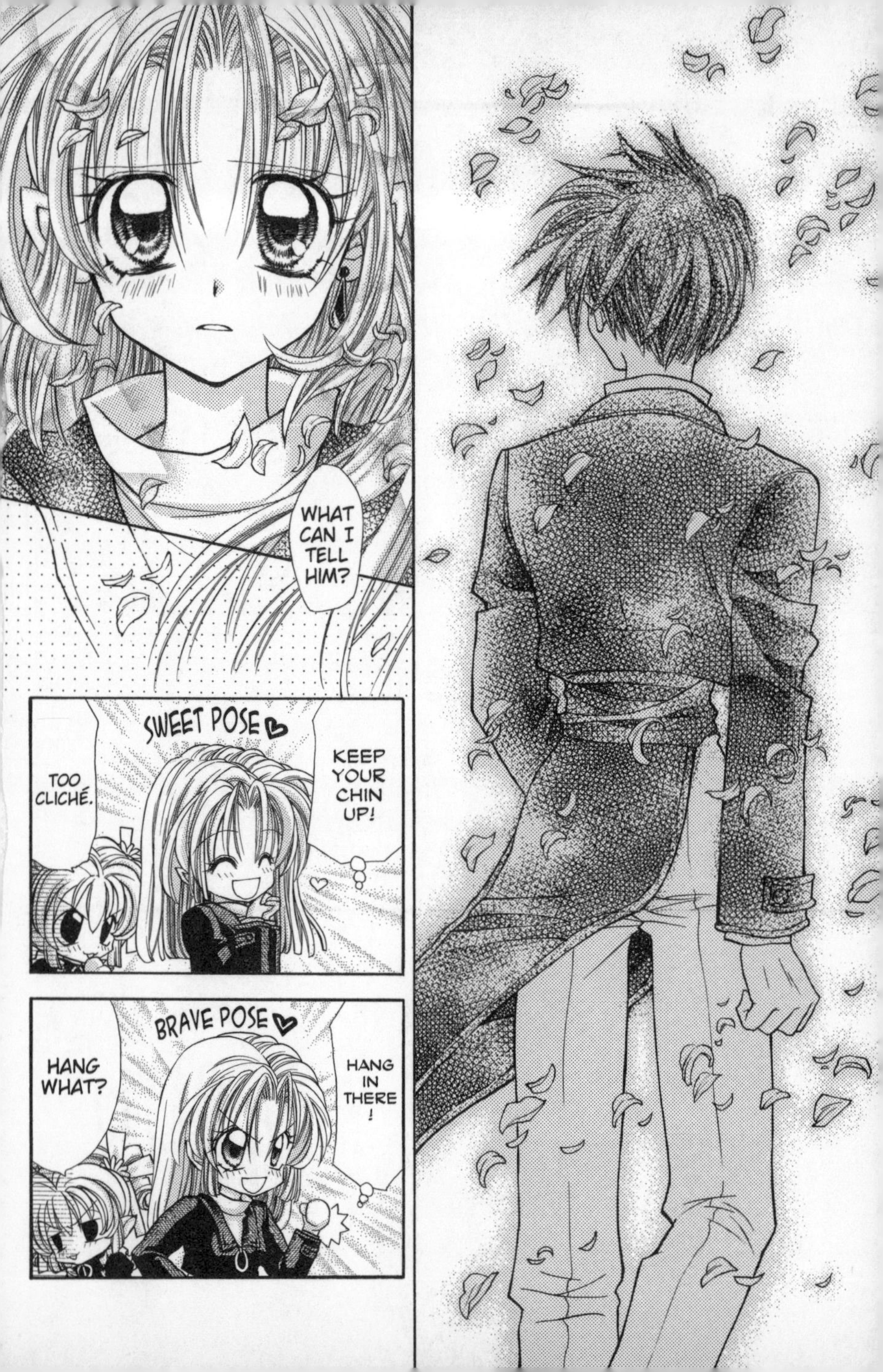
WHAT CAN I TELL HIM?
SWEET POSE ♥
KEEP YOUR CHIN UP!
TOO CLICHÉ.
BRAVE POSE ♥
HANG IN THERE!
HANG WHAT?

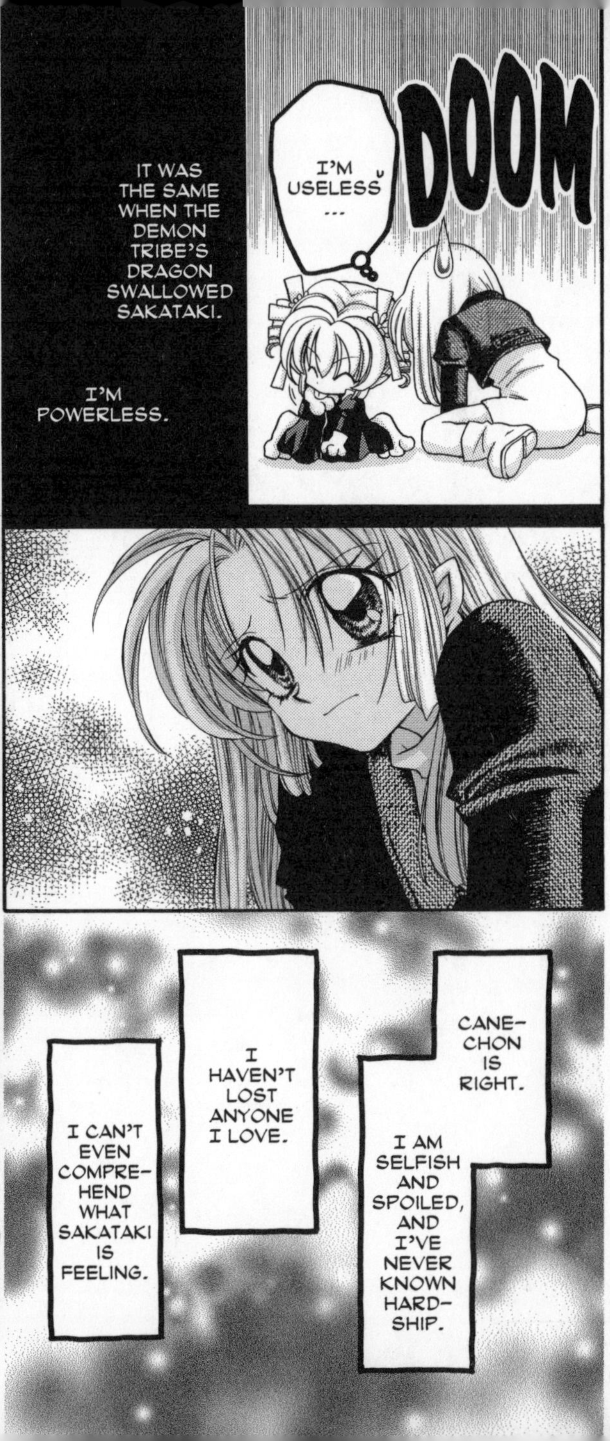
DOOM
I'M USELESS...
IT WAS THE SAME WHEN THE DEMON TRIBE'S DRAGON SWALLOWED SAKATAKI.
I'M POWERLESS.
CANE-CHON IS RIGHT.
I AM SELFISH AND SPOILED, AND I'VE NEVER KNOWN HARD-SHIP.
I HAVEN'T LOST ANYONE I LOVE.
I CAN'T EVEN COMPRE-HEND WHAT SAKATAKI IS FEELING.

ARINA ♡ TANEMURA'S

BENCHI O JOKIN

IT'S #42.

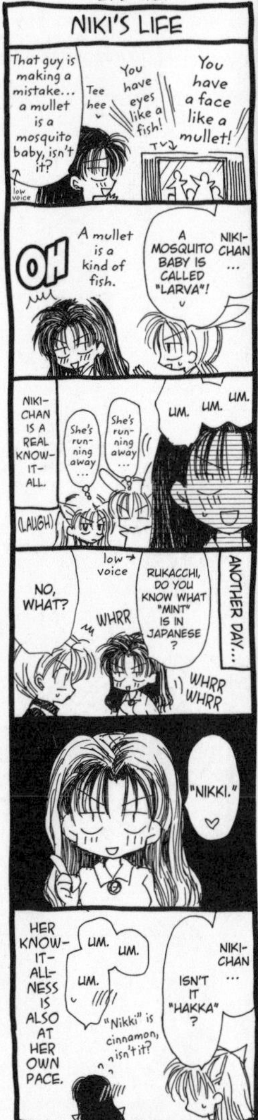
NIKI'S LIFE
You have a face like a mullet!
You have eyes like a fish!
Tee hee
TV
That guy is making a mistake... a mullet is a mosquito baby, isn't it?
low voice
NIKI-CHAN...
A MOSQUITO BABY IS CALLED "LARVA"!
A mullet is a kind of fish.
OH
UM.
UM.
UM.
She's running away...
She's running away...
NIKI-CHAN IS A REAL KNOW-IT-ALL.
(LAUGH)
ANOTHER DAY...
RUKACCHI, DO YOU KNOW WHAT "MINT" IS IN JAPANESE?
low voice
NO, WHAT?
WHRR
WHRR WHRR
"NIKKI."
NIKI-CHAN...
ISN'T IT "HAKKA"?
"Nikki" is cinnamon, isn't it?
UM.
UM.
UM.
HER KNOW-IT-ALLNESS IS ALSO AT HER OWN PACE.

A MOSQUITO BABY IS A LARVA.

MINT = HAKKA.

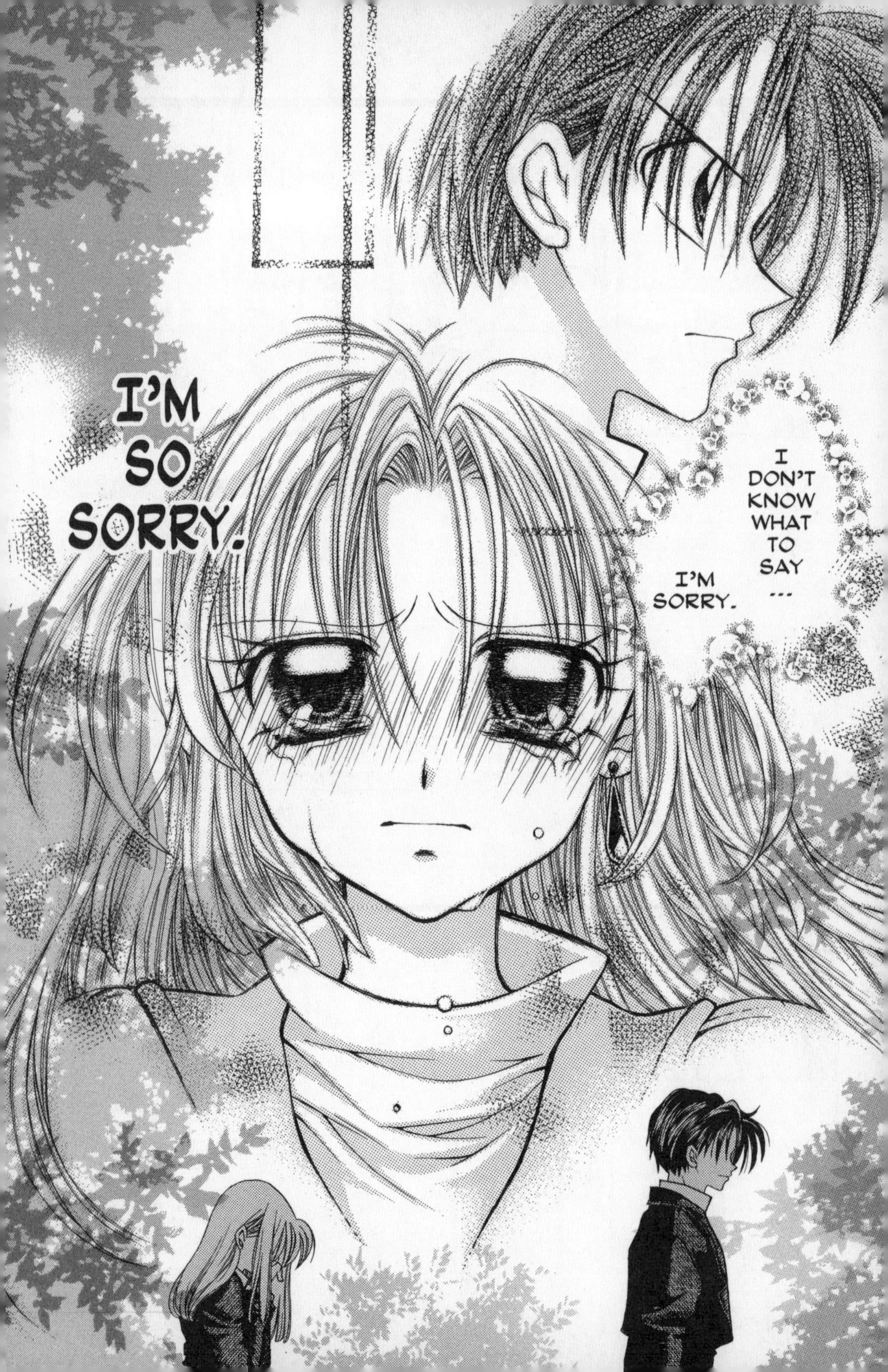
I DON'T KNOW WHAT TO SAY ...
I'M SORRY.
I'M SO SORRY.

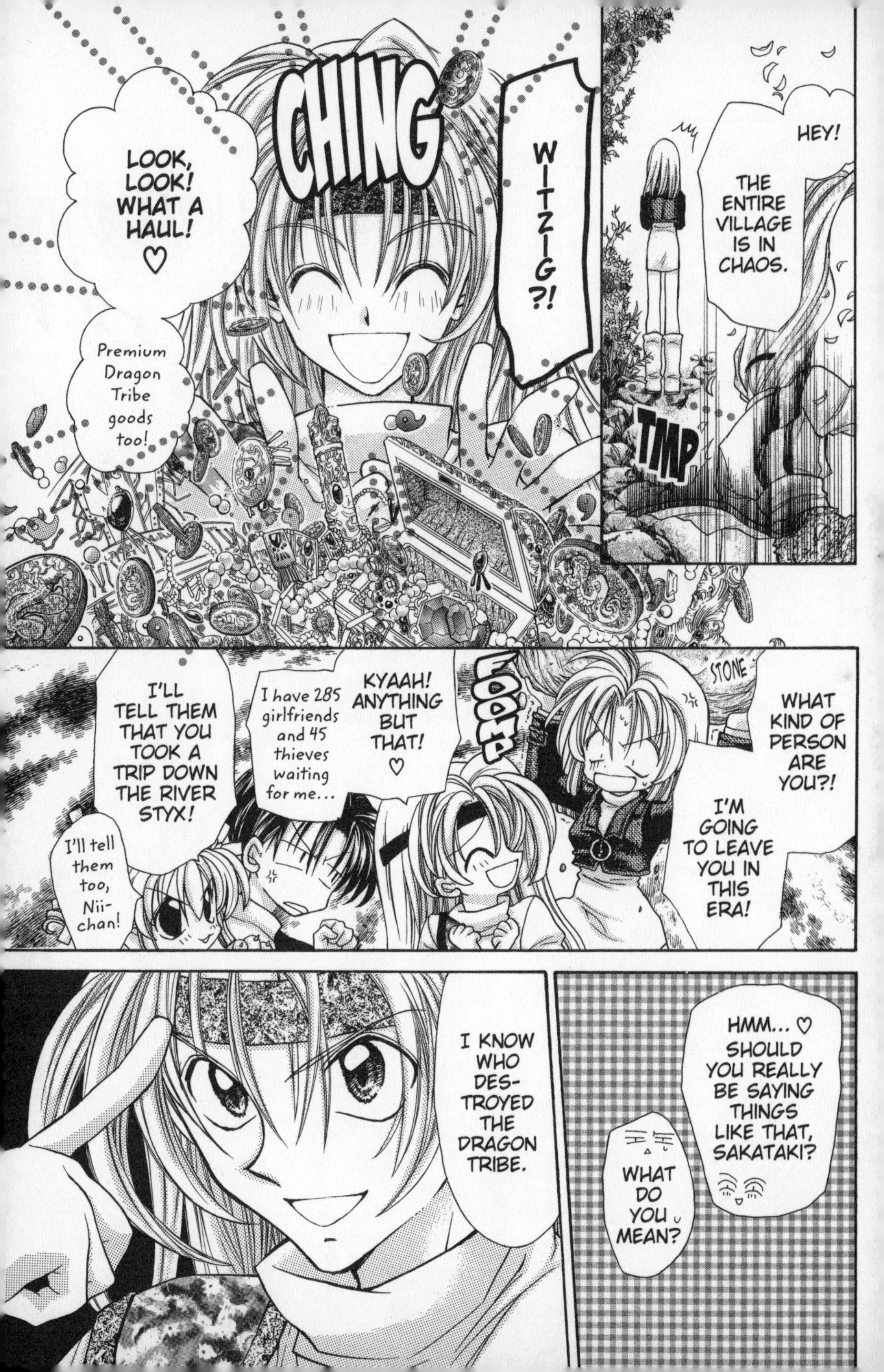
HEY!
THE ENTIRE VILLAGE IS IN CHAOS.
TMP
WITZIG?!
CHING
LOOK, LOOK! WHAT A HAUL! ♡
Premium Dragon Tribe goods too!
STONE
WHAT KIND OF PERSON ARE YOU?!
I'M GOING TO LEAVE YOU IN THIS ERA!
FOOMP
KYAAH! ANYTHING BUT THAT! ♡
I have 285 girlfriends and 45 thieves waiting for me...
I'LL TELL THEM THAT YOU TOOK A TRIP DOWN THE RIVER STYX!
I'll tell them too, Nii-chan!
HMM... ♡ SHOULD YOU REALLY BE SAYING THINGS LIKE THAT, SAKATAKI?
WHAT DO YOU MEAN?
I KNOW WHO DES-TROYED THE DRAGON TRIBE.

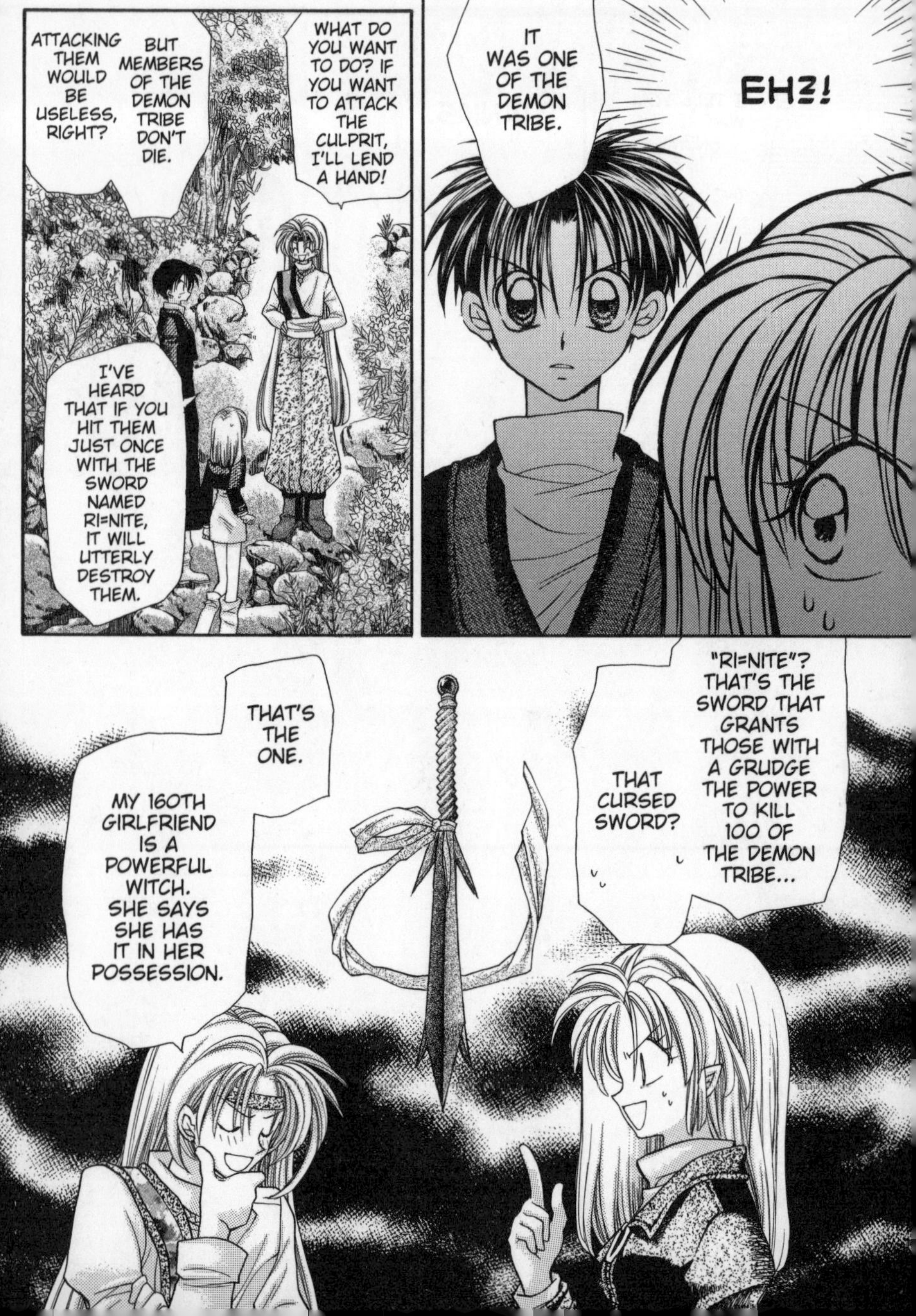
IT WAS ONE OF THE DEMON TRIBE.
EH?!
WHAT DO YOU WANT TO DO? IF YOU WANT TO ATTACK THE CULPRIT, I'LL LEND A HAND!
BUT MEMBERS OF THE DEMON TRIBE DON'T DIE.
ATTACKING THEM WOULD BE USELESS, RIGHT?
I'VE HEARD THAT IF YOU HIT THEM JUST ONCE WITH THE SWORD NAMED RI=NITE, IT WILL UTTERLY DESTROY THEM.
"RI=NITE"? THAT'S THE SWORD THAT GRANTS THOSE WITH A GRUDGE THE POWER TO KILL 100 OF THE DEMON TRIBE...
THAT CURSED SWORD?
THAT'S THE ONE.
MY 160TH GIRLFRIEND IS A POWERFUL WITCH. SHE SAYS SHE HAS IT IN HER POSSESSION.

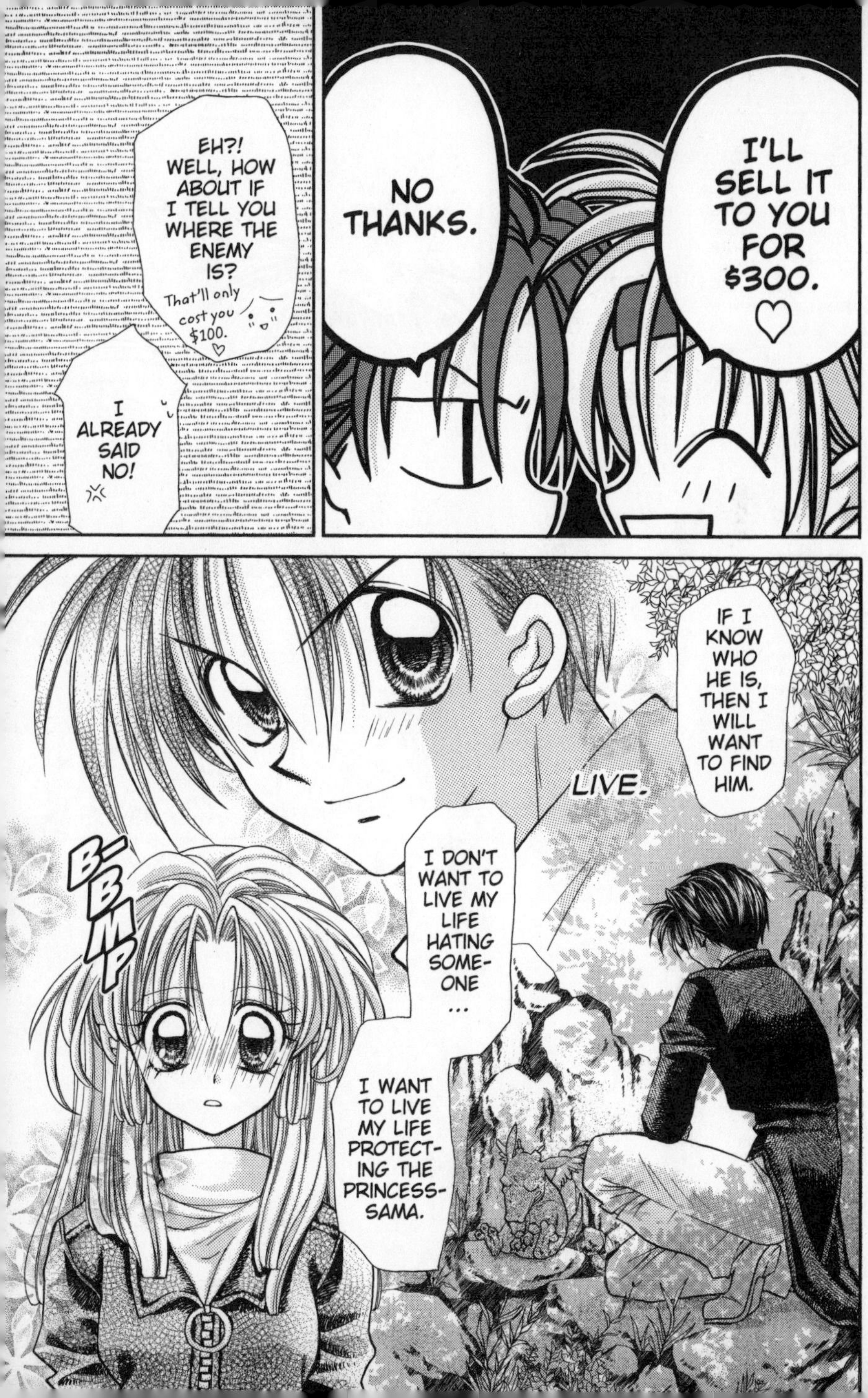
I'LL SELL IT TO YOU FOR $300. ♡
NO THANKS.
EH?! WELL, HOW ABOUT IF I TELL YOU WHERE THE ENEMY IS?
That'll only cost you $100. ♡
I ALREADY SAID NO!
IF I KNOW WHO HE IS, THEN I WILL WANT TO FIND HIM.
LIVE.
I DON'T WANT TO LIVE MY LIFE HATING SOME-ONE...
I WANT TO LIVE MY LIFE PROTECT-ING THE PRINCESS-SAMA.
B-BMP

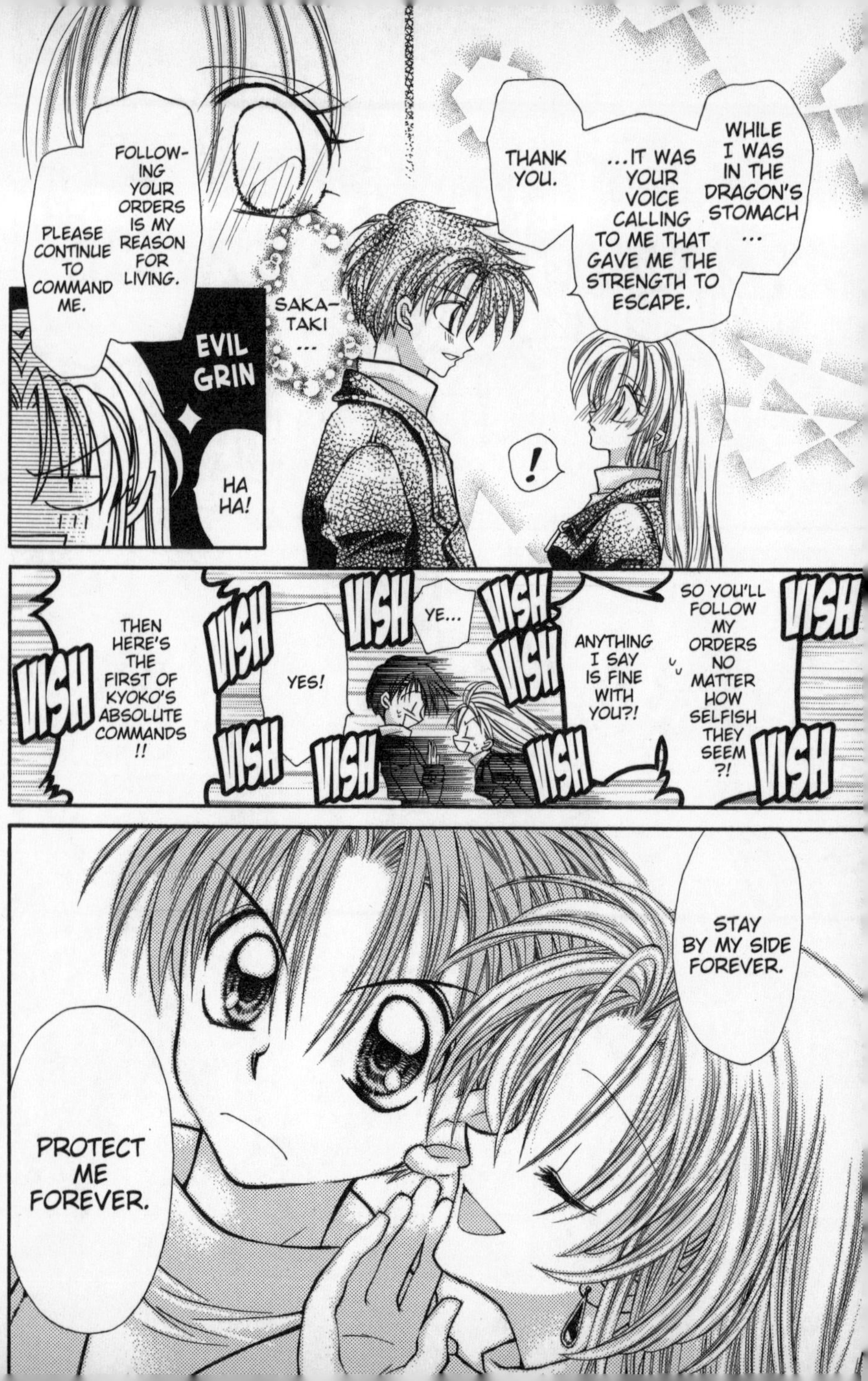
WHILE I WAS IN THE DRAGON'S STOMACH ...
...IT WAS YOUR VOICE CALLING TO ME THAT GAVE ME THE STRENGTH TO ESCAPE.
THANK YOU.
!
SAKA-TAKI ...
FOLLOW-ING YOUR ORDERS IS MY REASON FOR LIVING.
PLEASE CONTINUE TO COMMAND ME.
EVIL GRIN
HA HA!
VISH
SO YOU'LL FOLLOW MY ORDERS NO MATTER HOW SELFISH THEY SEEM?!
VISH
ANYTHING I SAY IS FINE WITH YOU?!
VISH VISH
VISH
YE...
VISH
YES!
VISH
VISH
THEN HERE'S THE FIRST OF KYOKO'S ABSOLUTE COMMANDS!!
VISH
VISH
STAY BY MY SIDE FOREVER.
PROTECT ME FOREVER.

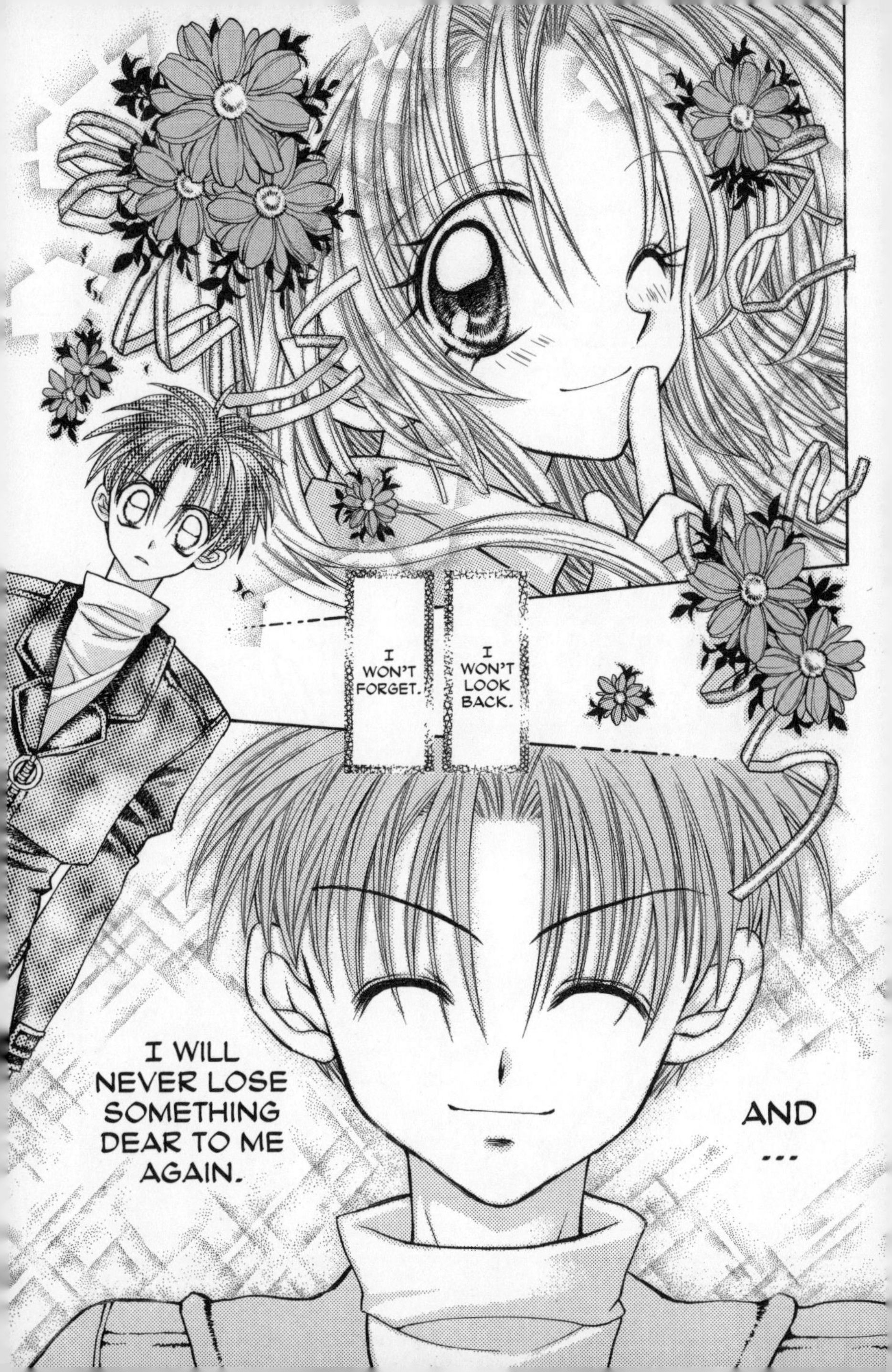
I WON'T LOOK BACK.
I WON'T FORGET.
AND ...
I WILL NEVER LOSE SOMETHING DEAR TO ME AGAIN.

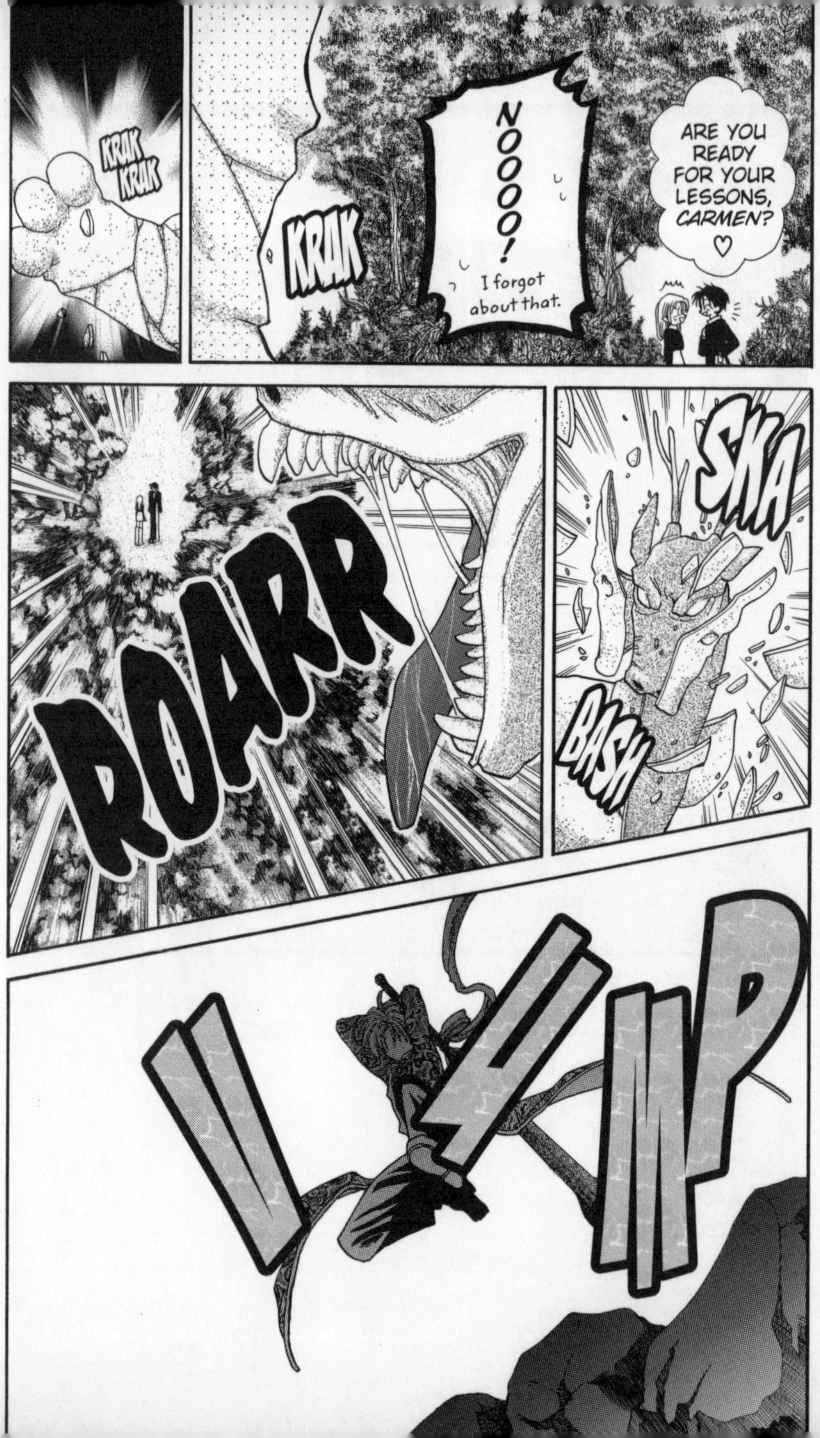
ARE YOU READY FOR YOUR LESSONS, CARMEN? ♡
NOOOOO! I forgot about that.
KRAK
KRAK KRAK
SKA
BASH
ROARR

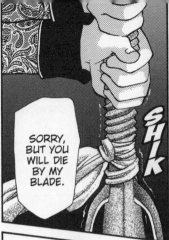

SHUNK
SORRY, BUT YOU WILL DIE BY MY BLADE.
SHIK
YOU SHOULD HAVE REMAINED IN YOUR SHELL ...
FORTUNE HAS DESERTED YOU. YOU'VE MADE ME ANGRY.
ZHK
ZHK
ZHK
ZHK
ZHK
DIE.

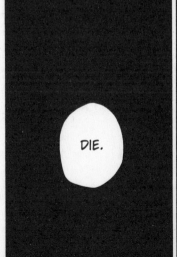

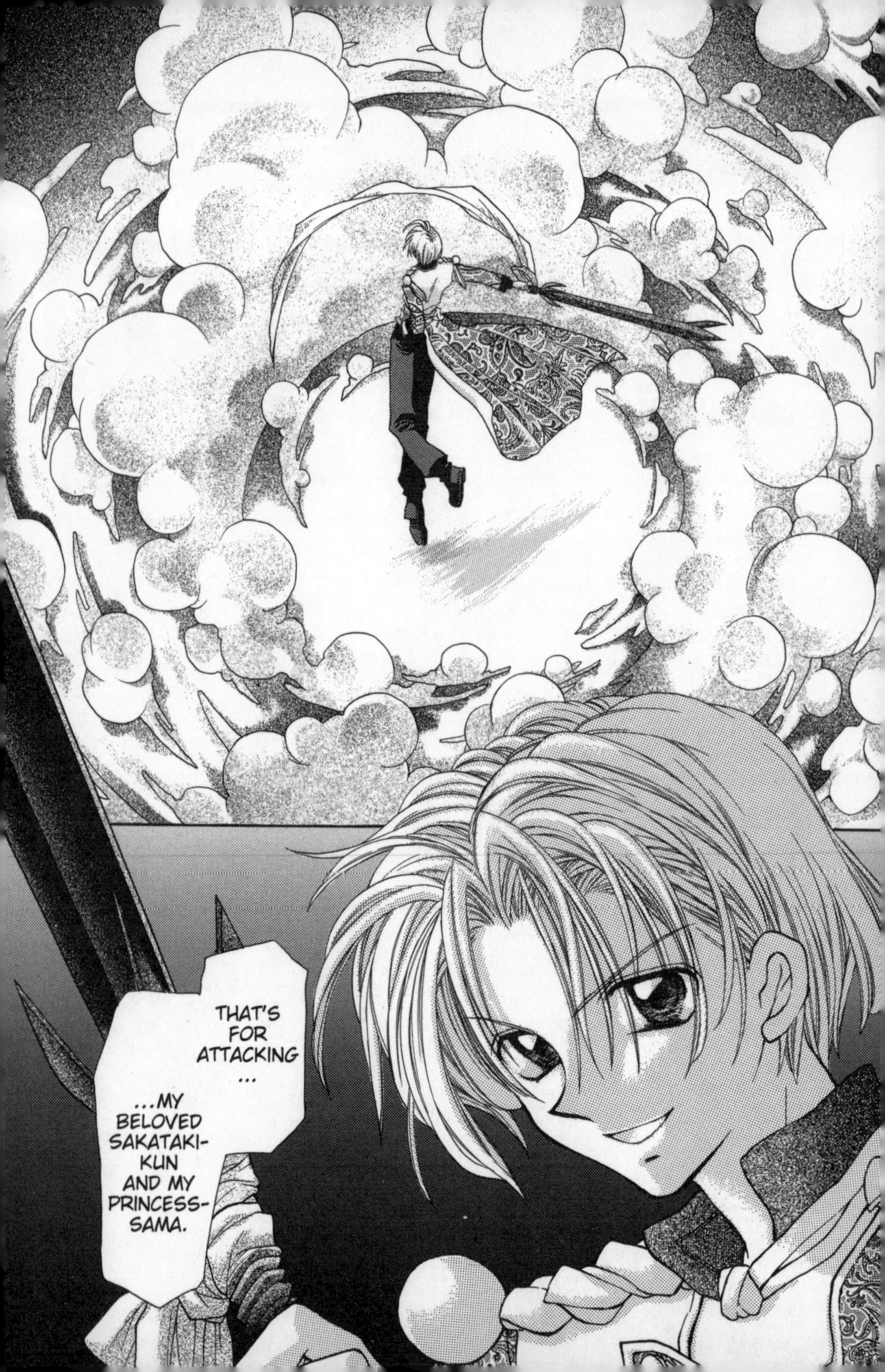
THAT'S FOR ATTACKING ...
...MY BELOVED SAKATAKI-KUN AND MY PRINCESS-SAMA.

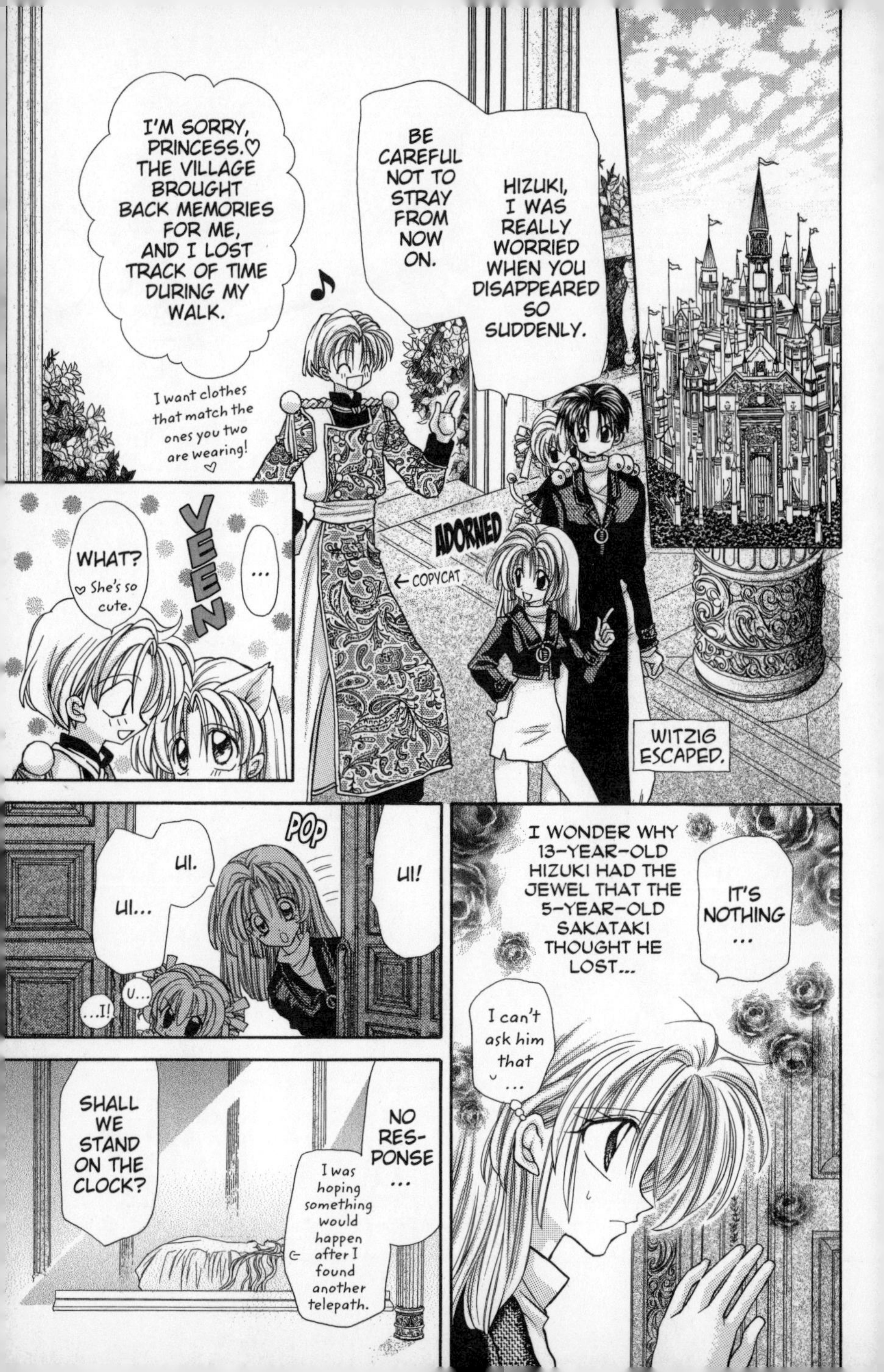
HIZUKI, I WAS REALLY WORRIED WHEN YOU DISAPPEARED SO SUDDENLY.
BE CAREFUL NOT TO STRAY FROM NOW ON.
I'M SORRY, PRINCESS.♡ THE VILLAGE BROUGHT BACK MEMORIES FOR ME, AND I LOST TRACK OF TIME DURING MY WALK.
I want clothes that match the ones you two are wearing! ♡
ADORNED
← COPYCAT
WITZIG ESCAPED.
...
VEEN
WHAT?
♡ She's so cute.
I WONDER WHY 13-YEAR-OLD HIZUKI HAD THE JEWEL THAT THE 5-YEAR-OLD SAKATAKI THOUGHT HE LOST...
IT'S NOTHING...
I can't ask him that...
POP
UI!
UI.
UI...
U...
...I!
NO RESPONSE...
I was hoping something would happen after I found another telepath.
SHALL WE STAND ON THE CLOCK?

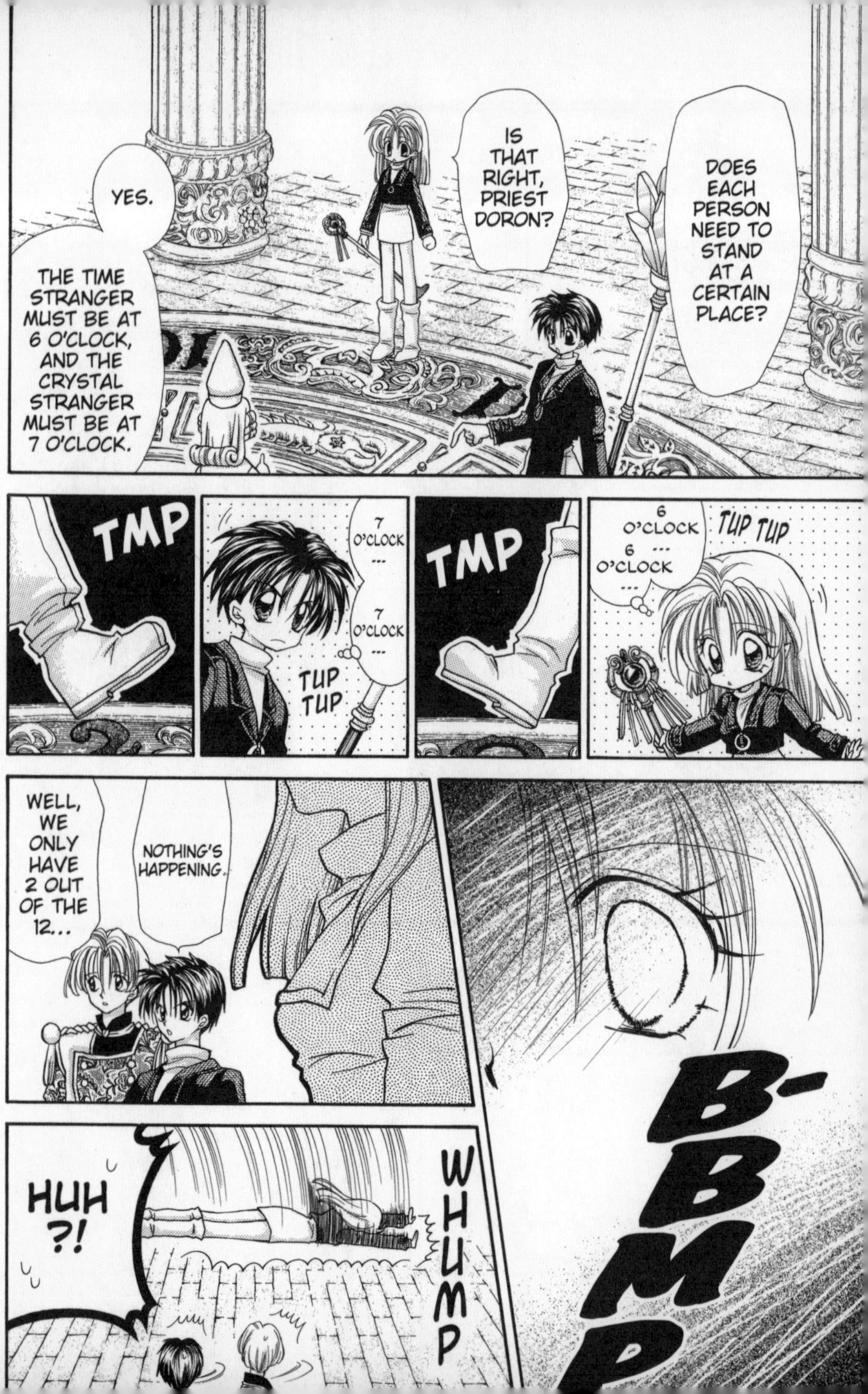
DOES EACH PERSON NEED TO STAND AT A CERTAIN PLACE?
IS THAT RIGHT, PRIEST DORON?
YES.
THE TIME STRANGER MUST BE AT 6 O'CLOCK, AND THE CRYSTAL STRANGER MUST BE AT 7 O'CLOCK.
TUP TUP
6 O'CLOCK ... 6 O'CLOCK ...
TMP
7 O'CLOCK ... 7 O'CLOCK ...
TUP TUP
TMP
B-BMP
NOTHING'S HAPPENING.
WELL, WE ONLY HAVE 2 OUT OF THE 12...
WHUMP
HUH?!

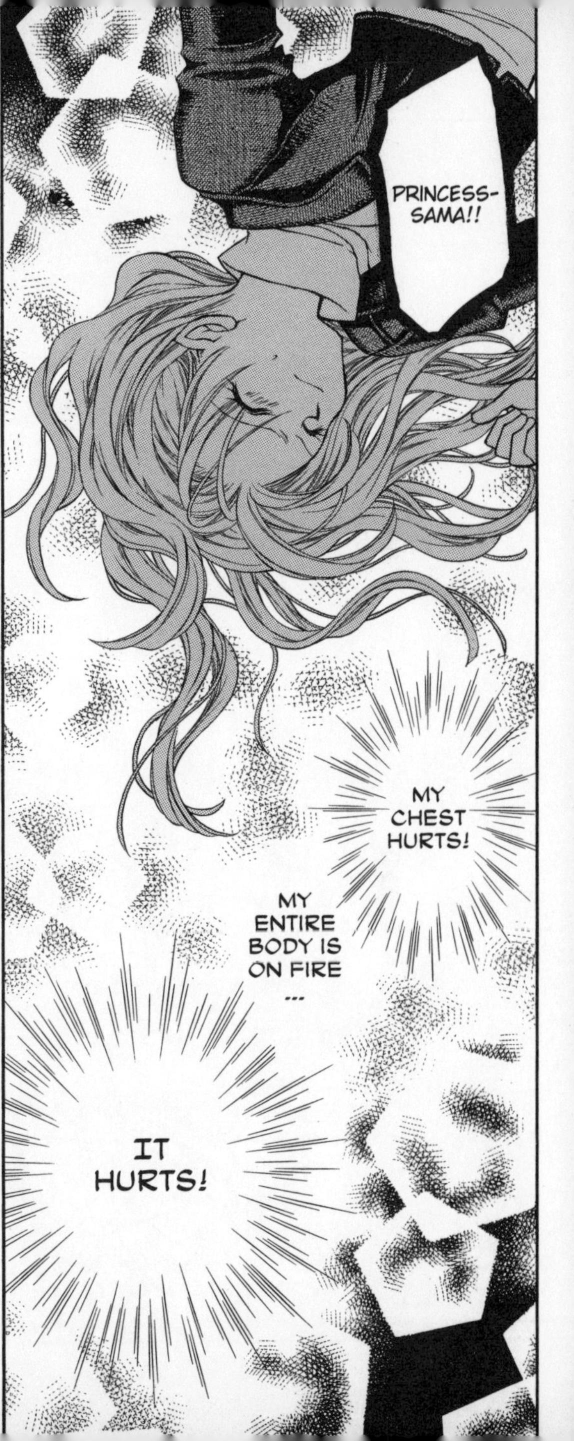
PRINCESS-SAMA!!
MY CHEST HURTS!
MY ENTIRE BODY IS ON FIRE...
IT HURTS!

BYE-BYE!!

I ALREADY USED UP A LOT OF THE SIDEBARS FOR CHARACTER INTRODUCTIONS. I DON'T THINK THERE WILL BE THAT MANY NEW CHARACTERS IN THE NEXT VOLUME. IT'S JUST THIS FIRST TIME, SO FORGIVE ME.

I AM TOTALLY FASCINATED WITH KYOKO'S WORLD RIGHT NOW. THIS KIND OF FANTASY SHOJO MANGA TENDS TO APPEAL TO A VERY NARROW RANGE OF READERS, SO I WAS WORRIED THAT MANY PEOPLE WOULDN'T LIKE IT. EVERYTHING SEEMS TO BE GOING REALLY WELL, THOUGH, AND I PLAN TO TRY EVEN HARDER THE NEXT TIME. PLEASE WAIT FOR THE NEXT VOLUME!!

PREVIEW

A secret look at what's in vol. 2!

CHAPTER 5: DEFINITELY A WONDERFUL LOVE SONG

WHAT IS THE STORY BEHIND KAREN'S TEARS?! KYOKO TRIES TO TRACK DOWN THE MISSING KAREN...

CHAPTER 6: EMPIRE OF SAND; PARADISE OF WATER

KYOKO HAS DISCOVERED WHAT THE STRANGERS HAVE IN COMMON. SHE TAKES AN AIRSHIP TO THE VILLAGE OF THE SNAKE TRIBE, LOCATED SOUTHEAST OF THE CASTLE, TO MEET WITH A PERSON OF INTEREST, BUT...

CHAPTER 7: YOU WANT TO PROTECT THE THINGS YOU CHERISH

WITZIG AND GINGA'S PAST TOGETHER IS REVEALED! ALSO, FIND OUT WHO KISSED KYOKO IN CHAPTER 4!

CHAPTER 8: A REPLICA OF THE PRINCESS

KYOKO IS WAVERING BETWEEN HER DUTIES AS A PRINCESS AND HER OWN WISHES. SHE CAN'T LET ANYONE KNOW ABOUT HER TEARS OR HER HEART'S DESIRE. DEJECTED, SHE AND SAKATAKI...

BONUS MANGA: LEAVE IT TO CHOCOLA

THE KING FORGETS THAT IT'S CHOCOLA'S BIRTHDAY AND DOESN'T COME TO HER PARTY. AN ANGRY CHOCOLA RUNS AWAY FROM THE CASTLE. HER DESTINATION: THE DESTROYERS ☆!

↑ The above-mentioned is subject to change without notice.

LET'S MEET AGAIN IN *TIME STRANGER KYOKO 2!*
ARINA T., 2002

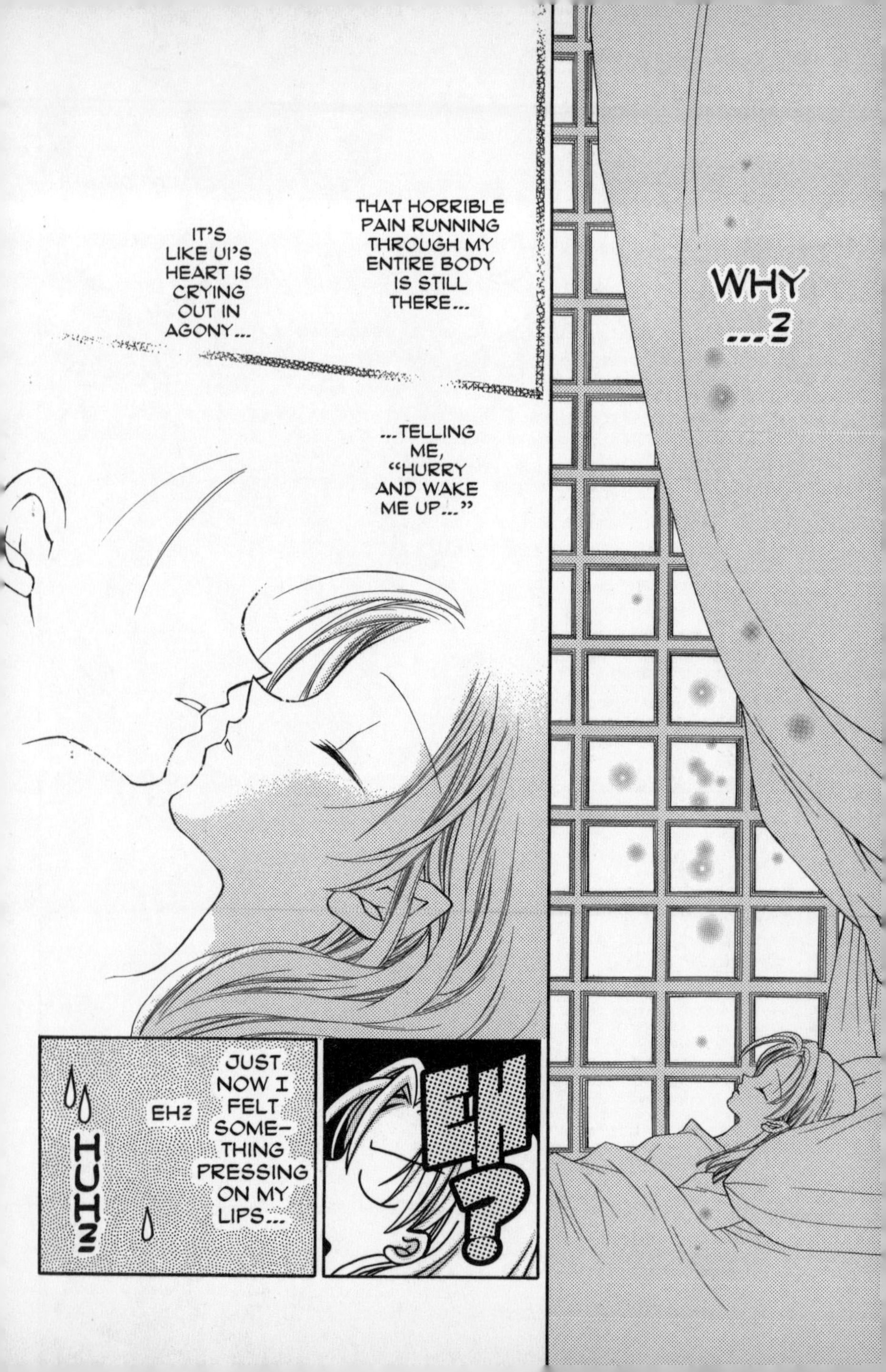
WHY ...?
THAT HORRIBLE PAIN RUNNING THROUGH MY ENTIRE BODY IS STILL THERE...
IT'S LIKE UI'S HEART IS CRYING OUT IN AGONY...
...TELLING ME, "HURRY AND WAKE ME UP..."
EH?!
JUST NOW I FELT SOME-THING PRESSING ON MY LIPS...
EH?
HUH?!

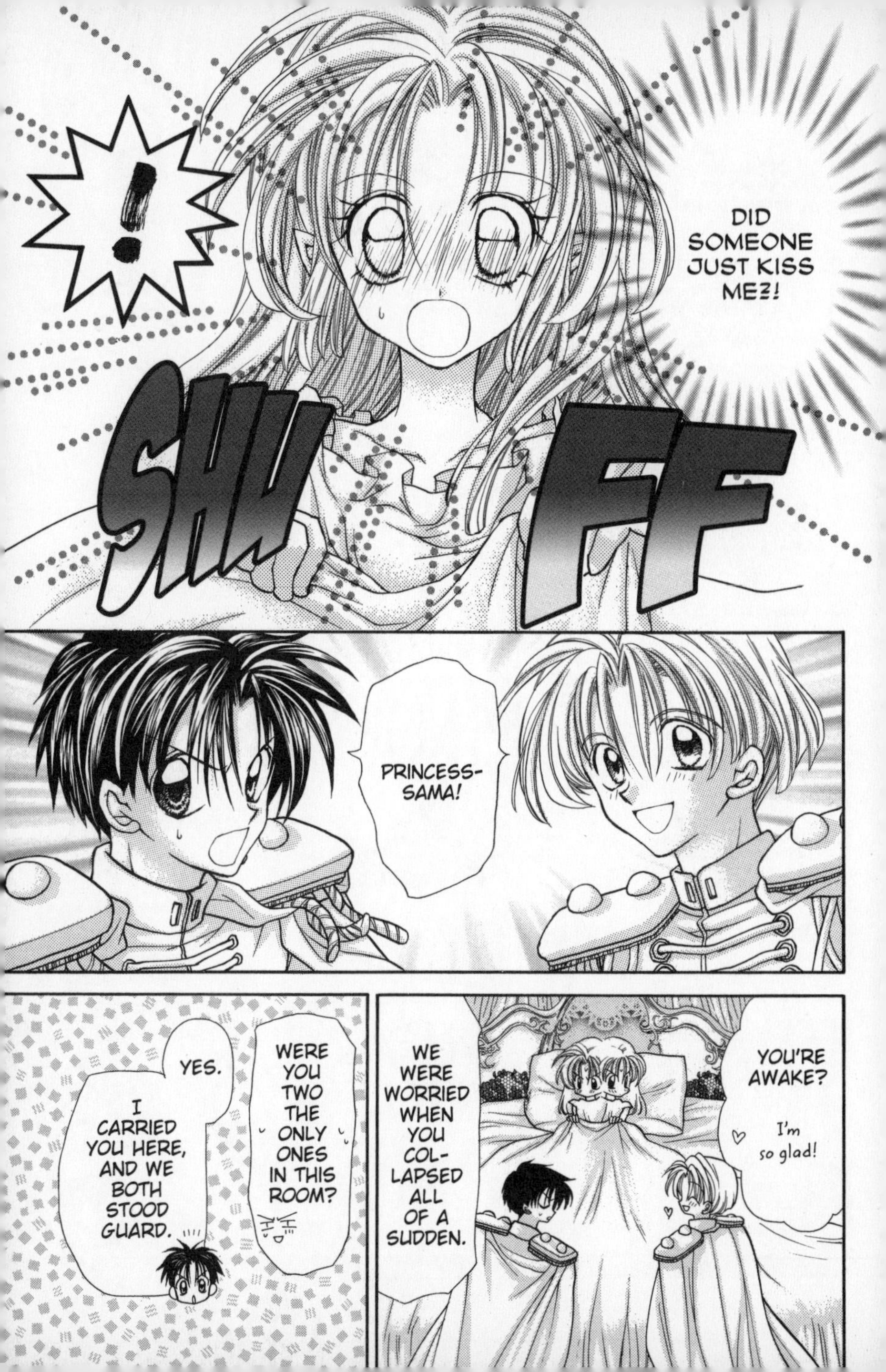
DID SOMEONE JUST KISS ME?!
!
SHUFF
PRINCESS-SAMA!
YOU'RE AWAKE?
I'm so glad!
WE WERE WORRIED WHEN YOU COL-LAPSED ALL OF A SUDDEN.
WERE YOU TWO THE ONLY ONES IN THIS ROOM?
YES.
I CARRIED YOU HERE, AND WE BOTH STOOD GUARD.

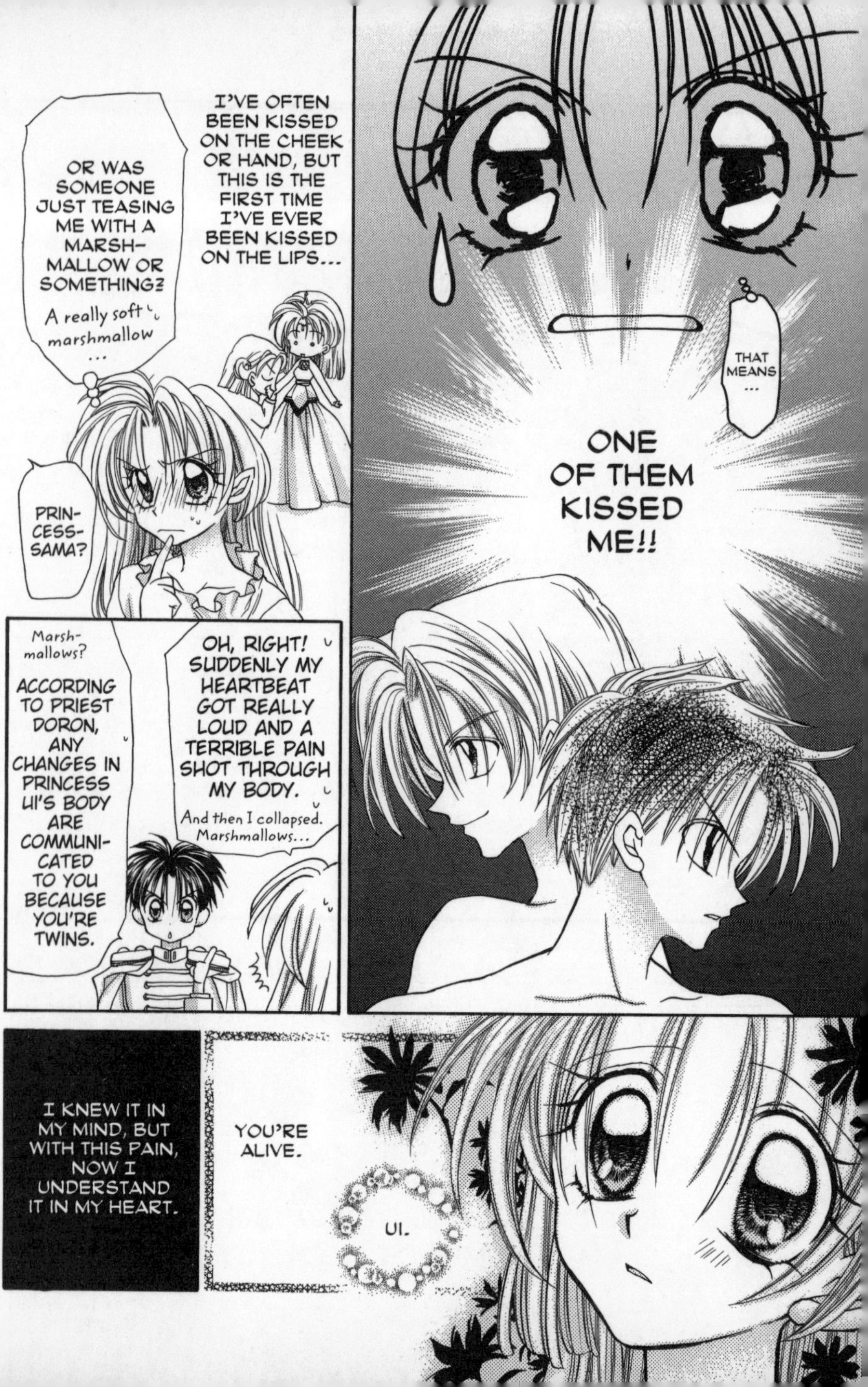

THAT MEANS...
ONE OF THEM KISSED ME!!
I'VE OFTEN BEEN KISSED ON THE CHEEK OR HAND, BUT THIS IS THE FIRST TIME I'VE EVER BEEN KISSED ON THE LIPS...
OR WAS SOMEONE JUST TEASING ME WITH A MARSH-MALLOW OR SOMETHING?
A really soft marshmallow...
PRIN-CESS-SAMA?
OH, RIGHT! SUDDENLY MY HEARTBEAT GOT REALLY LOUD AND A TERRIBLE PAIN SHOT THROUGH MY BODY.
And then I collapsed. Marshmallows...
Marsh-mallows?
ACCORDING TO PRIEST DORON, ANY CHANGES IN PRINCESS UI'S BODY ARE COMMUNI-CATED TO YOU BECAUSE YOU'RE TWINS.
YOU'RE ALIVE.
UI.
I KNEW IT IN MY MIND, BUT WITH THIS PAIN, NOW I UNDERSTAND IT IN MY HEART.

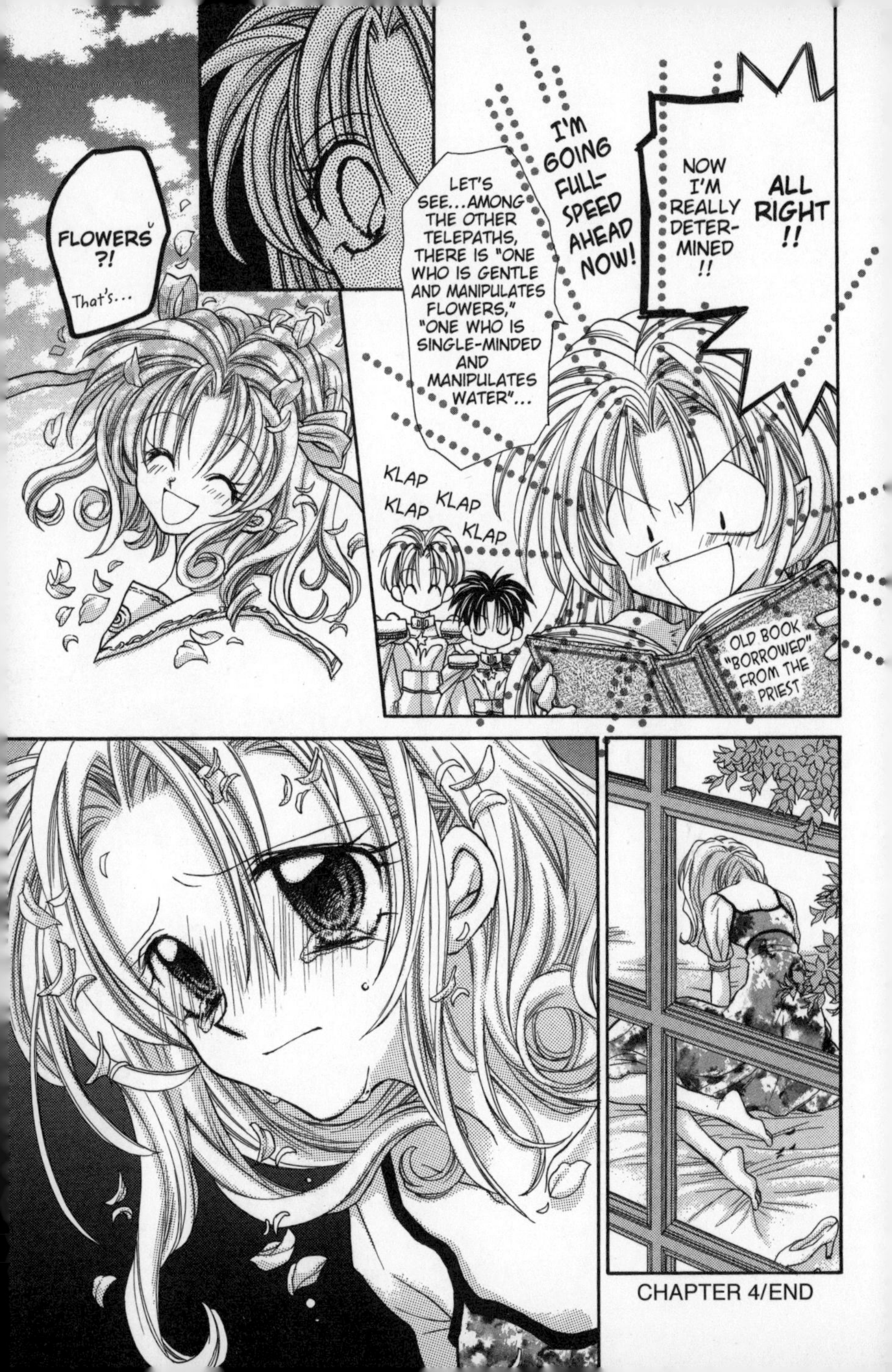
ALL RIGHT!!
NOW I'M REALLY DETERMINED!!
I'M GOING FULL-SPEED AHEAD NOW!
LET'S SEE...AMONG THE OTHER TELEPATHS, THERE IS "ONE WHO IS GENTLE AND MANIPULATES FLOWERS," "ONE WHO IS SINGLE-MINDED AND MANIPULATES WATER"...
KLAP KLAP KLAP KLAP
OLD BOOK "BORROWED" FROM THE PRIEST
FLOWERS?!
That's...

CHAPTER 4/END

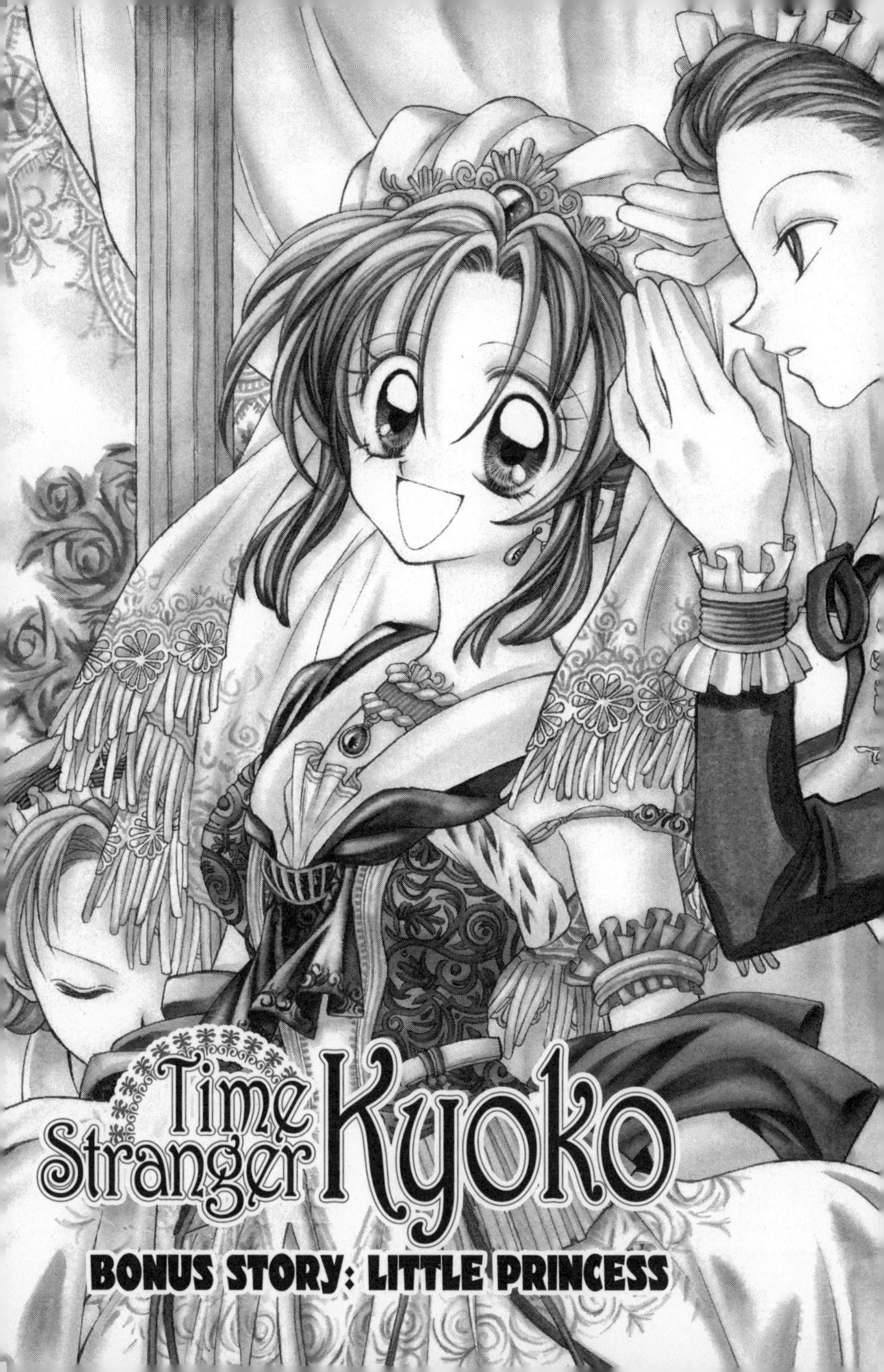
Time Stranger Kyoko
BONUS STORY: LITTLE PRINCESS

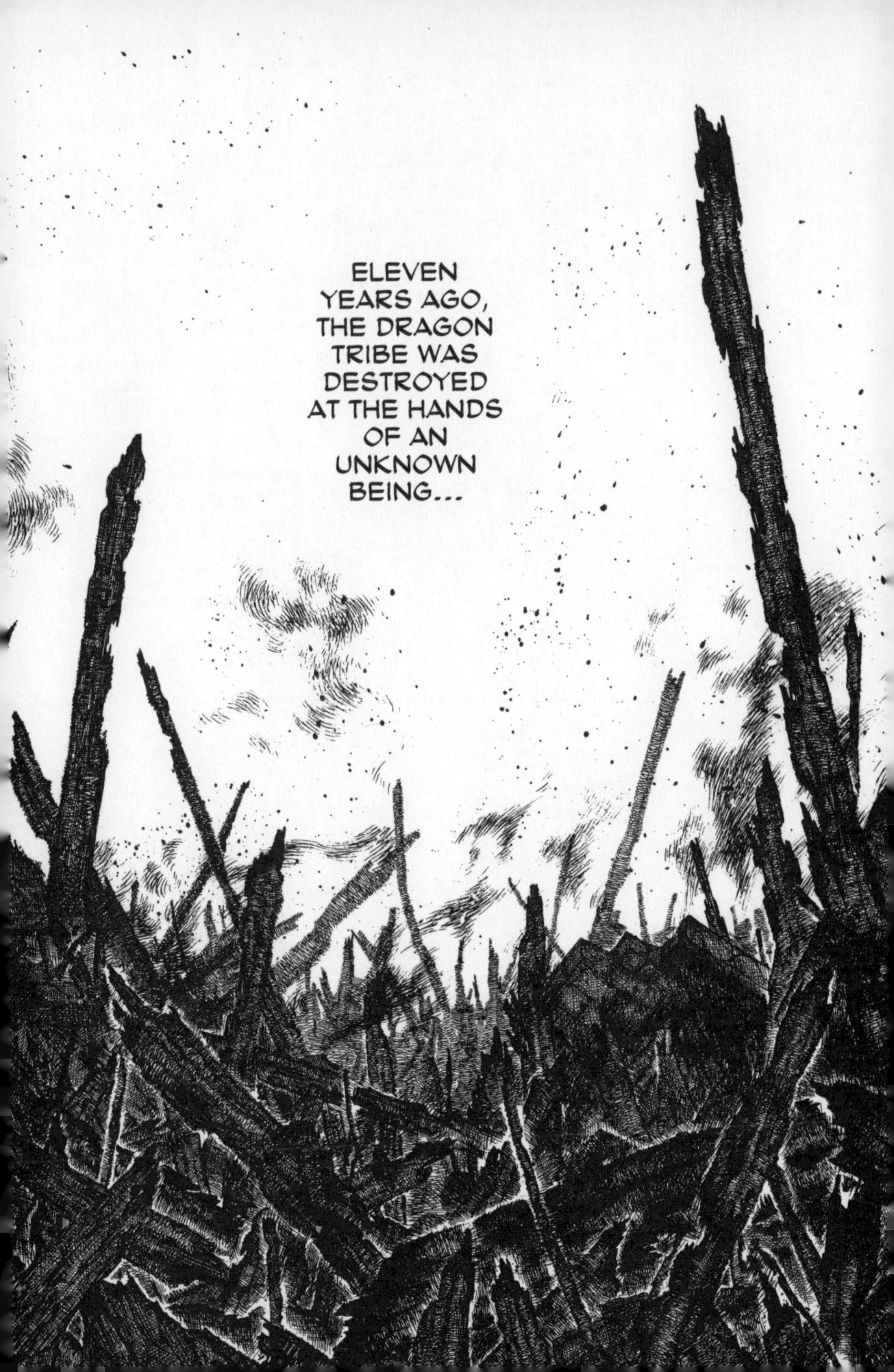
ELEVEN YEARS AGO, THE DRAGON TRIBE WAS DESTROYED AT THE HANDS OF AN UNKNOWN BEING...

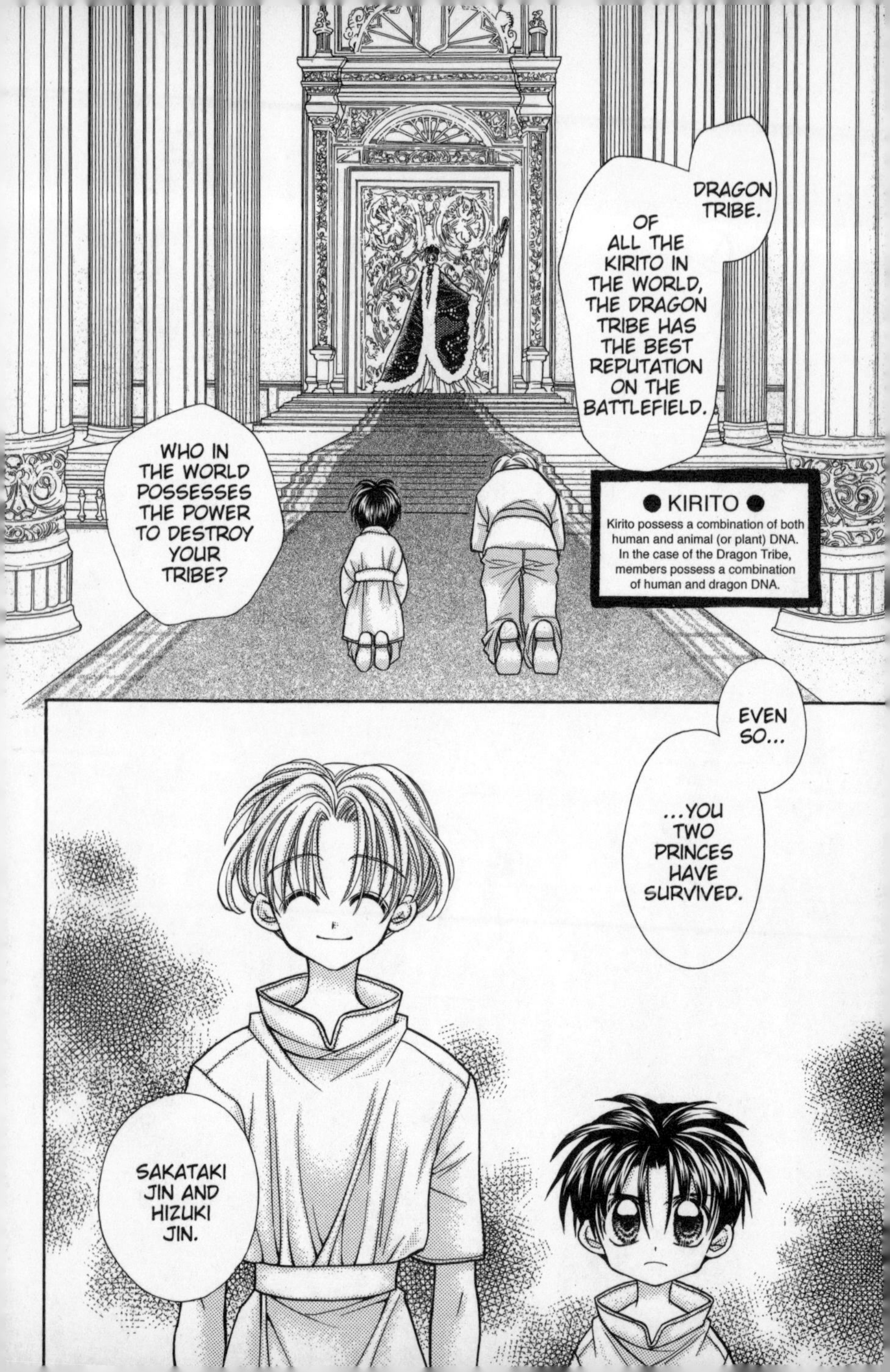
DRAGON TRIBE.
OF ALL THE KIRITO IN THE WORLD, THE DRAGON TRIBE HAS THE BEST REPUTATION ON THE BATTLEFIELD.
● KIRITO ●
Kirito possess a combination of both human and animal (or plant) DNA. In the case of the Dragon Tribe, members possess a combination of human and dragon DNA.
WHO IN THE WORLD POSSESSES THE POWER TO DESTROY YOUR TRIBE?
EVEN SO...
...YOU TWO PRINCES HAVE SURVIVED.
SAKATAKI JIN AND HIZUKI JIN.

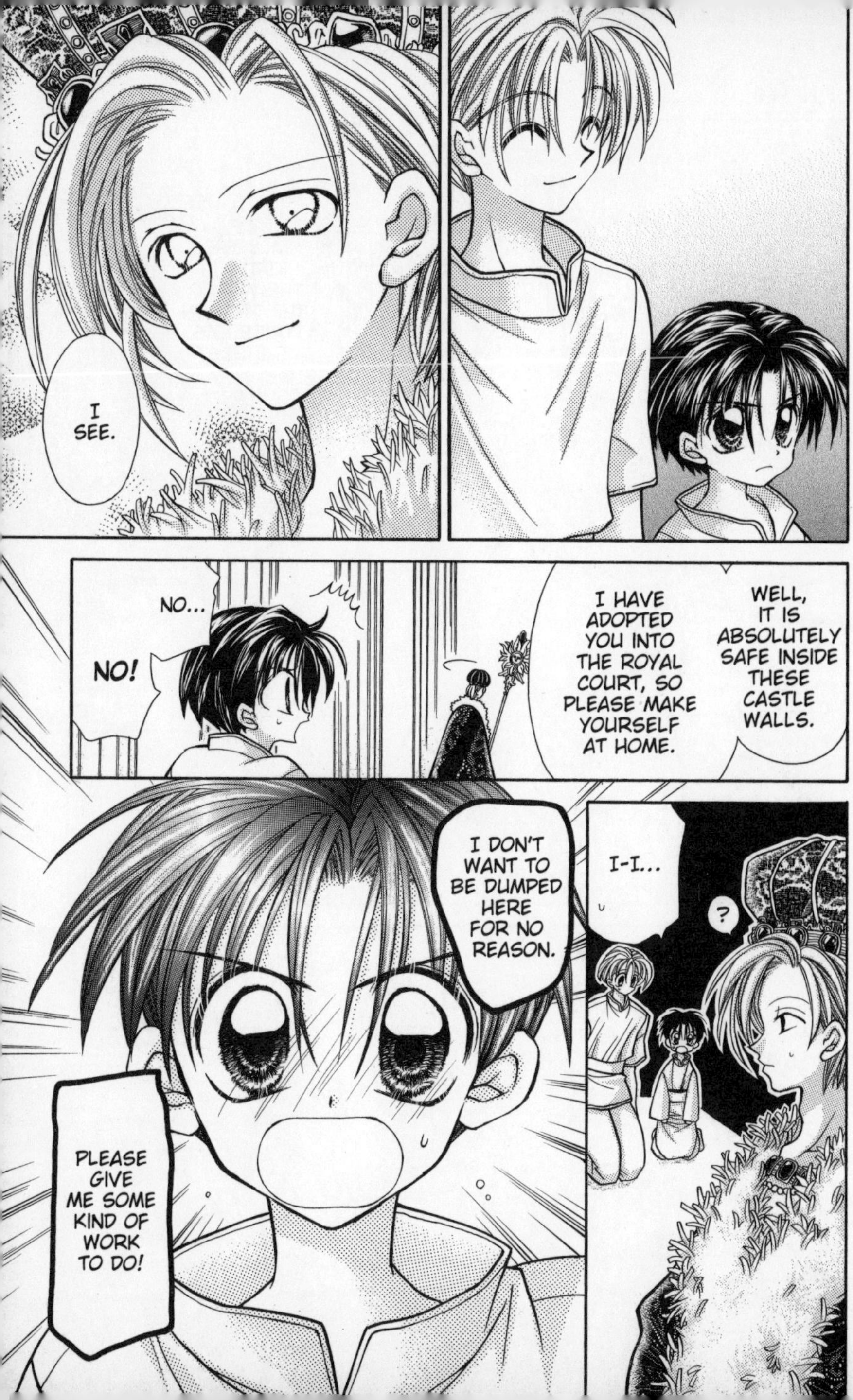
I SEE.
WELL, IT IS ABSOLUTELY SAFE INSIDE THESE CASTLE WALLS.
I HAVE ADOPTED YOU INTO THE ROYAL COURT, SO PLEASE MAKE YOURSELF AT HOME.
NO...
NO!
I-I...
?
I DON'T WANT TO BE DUMPED HERE FOR NO REASON.
PLEASE GIVE ME SOME KIND OF WORK TO DO!

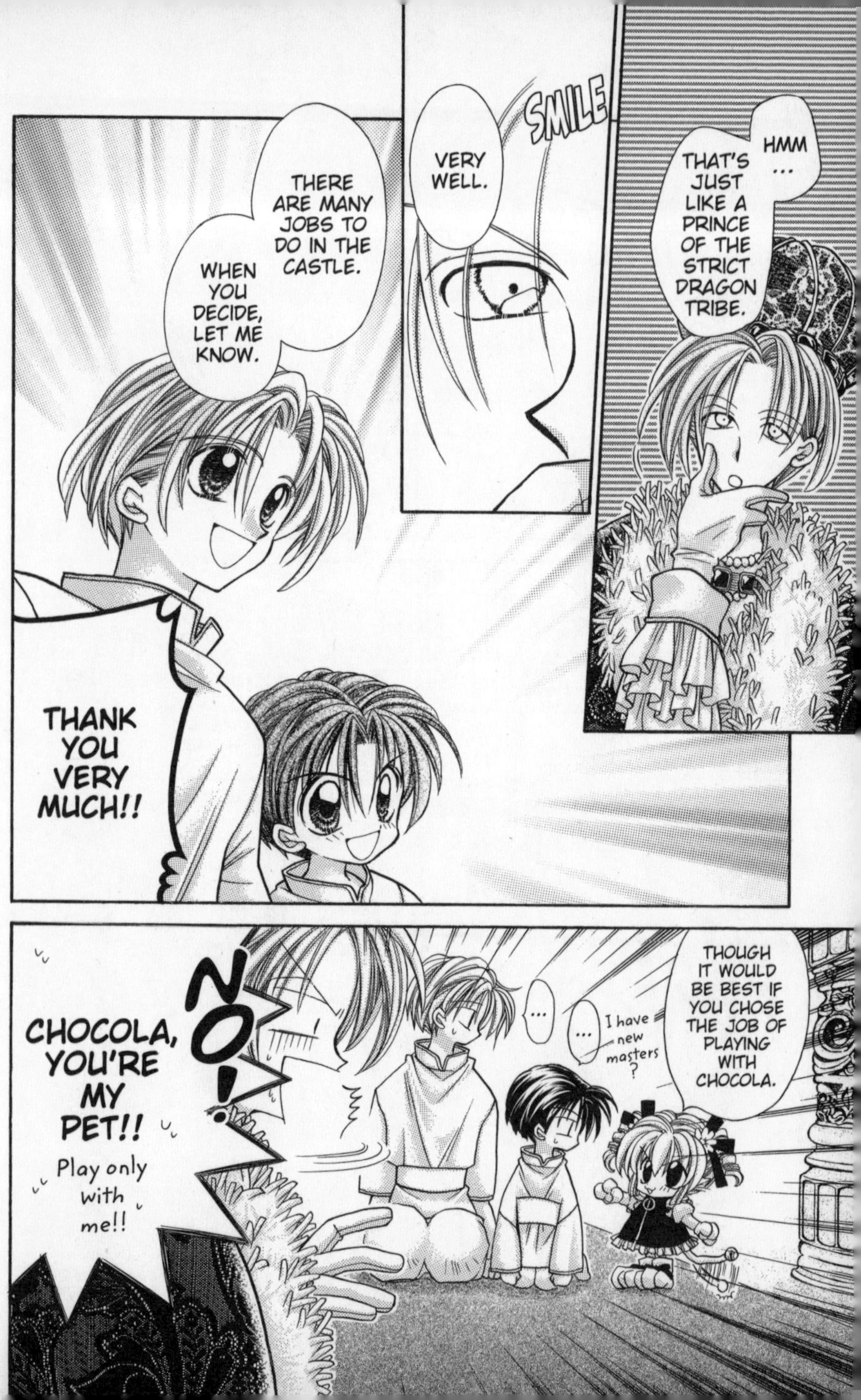
HMM ...
THAT'S JUST LIKE A PRINCE OF THE STRICT DRAGON TRIBE.
SMILE
VERY WELL.
THERE ARE MANY JOBS TO DO IN THE CASTLE.
WHEN YOU DECIDE, LET ME KNOW.
THANK YOU VERY MUCH!!
THOUGH IT WOULD BE BEST IF YOU CHOSE THE JOB OF PLAYING WITH CHOCOLA.
I have new masters?
...
...
NO!
CHOCOLA, YOU'RE MY PET!!
Play only with me!!

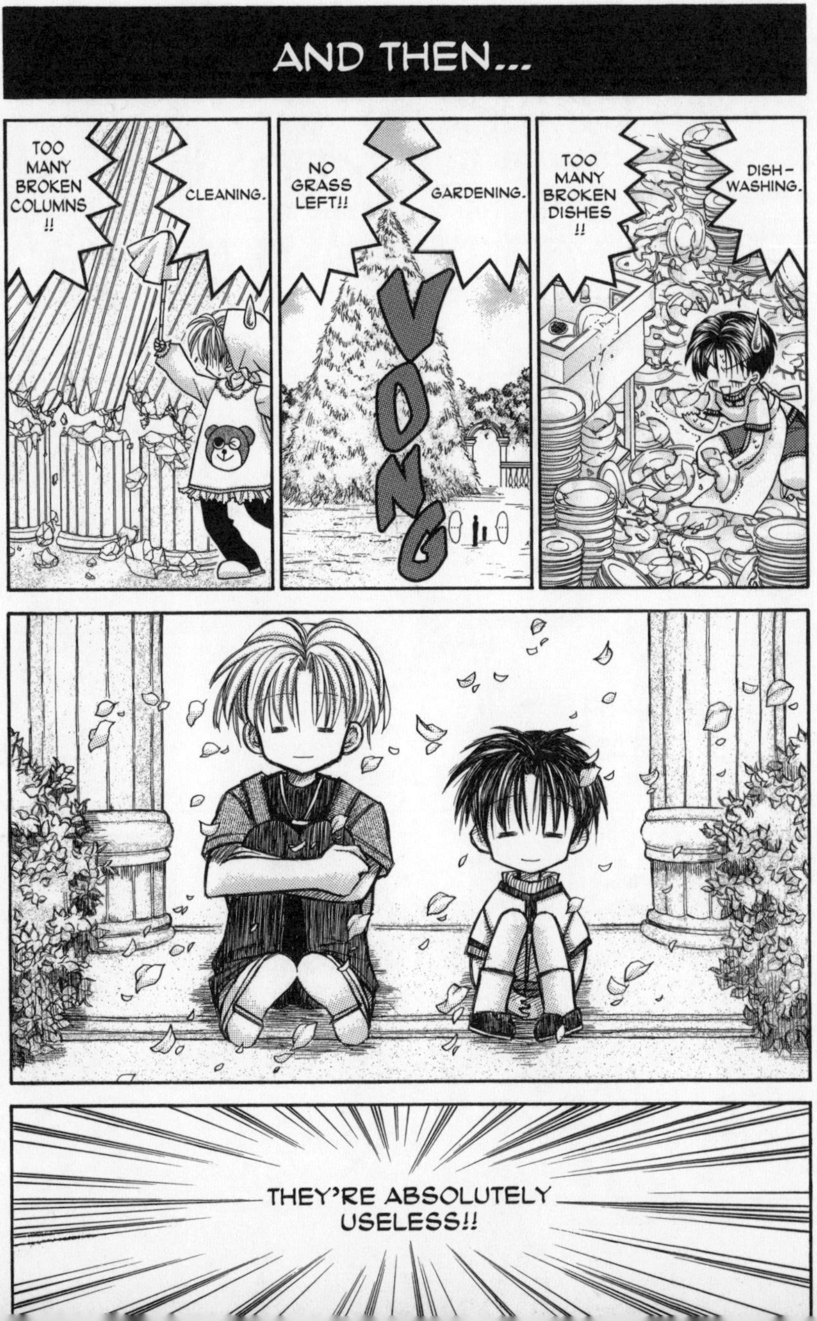
AND THEN...
DISH-WASHING.
TOO MANY BROKEN DISHES!!
GARDENING.
NO GRASS LEFT!!
VONG
CLEANING.
TOO MANY BROKEN COLUMNS!!
THEY'RE ABSOLUTELY USELESS!!

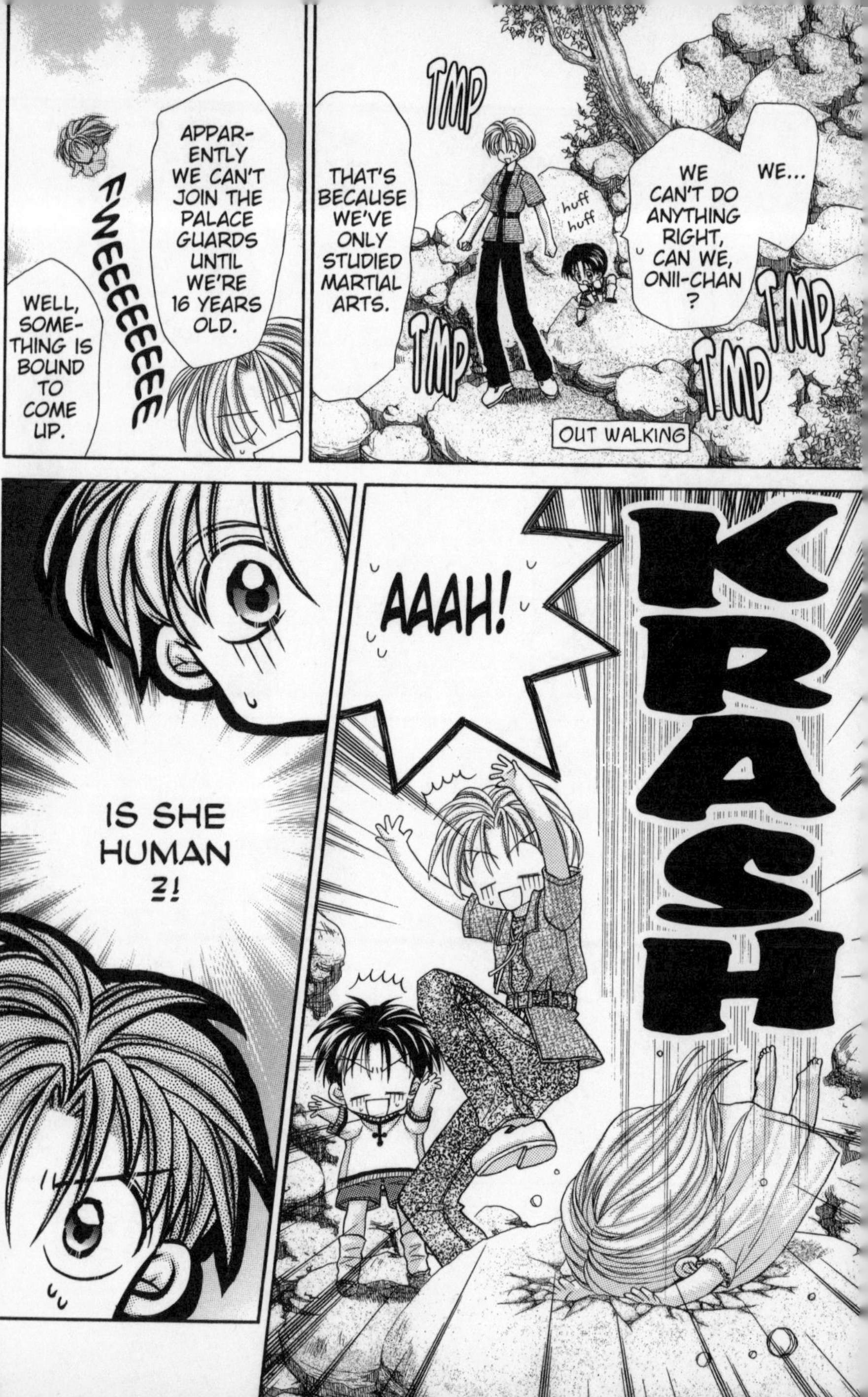
OUT WALKING
TMP
TMP
TMP
TMP
TMP
huff huff
WE...
WE CAN'T DO ANYTHING RIGHT, CAN WE, ONII-CHAN?
THAT'S BECAUSE WE'VE ONLY STUDIED MARTIAL ARTS.
APPARENTLY WE CAN'T JOIN THE PALACE GUARDS UNTIL WE'RE 16 YEARS OLD.
FWEEEEEEEEE
WELL, SOMETHING IS BOUND TO COME UP.
KRASH
AAAH!
IS SHE HUMAN?!

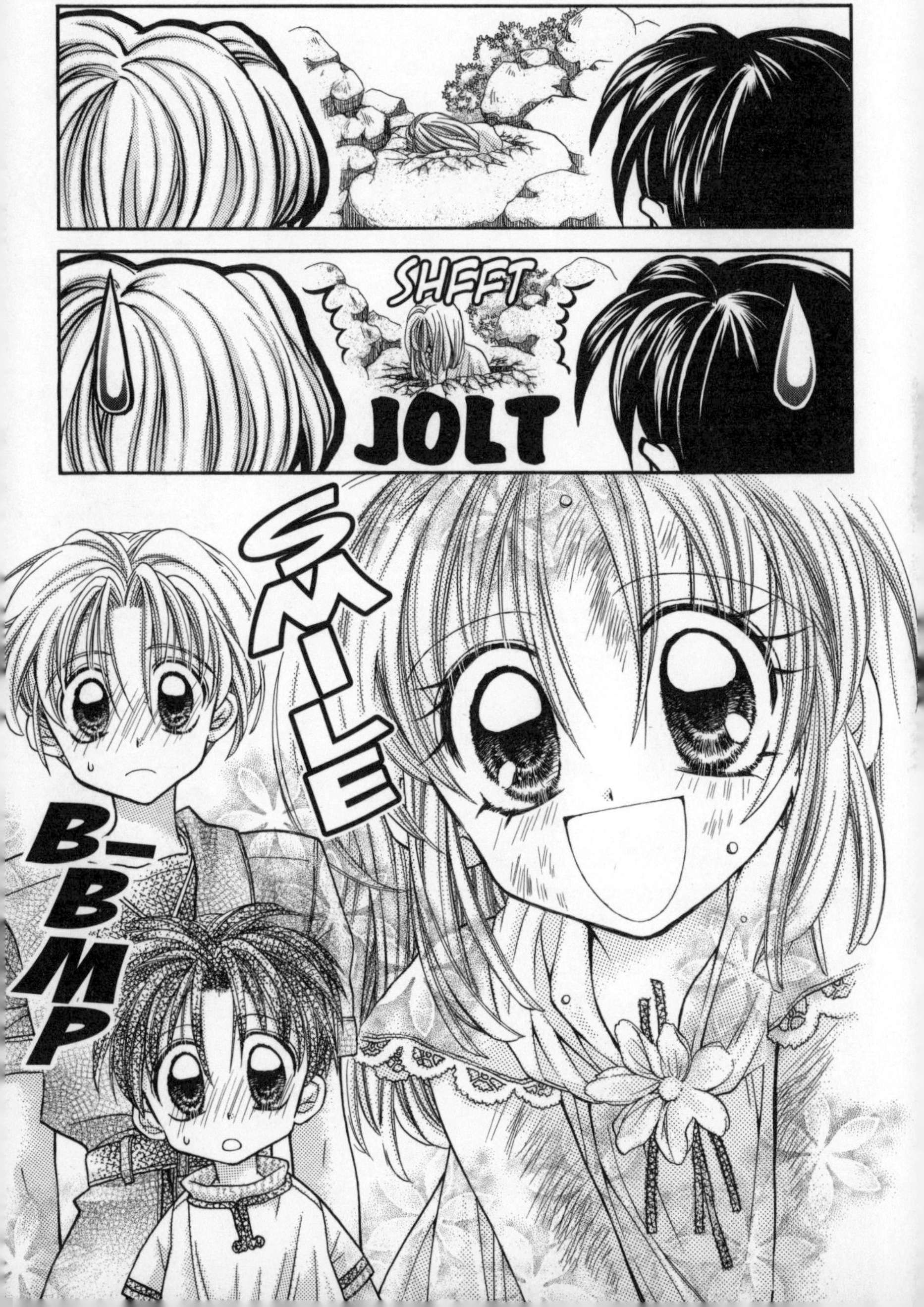
SHFFT
JOLT
SMILE
B-BMP

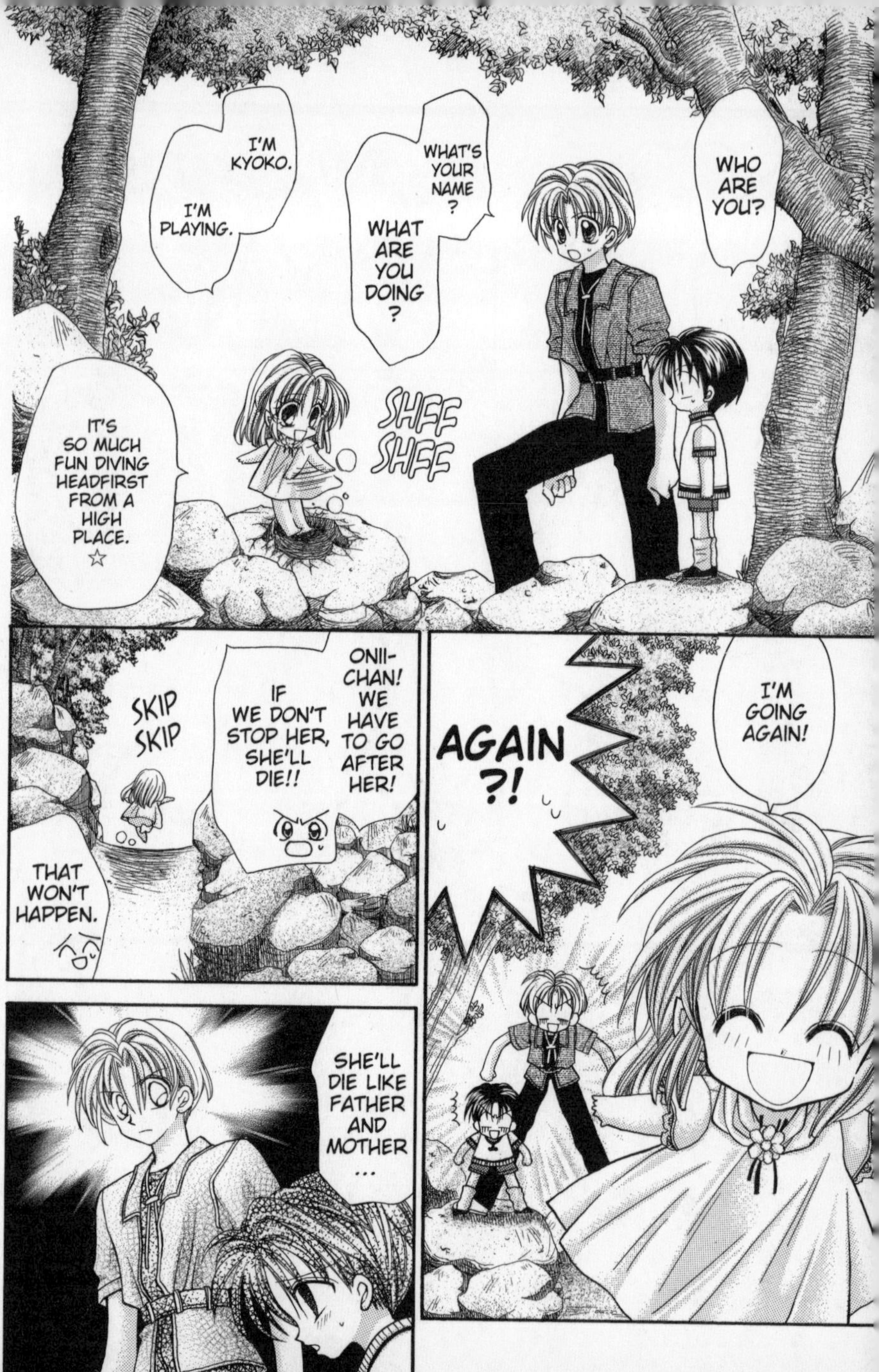
WHO ARE YOU?
WHAT'S YOUR NAME?
WHAT ARE YOU DOING?
I'M KYOKO.
I'M PLAYING.
SHFF SHFF
IT'S SO MUCH FUN DIVING HEADFIRST FROM A HIGH PLACE. ☆
I'M GOING AGAIN!
AGAIN?!
ONII-CHAN! WE HAVE TO GO AFTER HER!
IF WE DON'T STOP HER, SHE'LL DIE!!
SKIP SKIP
THAT WON'T HAPPEN.
SHE'LL DIE LIKE FATHER AND MOTHER...

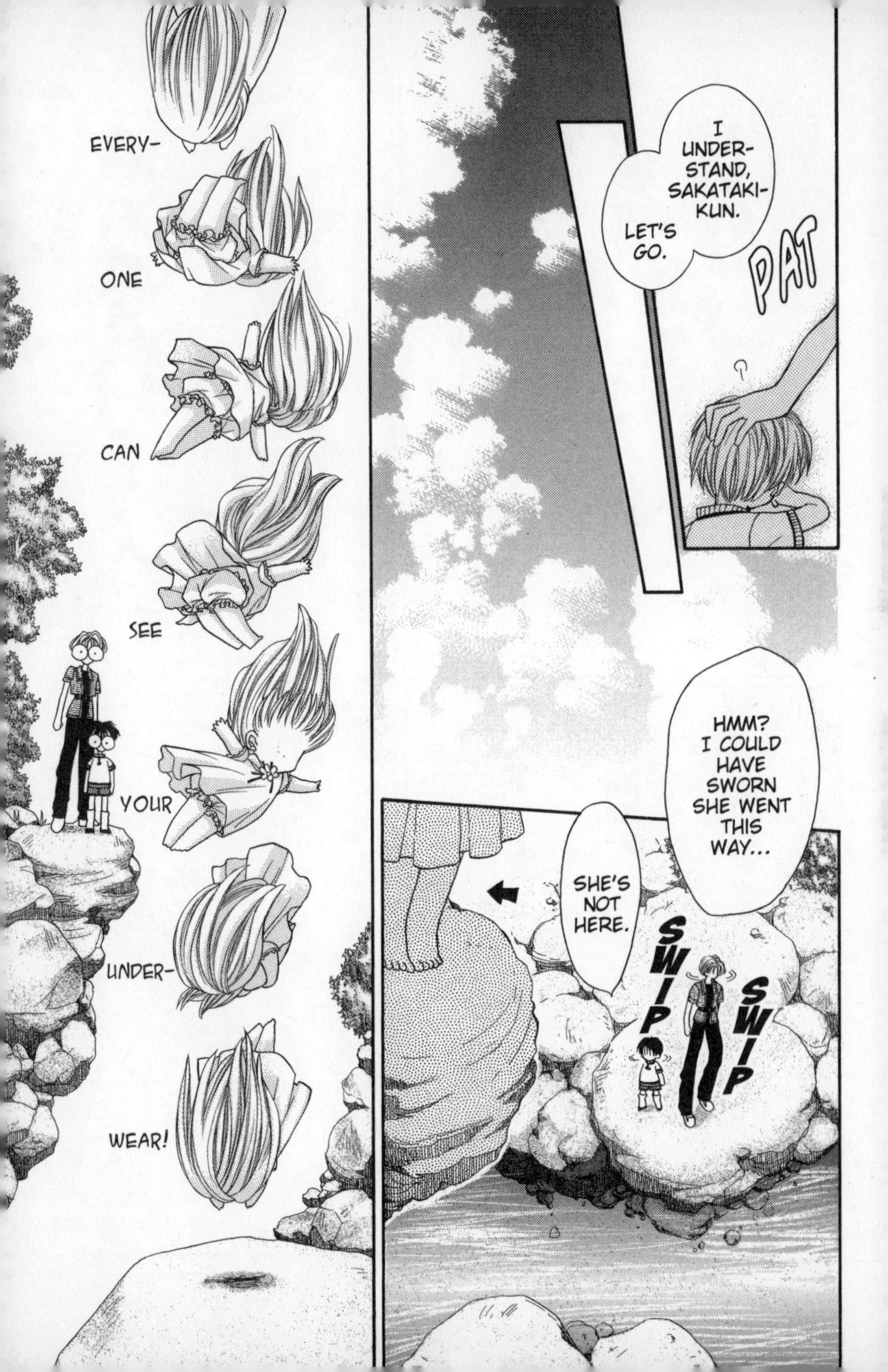
I UNDERSTAND, SAKATAKI-KUN.
LET'S GO.
PAT
HMM? I COULD HAVE SWORN SHE WENT THIS WAY...
SHE'S NOT HERE.
SWIP
SWIP
EVERY-
ONE
CAN
SEE
YOUR
UNDER-
WEAR!

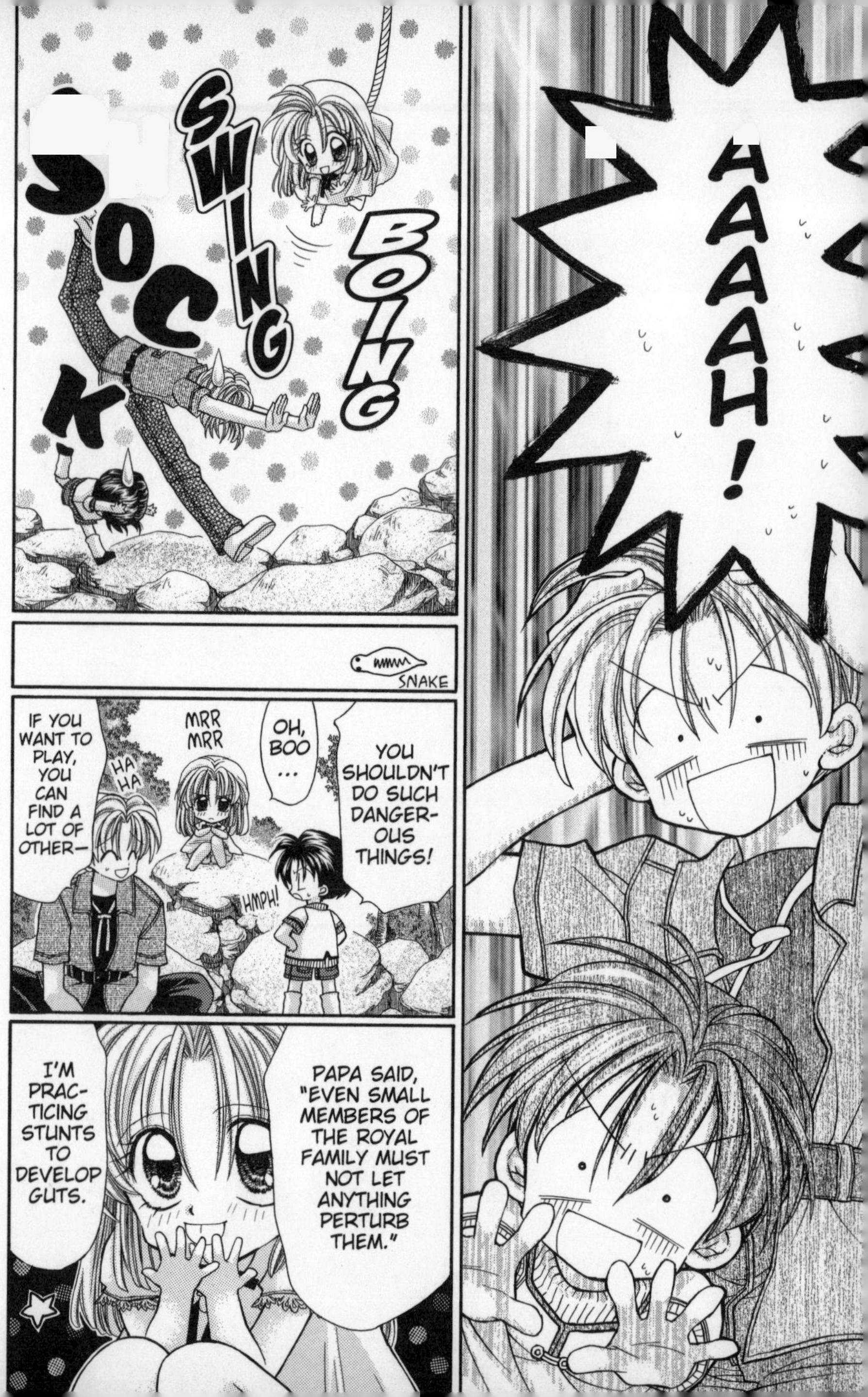
AAAAH!
BOING
SWING
SOCK
SNAKE
YOU SHOULDN'T DO SUCH DANGER-OUS THINGS!
OH, BOO...
MRR MRR
HMPH!
IF YOU WANT TO PLAY, YOU CAN FIND A LOT OF OTHER—
HA HA
PAPA SAID, "EVEN SMALL MEMBERS OF THE ROYAL FAMILY MUST NOT LET ANYTHING PERTURB THEM."
I'M PRAC-TICING STUNTS TO DEVELOP GUTS.

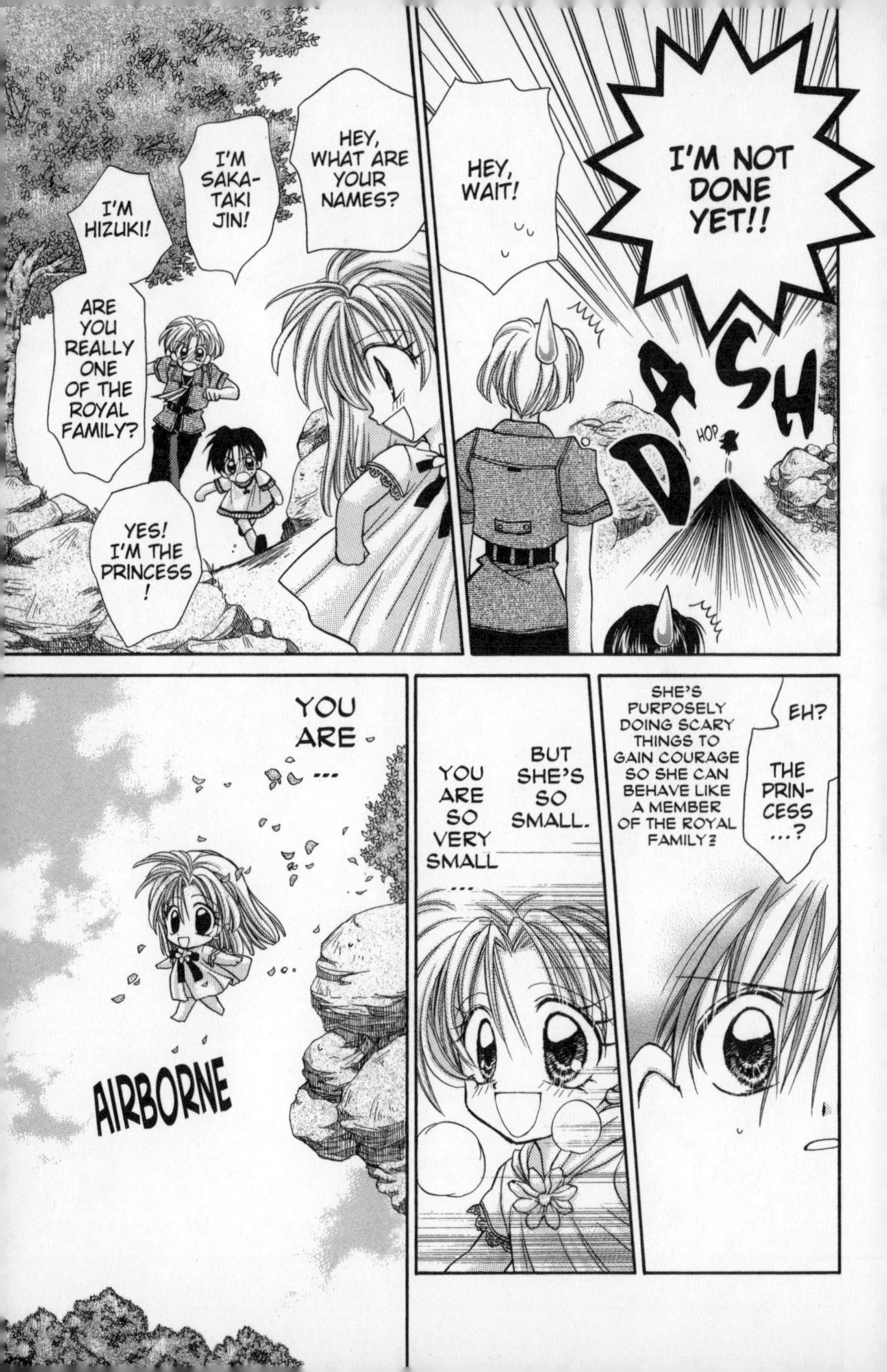
I'M NOT DONE YET!!
HEY, WAIT!
DASH
HOP
HEY, WHAT ARE YOUR NAMES?
I'M SAKA-TAKI JIN!
I'M HIZUKI!
ARE YOU REALLY ONE OF THE ROYAL FAMILY?
YES! I'M THE PRINCESS!
EH?
THE PRIN-CESS...?
SHE'S PURPOSELY DOING SCARY THINGS TO GAIN COURAGE SO SHE CAN BEHAVE LIKE A MEMBER OF THE ROYAL FAMILY?
BUT SHE'S SO SMALL.
YOU ARE SO VERY SMALL...
YOU ARE...
AIRBORNE

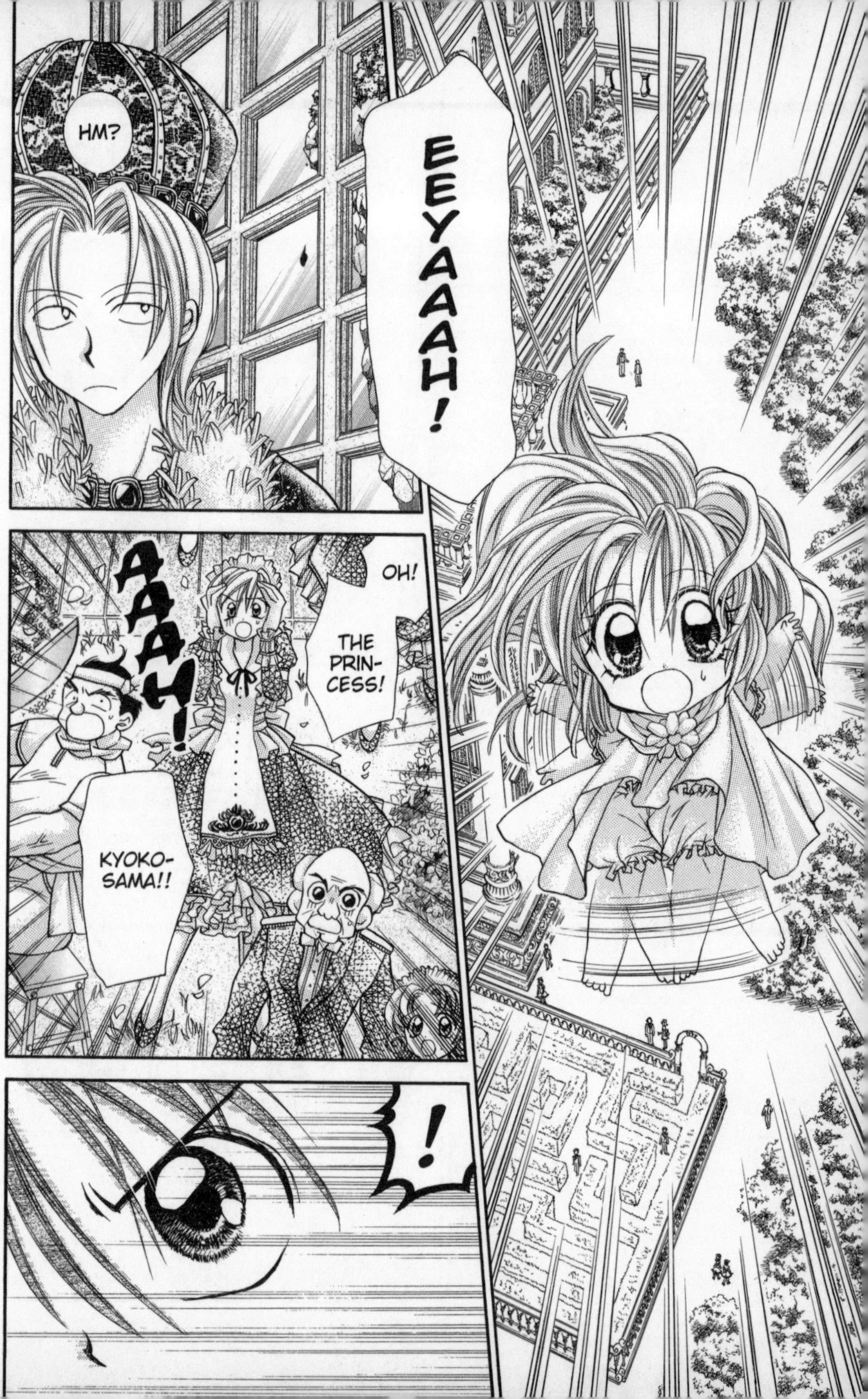
EEYAAAH!
HM?
OH!
THE PRIN-CESS!
AAAH!
KYOKO-SAMA!!
!

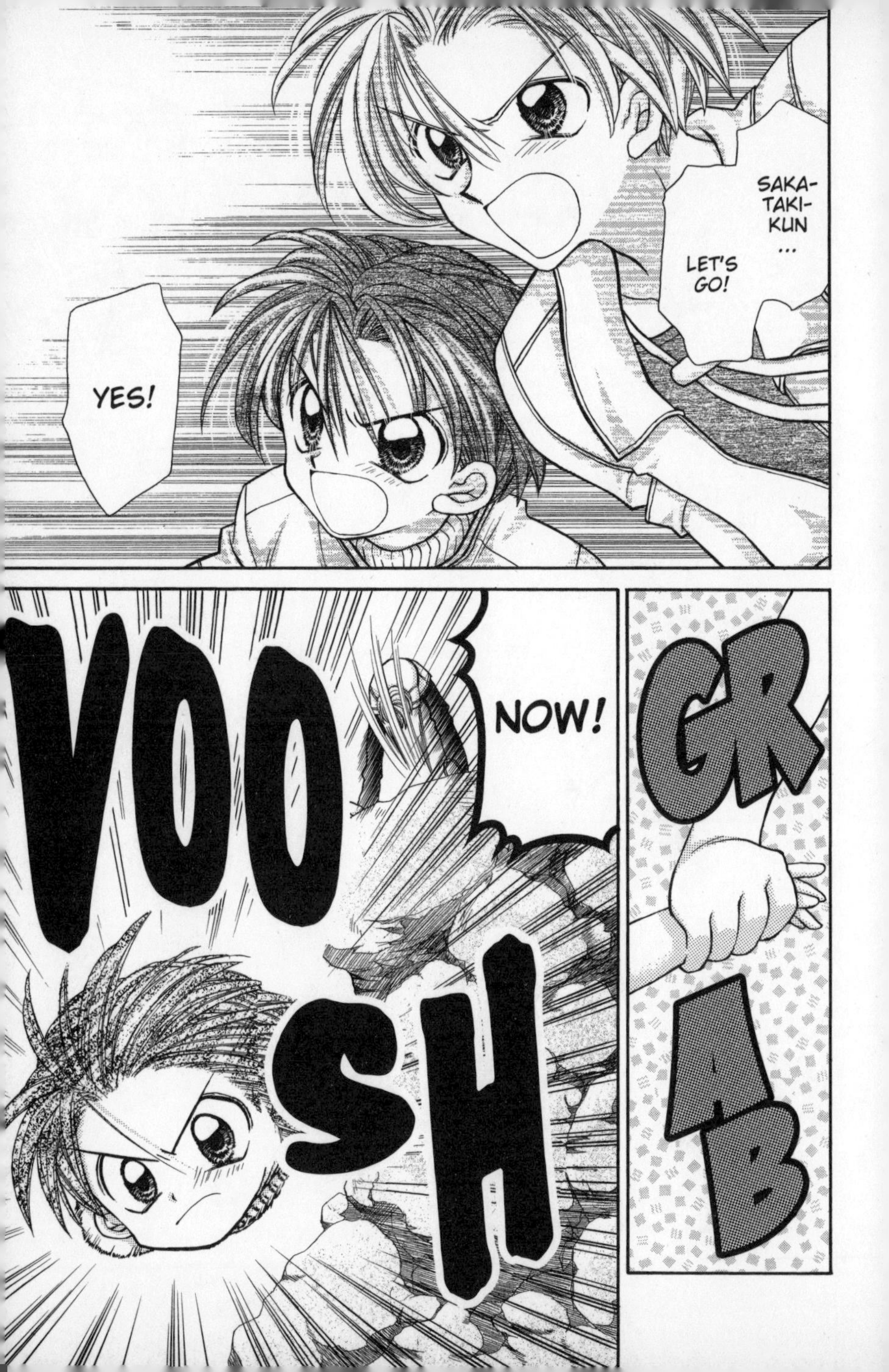
SAKA-TAKI-KUN ...
LET'S GO!
YES!
GRAB
NOW!
VOOSH

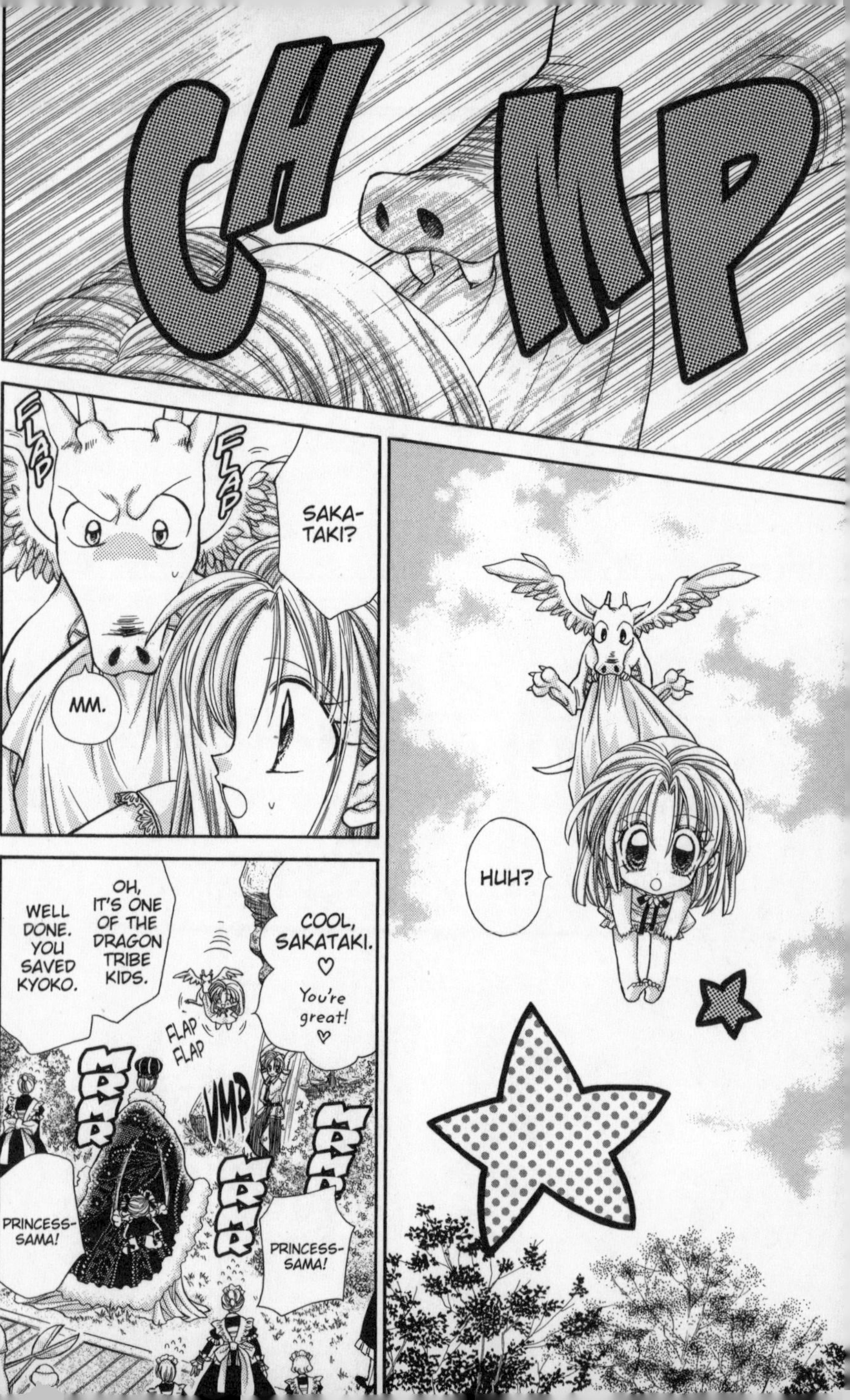
CHOMP
HUH?
FLAP
FLAP
SAKA-
TAKI?
MM.
COOL, SAKATAKI. ♡
You're great! ♡
OH, IT'S ONE OF THE DRAGON TRIBE KIDS.
WELL DONE. YOU SAVED KYOKO.
FLAP FLAP
VMP
MRMR
MRMR
MRMR
MRMR
PRINCESS-SAMA!
PRINCESS-SAMA!

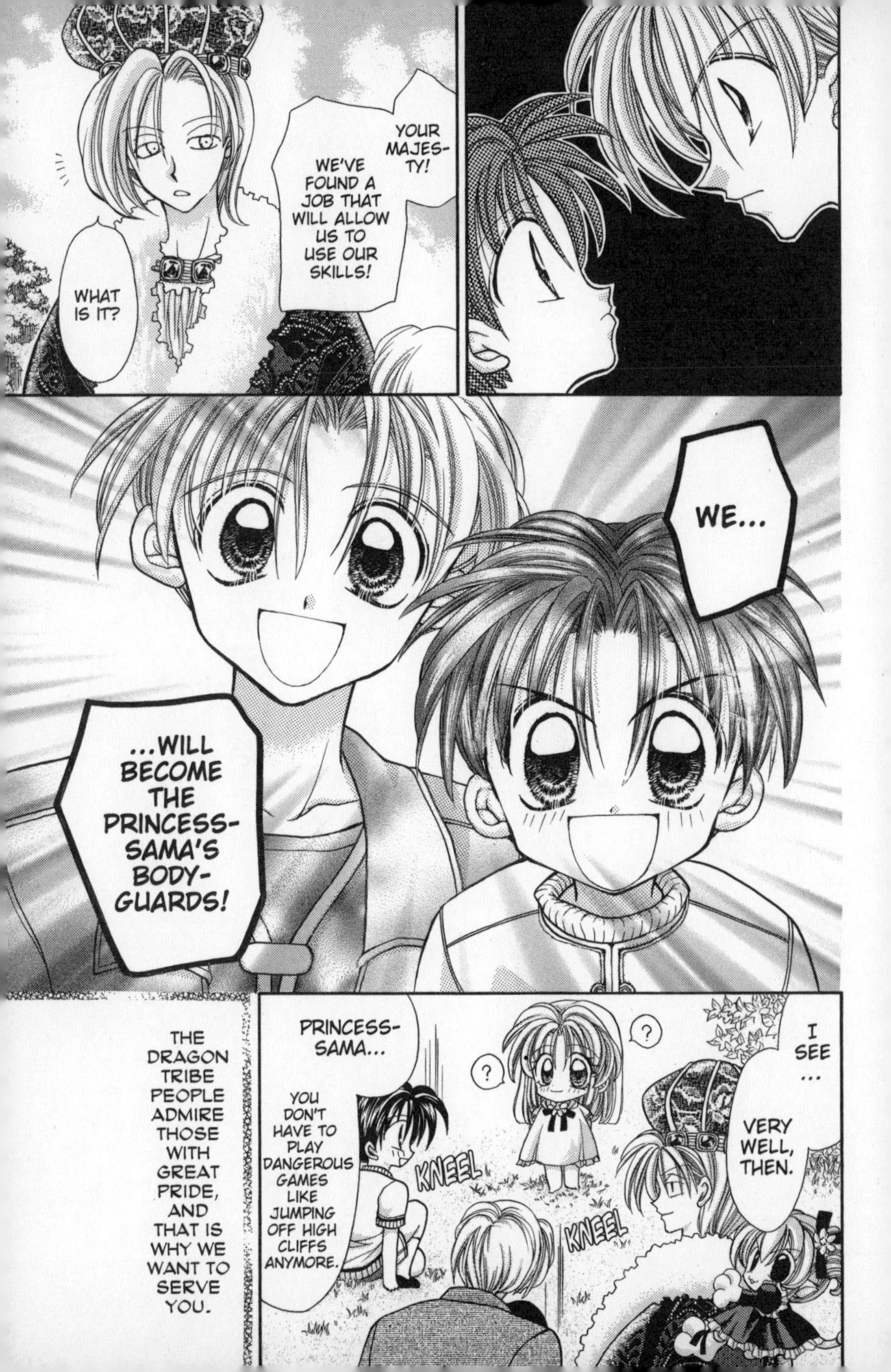
YOUR MAJESTY!
WE'VE FOUND A JOB THAT WILL ALLOW US TO USE OUR SKILLS!
WHAT IS IT?
WE...
...WILL BECOME THE PRINCESS-SAMA'S BODYGUARDS!
I SEE...
VERY WELL, THEN.
?
?
PRINCESS-SAMA...
YOU DON'T HAVE TO PLAY DANGEROUS GAMES LIKE JUMPING OFF HIGH CLIFFS ANYMORE.
KNEEL
KNEEL
THE DRAGON TRIBE PEOPLE ADMIRE THOSE WITH GREAT PRIDE, AND THAT IS WHY WE WANT TO SERVE YOU.

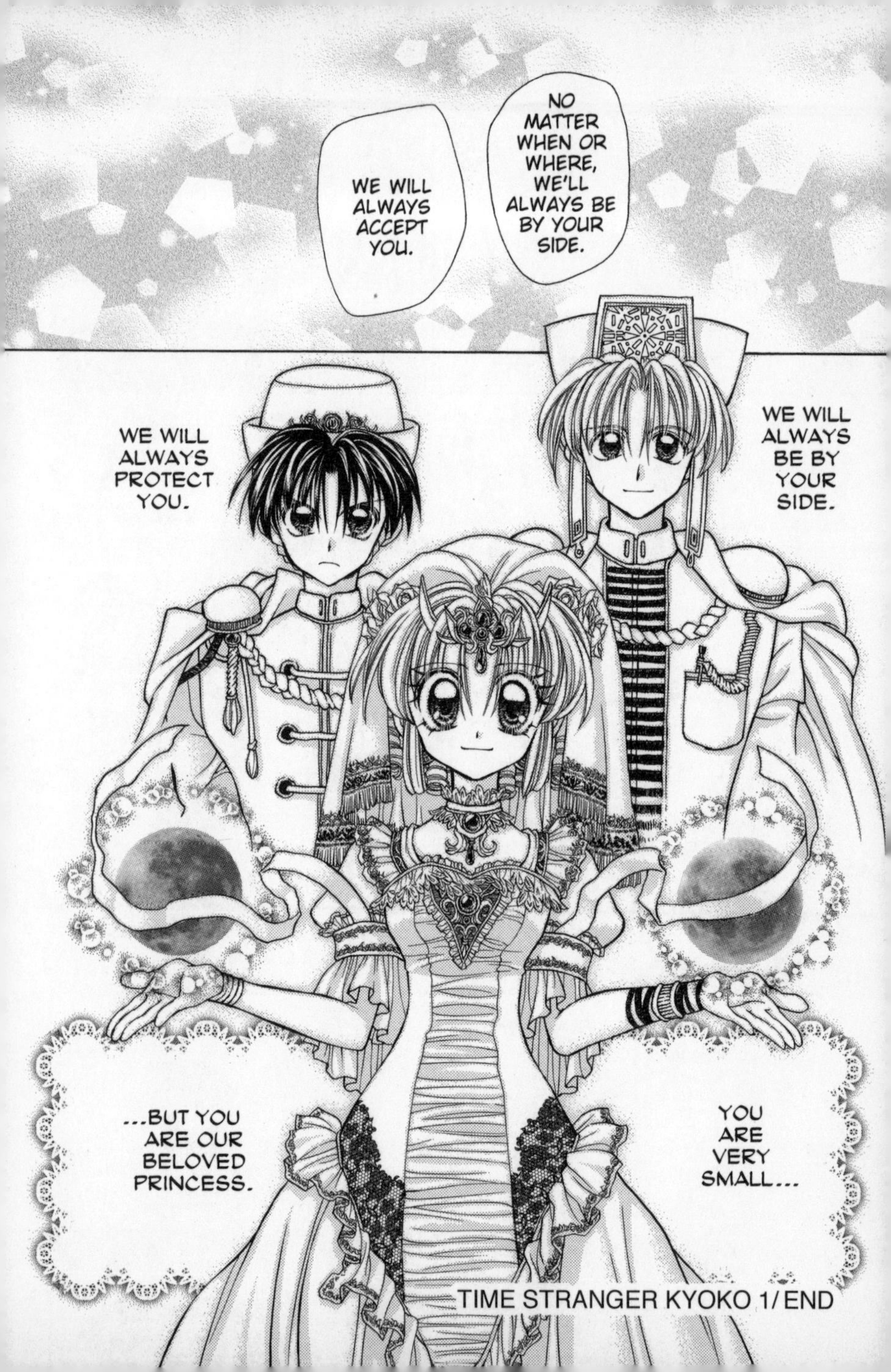
NO MATTER WHEN OR WHERE, WE'LL ALWAYS BE BY YOUR SIDE.
WE WILL ALWAYS ACCEPT YOU.
WE WILL ALWAYS BE BY YOUR SIDE.
WE WILL ALWAYS PROTECT YOU.
YOU ARE VERY SMALL...
...BUT YOU ARE OUR BELOVED PRINCESS.
TIME STRANGER KYOKO 1/END

Time Stranger Kyoko Notes

The suffixes *–kun* and *–chan* are added to a person's name to show familiarity. The suffix *–sama* is added to show respect for someone who is higher up in the social hierarchy. Witzig's "snake–chama" is a cute nickname for his snake.

Page 9: *Aniki* means "older brother."

Page 13: Eriko Kusuda is an essayist, translator and science writer. Kaoru Yumi is a ballerina–turned–actress.

Page 25: Antonio Inoki is a professional wrestler who is known for having a prominent chin.

Page 35: *Witzig* is German for "funny" or "amusing."

Page 71: Access is a character from *Kamikaze Kaitou Jeanne*. *Barefoot Gen* is a manga, anime and live–action series. "Ken" and Kaoru are characters in *Rurouni Kenshin*. KinKi Kids is a J–Pop group.

Page 101: *Pachin to Kishan*, or "snap and rattle," is a play on *Penchi de Shakin* (see *Full Moon* vol. 1, page 173). *Kisu* is a type of fish; *suki* means "to like."

Page 131: A *mangaka* is a manga creator.

Page 145: *Benchi o Jokin* is another play on *Penchi de Shakin*. This one means "to sterilize the bench."

Kyoko vol. 1 was my tenth published manga, so it was a kind of celebration. It felt a bit like fate. (*laughs*) It was my first serialized manga in about two and a half years, and at first I had writer's block, but now I'm writing like mad. I really like it. I'm going to do my best, so please read *Kyoko*.

Arina Tanemura was born in Aichi, Japan. She got her start in 1996, publishing *Nibanme no Koi no Katachi* (The Style of the Second Love) in *Ribon Original* magazine. Her early work includes a collection of short stories called *Kanshaku Dama no Yuutsu* (Short–Tempered Melancholic). Two of her titles, *Kamikaze Kaito Jeanne* and *Full Moon*, were made into popular TV series. Tanemura enjoys karaoke and is a huge *Lord of the Rings* fan.

TIME STRANGER KYOKO
VOL. 1

The Shojo Beat Manga Edition

STORY AND ART BY
ARINA TANEMURA

Translation/Mary Kennard
Adaptation/Heidi Vivolo
Touch-up Art & Lettering/Rina Mapa
Design/Yukiko Whitley
Editor/Nancy Thistlethwaite

Editor in Chief, Books/Alvin Lu
Editor in Chief, Magazines/Marc Weidenbaum
VP of Publishing Licensing/Rika Inouye
VP of Sales/Gonzalo Ferreyra
Sr. VP of Marketing/Liza Coppola
Publisher/Hyoe Narita

Printed in Canada

Published by VIZ Media, LLC
P.O. Box 77010
San Francisco, CA 94107

Shojo Beat Manga Edition
10 9 8 7 6 5 4 3 2 1
First printing, July 2008

store.viz.com

RATED T+ FOR OLDER TEEN

PARENTAL ADVISORY
TIME STRANGER KYOKO is rated T+ for Older Teen and is recommended for ages 16 and up. This volume contains sexual themes.
ratings.viz.com

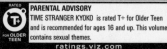

Arina Tanemura Series

The Gentlemen's Alliance †

Haine Otomiya joins Imperial Academy in pursuit of the boy she's loved since she was a child, unaware that he has many secrets of his own.

I•O•N

Chanting the letters of her first name has always brought Ion Tsuburagi good luck—but her good-luck charm is really the result of psychic powers!

Full Moon

Mitsuki Koyama dreams of becoming a pop star, but she is dying of throat cancer. Can she live out a lifetime of dreams in just one year?

Short-Tempered Melancholic

A collection of short stories including Arina Tanemura's debut manga, "In the Style of the Second Love"!

Time Stranger Kyoko

Kyoko Suomi must find 12 holy stones and 12 telepaths to awaken her sister who has been trapped in time since birth.

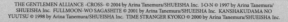

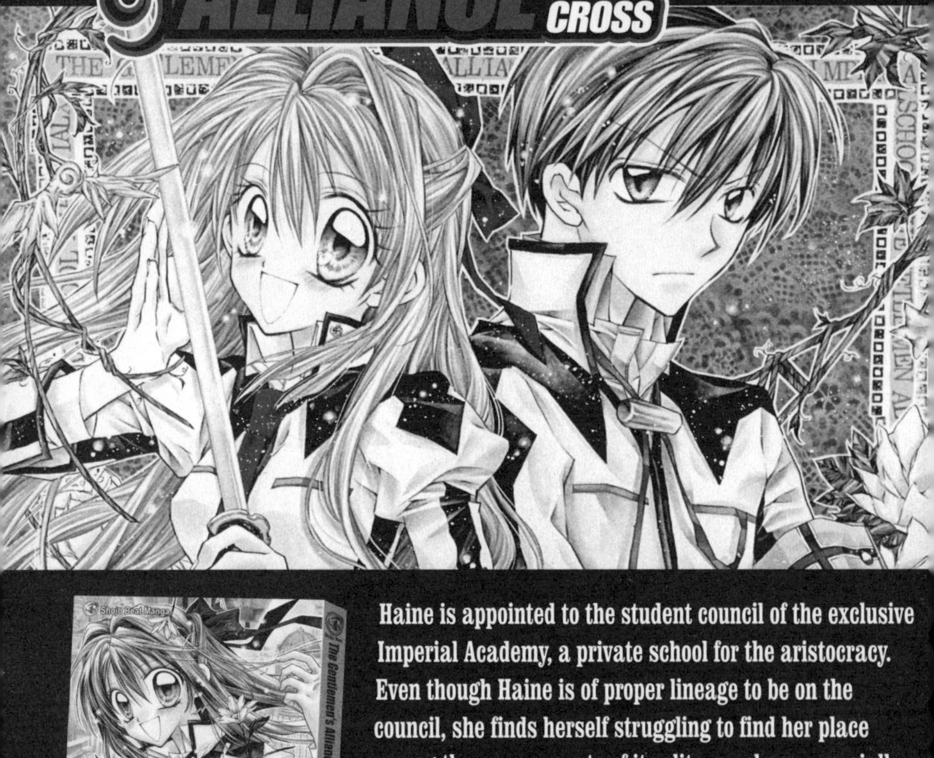

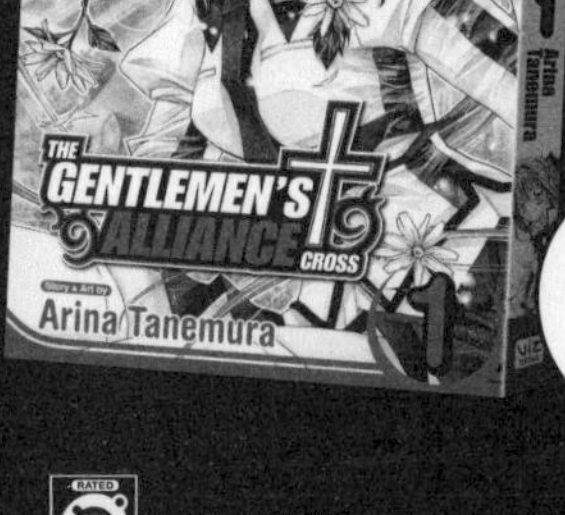
Shojo Beat Manga
The Gentlemen's Alliance
THE GENTLEMEN'S ALLIANCE CROSS
Arina Tanemura
1

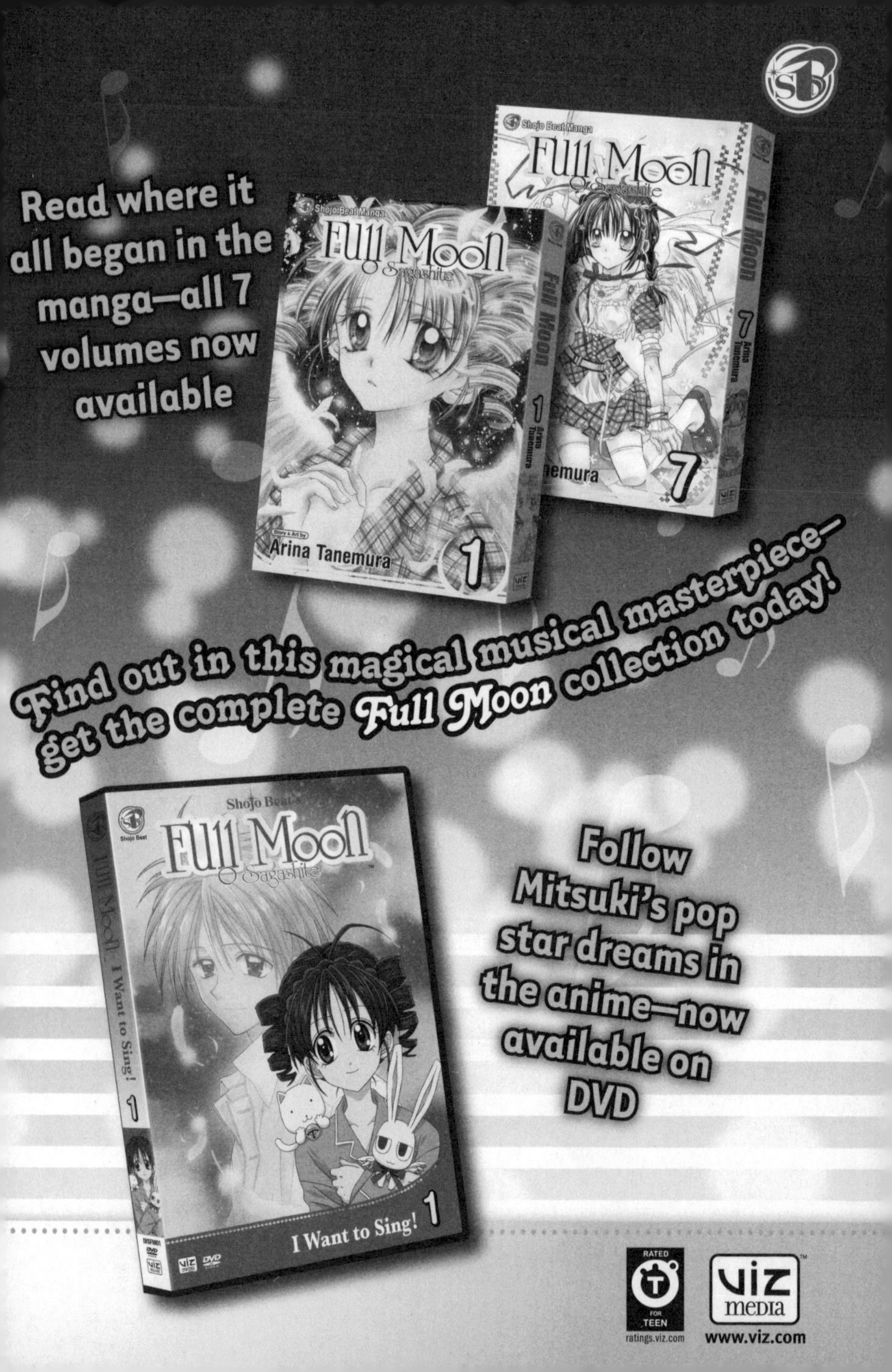
Read where it all began in the manga—all 7 volumes now available
Shojo Beat Manga
Full Moon O Sagashite
Story & Art by Arina Tanemura
1
Shojo Beat Manga
Full Moon O Sagashite
7
Find out in this magical musical masterpiece—get the complete Full Moon collection today!
Shojo Beat's
Full Moon O Sagashite
I Want to Sing! 1
Follow Mitsuki's pop star dreams in the anime—now available on DVD
RATED T FOR TEEN
ratings.viz.com
VIZ media
www.viz.com

Full Moon

O Sagashite

By Arina Tanemura

creator of *The Gentlemen's Alliance †*

Mitsuki loves singing, but a malignant throat tumor prevents her from pursuing her passion.

Can two fun-loving Shinigami give her singing career a magical jump-start?

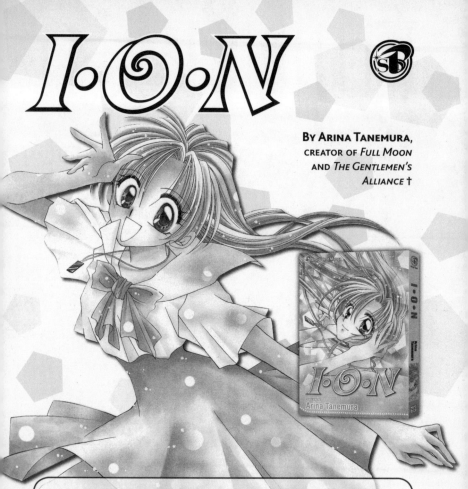

I·O·N

BY ARINA TANEMURA,
CREATER OF *FULL MOON*
AND *THE GENTLEMEN'S ALLIANCE* †

Ion Tsuburagi is a normal junior high girl with normal junior high problems. But when a mysterious substance grants her telekinetic powers, she finds herself struggling to keep everything together! Are her new abilities a blessing...or a curse?

Find out in *I·O·N*—manga on sale now!

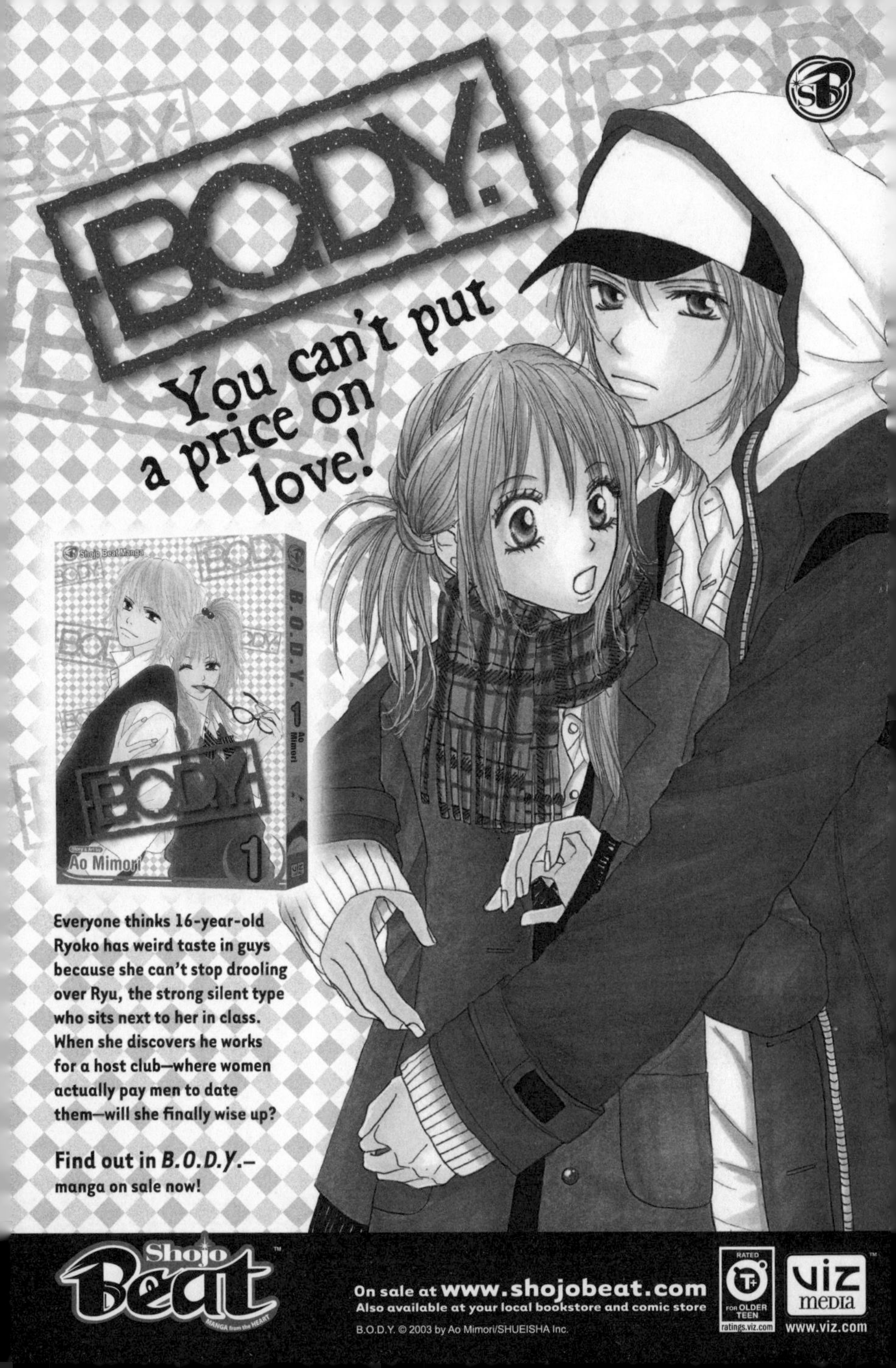
B.O.D.Y.
You can't put a price on love!
Shojo Beat Manga
B.O.D.Y.
1
Story & Art by
Ao Mimori
Everyone thinks 16-year-old Ryoko has weird taste in guys because she can't stop drooling over Ryu, the strong silent type who sits next to her in class. When she discovers he works for a host club—where women actually pay men to date them—will she finally wise up?
Find out in *B.O.D.Y.*—manga on sale now!
Shojo Beat
MANGA from the HEART
On sale at www.shojobeat.com
Also available at your local bookstore and comic store
B.O.D.Y. © 2003 by Ao Mimori/SHUEISHA Inc.
RATED T+ FOR OLDER TEEN
ratings.viz.com
VIZ media
www.viz.com

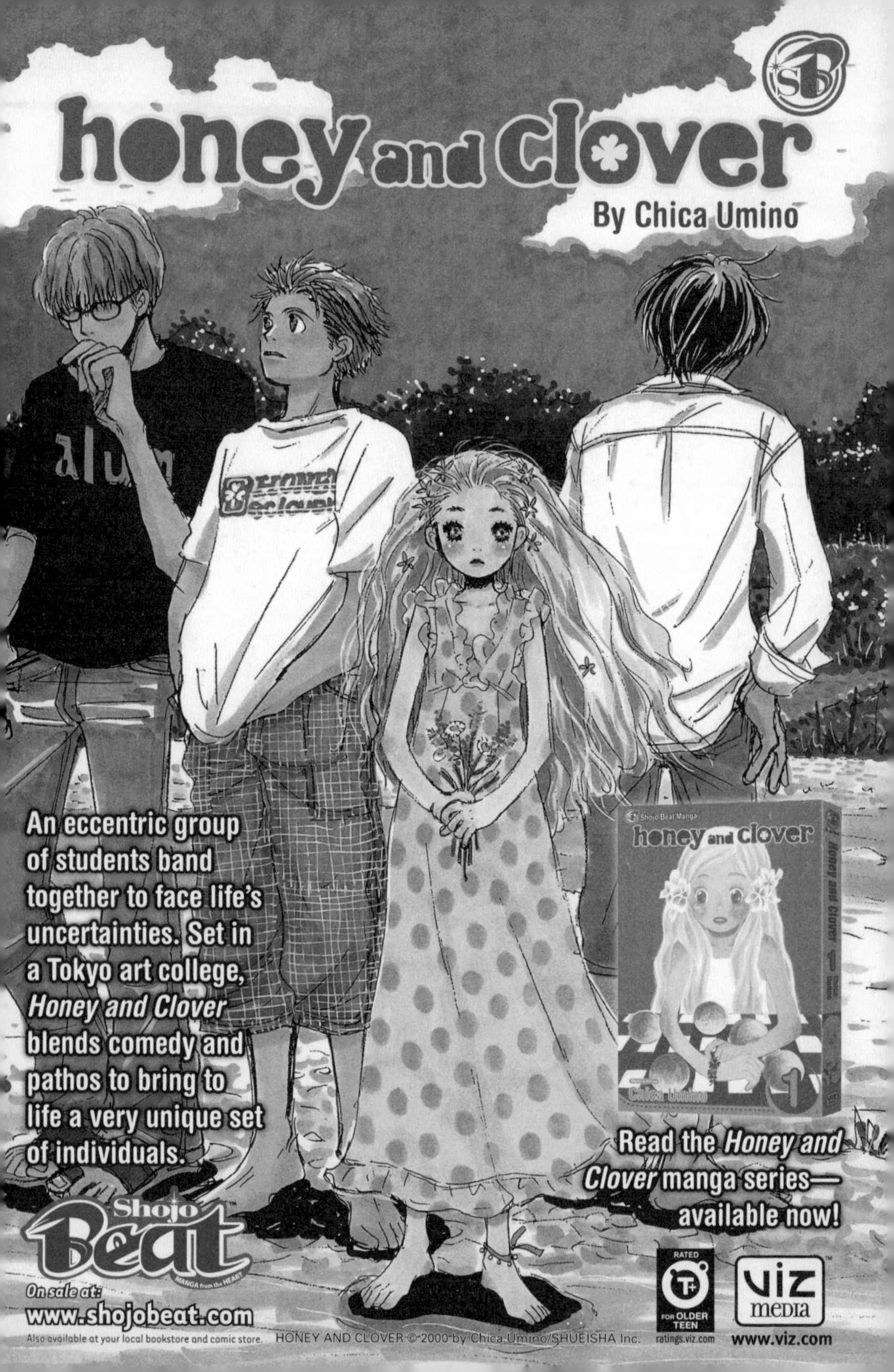
honey and clover
By Chica Umino
An eccentric group of students band together to face life's uncertainties. Set in a Tokyo art college, Honey and Clover blends comedy and pathos to bring to life a very unique set of individuals.
Read the Honey and Clover manga series—available now!
Shojo Beat
MANGA from the HEART
On sale at:
www.shojobeat.com
Also available at your local bookstore and comic store.
HONEY AND CLOVER © 2000 by Chica Umino/SHUEISHA Inc.
RATED T+ FOR OLDER TEEN
ratings.viz.com
VIZ MEDIA
www.viz.com

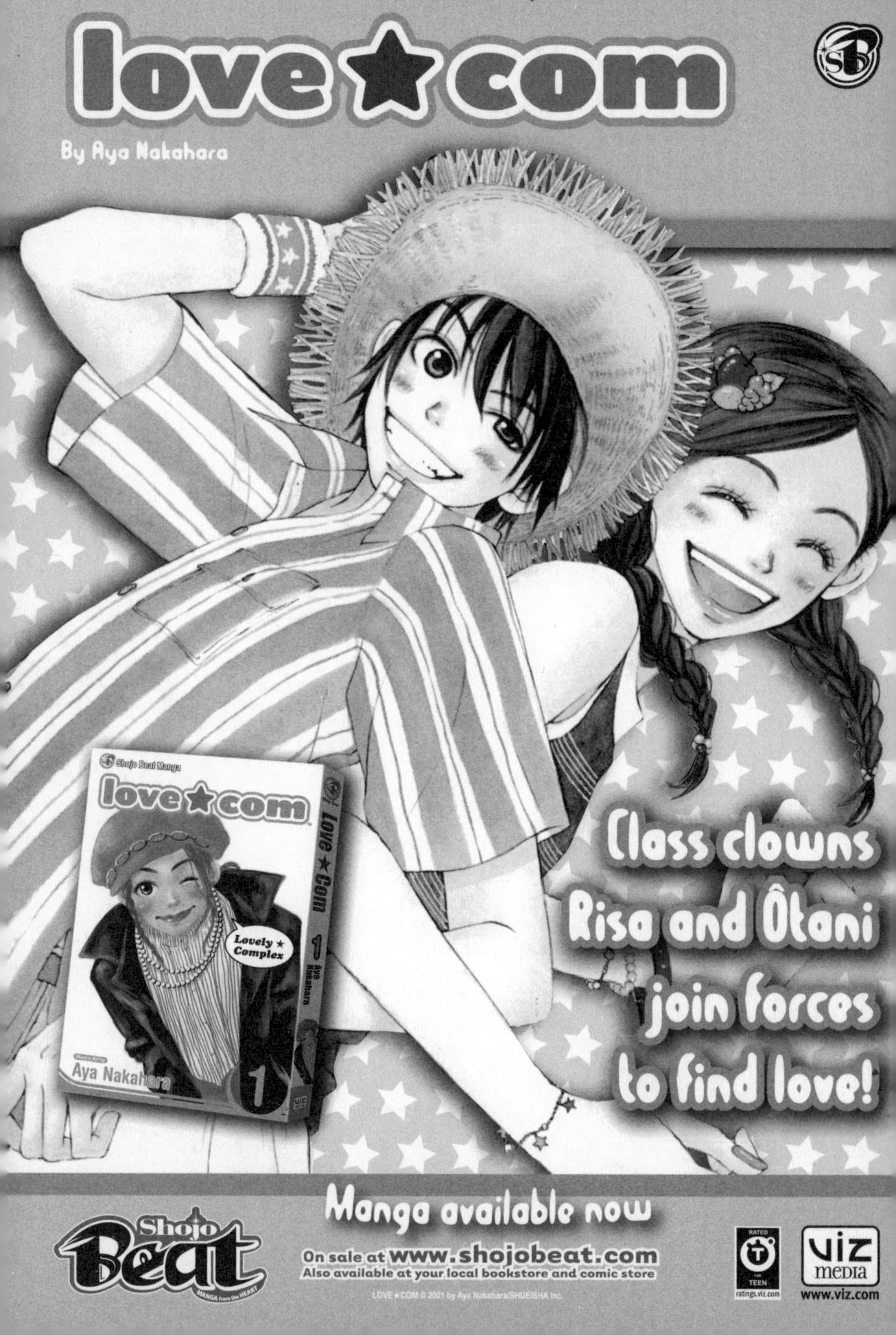

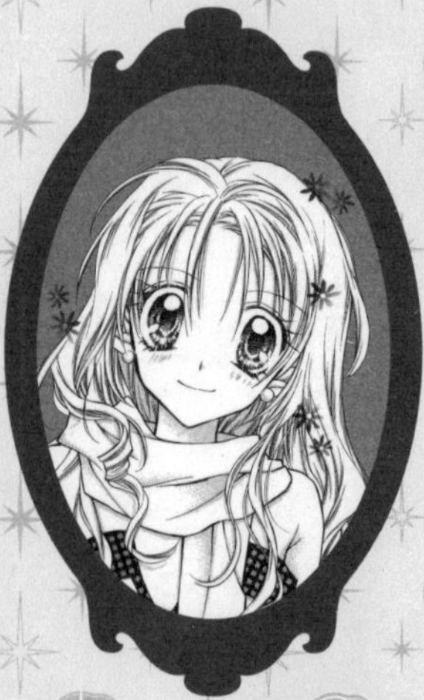

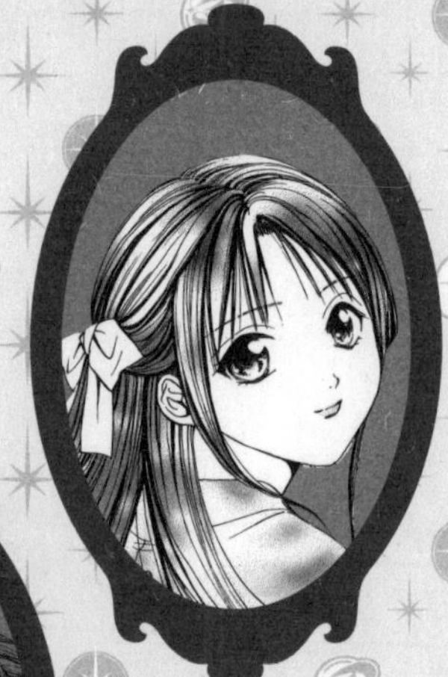

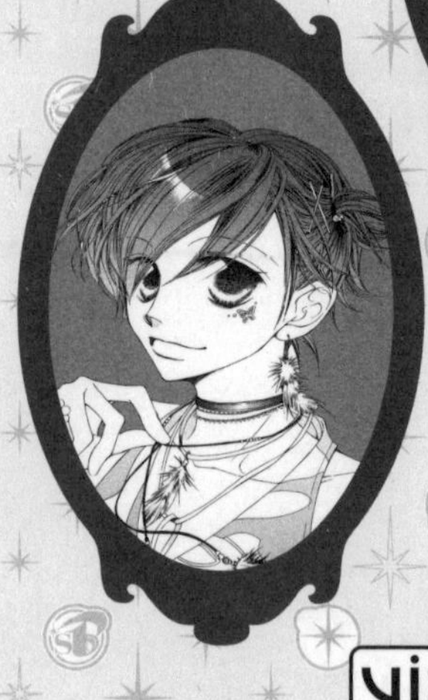

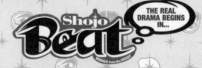